The Philokalia

VOLUME I

THE PHILOKALIA

Volume I

THE COMPLETE TEXT
compiled by
ST NIKODIMOS OF THE HOLY MOUNTAIN
and
ST MAKARIOS OF CORINTH

translated from the Greek
and edited by
G. E. H. PALMER
PHILIP SHERRARD
KALLISTOS WARE

with the assistance of
THE HOLY TRANSFIGURATION MONASTERY
(BROOKLINE)
CONSTANTINE CAVARNOS
BASIL OSBORNE
NORMAN RUSSELL

FABER AND FABER
London & Boston

First published in 1979
by Faber and Faber Limited
3 Queen Square London WC1N 3AU
Printed in Great Britain by
Western Printing Services Bristol
All rights reserved

British Library Cataloguing in Publication Data
The Philokalia   Vol. 1
1. Prayer – Early works to 1800
I. Nikodemos Hagioreites, Saint   II. Makarios, Saint
III. Palmer, G E H   IV. Sherrard, Philip
V. Ware, Kallistos
248'.3   BV209
ISBN 0–571–11377–x

CONTENTS

INTRODUCTION

The *Philokalia* is a collection of texts written between the fourth and the fifteenth centuries by spiritual masters of the Orthodox Christian tradition. It was compiled in the eighteenth century by two Greek monks, St Nikodimos of the Holy Mountain of Athos (1749–1809) and St Makarios of Corinth (1731–1805), and was first published at Venice in 1782. A second edition was published at Athens in 1893, and this included certain additional texts on prayer by Patriarch Kallistos not found in the 1782 edition. A third edition, in five volumes, was also published at Athens during the years 1957–1963 by the Astir Publishing Company. It is on the Astir edition that our English translation is based. Thus our translation, which we likewise hope to publish in five volumes, will reproduce all the texts included in the three Greek editions.

We depart notably from these editions in but four respects. First, we have not included the introduction written by St Nikodimos, and we have rewritten the notes which he placed before each text or series of texts written by a single author.

Second, we have used a more reliable version of a text if one is now available. Where that has been the case, we signify it in the relevant introductory note.

Third, we have attributed to Evagrios the work *On Prayer*, which in the Greek editions is attributed to St Neilos; the explanation for this change of attribution is in the note preceding Evagrios' texts.

Fourth, we have placed in an appendix the text, attributed to St Antony the Great, which opens the Greek editions; the reasons for this decision are likewise stated in the note introducing that text.

Where certain passages, or indeed entire sections, of individual texts attributed by St Nikodimos to particular authors are now known or suspected to have been written by other hands, we have indicated this either in the introductory notes to the texts in question or in footnotes. But in no case have we excised any such passage or section on the grounds that it is not by the author to whom St Nikodimos has attributed it. The distinction between genuine and spurious where all these writings are concerned must rest, not on the correctness of the attribution of their authorship, but on whether or not they belong to the spiritual tradition which the collection as a whole represents.

All the texts in the original *Philokalia* are in Greek, and all except two were first written in Greek, and even these two (written originally in Latin) were translated into Greek in Byzantine times. But the influence of the work has by no means been confined to the Greek-speaking world. It was Paisii Velichkovskii (1722–1794), a Russian monk who visited Mount Athos and later settled in Moldavia, who first translated a selection of the texts into Slavonic, published, with the title *Dobrotolubiye*, at Moscow in 1793 and reprinted at Moscow in 1822. This was the translation carried by the pilgrim in *The Way of a Pilgrim*; and indeed the impact of the *Philokalia* on Russian spirituality and culture in the nineteenth century was immense, as the writings of Dostoievsky, an assiduous reader of the book, alone sufficiently testify. A translation into Russian was made by Ignatii Brianchaninov (1807–1867) and was published in 1857. Yet another Russian translation, still with the title *Dobrotolubiye*, was made by Bishop Theophan the Recluse (1815–1894), who included in it several texts not in the original Greek edition, and deliberately omitted or paraphrased certain passages in some of the texts of the Greek edition. Bishop Theophan's translation was published at Moscow in five volumes at the expense of the Russian Monastery of St Panteleimon on Mount Athos. The first volume of the series, originally issued in 1877, was reprinted in 1883, 1885, 1905 and 1913. A photographic reprint of the 1883 edition was begun by the Monastery of the Holy Trinity, Jordanville, N.Y., in 1963. A Romanian translation, which also includes additional material, began to appear in 1946 under the editorship of Father Dumitru Staniloae; in 1976 the fifth volume of this edition appeared, and it is planned to complete it in eight volumes. A full French translation is in progress. Both the Romanian and the French translations are based on the original Greek.

The only previous translation into English of texts from the

Philokalia is that made by E. Kadloubovsky and G. E. H. Palmer in two volumes with the titles *Writings from the Philokalia on Prayer of the Heart* and *Early Fathers from the Philokalia*,[1] published in 1951 and 1954 respectively. This translation was made, not from the Greek original, but from Theophan's Russian translation, and covers slightly less than a third of the material of the Greek edition. It was because of this that the translators wrote in their Introduction to the second of these two English volumes that 'the only final solution to the problem of making the treasures contained in the *Philokalia* available to the West in a form as rich and as wisely balanced as the original is for someone with the necessary qualities . . . to undertake to translate the whole of the original Greek itself. We can only hope that this work will one day be achieved; it might well be one of the greatest single contributions to perpetuating in the West what is highest in the Christian tradition.' The present translation is a direct consequence of the hope expressed in that Introduction, written over twenty years ago.

What first determined the choice of texts made by St Nikodimos and St Makarios, and gives them their cohesion? 'Philokalia' itself means love of the beautiful, the exalted, the excellent, understood as the transcendent source of life and the revelation of Truth. It is through such love that, as the subtitle of the original edition puts it, 'the intellect is purified, illumined and made perfect'. The texts were collected with a view to this purification, illumination and perfection. They show the way to awaken and develop attention and consciousness, to attain that state of watchfulness which is the hallmark of sanctity. They describe the conditions most effective for learning what their authors call the art of arts and the science of sciences, a learning which is not a matter of information or agility of mind but of a radical change of will and heart leading man towards the highest possibilities open to him, shaping and nourishing the unseen part of his being, and helping him to spiritual fulfilment and union with God. The *Philokalia* is an itinerary through the labyrinth of time, a silent way of love and gnosis through the deserts and emptinesses of life, especially of modern life, a vivifying and fadeless presence. It is an active force revealing a spiritual path and inducing man to follow it. It is a summons to him to overcome his ignorance, to uncover the knowledge that lies within, to rid himself of illusion,

[1] Faber and Faber, London.

and to be receptive to the grace of the Holy Spirit who teaches all things and brings all things to remembrance.

The texts of the *Philokalia* are, then, guides to the practice of the contemplative life. They constitute, as St Nikodimos puts it in his introduction, 'a mystical school of inward prayer' where those who study may cultivate the divine seed implanted in their hearts at baptism and so grow in spirit that they become 'sons of God' (John 1 : 12), attaining through such deification 'the measure of the stature of the fulness of Christ' (Eph. 4: 13). The emphasis is therefore on inner work, on the cleansing of 'the inside of the cup and plate, so that their outside may also be clean' (Matt. 23 : 26). This does not mean that what one might call outer work – the keeping of the commandments and the practice of the moral virtues – is of no importance. On the contrary, such work is a pre-condition of that purification without which no real progress in inner work can be made. Indeed, in this respect outer and inner complement one another. Atrophy or defeat follow only when outer work is practised as an end in itself, and the one thing needful – the inner practice of guarding the intellect and of pure prayer – is neglected. St Nikodimos himself remarks that such neglect is only too common: many there are who wear their whole life away in outer work, with the result that grace diminishes in them and they fail to realize the illumination of consciousness and purity of heart which are the goal of the spiritual path that the *Philokalia* charts for us.

An advanced state which may be acquired through the pursuit of this path is described as *hesychia*, a word which not only bears the sense of tranquillity and silence (hence our translation: stillness) but also is linked through its Greek root with the idea of being seated, fixed, and so of being concentrated. It is therefore fitting that from this word should come the term hesychasm, frequently applied to the whole complex of theory and practice which constitutes the path itself. But here a certain caution is needed. Some modern historians, prone to over-simplification and schematization, have tended to speak of hesychasm as though it were a phenomenon of the later Byzantine world. They speak of the hesychast movement, and by this they mean the spiritual revival which, centred on Mount Athos in the thirteenth and fourteenth centuries, spread from there into neighbouring lands such as Bulgaria, Serbia and Russia. Yet hesychasm itself is far more than a local historical movement dating to the later Byzantine centuries. On the contrary it denotes the whole spiritual tradition going back to the earliest times and delineated in the *Philokalia*. If evidence for this is needed, it may be found in the fact that one of the central forms of the art and science which constitute hesychasm – namely, the invocation of the name of Jesus, or the Jesus Prayer, to give it its traditional title – is already integral to the spiritual method described in many of the texts included in this first volume, most if not all of which were written prior to the ninth century. Indeed, although the *Philokalia* is concerned with many other matters, it would not be too much to say that it is the recurrent references to the Jesus Prayer which more than anything else confer on it its inner unity.

It must be stressed, however, that this spiritual path known as hesychasm cannot be followed in a vacuum. Although most of the texts in the *Philokalia* are not specifically doctrinal, they all presuppose doctrine even when they do not state it. Moreover, this doctrine entails an ecclesiology. It entails a particular understanding of the Church and a view of salvation inextricably bound up with its sacramental and liturgical life. This is to say that hesychasm is not something that has developed independently of or alongside the sacramental and liturgical life of the Church. It is part and parcel of it. It too is an ecclesial tradition. To attempt to practise it, therefore, apart from active participation in this sacramental and liturgical life is to cut it off from its living roots. It is also to abuse the intention of its exponents and teachers and so to act with a presumption that may well have consequences of a disastrous kind, mental and physical.

There is a further point connected with this. The texts in the *Philokalia* were written by and for those actively living not only within the sacramental and liturgical framework of the Orthodox Church, but also within that of the Orthodox monastic tradition. They therefore presuppose conditions of life radically different from those in which most readers of this English translation are likely to find themselves. Is this tantamount to saying that the counsels they contain can be applied only within a monastic environment? Many hesychast writers affirm that this is not the case, and St Nikodimos himself, in his introduction to the original *Philokalia*, goes out of his way to stress that 'unceasing prayer' may or, rather, should be practised by all. Naturally, the monastic life provides conditions, such as quietness, solitude and regularity, indispensable for that concentration without which one cannot advance far along the spiritual path. But, provided that the basic condition of active participation in the sacramental and liturgical life of the Church is fulfilled, then this path is open to all to follow, each to the best of his or her ability and whatever the circumstances under which he or she lives. Indeed, in this respect the distinction between the monastic life and life 'in the world' is but relative: every human being, by virtue of the fact that he or she is created in the image of God, is summoned to be perfect, is summoned to love God with all his or her heart, soul and mind. In this sense all have the same vocation and all must follow the same spiritual path. Some no doubt will follow it further than others; and again for some the intensity of the desire with which they pursue it may well lead them to embrace a pattern of life more in harmony with its demands, and this pattern may well be provided by the monastic life. But the path with its goal is one and the same whether followed within or outside a monastic environment. What is essential is that one does not follow it in an arbitrary and ignorant manner. Personal guidance from a qualified teacher should always be sought for. If such guidance is not to be found, then active participation in the sacramental and liturgical life of the Church, always necessary, will have an added importance in the overcoming of obstacles and dangers inherent in any quest of a spiritual nature.

Certain key words occur and recur in these hesychastic writings. We have listed the most important of them in a glossary, specifying the English words we have used in translating them and the sense we attribute to them; and we have also indicated where they first occur in the translation itself.[1] But their real significance will be grasped only as the reader penetrates ever more deeply into the meaning of the passages in which they are to be found – indeed, as he penetrates ever more deeply into the theory *and* practice of the spiritual path they help to signpost.

Something similar applies with respect to the whole psychological understanding which these texts both presuppose and elucidate. In effect, one is confronted with a psychology, or science of the soul, many of whose fundamental features – particularly perhaps in relation to the role of the demons – are completely unrecognized by,

---

[1] Words listed in the Glossary are marked in the text with an asterisk*; see note on p. 20.

not to say at odds with, the theories of most modern psychologists. The contemporary reader, influenced directly or indirectly by these latter-day theories, may well be tempted to reject hesychastic psychology outright. But alternatively he may be led first to question his own outlook and assumptions and then to modify or even abandon them in the light of the understanding with which he is now confronted. In any case, how he reacts will depend very largely on the degree to which he perceives the inner coherence and relevance of this understanding, not only on the theoretical level but also in terms of his own experience. In this connection it should be remembered that, however much the external appearances and conditions of the world may change, such changes can never unroot the fundamental potentialities of the human state and of man's relationship with God; and as it is with these latter that the teaching and method of the *Philokalia* are concerned, the counsels it enshrines are as valid and effective today as they were at the times at which they were written.

This English translation of the *Philokalia* is produced under the auspices and with the financial assistance of a charitable trust, the Eling Trust. The work of initial translation has been done by a group of scholars and collaborators, namely the Holy Transfiguration Monastery at Brookline, Massachusetts, Dr Constantine Cavarnos of Boston, Father Basil Osborne of Oxford, and Father Norman Russell of the London Oratory. But the final version of the text has been prepared by and is the responsibility of the Editorial Committee set up by the Trustees of the Eling Trust, and consisting of G. E. H. Palmer, Dr Philip Sherrard and Archimandrite Kallistos Ware. The task of checking against the Greek text for consistency in interpretation in the English translation has been undertaken by the two last named members of this Committee, while all three have co-operated in establishing the definitive version of the translation itself. Although we have tried not to impose a uniformity of style, it is none the less inevitable that our translation should display less variety than the original texts. These texts were written by authors who lived at various times in a period that stretches over a thousand years and more, and who in addition came from many differing cultural backgrounds. Our translation extends over something like ten years, and all those who contributed to it share by and large in but a single culture. In spite of this we hope we have not suppressed entirely the distinctive flavour of the original texts. And we hope, too, that those who prepared the initial translations will forgive us for the many changes made to their texts for the reasons we have stated. The fact that we have made these changes in no way lessens our deep gratitude to them.

We would like to thank Father Palamas Koumantos of Simonopetra Monastery on Mount Athos for his assistance; the Monks of the Serbian Monastery of Chilandari on Mount Athos for their generous hospitality on two prolonged occasions; Mrs Ian Busby for her invaluable work; and Miss Marguerite Langford for her assistance.

Finally, the Eling Trust and the Editorial Committee would also like to express their gratitude to the Ingram Merrill Foundation of New York for a substantial grant provided to support this translation.

G. E. H. Palmer
Philip Sherrard
Bussock Mayne   Archimandrite Kallistos Ware
March 1977

NOTE ON BIBLICAL QUOTATIONS
AND REFERENCES

All Biblical passages have been translated directly from the Greek as given in the original *Philokalia*. This means that quotations from the Old Testament are normally based on the Greek Septuagint text. Where this differs significantly from the Hebrew, we have indicated the fact by adding the Roman numeral LXX after the reference.

Even though we follow the Septuagint text, in giving references we use the numbering and titles of the Hebrew, as reproduced in the Authorized Version (King James Bible), since this is more widely familiar in the Western world. In particular the following differences between the Hebrew and the Septuagint should be noted:

NUMBERING OF PSALMS

Hebrew (*Authorized Version*)	Greek (*Septuagint*)
1–8	1–8
9 and 10	9
11–113	Subtract one from the number of each Psalm in the Hebrew
114 and 115	113
116:1–9	114
116:10–16	115
117–146	Subtract one from the number of each Psalm in the Hebrew
147:1–11	146
147:12–20	147
148–150	148–150

TITLES OF BOOKS

Hebrew (Authorized Version)	*Greek (Septuagint)*
1 Samuel	1 Kingdoms
2 Samuel	2 Kingdoms
1 Kings	3 Kingdoms
2 Kings	4 Kingdoms

Where authors in the *Philokalia* merely refer to a passage or paraphrase it, but do not quote it exactly, 'cf.' is added before the reference.

Note: throughout the text, an asterisk* is used to denote a word defined in the Glossary when it occurs for the first time, but not thereafter. Where the reference is to a word other than that which appears in the text, the Glossary entry is indicated in a numbered footnote thus: 1. Age.*

ST ISAIAH THE SOLITARY

Introductory Note

There is some uncertainty about the identity of the author of the *Twenty-Seven Texts* that follow. According to St Nikodimos, St Isaiah the Solitary lived around the year 370 and was a contemporary of St Makarios the Great of Egypt. Most historians today consider him to be later in date. He is now usually identified with a monk Isaiah, who lived initially at Sketis in Egypt, and who then moved to Palestine at some date subsequent to 431, eventually dying in great old age as a recluse near Gaza on 11 August 491 (according to others, in 489). Whichever date is preferred, it is evident that the author reflects the authentic spirituality of the Desert Fathers of Egypt and Palestine during the fourth and fifth centuries. St Nikodimos commends in particular his advice on the rebuttal of demonic provocations and on the need to be attentive to the conscience.

St Nikodimos here gives no more than short extracts from a much longer work, as yet untranslated into English.[1]

---

[1] Greek text edited by the monk Avgoustinos (Jerusalem, 1911; reprinted, Volos, 1962;) French translation by Dom Hervé de Broc, *Abbé Isaïe: Recueil ascétique*, with an introduction by Dom L. Regnault (Collection Spiritualité Orientale, No. 7, 2nd edition, Abbaye de Bellefontaine, 1976).

On Guarding the Intellect:
Twenty-Seven Texts

1. There is among the passions* an anger of the intellect, and this anger is in accordance with nature. Without anger a man cannot attain purity: he has to feel angry with all that is sown in him by the enemy. When Job felt this anger he reviled his enemies, calling them 'dishonourable men of no repute, lacking everything good, whom I would not consider fit to live with the dogs that guard my flocks' (cf. Job 30:1, 4. LXX). He who wishes to acquire the anger that is in accordance with nature must uproot all self-will, until he establishes within himself the state natural to the intellect.

2. If you find yourself hating your fellow men and resist this hatred, and you see that it grows weak and withdraws, do not rejoice in your heart; for this withdrawal is a trick of the evil spirits. They are preparing a second attack worse than the first; they have left their troops behind the city and ordered them to remain there. If you go out to attack them, they will flee before you in weakness. But if your heart is then elated because you have driven them away, and you leave the city, some of them will attack you from the rear while the rest will stand their ground in front of you; and your wretched soul will be caught between them with no means of escape. The city is prayer. Resistance is rebuttal* through Christ Jesus. The foundation is incensive power*.

3. Let us stand firm in the fear of God, rigorously practising the virtues[1] and not giving our conscience cause to stumble. In the fear of God let us keep our attention fixed within ourselves, until our conscience achieves its freedom. Then there will be a union between it and us, and thereafter it will be our guardian, showing us each thing that we must uproot. But if we do not obey our

[1] Practice* of the virtues.

conscience, it will abandon us and we shall fall into the hands of our enemies, who will never let us go. This is what our Lord taught us when He said: 'Come to an agreement with your adversary quickly while you are with him in the road, lest he hand you over to the judge, and the judge deliver you to the officer and you are cast into prison' (Matt. 5:25). The conscience is called an 'adversary' because it opposes us when we wish to carry out the desires of our flesh;* and if we do not listen to our conscience, it delivers us into the hands of our enemies.

4. If God sees that the intellect has entirely submitted to Him and puts its hope in Him alone, He strengthens it, saying: 'Have no fear Jacob my son, my little Israel' (Isa. 41:14. LXX), and: 'Have no fear: for I have delivered you, I have called you by My name; you are Mine. If you pass through water, I shall be with you, and the rivers will not drown you. If you go through fire, you will not be burnt, and the flames will not consume you. For I am the Lord your God, the Holy One of Israel, who saves you' (cf. Isa. 43:1-3. LXX).

5. When the intellect hears these words of reassurance, it says boldly to its enemies: 'Who would fight with me? Let him stand against me. And who would accuse me? Let him draw near to me. Behold, the Lord is my helper; who will harm me? Behold, all of you are like an old moth-eaten garment' (cf. Isa. 50:8-9. LXX).

6. If your heart* comes to feel a natural hatred for sin,* it has defeated the causes of sin and freed itself from them. Keep hell's torments in mind; but know that your Helper is at hand. Do nothing that will grieve Him, but say to Him with tears: 'Be merciful and deliver me, O Lord, for without Thy help I cannot escape from the hands of my enemies.' Be attentive to your heart, and He will guard you from all evil.

7. The monk should shut all the gates of his soul, that is, the senses, so that he is not lured astray. When the intellect sees that it is not dominated by anything, it prepares itself for immortality, gathering its senses together and forming them into one body.

8. If your intellect is freed from all hope in things visible, this is a sign that sin has died in you.

9. If your intellect is freed, the breach between it and God is eliminated.

10. If your intellect is freed from all its enemies and attains the sabbath rest, it lives in another age,* a new age in which it contemplates things new and undecaying. For 'wherever the dead body is, there will the eagles be gathered together' (Matt. 24:28).

11. The demons cunningly withdraw for a time in the hope that we will cease to guard* our heart, thinking we have now attained peace; then they suddenly attack our unhappy soul and seize it like a sparrow. Gaining possession of it, they drag it down mercilessly into all kinds of sin, worse than those which we have already committed and for which we have asked forgiveness. Let us stand, therefore, with fear of God and keep guard over our heart, practising the virtues which check the wickedness of our enemies.

12. Our teacher Jesus Christ, out of pity for mankind and knowing the utter mercilessness of the demons, severely commands us: 'Be ready at every hour, for you do not know when the thief will come; do not let him come and find you asleep' (cf. Matt. 24:42–43). He also says: 'Take heed, lest your hearts be overwhelmed with debauchery and drunkenness and the cares of this life, and the hour come upon you unawares' (cf. Luke 21:34). Stand guard, then, over your heart and keep a watch on your senses; and if the remembrance* of God dwells peaceably within you, you will catch the thieves when they try to deprive you of it. When a man has an exact knowledge about the nature of thoughts,* he recognizes those which are about to enter and defile him, troubling the intellect with distractions and making it lazy. Those who recognize these evil thoughts for what they are remain undisturbed and continue in prayer to God.

13. Unless a man hates all the activity of this world, he cannot worship God. What then is meant by the worship of God? It means that we have nothing extraneous in our intellect when we are praying to Him: neither sensual pleasure* as we bless Him, nor malice as we sing His praise, nor hatred as we exalt Him, nor jealousy to hinder us as we speak to Him and call Him to mind. For all these things are full of darkness; they are a wall imprisoning our wretched soul, and if the soul has them in itself it cannot worship God with purity. They obstruct its ascent and prevent it from meeting God; they hinder it from blessing Him inwardly and praying to Him with sweetness of heart, and so receiving His illumination. As a result the intellect is always shrouded in darkness and cannot

advance in holiness, because it does not make the effort to uproot these thoughts by means of spiritual knowledge.*

14. When the intellect rescues the soul's senses from the desires of the flesh and imbues them with dispassion,* the passions shamelessly attack the soul, trying to hold its senses fast in sin; but if the intellect then continually calls upon God in secret, He, seeing all this, will send His help and destroy all the passions at once.

15. I entreat you not to leave your heart unguarded, so long as you are in the body. Just as a farmer cannot feel confident about the crop growing in his fields, because he does not know what will happen to it before it is stored away in his granary, so a man should not leave his heart unguarded so long as he still has breath in his nostrils. Up to his last breath he cannot know what passion will attack him; so long as he breathes, therefore, he must not leave his heart unguarded, but should at every moment pray to God for His help and mercy.

16. He who receives no help when at war should feel no confidence when at peace.

17. When a man severs himself from evil, he gains an exact understanding of all the sins he has committed against God; for he does not see his sins unless he severs himself from them with a feeling of revulsion. Those who have reached this level pray to God with tears, and are filled with shame when they recall their evil love of the passions. Let us therefore pursue the spiritual way with all our strength, and God in His great mercy will help us. And if we have not guarded our hearts as our fathers guarded theirs, at least in obedience to God let us do all we can to keep our bodies sinless, trusting that at this time of spiritual dearth He will grant mercy to us together with His saints.

18. Once you have begun to seek God with true devotion and with all your heart, then you cannot possibly imagine that you already conform to His will. So long as your conscience reproves you for anything that you have done contrary to nature, you are not yet free: the reproof means that you are still under trial and have not yet been acquitted. But if you find when you are praying that nothing at all accuses you of evil, then you are free and by God's will have entered into His peace.

If you see growing within yourself a good crop, no longer choked by the tares of the evil one; if you find that the demons have reluctantly withdrawn, convinced that it is no use making further attacks on your senses; if 'a cloud overshadows your tent' (cf. Exod. 40:34), and 'the sun does not burn you by day, nor the moon by night' (Ps. 121:6); if you find yourself equipped to pitch your tent and keep it as God wishes – if all this has happened, then you have gained the victory with God's help, and henceforward He will Himself overshadow your tent, for it is His.

So long as the contest continues, a man is full of fear and trembling, wondering whether he will win today or be defeated, whether he will win tomorrow or be defeated: the struggle and stress constrict his heart. But when he has attained dispassion, the contest comes to an end; he receives the prize of victory and has no further anxiety about the three that were divided, for now through God they have made peace with one another. These three are the soul, the body and the spirit. When they become one through the energy of the Holy Spirit, they cannot again be separated. Do not think, then, that you have died to sin, so long as you suffer violence, whether waking or sleeping, at the hands of your opponents. For while a man is still competing in the arena, he cannot be sure of victory.

19. When the intellect grows strong, it makes ready to pursue the love which quenches all bodily passions and which prevents anything contrary to nature from gaining control over the heart. Then the intellect, struggling against what is contrary to nature, separates this from what is in accordance with nature.

20. Examine yourself daily in the sight of God, and discover which of the passions is in your heart. Cast it out, and so escape His judgment.

21. Be attentive to your heart and watch your enemies, for they are cunning in their malice. In your heart be persuaded of this: it is impossible for a man to achieve good through evil means. That is why our Saviour told us to be watchful, saying: 'Strait is the gate, and narrow is the way that leads to life, and few there are that find it' (Matt. 7:14).

22. Be attentive to yourself, so that nothing destructive can separate you from the love of God. Guard your heart, and do not grow listless and say: 'How shall I guard it, since I am a sinner?' For when a man abandons his sins and returns to God, his repentance* regenerates him and renews him entirely.

23. Holy Scripture speaks everywhere about the guarding of the

heart, in both the Old and the New Testaments. David says in the Psalms: 'O sons of men, how long will you be heavy of heart?' (Ps. 4:2. LXX), and again: 'Their heart is vain' (Ps. 5:9. LXX); and of those who think futile thoughts, he says: 'For he has said in his heart, I shall not be moved' (Ps. 10:6), and: 'He has said in his heart, God has forgotten' (Ps. 10:11).

A monk should consider the purpose of each text in Scripture, to whom it speaks and on what occasions. He should persevere continually in the ascetic struggle and be on his guard against the provocations* of the enemy. Like a pilot steering a boat through the waves, he should hold to his course, guided by grace. Keeping his attention fixed within himself, he should commune with God in stillness,* guarding his thoughts from distraction and his intellect from curiosity.

24. In storms and squalls we need a pilot, and in this present life we need prayer; for we are susceptible to the provocations of our thoughts, both good and bad. If our thought is full of devotion and love of God, it rules over the passions. As hesychasts,[1] we should discriminate between virtue and vice with discretion and watchfulness;* and we should know which virtues to practise when in the presence of our brethren and elders and which to pursue when alone. We should know which virtue comes first, and which second or third; which passions attack the soul and which the body, and also which virtues concern the soul and which the body. We should know which virtue pride uses in order to assault the intellect, and which virtue leads to vainglory, wrath* or gluttony. For we ought to purify our thoughts from 'all the self-esteem that exalts itself against the knowledge of God' (2 Cor. 10:5).

25. The first virtue is detachment, that is, death in relation to every person or thing. This produces the desire* for God, and this in turn gives rise to the anger that is in accordance with nature, and that flares up against all the tricks of the enemy. Then the fear of God will establish itself within us, and through this fear love will be made manifest.

26. At the time of prayer, we should expel from our heart the provocation of each evil thought, rebutting it in a spirit of devotion so that we do not prove to be speaking to God with our lips, while pondering wicked thoughts in our heart. God will not accept from

[1] Stillness.*

the hesychast a prayer that is turbid and careless, for everywhere Scripture tells us to guard the soul's organs of perception. If a monk submits his will to the law of God, then his intellect will govern in accordance with this law all that is subordinate to itself. It will direct as it should all the soul's impulses, especially its incensive power and desire, for these are subordinate to it.

We have practised virtue and done what is right, turning our desire towards God and His will, and directing our incensive power, or wrath, against the devil and sin. What then do we still lack? Inward meditation.

27. If some shameful thought is sown in your heart as you are sitting in your cell, watch out. Resist the evil, so that it does not gain control over you. Make every effort to call God to mind, for He is looking at you, and whatever you are thinking in your heart is plainly visible to Him. Say to your soul: 'If you are afraid of sinners like yourself seeing your sins, how much more should you be afraid of God who notes everything?' As a result of this warning the fear of God will be revealed in your soul, and if you cleave to Him you will not be shaken by the passions; for it is written: 'They that trust in the Lord shall be as Mount Zion; he that dwells in Jerusalem shall never be shaken' (Ps. 125: 1. LXX). Whatever you are doing, remember that God sees all your thoughts, and then you will never sin. To Him be glory through all the ages. Amen.

EVAGRIOS THE SOLITARY

Introductory Note

Evagrios the Solitary, also known as Evagrios Pontikos, was born in 345 or 346, probably at Ibora in Pontus, although according to another opinion he was a native of Iberia (Georgia). A disciple of the Cappadocian Fathers, he was ordained reader by St Basil the Great and deacon by St Gregory the Theologian (Gregory of Nazianzos), and he accompanied the latter to the Council of Constantinople in 381 (the second Ecumenical Council). Evagrios was never ordained priest. After a brief stay in Jerusalem, he went in 383 to Egypt, where he spent the remaining sixteen years of his life. After two years at Nitria, where he became a monk, he moved to the more remote desert of Kellia, dying there in 399. While in Egypt he had as his spiritual father the priest of Kellia, St Makarios of Alexandria, and it is probable that he also knew St Makarios the Egyptian, the priest and spiritual father of Sketis. In the person of these two saints, he came into contact with the first generation of the Desert Fathers and with their spirituality in its purest form.

In the numerous writings of Evagrios there may be discerned two tendencies, the one 'speculative' and the other 'practical'. On the 'speculative' side he relies heavily upon Origen (c. 185–c. 254), borrowing from him in particular certain theories about the pre-existence of human souls and the *apokatastasis* or final restoration of all things in Christ. These theories were condemned at the fifth Ecumenical Council (553). On the 'practical' side he draws upon the living experience of the Desert Fathers of Egypt, mainly Copts, among whom he spent the last years of his life. He possessed to an exceptional degree the gifts of psychological insight and vivid description, together with the ability to analyse and define with remarkable precision the various stages on the spiritual way. Here his teachings, so far from being condemned, have exercised a decisive influence upon subsequent writers. His disciple St John

Cassian, while abandoning the suspect theories that Evagrios derived from Origen, transmitted the 'practical' aspect of Evagrios' teachings to the Latin West. In the Greek East the technical vocabulary devised by Evagrios remained thereafter standard: it can be found, for example, in the writings of St Diadochos of Photiki, St John Klimakos and St Maximos the Confessor, as also within the Syriac tradition, in the *Mystic Treatises* of St Isaac of Nineveh. The works included by St Nikodimos in the *Philokalia* all belong to the 'practical' side of Evagrios, and contain little if any trace of suspect speculations.

Several of Evagrios' works have come down under the name of other authors. This is the case with the writing *On Prayer*, which in the Greek *Philokalia* is ascribed to Neilos; but recent research has made it plain beyond any reasonable doubt that this is a writing of Evagrios.[1]

---

[1] See the studies by I. Hausherr, 'Le Traité de l'Oraison d'Evagre le Pontique', in *Revue d'Ascétique et de Mystique*, XV (1934), pp. 34–93, 113–70; and *Les leçons d'un contemplatif. Le Traité de l'Oraison d'Evagre le Pontique* (Paris, 1960). The Evagrian authorship of the work *On Prayer* is accepted by a previous English translator, John Eudes Bamberger, in his introduction to *Evagrius Ponticus: The Praktikos; Chapters on Prayer* (Cistercian Studies Series, No. 4, Spencer, Mass., 1970 [i.e. 1972]).

Outline Teaching on Asceticism and Stillness in the Solitary Life

In Jeremiah it is said: 'And you shall not take a wife in this place, for thus says the Lord concerning the sons and daughters born in this place: . . . they shall die grievous deaths' (Jer. 16: 1–4). This shows that, in the words of the Apostle, 'He that is married cares for the things that are of the world, how he may please his wife', and he is inwardly divided, and 'she that is married cares for the things of the world, how she may please her husband' (1 Cor. 7: 32–34). It is clear that the statement in Jeremiah, 'they shall die grievous deaths', refers not only to the sons and daughters born as a result of marriage, but also to those born in the heart, that is, to worldly thoughts and desires: these too will die from the weak and sickly spirit of this world, and will have no place in heavenly life. On the other hand, as the Apostle says, 'he that is unmarried cares for the things that belong to the Lord, how he may please the Lord' (1 Cor. 7: 32); and he produces the fruits of eternal life, which always keep their freshness.

Such is the solitary. He should therefore abstain from women and not beget a son or daughter in the place of which Jeremiah speaks. He must be a soldier of Christ, detached from material things, free from cares and not involved in any trade or commerce; for, as the Apostle says, 'In order to please the leader who has chosen him, the soldier going to war does not entangle himself in the affairs of this world' (2 Tim. 2: 4). Let the monk follow this course, especially since he has renounced the materiality of this world in order to win the blessings of stillness. For the practice of stillness is full of joy and beauty; its yoke is easy and its burden light.

Do you desire, then, to embrace this life of solitude, and to seek out the blessings of stillness? If so, abandon the cares of the world, and the principalities and powers that lie behind them; free yourself from attachment to material things, from domination by passions and desires, so that as a stranger to all this you may attain true stillness. For only by raising himself above these things can a man achieve the life of stillness.

Keep to a sparse and plain diet, not seeking a variety of tempting dishes. Should the thought come to you of getting extravagant foods in order to give hospitality, dismiss it, do not be deceived by it: for in it the enemy lies in ambush, waiting to tear you away from stillness. Remember how the Lord rebukes Martha (the soul that is over-busy with such things) when He says: 'You are anxious and troubled about many things: one thing alone is needful' (Luke 10:41–42) – to hear the divine word; after that, one should be content with anything that comes to hand. He indicates all this by adding: 'Mary has chosen what is best, and it cannot be taken away from her' (Luke 10:42). You also have the example of how the widow of Zarephath gave hospitality to the Prophet (cf. 1 Kings 17:9–16). If you have only bread, salt or water, you can still meet the dues of hospitality. Even if you do not have these, but make the stranger welcome and say something helpful, you will not be failing in hospitality; for 'is not a word better than a gift?' (Ecclus. 18:17). This is the view you should take of hospitality. Be careful, then, and do not desire wealth for giving to the poor. For this is another trick of the evil one, who often arouses self-esteem and fills your intellect with worry and restlessness. Think of the widow mentioned in the Gospel by our Lord: with two mites she surpassed the generous gifts of the wealthy. For He says: 'They cast into the treasury out of their abundance; but she . . . cast in all her livelihood' (Mark 12:44).

With regard to clothes, be content with what is sufficient for the needs of the body. 'Cast your burden upon the Lord' (Ps. 55:22) and He will provide for you, since 'He cares for you' (1 Pet. 5:7). If you need food or clothes, do not be ashamed to accept what others offer you. To be ashamed to accept is a kind of pride. But if you have more than you require, give to those in need. It is in this way that God wishes His children to manage their affairs. That is why, writing to the Corinthians, the Apostle said about those who were in want: 'Your abundance should supply their want, so that their abundance likewise may supply your want; then there will be equality, as it is written: "He that gathered much had nothing over; and he that gathered little had no lack"' (2 Cor. 8:14–15; Exod. 16:18). So if you have all you need for the moment, do not be anxious about the future, whether it is one day ahead or a week or months. For when tomorrow comes, it will supply what you need, if you seek above all else the kingdom of heaven and the righteousness of God; for the Lord says: 'Seek the kingdom of God and His righteousness; and all these things as well will be given to you' (cf. Matt. 6:33).

Do not have a servant, for if you do you will no longer have only yourself to provide for; and in that case the enemy may trip you up through the servant and disturb your mind with worries about laying in extravagant foods. Should you have the thought of getting a servant to allow your body a little ease, call to mind what is more important – I mean spiritual peace, for spiritual peace is certainly more important than bodily ease. Even if you have the idea that taking a servant would be for the servant's benefit, do not accept it. For this is not our work; it is the work of others, of the holy Fathers who live in communities and not as solitaries. Think only of what is best for yourself, and safeguard the way of stillness.

Do not develop a habit of associating with people who are materially minded and involved in worldly affairs. Live alone, or else with brethren who are detached from material things and of one mind with yourself. For if one associates with materially minded people involved in worldly affairs, one will certainly be affected by their way of life and will be subject to social pressures, to vain talk and every other kind of evil: anger, sorrow,* passion for material things, fear of scandals. Do not get caught up in concern for your parents or affection for your relatives; on the contrary, avoid meeting them frequently, in case they rob you of the stillness you have in your cell and involve you in their own affairs. 'Let the dead bury their dead,' says the Lord; 'but come, follow me' (cf. Matt. 8:22).

If you find yourself growing strongly attached to your cell, leave it, do not cling to it, be ruthless. Do everything possible to attain stillness and freedom from distraction, and struggle to live according to God's will, battling against invisible enemies. If you cannot attain stillness where you now live, consider living in exile, and try and make up your mind to go. Be like an astute business man: make stillness your criterion for testing the value of everything, and choose always what contributes to it.

Indeed, I urge you to welcome exile. It frees you from all the entanglements of your own locality, and allows you to enjoy the blessings of stillness undistracted. Do not stay in a town, but persevere in the wilderness. 'Lo,' says the Psalm, 'then would I wander far off, and remain in the wilderness' (Ps. 55:7). If possible, do not visit a town at all. For you will find there nothing of benefit, nothing useful, nothing profitable for your way of life. To quote the Psalm again, 'I have seen violence and strife in the city' (Ps. 55:9). So seek out places that are free from distraction, and solitary. Do not be afraid of the noises you may hear. Even if you should see some demonic fantasy,* do not be terrified or flee from the training ground so apt for your progress. Endure fearlessly, and you will see the great things of God, His help, His care, and all the other assurances of salvation. For as the Psalm says, 'I waited for Him who delivers me from distress of spirit and the tempest' (Ps. 55:8. LXX).

Do not let restless desire overcome your resolution; for 'restlessness of desire perverts the guileless intellect' (Wisd. 4:12). Many temptations* result from this. For fear that you may go wrong, stay rooted in your cell. If you have friends, avoid constant meetings with them. For if you meet only on rare occasions, you will be of more help to them. And if you find that harm comes through meeting them, do not see them at all. The friends that you do have should be of benefit to you and contribute to your way of life. Avoid associating with crafty or aggressive people, and do not live with anyone of that kind but shun their evil purposes; for they do not dwell close to God or abide with Him. Let your friends be men of peace, spiritual brethren, holy fathers. It is of such that the Lord speaks when he says: 'My mother and brethren and fathers are those who do the will of My Father who is in heaven' (cf. Matt. 12:49–50). Do not pass your time with people engaged in worldly affairs or share their table, in case they involve you in their illusions and draw you away from the science of stillness. For this is what they want to do. Do not listen to their words or accept the thoughts of their hearts, for they are indeed harmful. Let the labour and longing of your heart be for the faithful of the earth, to become like them in mourning. For 'my eyes will be on the faithful of the land, that they may dwell with me' (Ps. 101:6). If someone who lives in accordance with the love of God comes to you and invites you to eat, go if you wish, but return quickly to your cell. If possible, never sleep outside your cell, so that the gift of stillness may always be with you. Then you will be unhindered on your chosen path.

Do not hanker after fine foods and deceitful pleasures. For 'she that indulges in pleasure is dead while still alive', as the Apostle says (1 Tim. 5:6). Do not fill your belly with other people's food in case you develop a longing for it, and this longing makes you want to eat at their table. For it is said: 'Do not be deceived by the filling of the belly' (Prov. 24:15. LXX). If you find yourself continually invited outside your cell, decline the invitations. For continual absence from your cell is harmful. It deprives you of the grace of stillness, darkens your mind, withers your longing for God. If a jar of wine is left in the same place for a long time, the wine in it becomes clear, settled and fragrant. But if it is moved about, the wine becomes turbid and dull, tainted throughout by the lees. So you, too, should stay in the same place and you will find how greatly this benefits you. Do not have relationships with too many people, lest your intellect becomes distracted and so disturbs the way of stillness.

Provide yourself with such work for your hands as can be done, if possible, both during the day and at night, so that you are not a burden to anyone, and indeed can give to others, as Paul the Apostle advises (cf. 1 Thess. 2:9; Eph. 4:28). In this manner you will overcome the demon of listlessness and drive away all the desires suggested by the enemy; for the demon of listlessness takes advantage of idleness. 'Every idle man is full of desires' (Prov. 13:4. LXX).

When buying or selling you can hardly avoid sin. So, in either case, be sure you lose a little in the transaction. Do not haggle about the price from love of gain, and so indulge in actions harmful to the soul – quarrelling, lying, shifting your ground and so on – thus bringing our way of life into disrepute. Understanding things in this manner, be on your guard when buying and selling. If possible it is best to place such business in the hands of someone you trust, so that, being thus relieved of the worry, you can pursue your calling with joy and hope.

In addition to all that I have said so far, you should consider now other lessons which the way of stillness teaches, and do what I tell you. Sit in your cell, and concentrate your intellect; remember the day of death, visualize the dying of your body, reflect on this calamity, experience the pain, reject the vanity of this world, its compromises and crazes, so that you may continue in the way of stillness and not weaken. Call to mind, also, what is even now going on in hell. Think of the suffering, the bitter silence, the terrible moaning, the great fear and agony, the dread of what is to come, the unceasing pain, the endless weeping. Remember, too, the day of your resurrection and how you will stand before God. Imagine that fearful and awesome judgment-seat. Picture all that awaits those who sin: their shame before God the Father and His Anointed, before angels, archangels, principalities and all mankind; think of all the forms of punishment: the eternal fire, the worm that does not die, the abyss of darkness, the gnashing of teeth, the terrors and the torments. Then picture all the blessings that await the righteous: intimate* communion with God the Father and His Anointed, with angels, archangels, principalities and all the saints, the kingdom and its gifts, the gladness and the joy.

Picture both these states: lament and weep for the sentence passed on sinners; mourn while you are doing this, frightened that you, too, may be among them. But rejoice and be glad at the blessings that await the righteous, and aspire to enjoy them and to be delivered from the torments of hell. See to it that you never forget these things, whether inside your cell or outside it. This will help you to escape thoughts that are defiling and harmful.

Fast before the Lord according to your strength, for to do this will purge you of your iniquities and sins; it exalts the soul, sanctifies the mind, drives away the demons, and prepares you for God's presence. Having already eaten once, try not to eat a second time the same day, in case you become extravagant and disturb your mind. In this way you will have the means for helping others and for mortifying the passions of your body. But if there is a meeting of the brethren, and you have to eat a second and a third time, do not be disgruntled and surly. On the contrary, do gladly what you have to do, and when you have eaten a second or a third time, thank God that you have fulfilled the law of love and that He himself is providing for you. Also, there are occasions when, because of a bodily sickness, you have to eat a second and a third time or more often. Do not be sad about this; when you are ill you should modify your ascetic labours for the time being, so that you may regain the strength to take them up once more.

As far as abstinence from food is concerned, the divine Logos*
did not prohibit the eating of anything, but said: 'See, even as I have
given you the green herb I have given you all things; eat, asking
no questions; it is not what goes into the mouth that defiles a man'
(cf. Gen. 9:3; 1 Cor. 10:25; Matt. 15:11). To abstain from food,
then, should be a matter of our own choice and an ascetic labour.

Gladly bear vigils, sleeping on the ground and all other hardships,
looking to the glory that will be revealed to you and to all the
saints; 'for the sufferings of this present time', says the Apostle, 'are
not worthy to be compared with the glory which shall be revealed
in us' (Rom. 8:18).

If you are disheartened, pray, as the Apostle says (cf. Jas. 5:13).
Pray with fear, trembling, effort, with inner watchfulness and
vigilance. To pray in this manner is especially necessary because the
enemies are so malignant. For it is just when they see us at prayer
that they come and stand beside us, ready to attack, suggesting to our
intellect the very things we should not think about when praying;
in this way they try to take our intellect captive and to make our
prayer and supplication vain and useless. For prayer is truly vain and
useless when not performed with fear and trembling, with inner
watchfulness and vigilance. When someone approaches an earthly
king, he entreats him with fear, trembling and attention; so much
the more, then, should we stand and pray in this manner before God
the Father, the Master of all, and before Christ the King of Kings.
For it is He whom the whole spiritual host and the choir of angels
serve with fear and glorify with trembling; and they sing in unceasing
praise to Him, together with the Father who has no origin, and
with the all-holy and coeternal Spirit, now and ever through all the
ages. Amen.

Texts on Discrimination*
in respect of Passions and Thoughts

1. Of the demons opposing us in the practice of the ascetic life, there are three groups who fight in the front line: those entrusted with the appetites of gluttony, those who suggest avaricious thoughts, and those who incite us to seek the esteem of men. All the other demons follow behind and in their turn attack those already wounded by the first three groups. For one does not fall into the power of the demon of unchastity, unless one has first fallen because of gluttony; nor is one's anger aroused unless one is fighting for food or material possessions or the esteem of men. And one does not escape the demon of dejection, unless one no longer experiences suffering when deprived of these things. Nor will one escape pride, the first offspring of the devil, unless one has banished avarice, the root of all evil, since poverty makes a man humble, according to Solomon (cf. Prov. 10:4. LXX). In short, no one can fall into the power of any demon, unless he has been wounded by those of the front line. That is why the devil suggested these three thoughts to the Saviour: first he exhorted Him to turn stones into bread; then he promised Him the whole world, if Christ would fall down and worship him; and thirdly he said that, if our Lord would listen to him, He would be glorified and suffer nothing in falling from the pinnacle of the temple. But our Lord, having shown Himself superior to these temptations, commanded the devil to 'get behind Him'. In this way He teaches us that it is not possible to drive away the devil, unless we scornfully reject these three thoughts (cf. Matt. 4:1-10).

2. All thoughts inspired by the demons produce within us conceptions of sensory objects; and in this way the intellect, with such conceptions imprinted on it, bears the forms of these objects within itself. So, by recognizing the object presented to it, the

intellect knows which demon is approaching. For example, if the face of a person who has done me harm or insulted me appears in my mind, I recognize the demon of rancour approaching. If there is a suggestion of material things or of esteem, again it will be clear which demon is troubling me. In the same way with other thoughts, we can infer from the object appearing in the mind which demon is close at hand, suggesting that object to us. I do not say that all thoughts of such things come from the demons; for when the intellect is activated by man it is its nature to bring forth the images of past events. But all thoughts producing anger or desire in a way that is contrary to nature are caused by demons. For through demonic agitation the intellect mentally commits adultery and becomes incensed. Thus it cannot receive the vision of God, who sets us in order; for the divine splendour only appears to the intellect during prayer, when the intellect is free from conceptions of sensory objects.

3. Man cannot drive away impassioned thoughts unless he watches over his desire and incensive power. He destroys desire through fasting, vigils and sleeping on the ground, and he tames his incensive power through long-suffering, forbearance, forgiveness and acts of compassion. For with these two passions are connected almost all the demonic thoughts which lead the intellect to disaster and perdition. It is impossible to overcome these passions unless we can rise above attachment to food and possessions, to self-esteem and even to our very body, because it is through the body that the demons often attempt to attack us. It is essential, then, to imitate people who are in danger at sea and throw things overboard because of the violence of the winds and the threatening waves. But here we must be very careful in case we cast things overboard just to be seen doing so by men. For then we shall get the reward we want; but we shall suffer another shipwreck, worse than the first, blown off our course by the contrary wind of the demon of self-esteem. That is why our Lord, instructing the intellect, our helmsman, says in the Gospels: 'Take heed that you do not give alms in front of others, to be seen by them; for unless you take heed, you will have no reward from your Father in heaven.' Again, He says: 'When you pray, you must not be as the hypocrites are: for they love to pray standing in synagogues and at street-corners, so as to be seen by men. Truly I say to you, they get the reward they want. . . . Moreover when you fast, do not put on a gloomy face, like the hypocrites;

for they disfigure their faces, so that they may be seen by men to be fasting. Truly I say to you, they get the reward they want' (cf. Matt. 6:1–18). Observe how the Physician of souls here corrects our incensive power through acts of compassion, purifies the intellect through prayer, and through fasting withers desire. By means of these virtues the new Adam is formed, made again according to the image of his Creator – an Adam in whom, thanks to dispassion, there is 'neither male nor female' and, thanks to singleness of faith, there is 'neither Greek nor Jew, circumcision nor uncircumcision, barbarian, Scythian, bond nor free; but Christ is all, and in all' (Gal. 3:28; Col. 3:10–11).

4. We shall now enquire how, in the fantasies that occur during sleep, the demons imprint shapes and forms on our intellect. Normally the intellect receives these shapes and forms either through the eyes when it is seeing, or through the ears when it is hearing, or through some other sense, or else through the memory, which stirs up and imprints on the intellect things which it has experienced through the body. Now it seems to me that in our sleep, when the activity of our bodily senses is suspended, it is by arousing the memory that the demons make this imprint. But, in that case, how do the demons arouse the memory? Is it through the passions? Clearly this is so, for those in a state of purity and dispassion no longer experience demonic fantasies in sleep. There is also an activity of the memory that is not demonic: it is caused by ourselves or by the angelic powers, and through it we may meet with saints and delight in their company. We should notice in addition that during sleep the memory stirs up, without the body's participation, those very images which the soul has received in association with the body. This is clear from the fact that we often experience such images during sleep, when the body is at rest.

Just as it is possible to think of water both while thirsty and while not thirsty, so it is possible to think of gold with greed and without greed. The same applies to other things. Thus if we can discriminate in this way between one kind of fantasy and another, we can then recognize the artfulness of the demons. We should be aware, too, that the demons also use external things to produce fantasies, such as the sound of waves heard at sea.

5. When our incensive power is aroused in a way contrary to nature, it greatly furthers the aim of the demons and is an ally in all

their evil designs. Day and night, therefore, they are always trying to provoke it. And when they see it tethered by gentleness, they at once try to set it free on some seemingly just pretext; in this way, when it is violently aroused, they can use it for their shameful purposes. So it must not be aroused either for just or for unjust reasons; and we must not hand a dangerous sword to those too readily incensed to wrath, for it often happens that people become excessively worked up for quite trivial reasons. Tell me, why do you rush into battle so quickly, if you are really above caring about food, possessions and glory? Why keep a watchdog if you have renounced everything? If you do, and it barks and attacks other men, it is clear that there are still some possessions for it to guard. But since I know that wrath is destructive of pure prayer, the fact that you cannot control it shows how far you are from such prayer. I am also surprised that you have forgotten the saints: David who exclaims, 'Cease from anger, and put aside your wrath' (Ps. 37:8. LXX); and Ecclesiastes who urges us, 'Remove wrath from your heart, and put away evil from your flesh' (Eccles. 11:10. LXX); while the Apostle commands that always and everywhere men should 'lift up holy hands, without anger and without quarrelling' (1 Tim. 2:8). And do we not learn the same from the mysterious and ancient custom of putting dogs out of the house during prayer? This indicates that there should be no wrath in those who pray. 'Their wine is the wrath of serpents' (Deut. 32:33. LXX); that is why the Nazarenes abstained from wine.

It is needless to insist that we should not worry about clothes or food. The Saviour Himself forbids this in the Gospels: 'Do not worry about what to eat or drink, or about what to wear' (cf. Matt. 6:25). Such anxiety is a mark of the Gentiles and unbelievers, who reject the providence of the Lord and deny the Creator. An attitude of this kind is entirely wrong for Christians who believe that even two sparrows which are sold for a farthing are under the care of the holy angels (cf. Matt. 10:29). The demons, however, after arousing impure thoughts, go on to suggest worries of this kind, so that 'Jesus conveys Himself away', because of the multitude of concerns in our mind (cf. John 5:13). The divine word can bear no fruit, being choked by our cares. Let us, then, renounce these cares, and throw them down before the Lord, being content with what we have at the moment; and living in poverty and rags, let us day by day rid ourselves of all that fills us with self-esteem. If anyone thinks it shameful to live in rags, he should remember St Paul, who 'in cold and nakedness' patiently awaited the 'crown of righteousness' (2 Cor. 11:27; 2 Tim. 4:8). The Apostle likened this world to a contest in an arena (cf. 1 Cor. 9:24); how then can someone clothed with anxious thoughts run for 'the prize of the high calling of God' (Phil. 3:14), or 'wrestle against principalities, against powers, against the rulers of the darkness of this world' (Eph. 6:12)? I do not see how this is possible; for just as a runner is obstructed and weighed down by clothing, so too is the intellect by anxious thoughts – if indeed the saying is true that the intellect is attached to its own treasure; for it is said, 'where your treasure is, there will your heart be also' (Matt. 6:21).

6. Sometimes thoughts are cut off, and sometimes they do the cutting off. Evil thoughts cut off good thoughts, and in turn are cut off by good thoughts. The Holy Spirit therefore notes to which thought we give priority and condemns or approves us accordingly. What I mean is something like this: the thought occurs to me to give hospitality and it is for the Lord's sake; but when the tempter attacks, this thought is cut off and in its place he suggests giving hospitality for the sake of display. Again, the thought comes to me of giving hospitality so as to appear hospitable in the eyes of others. But this thought in its turn is cut off when a better thought comes, which leads me to practise this virtue for the Lord's sake and not so as to gain esteem from men.

7. We have learnt, after much observation, to recognize the difference between angelic thoughts, human thoughts, and thoughts that come from demons. Angelic thought is concerned with the true nature of things and with searching out their spiritual essences.[1] For example, why was gold created and scattered like sand in the lower regions of the earth, to be found only with much toil and effort? And how, when found, is it washed in water and committed to the fire, and then put into the hands of craftsmen who fashion it into the candlestick of the tabernacle and the censers and the vessels (cf. Exod. 25:22–39) from which, by the grace of our Saviour, the king of Babylon no longer drinks (cf. Dan. 5:2, 3)? A man such as Cleopas brings a heart burning with these mysteries (cf. Luke 24:32). Demonic thought, on the other hand, neither knows nor can

---

[1] Inner essences.*

know such things. It can only shamelessly suggest the acquisition of physical gold, looking forward to the wealth and glory that will come from this. Finally, human thought neither seeks to acquire gold nor is concerned to know what it symbolizes, but brings before the mind simply the image of gold, without passion or greed. The same principle applies to other things as well.

8. There is a demon, known as the deluder, who visits the brethren especially at dawn, and leads the intellect about from city to city, from village to village, from house to house, pretending that no passions are aroused through such visits; but then the intellect goes on to meet and talk with old acquaintances at greater length, and so allows its own state to be corrupted by those it encounters. Little by little it falls away from the knowledge[1] of God and holiness, and forgets its calling. Therefore the solitary must watch this demon, noting where he comes from and where he ends up; for this demon does not make this long circuit without purpose and at random, but because he wishes to corrupt the state of the solitary, so that his intellect, over-excited by all this wandering, and intoxicated by its many meetings, may immediately fall prey to the demons of unchastity, anger or dejection – the demons that above all others destroy its inherent brightness.

But if we really want to understand the cunning of this demon, we should not be hasty in speaking to him, or tell others what is taking place, how he is compelling us to make these visits in our mind and how he is gradually driving the intellect to its death – for then he will flee from us, as he cannot bear to be seen doing this; and so we shall not grasp any of the things we are anxious to learn. But, instead, we should allow him one more day, or even two, to play out his role, so that we can learn about his deceitfulness in detail; then, mentally rebuking him, we put him to flight. But because during temptation the intellect is clouded and does not see exactly what is happening, do as follows after the demon has withdrawn. Sit down and recall in solitude the things that have happened: where you started and where you went, in what place you were seized by the spirit of unchastity, dejection or anger and how it all happened. Examine these things closely and commit them to memory, so that you will then be ready to expose the demon when he next approaches you. Try to become conscious of the weak spot

[1] Spiritual knowledge.*

in yourself which he hid from you, and you will not follow him again.
If you wish to enrage him, expose him at once when he reappears,
and tell him just where you went first, and where next, and so on.
For he becomes very angry and cannot bear the disgrace. And the
proof that you spoke to him effectively is that the thoughts he
suggested leave you. For he cannot remain in action when he is
openly exposed.

The defeat of this demon is followed by heavy sleepiness and
deadness, together with a feeling of great coldness in the eyelids,
countless yawnings, and heaviness in the shoulders. But if you pray
intensely all this is dispersed by the Holy Spirit.

9. Hatred against the demons contributes greatly to our salvation and helps our growth in holiness. But we do not of ourselves
have the power to nourish this hatred into a strong plant, because the
pleasure-loving spirits restrict it and encourage the soul again to
indulge in its old habitual loves. But this indulgence – or rather this
gangrene that is so hard to cure – the Physician of souls heals by
abandoning us. For He permits us to undergo some fearful suffering night and day, and then the soul returns again to its original
hatred, and learns like David to say to the Lord: 'I hate them with
perfect hatred: I count them my enemies' (Ps. 139:22). For a man
hates his enemies with perfect hatred when he sins neither in act nor
in thought – which is a sign of complete dispassion.

10. Now what am I to say about the demon who makes the soul
obtuse? For I am afraid to write about him: how, at his approach,
the soul departs from its own proper state and strips itself of
reverence and the fear of God, no longer regarding sin as sin, or
wickedness as wickedness; it looks on judgment and the eternal
punishment of hell as mere words; it laughs at the fire which causes
the earth to tremble; and, while supposedly confessing God, it has
no understanding of His commandments. You may beat your breast
as such a soul draws near to sin, but it takes no notice. You recite
from the Scripture, yet it is wholly indifferent and will not hear.
You point out its shame and disgrace among men, and it ignores
you, like a pig that closes its eyes and charges through a fence. This
demon gets into the soul by way of long-continuing thoughts of
self-esteem; and unless 'those days are shortened, no flesh will be
saved' (Matt. 24:22).

This is one of those demons that seldom approach brethren living in a community. The reason is clear: when people round us fall into misfortune, or are afflicted by illness, or are suffering in prison, or meet sudden death, this demon is driven out; for the soul has only to experience even a little compunction or compassion and the callousness caused by the demon is dissolved. We solitaries lack these things, because we live in the wilderness and sickness is rare among us. It was to banish this demon especially that the Lord enjoined us in the Gospels to call on the sick and visit those in prison. For 'I was sick,' He says, 'and you visited Me' (Matt. 25:36).

But you should know this: if an anchorite falls in with this demon, yet does not admit unchaste thoughts or leave his cell out of listlessness, this means he has received the patience and self-restraint that come from heaven, and is blessed with dispassion. Those, on the other hand, who profess to practise godliness, yet choose to have dealings with people of the world, should be on their guard against this demon. I feel ashamed to say or write more about him.

11. All the demons teach the soul to love pleasure; only the demon of dejection refrains from doing this, since he corrupts the thoughts of those he enters by cutting off every pleasure of the soul and drying it up through dejection, for 'the bones of the dejected are dried up' (Prov. 17:22. LXX). Now if this demon attacks only to a moderate degree, he makes the anchorite more resolute; for he encourages him to seek nothing worldly and to shun all pleasures. But when the demon remains for longer, he encourages the soul to give up, or forces it to run away. Even Job was tormented by this demon, and it was because of this that he said: 'O that I might lay hands upon myself, or at least ask someone else to do this for me' (Job 30:24. LXX).

The symbol of this demon is the viper. When used in moderation for man's good, its poison is an antidote against that of other venomous creatures, but when taken in excess it kills whoever takes it. It was to this demon that Paul delivered the man at Corinth who had fallen into sin. That is why he quickly wrote again to the Corinthians saying: 'Confirm your love towards him . . . lest perhaps he should be swallowed up with too great dejection' (2 Cor. 2:7–8). He knew that this spirit, in troubling men, can also bring about true repentance. It was for this reason that St John the Baptist gave the name 'progeny of vipers' to those who were goaded by this spirit to seek refuge in God, saying: 'Who has warned you to flee from the anger to come? Bring forth fruits, then, that testify to your repentance; and do not think that you can just say within yourselves, We have Abraham as our father' (Matt. 3:7–9). But if a man imitates Abraham and leaves his country and kindred (cf. Gen. 12:1), he thereby becomes stronger than this demon.

12. He who has mastery over his incensive power has mastery also over the demons. But anyone who is a slave to it is a stranger to the monastic life and to the ways of our Saviour, for as David said of the Lord: 'He will teach the gentle His ways' (Ps. 25:9). The intellect of the solitary is hard for the demon to catch, for it shelters in the land of gentleness. There is scarcely any other virtue which the demons fear as much as gentleness. Moses possessed this virtue, for he was called 'very gentle, above all men' (Num. 12:3). And David showed that it makes men worthy to be remembered by God when he said: 'Lord, remember David and all his gentleness' (Ps. 132:1. LXX). And the Saviour Himself also enjoined us to imitate Him in His gentleness, saying: 'Learn from Me; for I am gentle and humble in heart: and you will find rest for your souls' (Matt. 11:29). Now if a man abstains from food and drink, but becomes incensed to wrath because of evil thoughts, he is like a ship sailing the open sea with a demon for pilot. So we must keep this watchdog under careful control, training him to destroy only the wolves and not to devour the sheep, and to show the greatest gentleness towards all men.

13. In the whole range of evil thoughts, none is richer in resources than self-esteem; for it is to be found almost everywhere, and like some cunning traitor in a city it opens the gates to all the demons. So it greatly debases the intellect of the solitary, filling it with many words and notions, and polluting the prayers through which he is trying to heal all the wounds of his soul. All the other demons, when defeated, combine to increase the strength of this evil thought; and through the gateway of self-esteem they all gain entry into the soul, thus making a man's last state worse than his first (cf. Matt. 12:45). Self-esteem gives rise in turn to pride, which cast down from heaven to earth the highest of the angels, the seal of God's likeness and the crown of all beauty. So turn quickly away from pride and do not dally with it, in case you surrender your life to others and your substance to the merciless (cf. Prov. 5:9). This demon is driven away by intense prayer and by not doing or

saying anything that contributes to the sense of your own importance.

14. When the intellect of the solitary attains some small degree of dispassion, it mounts the horse of self-esteem and immediately rides off into cities, taking its fill of the lavish praise accorded to its repute. But by God's providence the spirit of unchastity now confronts it and shuts it up in a sty of dissipation. This is to teach it to stay in bed until it is completely recovered and not to act like disobedient patients who, before they are fully cured of their disease, start taking walks and baths and so fall sick again. Let us sit still and keep our attention fixed within ourselves, so that we advance in holiness and resist vice more strongly. Awakened in this way to spiritual knowledge, we shall acquire contemplative insight into many things; and ascending still higher, we shall receive a clearer vision of the light of our Saviour.

15. I cannot write about all the villainies of the demons; and I feel ashamed to speak about them at length and in detail, for fear of harming the more simple-minded among my readers. But let me tell you about the cunning of the demon of unchastity. When a man has acquired dispassion in the appetitive* part of his soul and shameful thoughts cool down within him, this demon at once suggests images of men and women playing with one another, and makes the solitary a spectator of shameful acts and gestures. But this temptation need not be permanent; for intense prayer, a very frugal diet, together with vigils and the development of spiritual contemplation, drive it away like a light cloud. There are times when this cunning demon even touches the flesh, inflaming it to uncontrolled desire; and it devises endless other tricks which need not be described.

Our incensive power is also a good defence against this demon. When it is directed against evil thoughts of this kind, such power fills the demon with fear and destroys his designs. And this is the meaning of the statement: 'Be angry, and do not sin' (Ps. 4:4). Such anger is a useful medicine for the soul at times of temptation.

The demon of anger employs tactics resembling those of the demon of unchastity. For he suggests images of our parents, friends or kinsmen being gratuitously insulted; and in this way he excites our incensive power, making us say or do something vicious to those who appear in our minds. We must be on our guard against these fantasies and expel them quickly from our mind, for if we dally with them, they will prove a blazing firebrand to us during prayer. People prone to anger are specially liable to fall into these temptations; and if they do, then they are far from pure prayer and from the knowledge of our Saviour Jesus Christ.

16. As sheep to a good shepherd, the Lord has given to man intellections* of this present world; for it is written: 'He has given intellection to the heart of every man' (cf. Heb. 10:16). To help man He has given him incensive power and desire, so that with the first he may drive away wolflike intellections, while with the second he may lovingly tend the sheep, even though he is often exposed to rains and winds. In addition, God has given man the law, so that he may shepherd the sheep; He has given him green pastures and refreshing water (cf. Ps. 23:2), a psaltery and harp, a rod and staff. In this way he gathers hay from the mountains, and is fed and clothed from his flock; for it is written, 'Does anyone feed a flock and not drink its milk?' (1 Cor. 9:7). Therefore the solitary ought to guard this flock night and day, making sure that none of the lambs is caught by wild beasts or falls into the hands of thieves. Should this happen in some valley, he must at once snatch the creature from the mouth of the lion or the bear (cf. 1 Sam. 17:35).

What does it mean for the lambs to be caught by wild beasts? It means that when we think about our brother we feed on hatred; when we think about a woman we are moved with shameful lust; when we think about gold and silver we are filled with greed; and likewise when we think about gifts received from God, our mind is gorged with self-esteem. The same happens in the case of other intellections if they are seized by the passions.

We must not only guard this flock by day, but also keep watch at night; for by having fantasies of shameful and evil things we may lose some of the sheep entrusted to us. And this is the meaning of Jacob's words: 'I did not bring you a sheep which was caught by wild beasts; I made good of myself the thefts of the day and the thefts of the night. I was parched with heat by day, and chilled with frost by night, and sleep departed from my eyes' (Gen. 31:39–40. LXX).

If a certain listlessness overtakes us as a result of our efforts, we should climb a little up the rock of spiritual knowledge and play on the harp, plucking the strings with the skills of such knowledge. Let us pasture our sheep below Mount Sinai, so that the God of our fathers may speak to us, too, out of the bush (cf. Exod. 3) and show us the inner essence of signs and wonders.

17. Our spiritual nature, which had become dead through wickedness, is raised once more by Christ through the contemplation* of all the ages of creation. And through the spiritual knowledge that He gives of Himself, the Father raises the soul which has died the death of Christ. And this is the meaning of Paul's statement: 'If we have died with Christ, we believe that we shall also live with Him' (cf. 2 Tim. 2:11).

18. When the intellect has shed its fallen state and acquired the state of grace, then during prayer it will see its own nature like a sapphire or the colour of heaven. In Scripture this is called the realm of God that was seen by the elders on Mount Sinai (cf. Exod. 24:10).

19. Of the unclean demons, some tempt man in so far as he is man, while others disturb him in so far as he is a non-rational animal. The first, when they approach us, suggest to us notions of self-esteem, pride, envy or censoriousness, notions by which non-rational animals are not affected; whereas the second, when they approach, arouse incensive power and desire in a manner contrary to nature. For these passions are common to us and to animals, and lie concealed beneath our rational and spiritual nature. Hence the Holy Spirit says of the thoughts that come to men in so far as they are men: 'I have said, you are gods, and all of you are children of the most High. But you shall die as men, and fall as one of the princes' (Ps. 82:6–7). But what does He say of the thoughts which stir in men non-rationally? 'Do not be as the horse and mule, which have no understanding: whose mouth must be controlled with bit and bridle in case they attack you' (Ps. 32:9). Now if 'the soul that sins shall die' (Ezek. 18:4), it is clear that in so far as we die as men we are buried by men, but in so far as we are slain or fall as non-rational animals, we are devoured by vultures and ravens whose young 'cry' to the Lord (Ps. 147:9) and 'roll themselves in blood' (Job 39:30. LXX). 'He that has ears to hear, let him hear' (Matt. 11:15).

20. When one of the enemy approaches you and wounds you, and you wish to turn his sword back into his own heart (cf. Ps. 37:15), then do as follows: analyse in yourself the sinful thought that has wounded you, what it is, what it consists of, and what in it

especially afflicts the intellect. Suppose, for instance, that a thought full of avarice is suggested to you. Distinguish between the component elements: the intellect which has accepted the thought, the intellection of gold, gold itself, and the passion of avarice. Then ask: in which of these does the sin consist? Is it the intellect? But how then can the intellect be the image of God? Is it the intellection of gold? But what sensible person would ever say that? Then is gold itself the sin? In that case, why was it created? It follows, then, that the cause of the sin is the fourth element, which is neither an objective reality, nor the intellection of something real, but is a certain noxious pleasure which, once it is freely chosen, compels the intellect to misuse what God has created. It is this pleasure that the law of God commands us to cut off. Now as you investigate the thought in this way and analyse it into its components, it will be destroyed; and the demon will take to flight once your mind is raised to a higher level by this spiritual knowledge.

But before using his own sword against him, you may choose first to use your sling against him. Then take a stone from your shepherd's bag and sling it (cf. 1 Sam. 17) by asking these questions: how is it that angels and demons affect our world whereas we do not affect their worlds, for we cannot bring the angels closer to God, and we cannot make the demons more impure? And how was Lucifer, the morning star, cast down to the earth (cf. Isa. 14:12), 'making the deep boil like a brazen cauldron' (Job 41:31. LXX), disturbing all by his wickedness and seeking to rule over all? Insight into these things grievously wounds the demon and puts all his troops to flight. But this is possible only for those who have been in some measure purified and gained a certain vision of the inner essences of created things; whereas the impure have no insight into these essences, and even if they have been taught by others how to outwit the enemy they will fail because of the great clouds of dust and the turmoil aroused by their passions at the time of battle. For the enemy's troops must be made quiet, so that Goliath alone can face our David. In combat with all unclean thoughts, then, let us use these two methods: analysis of the thought attacking us, and the asking of questions about inner essences.

21. Whenever unclean thoughts have been driven off quickly, we should try to find out why this has happened. Did the enemy fail to overpower us because there was no possibility of the thought

becoming action? Or was it because of the degree of dispassion we have attained? For example, if a solitary imagines himself entrusted with the spiritual rule of a city, he does not dwell on this thought for long because clearly it cannot be realized in practice. But if someone does become the spiritual guide of a city and yet remains unaffected, that means he is blessed with dispassion. The same criterion can be applied to other thoughts. We need to know these things in order to estimate our commitment and strength, and to perceive whether we have crossed the Jordan and are near the palm-trees, or are still in the wilderness and harassed by the enemy.

The demon of avarice, it seems to me, is extraordinarily complex and is baffling in his deceits. Often, when frustrated by the strictness of our renunciation, he immediately pretends to be a steward and a lover of the poor; he urges us to prepare a welcome for strangers who have not yet arrived or to send provisions to absent brethren. He makes us mentally visit prisons in the city and ransom those on sale as slaves. He suggests that we should attach ourselves to wealthy women, and advises us to be obsequious to others who have a full purse. And so, after deceiving the soul, little by little he engulfs it in avaricious thoughts and then hands it over to the demon of self-esteem. The latter calls up in our imagination crowds of admirers who praise the Lord for the works of mercy we have performed; he makes us picture people talking to one another about how we deserve to be ordained, and he suggests to us that the present priest is bound to die before long. So our wretched intellect, entangled by these thoughts, attacks anyone who (as it imagines) opposes the idea of our ordination, while on those who support the idea it lavishes gifts and flattery. Some of our critics we bring in our mind's eye before the judges and demand their expulsion from the city. As these thoughts circle in our mind, the demon of pride suddenly appears, filling our cell with lightning and visions of terror and trying to make us mad. But let us call down destruction upon all such thoughts and thankfully live in poverty. 'For we brought nothing into the world, and it is certain that we can take nothing out of it. Having food and raiment, let us be content with them' (1 Tim. 6:7–8), remembering the words of St Paul: 'Avarice is the root of all evil' (1 Tim. 6:10).

22. All the impure thoughts that persist in us because of our passions bring the intellect down to ruin and perdition. Just as the

idea of bread persists in a hungry man because of his hunger, and the idea of water in a thirsty man because of his thirst, so ideas of material things and of the shameful thoughts that follow a surfeit of food and drink persist in us because of the passions. The same is true about thoughts of self-esteem and other ideas. It is not possible for an intellect choked by such ideas to appear before God and receive the crown of righteousness. It is through being dragged down by such thoughts that the wretched intellect, like the man in the Gospels, declines the invitation to the supper of the knowledge of God (cf. Luke 14:18); and the man who was bound hand and foot and cast into outer darkness (cf. Matt. 22:13) was clothed in a garment woven of these thoughts, and so was judged by the Lord, who had invited him, not to be worthy of the wedding feast. For the true wedding garment is the dispassion of the deiform soul which has renounced worldly desires.

In the texts *On Prayer* it is explained why dwelling on ideas of sensory objects destroys true knowledge of God.

23. As we stated at the beginning, there are three chief groups of demons opposing us in the practice of the ascetic life, and after them follows the whole army of the enemy. These three groups fight in the front line, and with impure thoughts seduce our souls into wrongdoing. They are the demons set over the appetites of gluttony, those who suggest to us avaricious thoughts, and those who incite us to seek esteem in the eyes of men. If you long for pure prayer, keep guard over your incensive power; and if you desire self-restraint, control your belly, and do not take your fill even of bread and water. Be vigilant in prayer and avoid all rancour. Let the teachings of the Holy Spirit be always with you; and use the virtues as your hands to knock at the doors of Scripture. Then dispassion of heart will arise within you, and during prayer you will see your intellect shine like a star.

Extracts from the Texts on Watchfulness

1. A monk should always act as if he was going to die tomorrow; yet he should treat his body as if it was going to live for many years. The first cuts off the inclination to listlessness, and makes the monk more diligent; the second keeps his body sound and his self-control well balanced.

2. He who has attained spiritual knowledge and has enjoyed the delight that comes from it will no longer succumb to the demon of self-esteem, even when he offers him all the delights of the world; for what could the demon promise him that is greater than spiritual contemplation? But so long as we have not tasted this knowledge, let us devote ourselves eagerly to the practice of the virtues, showing God that our aim in everything is to attain knowledge of Him.

3. We should examine the ways of the monks who have preceded us, and achieve our purpose by following their example. One of their many helpful counsels is that a frugal and balanced diet, accompanied by the presence of love, quickly brings a monk into the harbour of dispassion.

4. Once I visited St Makarios[1] at noon and, burning with intense thirst, I asked for a drink of water. But he said: 'Be satisfied with the shade, for at this moment there are many travellers who lack even that.' Then, as I was telling him of my difficulties in practising self-restraint, he said: 'Take heart, my son; for during the whole of twenty years I myself have never had my fill of bread, water or sleep; but I have carefully measured my bread and water, and snatched some sleep by leaning a little against the wall.'

5. Spiritual reading, vigils and prayer bring the straying intellect

[1] St Makarios of Alexandria, who died c. 393-4, aged nearly a hundred, was priest and superior at the monastic centre of Kellia, not far from Nitria (Egypt). Evagrios became his disciple when he settled at Kellia in 385.

to stability. Hunger, exertion and withdrawal from the world wither burning lust. Reciting the psalms, long-suffering and compassion curb our incensive power when it is unruly. Anything untimely or pushed to excess is short-lived and harmful rather than helpful.

On Prayer:
One Hundred and Fifty-Three Texts

PROLOGUE

When suffering from the fever of unclean passions, my intellect afflicted with shameful thoughts, I have often been restored to health by your letters, as I used to be by the counsel of our great guide and teacher.[1] This is not to be wondered at, since like the blessed Jacob you have earned a rich inheritance. Through your efforts to win Rachel you have been given Leah (cf. Gen. 29:25),[2] and now you seek to be given Rachel also, since you have laboured a further seven years for her sake.

For myself, I cannot deny that although I have worked hard all night I have caught nothing. Yet at your suggestion I have again let down the nets, and I have made a large catch. They are not big fish, but there are a hundred and fifty-three of them (cf. John 21:11). These, as you requested, I am sending you in a creel of love, in the form of a hundred and fifty-three texts.

I am delighted to find you so eager for texts on prayer – eager not simply for those written on paper with ink but also for those which are fixed in the intellect through love and generosity. But since 'all things go in pairs, one complementing the other', as the wise Jesus puts it (Ecclus. 42:24), please accept the letter and understand its spirit, since every written word presupposes the intellect: for where there is no intellect there is no written word. The way of prayer is also twofold: it comprises practice of the virtues and contemplation. The same applies to numbers: literally they are quantities, but they can also signify qualities.

I have divided this discourse on prayer into one hundred and fifty-three texts. In this way I send you an evangelical feast, so that

---

[1] St Makarios of Alexandria (see p. 53).
[2] Here Leah symbolizes the practice of the virtues and Rachel contemplation.

you may delight in a symbolical number that combines a triangular with a hexagonal figure.[1] The triangle indicates spiritual knowledge

[1] The number 153 recalls the draught of 'great fishes' caught by Simon Peter and the Apostles (John 21 : 11). In this passage Evagrios makes use of a numerical symbolism widely employed in the ancient and medieval world:

i. A *triangular* number is the sum total of a continuous series of numerals, starting from the number 1. Thus 3(= 1 + 2), 6(= 1 + 2 + 3) and 10(= 1 +2 + 3 + 4) are all triangular numbers.

ii. A *square* number is obtained by numbering from 1 but omitting one numeral each time. Thus 4(= 1 + 3), 9(= 1 + 3 + 5) and 16(= 1 + 3 + 5 + 7) are square numbers.

iii. To obtain a *pentagonal* number, two numerals are omitted each time: 1 + 4 + 7 + 10 . . . etc.; to obtain a *hexagonal* number, three numerals are omitted: 1 + 5 + 9 + 13 . . . etc.

iv. A *circular* or *spherical* number is one which, when multiplied by itself, reproduces itself again as the last digit: e.g. 5 × 5 = 25; 6 × 6 = 36.

Applying this to the number 153, Evagrios concludes:

a. 153 is *triangular*, being the sum of all numerals up to 17 (inclusive).

b. It is *hexagonal*, being the sum of 1 + 5 + 9 + 13 . . . up to 33 (inclusive).

c. It is the sum of 100 (a *square* number) and of 53; and 53 is in its turn the sum of 28 (a *triangular* number: = 1 + 2 + 3 + 4 + 5 + 6 + 7) and 25 (a *circular/ spherical* number: = 5 × 5).

The following diagrams show the manner in which the various series quoted above correspond to the names which denote them:

i. *Triangular numbers:*

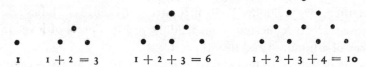

    1   1 + 2 = 3   1 + 2 + 3 = 6   1 + 2 + 3 + 4 = 10

ii. *Square numbers:*

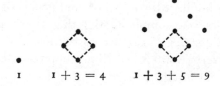

    1   1 + 3 = 4   1 + 3 + 5 = 9

iii. *Hexagonal numbers:*

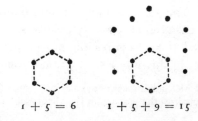

    1   1 + 5 = 6   1 + 5 + 9 = 15

of the Trinity, the hexagon indicates the ordered creation of the world in six days. The number one hundred is square, while the number fifty-three is triangular and spherical; for twenty-eight is triangular, and twenty-five is spherical, five times five being twenty-five. In this way, you have a square figure to express the fourfold nature of the virtues, and also a spherical number, twenty-five, which by form represents the cyclic movement of time and so indicates true knowledge of this present age. For week follows week and month follows month, and time revolves from year to year, and season follows season, as we see from the movement of the sun and moon, of spring and summer, and so on. The triangle can signify knowledge of the Holy Trinity. Or you can regard the total sum, one hundred and fifty-three, as triangular and so signifying respectively the practice of the virtues, contemplation of the divine in nature, and theology* or spiritual knowledge of God; faith, hope and love (cf. 1 Cor. 13:13); or gold, silver and precious stones (cf. 1 Cor. 3:12). So much, then, for this number.

Do not despise the humble appearance of these texts, for you know how to be content with much or little (cf. Phil. 4:12). You will recall how Christ did not reject the widow's mites (cf. Mark 12:44), but accepted them as greater than the rich gifts of many others. Showing in this way charity and love towards your true brethren, pray for one who is sick that he may 'take up his bed' and walk (Mark 2:11) by the grace of Christ. Amen.

1. Should one wish to make incense, one will mingle, according to the Law, fragrant gum, cassia, aromatic shell and myrrh in equal amounts (cf. Exod. 30:34). These are the four virtues. With their full and balanced development, the intellect will be safe from betrayal.

2. When the soul has been purified through the keeping of all the commandments, it makes the intellect steadfast and able to receive the state needed for prayer.

3. Prayer is communion of the intellect with God. What state, then, does the intellect need so that it can reach out to its Lord without deflection and commune with Him without intermediary?

4. When Moses tried to draw near to the burning bush he was forbidden to approach until he had loosed his sandals from his feet (cf. Exod. 3:5). If, then, you wish to behold and commune with

Him who is beyond sense-perception and beyond concept, you must free yourself from every impassioned thought.

5. First pray for the gift of tears, so that through sorrowing you may tame what is savage in your soul. And having confessed your transgressions to the Lord, you will obtain forgiveness from Him.

6. Pray with tears and all you ask will be heard. For the Lord rejoices greatly when you pray with tears.

7. If you do shed tears during your prayer, do not exalt yourself, thinking you are better than others. For your prayer has received help so that you can confess your sins readily and make your peace with the Lord through your tears. Therefore do not turn the remedy for passions into a passion, and so again provoke to anger Him who has given you this grace.

8. Many people, shedding tears for their sins, forget what tears are for, and so in their folly go astray.

9. Persevere with patience in your prayer, and repulse the cares and doubts that arise within you. They disturb and trouble you, and so slacken the intensity of your prayer.

10. When the demons see you truly eager to pray, they suggest an imaginary need for various things, and then stir up your remembrance of these things, inciting the intellect to go after them; and when it fails to find them, it becomes very depressed and miserable. And when the intellect is at prayer, the demons keep filling it with the thought of these things, so that it tries to discover more about them and thus loses the fruitfulness of its prayer.

11. Try to make your intellect deaf and dumb during prayer; you will then be able to pray.

12. Whenever a temptation or a feeling of contentiousness comes over you, immediately arousing you to anger or to some senseless word, remember your prayer and how you will be judged about it, and at once the disorderly movement within you will subside.

13. Whatever you do to avenge yourself against a brother who has done you a wrong will prove a stumbling-block to you during prayer.

14. Prayer is the flower of gentleness and of freedom from anger.

15. Prayer is the fruit of joy and thankfulness.

16. Prayer is the remedy for gloom and despondency.

17. 'Go and sell all you have and give to the poor' (Matt. 19:21);

and 'deny yourself, taking up your cross' (Matt. 16:24). You will then be free from distraction when you pray.

18. If you wish to pray as you should, deny yourself all the time, and when any kind of affliction troubles you, meditate on prayer.

19. If you endure something painful out of love for wisdom, you will find the fruit of this during prayer.

20. If you desire to pray as you ought, do not grieve anyone; otherwise you 'run in vain' (Phil. 2:16).

21. 'Leave your gift before the altar; first go away and be reconciled with your brother' (Matt. 5:24), and when you return you will pray without disturbance. For rancour darkens the intellect of one who prays, and extinguishes the light of his prayers.

22. Those who store up grievances and rancour in themselves are like people who draw water and pour it into a cask full of holes.

23. If you patiently accept what comes, you will always pray with joy.

24. When you pray as you should, thoughts will come to you which make you feel that you have a real right to be angry. But anger with your neighbour is never right. If you search you will find that things can always be arranged without anger. So do all you can not to break out into anger.

25. Take care that, while appearing to cure someone else, you yourself do not remain uncured, in this way thwarting your prayer.

26. If you are sparing with your anger you will yourself be spared, and you will show your good sense and will be one of those who pray.

27. If you arm yourself against anger, then you will never succumb to any kind of desire. Desire provides fuel for anger, and anger disturbs spiritual vision, disrupting the state of prayer.

28. Do not pray only with outward forms and gestures, but with reverence and awe try to make your intellect conscious of spiritual prayer.

29. Sometimes as soon as you start to pray, you pray well; at other times, in spite of great exertion, you do not reach your goal. This is to make you exert yourself still more, so that, having gained the gift of prayer, you keep it safe.

30. When an angel comes to us, all who trouble us withdraw at once; then the intellect is completely calm and prays soundly. But at other times, when the attacks of the demons are particularly strong,

the intellect does not have a moment's respite. This is because it is weakened by the passions to which it has succumbed in the past. But if it goes on searching, it will find; and if it knocks, the door will be opened (cf. Matt. 7:8).

31. Do not pray for the fulfilment of your wishes, for they may not accord with the will of God. But pray as you have been taught, saying: Thy will be done in me (cf. Luke 22:42). Always entreat Him in this way – that His will be done. For He desires what is good and profitable for you, whereas you do not always ask for this.

32. Often when I have prayed I have asked for what I thought was good, and persisted in my petition, stupidly importuning the will of God, and not leaving it to Him to arrange things as He knows is best for me. But when I have obtained what I asked for, I have been very sorry that I did not ask for the will of God to be done; because the thing turned out not to be as I had thought.

33. What is good, except God? Then let us leave to Him everything that concerns us and all will be well. For He who is good is naturally also a giver of good gifts.

34. Do not be distressed if you do not at once receive from God what you ask. He wishes to give you something better – to make you persevere in your prayer. For what is better than to enjoy the love of God and to be in communion with Him?

35. Undistracted prayer is the highest intellection of the intellect.

36. Prayer is the ascent of the intellect to God.

37. If you long for prayer, renounce all to gain all.

38. Pray first for the purification of the passions; secondly, for deliverance from ignorance and forgetfulness; and thirdly, for deliverance from all temptation, trial and dereliction.

39. In your prayer seek only righteousness and the kingdom of God, that is, virtue and spiritual knowledge; and everything else 'will be given to you' (Matt. 6:33).

40. It is right to pray not only for your own purification, but also for that of all your fellow men, and so to imitate the angels.

41. See whether you stand truly before God in your prayer, or are overcome by the desire for human praise, using prolonged prayer as a disguise.

42. Whether you pray with brethren or alone, try to pray not simply as a routine, but with conscious awareness of your prayer.

43. Conscious awareness of prayer is concentration accompanied

by reverence, compunction* and distress of soul as it confesses its sins with inward sorrow.

44. If your intellect is still distracted during prayer, you do not yet know what it is to pray as a monk; but your prayer is still worldly, embellishing the outer tabernacle.

45. When you pray, keep close watch on your memory, so that it does not distract you with recollections of your past. But make yourself aware that you are standing before God. For by nature the intellect is apt to be carried away by memories during prayer.

46. While you are praying, the memory brings before you fantasies either of past things, or of recent concerns, or of the face of someone who has irritated you.

47. The demon is very envious of us when we pray, and uses every kind of trick to thwart our purpose. Therefore he is always using our memory to stir up thoughts of various things and our flesh to arouse the passions, in order to obstruct our way of ascent to God.

48. When after many attempts the cunning demon fails to hinder the prayer of the righteous man, he slackens his efforts a little, and then gets his own back when the man has finished praying. Either he provokes the man to anger, and so destroys the good effects of the prayer, or else he excites him to senseless pleasure, and so degrades his intellect.

49. Having prayed as you should, expect the demon to attack you; so stand on guard, ready to protect the fruits of your prayer. For this from the start has been your appointed task: to cultivate and to protect (cf. Gen. 2 : 15). Therefore, having cultivated, do not leave the fruits unprotected; otherwise you will gain nothing from your prayer.

50. The warfare between us and the demons is waged solely on account of spiritual prayer. For prayer is extremely hateful and offensive to them, whereas it leads us to salvation and peace.

51. What is it that the demons wish to excite in us? Gluttony, unchastity, avarice, anger, rancour, and the rest of the passions, so that the intellect grows coarse and cannot pray as it ought. For when the passions are aroused in the non-rational part of our nature, they do not allow the intellect to function properly.

52. We practise the virtues in order to achieve contemplation of the inner essences (*logoi*) of created things, and from this we pass to

contemplation of the Logos who gives them their being; and He manifests Himself when we are in the state of prayer.

53. The state of prayer is one of dispassion, which by virtue of the most intense love[1] transports to the noetic* realm the intellect that longs for wisdom.

54. He who wishes to pray truly must not only control his incensive power and his desire, but must also free himself from every impassioned thought.

55. He who loves God is always communing with Him as his Father, repulsing every impassioned thought.

56. One who has attained dispassion has not necessarily achieved pure prayer. For he may still be occupied with thoughts which, though dispassionate, distract him and keep him far from God.

57. When the intellect no longer dallies with dispassionate thoughts about various things, it has not necessarily reached the realm of prayer; for it may still be contemplating the inner essences of these things. And though such contemplation is dispassionate, yet since it is of created things, it impresses their forms upon the intellect and keeps it away from God.

58. If the intellect has not risen above the contemplation of the created world, it has not yet beheld the realm of God perfectly. For it may be occupied with the knowledge of intelligible things and so involved in their multiplicity.

59. If you wish to pray, you have need of God, 'who gives prayer to him who prays' (1 Sam. 2:9. LXX). Invoke Him, then, saying: 'Hallowed be Thy name, Thy kingdom come' (Matt. 6:9–10) – that is, the Holy Spirit and Thy only-begotten Son. For so He taught us, saying: 'Worship the Father in spirit and in truth' (John 4:24).

60. He who prays in spirit and in truth is no longer dependent on created things when honouring the Creator, but praises Him for and in Himself.

61. If you are a theologian,* you will pray truly. And if you pray truly, you are a theologian.

62. When your intellect in its great longing for God gradually withdraws from the flesh and turns away from all thoughts that have their source in your sense-perception, memory or soul-body temperament,* and when it becomes full of reverence and joy,

[1] Intense longing.*

then you may conclude that you are close to the frontiers of prayer.

63. The Holy Spirit, out of compassion for our weakness, comes to us even when we are impure. And if only He finds our intellect truly praying to Him, He enters it and puts to flight the whole array of thoughts and ideas circling within it, and He arouses it to a longing for spiritual prayer.

64. While all else produces thoughts, ideas and speculations in the intellect through changes in the body, the Lord does the opposite: by entering the intellect, He fills it with whatever knowledge He wishes; and through the intellect He calms the uncontrolled impulses in the body.

65. Whoever loves true prayer and yet becomes angry or resentful is his own enemy. He is like a man who wants to see clearly and yet inflicts damage on his own eyes.

66. If you long to pray, do nothing that is opposed to prayer, so that God may draw near and be with you.

67. When you are praying, do not shape within yourself any image of the Deity, and do not let your intellect be stamped with the impress of any form; but approach the Immaterial in an immaterial manner, and then you will understand.

68. Be on your guard against the tricks of the demons. While you are praying purely and calmly, sometimes they suddenly bring before you some strange and alien form, making you imagine in your conceit that the Deity is there. They are trying to persuade you that the object suddenly disclosed to you is the Deity, whereas the Deity does not possess quantity and form.

69. When the jealous demon fails to stir up our memory during prayer, he disturbs the soul-body temperament, so as to form some strange fantasy in the intellect. Since your intellect is usually preoccupied with thoughts it is easily diverted: instead of pursuing immaterial and formless knowledge, it is deceived, mistaking smoke for light.

70. Stand on guard and protect your intellect from thoughts while you pray. Then your intellect will complete its prayer and continue in the tranquillity that is natural to it. In this way He who has compassion on the ignorant will come to you, and you will receive the blessed gift of prayer.

71. You cannot attain pure prayer while entangled in material

things and agitated by constant cares. For prayer means the shedding of thoughts.

72. A man who is tied up cannot run. Nor can the intellect that is a slave to passion perceive the realm of spiritual prayer. For it is dragged about by impassioned thoughts and cannot stay still.

73. When the intellect attains prayer that is pure and free from passion, the demons attack no longer with sinister thoughts but with thoughts of what is good. For they suggest to it an illusion of God's glory in a form pleasing to the senses, so as to make it think that it has realized the final aim of prayer. A man who possesses spiritual knowledge has said that this illusion results from the passion of self-esteem and from the demon's touch on a certain area of the brain.

74. I think that the demon, by touching this area, changes the light surrounding the intellect as he likes. In this way he uses the passion of self-esteem to stir up in the intellect a thought which fatuously attributes form and location to divine and principial knowledge. Not being disturbed by impure and carnal passions, but supposing itself to be in a state of purity, the intellect imagines that there is no longer any adverse energy within it. It then mistakes for a divine manifestation the appearance produced in it by the demon, who cunningly manipulates the brain and converts the light surrounding the intellect into a form, as we have described.

75. When the angel of God comes to us, with his presence alone he puts an end to all adverse energy within the intellect and makes its light energize without illusion.*

76. The statement in the Apocalypse that the angel brought incense and offered it with the prayers of the saints (cf. Rev. 8 : 3) refers, I think, to this grace which is energized through the angel. For it instils knowledge of true prayer, so that the intellect stands firm, free from all agitation, listlessness and negligence.

77. The bowls of incense which the twenty-four elders offered are said to be the prayers of the saints. By a bowl should be understood friendship with God or perfect spiritual love, whereby prayer is energized in spirit and in truth.

78. When you think that you do not need tears for your sins during prayer, reflect on this: you should always be in God, and yet you are still far from Him. Then you will weep with greater feeling.

79. Surely, when you do realize where you are, you will gladly sorrow and, like Isaiah, will reproach yourself because, being unclean, and dwelling in the midst of an unclean people – that is, of enemies – you dare to stand before the Lord of hosts (cf. Isa. 6:5).

80. If you pray truly, you will gain great assurance; angels will come to you as they came to Daniel, and they will illuminate you with knowledge of the inner essences of created things (cf. Dan. 2:19).

81. Know that the holy angels encourage us to pray and stand beside us, rejoicing and praying for us (cf. Tobit. 12:12). Therefore, if we are negligent and admit thoughts from the enemy, we greatly provoke the angels. For while they struggle hard on our behalf we do not even take the trouble to pray to God for ourselves, but we despise their services to us and, abandoning their Lord and God, we consort with unclean demons.

82. Pray gently and calmly, sing with understanding and rhythm; then you will soar like a young eagle high in the heavens.

83. Psalmody calms the passions and curbs the uncontrolled impulses in the body; and prayer enables the intellect to activate its own energy.

84. Prayer is the energy which accords with the dignity of the intellect; it is the intellect's true and highest activity.

85. Psalmody appertains to the wisdom of the world of multiplicity; prayer is the prelude to the immaterial knowledge of the One.[1]

86. Spiritual knowledge has great beauty: it is the helpmate of prayer, awakening the noetic power of the intellect to contemplation of divine knowledge.

87. If you have not yet received the gift of prayer or psalmody, persevere patiently and you will receive it.

88. 'And He spake a parable to them to this end, that men ought always to pray, and not to lose heart.' So do not lose heart and despair because you have not yet received the gift of prayer. You will receive it later. In the same parable we read: 'Though I do not fear God, or man's opinion, yet because this widow troubles me, I will vindicate her.' Similarly, God will speedily vindicate those who cry

---

[1] For 'immaterial knowledge of the One', the Greek text in the *Philokalia* reads 'immaterial and multiple knowledge'. We have adopted the emendation suggested by Hausherr.

to Him day and night (cf. Luke 18:1–8). Take heart, then, and persevere diligently in holy prayer.

89. You should wish for your affairs to turn out, not as you think best, but according to God's will. Then you will be undisturbed and thankful in your prayer.

90. Even if you think you are with God, be on your guard against the demon of unchastity. For he is very wily and jealous: he tries to outwit the activity and watchfulness of your intellect and to draw it away from God, when it stands before Him with reverence and fear.

91. If you cultivate prayer, be ready for the attacks of demons and endure them resolutely; for they will come at you like wild beasts and maltreat your whole body.

92. Prepare yourself like an experienced fighter, and even if you see a sudden apparition do not be shaken; and should you see a sword drawn against you, or a torch thrust into your face, do not be alarmed. Should you see even some loathsome and bloody figure, do not panic; but stand fast, boldly affirming your faith, and you will be more resolute in confronting your enemies.

93. He who bears distress patiently will attain joy, and he who endures the repulsive will know delight.

94. Take care that the crafty demons do not deceive you with some vision; be on your guard, turn to prayer and ask God to show you if the intellection comes from Him and, if it does not, to dispel the illusion at once. Do not be afraid, for if you pray fervently to God, the demons will retreat, lashed by His unseen power.

95. You should be aware of this trick: at times the demons split into two groups; and when you call for help against one group, the other will come in the guise of angels and drive away the first, so that you are deceived into believing that they are truly angels.

96. Cultivate great humility and courage, and you will escape the power of the demons; 'no plague shall come near your dwelling, for He shall give His angels charge over you' (Ps. 91:10–11). And they will invisibly repel all the energy of the enemy.

97. He who practises pure prayer will hear the demons crashing and banging, shouting and cursing; yet he will not be overwhelmed or go out of his mind. But he will say to God: 'I will fear no evil, for Thou art with me' (Ps. 23:4), and other words of this kind.

98. At the time of such trials, use a brief but intense prayer.

99. If the demons suddenly threaten to appear out of the air, to

make you panic and to take possession of your intellect, do not be frightened and pay no attention to their threats. For they are trying to terrify you, to see if you take notice of them or scorn them utterly.

100. When you stand in prayer before God the Almighty, who created all things and takes thought for all, why are you so foolish as to forget the fear of God and to be scared of mosquitoes and cockroaches? Have you not heard it said, 'You shall fear the Lord your God' (Deut. 6:13); or again 'Fear and dread shall fall upon them' (Exod. 15:16)?

101. Bread is food for the body and holiness is food for the soul; spiritual prayer is food for the intellect.

102. When you are in the inner temple pray not as the Pharisee but as the publican, so that you too are set free by the Lord (cf. Luke 18:10–14).

103. Try not to pray against anyone in your prayer, so that you do not destroy what you are building, and make your prayer loathsome.

104. Learn from the man who owed the ten thousand talents that, if you do not forgive your debtor, you yourself will not be forgiven. For it is said, 'He delivered him to the tormentors' (Matt. 18:34).

105. Detach yourself from concern for the body when you pray: do not let the sting of a flea or a fly, the bite of a louse or a mosquito, deprive you of the fruits of your prayer.

106. We have heard that the evil one attacked a certain saint so fiercely as he prayed that, when the saint lifted up his hands, the evil one changed himself into a lion and raising his front legs fixed his claws into the saint's thighs; and he kept them there until the saint lowered his hands, which was only when he had come to the end of his usual prayers.

107. There is too the case of that great monk, John the Small. He lived the hesychastic life in a pit, and his communion with God was not interrupted even when a demon in the form of a serpent wound itself round him, chewed his flesh and spat it out into his face.

108. You have surely read the lives of the monks of Tabennesis. When Abba Theodore was preaching to the brethren, two vipers crawled under his feet; but he calmly made an arch of his feet and let them stay there until he had finished his sermon. Then he showed the vipers to the brethren and told them what had happened.

109. We read how, when another spiritual brother was praying, a viper came and wound itself round his leg. But he did not lower his hands until he had finished all his usual prayers; and because he loved God more than himself, he was not harmed at all.

110. Do not let your eyes be distracted during prayer, but detach yourself from concern with body and soul, and give all your attention to the intellect.

111. Another saint living the hesychastic life in the desert was attacked, as he was praying, by demons who for two weeks tossed him like a ball in the air, catching him in his rush-mat. They were completely unsuccessful in distracting his mind from fiery prayer.

112. When another monk was practising inner prayer as he journeyed in the desert, two angels came and walked on either side of him. But he paid no heed to them, for he did not wish to lose what was better. He remembered the words of the Apostle: 'Neither angels, nor principalities, nor powers . . . shall be able to separate us from the love of Christ' (Rom. 8:38–39).

113. The monk becomes equal to the angels through prayer, because of his longing to 'behold the face of the Father who is in heaven' (cf. Matt. 18:10).

114. Never try to see a form or shape during prayer.

115. Do not long to have a sensory image of angels or powers or Christ, for this would be madness: it would be to take a wolf as your shepherd and to worship your enemies, the demons.

116. Self-esteem is the start of illusions in the intellect. Under its impulse, the intellect attempts to enclose the Deity in shapes and forms.

117. I shall say again what I have said elsewhere: blessed is the intellect that is completely free from forms during prayer.

118. Blessed is the intellect that, undistracted in its prayer, acquires an ever greater longing for God.

119. Blessed is the intellect that during prayer is free from materiality and stripped of all possessions.

120. Blessed is the intellect that has acquired complete freedom from sensations during prayer.

121. Blessed is the monk who regards every man as God after God.

122. Blessed is the monk who looks with great joy on everyone's salvation and progress as if they were his own.

123. Blessed is the monk who regards himself as 'the offscouring of all things' (1 Cor. 4:13).

124. A monk is one who is separated from all and united with all.

125. A monk is one who regards himself as linked with every man, through always seeing himself in each.

126. The man who always dedicates his first thoughts to God has perfect prayer.

127. If you want to pray as a monk, shun all lies and take no oath. Otherwise you vainly pretend to be what you are not.

128. If you wish to pray in spirit, be detached from the flesh, and no cloud will darken you during prayer.

129. Entrust to God the needs of your body, and it will be clear that you entrust to Him the needs of your spirit also.

130. If you receive what has been promised, you will reign over all things; and, keeping these promises in mind, you will gladly endure your present poverty, spiritual and material.

131. Do not shun poverty and affliction, the fuel that gives wings to prayer.

132. Let the virtues of the body lead you to those of the soul; and the virtues of the soul to those of the spirit; and these, in turn, to immaterial and principial knowledge.

133. If you are praying to overcome some thought, and it subsides easily, examine carefully how this has come about; otherwise you may be deluded into attributing the cause to yourself.

134. There are times when the demons suggest thoughts to you and then urge you to rebut them with prayer; whereupon they withdraw of their own accord, so as to deceive you into imagining that you have begun to overcome such thoughts and to rout the demons.

135. If you pray to overcome a passion or a demon who is troubling you, remember the words: 'I will pursue my enemies, and overtake them; and I will not turn back until they are consumed. I will dash them to pieces and they shall not be able to stand: they shall fall under my feet' (Ps. 18:37–38. LXX). Say this when needed and so arm yourself with humility against your enemies.

136. Do not think that you have acquired holiness unless you have reached the point of shedding your blood to attain it. For, according to the Apostle, we must battle unremittingly against sin even if it means death (cf. Eph. 6:11–17; Heb. 12:4).

137. If you do good to one person, you may be wronged by another and so feel injured, and say or do something stupid, thus dissipating by your bad action what you gained by your good action. This is just what the demons want; so always be attentive.

138. Be ready for the attacks of the demons, and think how to avoid becoming their slave.

139. At night the cunning demons try to disturb the spiritual teacher by direct attack; in the daytime, they attack him through other people, besieging him with slander, distraction and danger.

140. Do not try to avoid the fullers. Let them beat, trample, stretch and smooth; and your garments will be all the brighter.

141. So long as you have not renounced the passions, and your intellect is still opposed to holiness and truth, you will not find the fragrance of incense in your breast.

142. Do you have a longing for prayer? Then leave the things of this world and live your life in heaven, not just theoretically but in angelic action and godlike knowledge.

143. If it is only in times of adversity that you remember the Judge and how awe-inspiring and impartial He is, you have not yet learned 'to serve the Lord with fear and rejoice in Him with trembling' (Ps. 2:11). For even in a state of spiritual peace and blessedness you still worship Him with reverence and awe.

144. Until a man is completely changed by repentance, he will be wise always to remember his sins with sorrow and to recall the eternal fire which they justly deserve.

145. If a man, still enmeshed in sin and anger, dares shamelessly to reach out for knowledge of divine things, or even to embark upon immaterial prayer, he deserves the rebuke given by the Apostle; for it is dangerous for him to pray with head bare and uncovered. Such a soul, he says, ought 'to have a veil on her head because of the angels' who are present (cf. 1 Cor. 11:5–7), and to be clothed in due reverence and humility.

146. Just as persistent staring at the sun in its noonday brilliance will not cure a man suffering from ophthalmia, so the counterfeit practice of fearful and supernal prayer – which is properly to be performed in spirit and in truth – will in no way benefit an intellect that is passionate and impure; on the contrary, such practice will provoke the wrath of God against the intellect.

147. If He who is in want of nothing and shows no favours did

not receive the man coming with a gift to the altar until he was reconciled with his neighbour who had something against him (cf. Matt. 5:23–24), consider how much we must be on guard and use discrimination if we are to offer at the spiritual altar incense that is acceptable to God.

148. Do not delight in words or in glory. Otherwise the demons will no longer work behind your back, but openly before your face; and they will laugh you to scorn during prayer, drawing you away and enticing you into strange thoughts.

149. If you seek prayer attentively you will find it; for nothing is more essential to prayer than attentiveness. So do all you can to acquire it.

150. As sight is superior to all the other senses, so prayer is more divine than all the other virtues.

151. The value of prayer lies not in mere quantity but in its quality. This is shown by the contrast of the two men who went up into the temple (cf. Luke 18:10), and by the injunction: 'When you pray, do not use vain repetitions' (Matt. 6:7).

152. So long as you give attention to the beauty of the body, and your intellect delights in the outside of the tabernacle, you have not yet perceived the realm of prayer and are still far from treading its blessed path.

153. If when praying no other joy can attract you, then truly you have found prayer.

ST JOHN CASSIAN

Introductory Note

St John Cassian, often styled 'Cassian the Roman' in Greek sources, was born around the year 360, probably in Roman Scythia. As a young man he joined a monastery in Bethlehem, but around 385–6 he travelled with his friend Germanos to Egypt, where he remained until 399, becoming a disciple of Evagrios. During 401–5 he was at Constantinople, where he was ordained deacon; here he became a disciple and ardent supporter of St John Chrysostom. In 405 he travelled to the West, remaining for some years in Rome and then moving to Gaul. Either in Rome or in Gaul he was ordained priest. Around 415 he founded two monasteries near Marseilles, one for men and the other for women. His two main works are the *Institutes* and the *Conferences*, both written in Latin around the years 425–8. In these Cassian summarized the spiritual teaching which he had received in Egypt, adapting it to the somewhat different conditions of the West. His writings exercised a formative influence on Latin monasticism and are especially commended in the *Rule* of St Benedict. Cassian died around 435 and is commemorated in the Orthodox Church as a saint, his feast-day falling on 29 February.

St Nikodimos included in the *Philokalia* a Greek summary of certain parts of Cassian's main writings. The first text, *On the Eight Vices*, is taken from the *Institutes*, Books V-XII; the second text, *On the Holy Fathers of Sketis and on Discrimination*, comes from the *Conferences*, Books I-II. In both cases the Greek version considerably abbreviates the Latin original.[1]

---

[1] There is a full English translation of the *Institutes* and the *Conferences* by E. C. S. Gibson, in P. Schaff and H. Wace (editors), *A Select Library of Nicene and Post-Nicene Fathers of the Christian Church*, Second Series, Vol. XI (Oxford/New York, 1894; reprinted, Grand Rapids, 1955). The best study on Cassian in English is O. Chadwick, *John Cassian. A Study in Primitive Monasticism* (Cambridge, 1950; 2nd edition, Cambridge, 1968).

On the Eight Vices
WRITTEN FOR BISHOP KASTOR

Having composed the treatise on coenobitic institutions, I am now once more encouraged by your prayers to attempt to write something about the eight vices: gluttony, unchastity, avarice, anger, dejection, listlessness, self-esteem and pride.

ON CONTROL OF THE STOMACH

I shall speak first about control of the stomach, the opposite to gluttony, and about how to fast and what and how much to eat. I shall say nothing on my own account, but only what I have received from the Holy Fathers. They have not given us only a single rule for fasting or a single standard and measure for eating, because not everyone has the same strength; age, illness or delicacy of body create differences. But they have given us all a single goal: to avoid over-eating and the filling of our bellies. They also found a day's fast to be more beneficial and a greater help toward purity than one extending over a period of three, four, or even seven days. Someone who fasts for too long, they say, often ends up by eating too much food. The result is that at times the body becomes enervated through undue lack of food and sluggish over its spiritual exercises, while at other times, weighed down by the mass of food it has eaten, it makes the soul listless and slack.

They also found that the eating of greens or pulse did not agree with everyone, and that not everyone could live on dry bread. One man, they said, could eat two pounds of dry bread and still be hungry, while another might eat a pound, or only six ounces, and be satisfied. As I said, the Fathers have handed down a single basic rule of self-control: 'do not be deceived by the filling of the belly' (Prov. 24:15. LXX), or be led astray by the pleasure of the palate. It is not only the variety of foodstuffs that kindles the fiery darts of unchastity, but also their quantity. Whatever the kind of food with which it is filled, the belly engenders the seed of profligacy. It is not only too much wine that besots our mind: too much water or too much of anything makes it drowsy and stupefied. The Sodomites were destroyed not because of too much wine or too much of other foods, but because of a surfeit of bread, as the Prophet tells us (cf. Ezek. 16:49).

Bodily illness is not an obstacle to purity of heart, provided we give the body what its illness requires, not what gratifies our desire for pleasure. Food is to be taken in so far as it supports our life, but not to the extent of enslaving us to the impulses of desire. To eat moderately and reasonably is to keep the body in health, not to deprive it of holiness.

A clear rule for self-control handed down by the Fathers is this: stop eating while still hungry and do not continue until you are satisfied. When the Apostle said, 'Make no provision to fulfil the desires of the flesh' (Rom. 13:14), he was not forbidding us to provide for the needs of life; he was warning us against self-indulgence. Moreover, by itself abstinence from food does not contribute to perfect purity of soul unless the other virtues are active as well. Humility, for example, practised through obedience in our work and through bodily hardship, is a great help. If we avoid avarice not only by having no money, but also by not wanting to have any, this leads us towards purity of soul. Freedom from anger, from dejection, self-esteem and pride also contributes to purity of soul in general, while self-control and fasting are especially important for bringing about that specific purity of soul which comes through restraint and moderation. No one whose stomach is full can fight mentally against the demon of unchastity. Our initial struggle therefore must be to gain control of our stomach and to bring our body into subjection not only through fasting but also through vigils, labours and spiritual reading, and through concentrating our heart on fear of Gehenna and on longing for the kingdom of heaven.

ON THE DEMON OF UNCHASTITY AND
THE DESIRE OF THE FLESH

Our second struggle is against the demon of unchastity and the desire of the flesh, a desire which begins to trouble man from the time of his youth. This harsh struggle has to be fought in both soul and body, and not simply in the soul, as is the case with other faults. We therefore have to fight it on two fronts.

Bodily fasting alone is not enough to bring about perfect self-restraint and true purity; it must be accompanied by contrition of heart, intense prayer to God, frequent meditation on the Scriptures, toil and manual labour. These are able to check the restless impulses of the soul and to recall it from its shameful fantasies. Humility of soul helps more than everything else, however, and without it no one can overcome unchastity or any other sin. In the first place, then, we must take the utmost care to guard the heart from base thoughts, for, according to the Lord, 'out of the heart proceed evil thoughts, murders, adulteries, unchastity' and so on (Matt. 15:19).

We are told to fast not only to mortify our body, but also to keep our intellect watchful, so that it will not be obscured because of the amount of food we have eaten and thus be unable to guard its thoughts. We must not therefore expend all our effort in bodily fasting; we must also give attention to our thoughts and to spiritual meditation, since otherwise we will not be able to advance to the heights of true purity and chastity. As our Lord has said, we should 'cleanse first the inside of the cup and plate, so that their outside may also be clean' (Matt. 23:26).

If we are really eager, as the Apostle puts it, to 'struggle lawfully' and to 'be crowned' (2 Tim: 2:5) for overcoming the impure spirit of unchastity, we should not trust in our own strength and ascetic practice, but in the help of our Master, God. No one ceases to be attacked by this demon until he truly believes that he will be healed and reach the heights of purity not through his own effort and labour, but through the aid and protection of God. For such a victory is beyond man's natural powers. Indeed, he who has trampled down the pleasures and provocations of the flesh is in a certain sense outside the body. Thus, no one can soar to this high and heavenly prize of holiness on his own wings and learn to imitate the angels, unless the grace of God leads him upwards from this earthly mire.

No virtue makes flesh-bound man so like a spiritual angel as does self-restraint, for it enables those still living on earth to become, as the Apostle says, 'citizens of heaven' (cf. Phil. 3:20). A sign that we have acquired this virtue perfectly is that our soul ignores those images which the defiled fantasy produces during sleep; for even if the production of such images is not a sin, nevertheless it is a sign that the soul is ill and has not been freed from passion. We should therefore regard the defiled fantasies that arise in us during sleep as the proof of previous indolence and weakness still existing in us, since the emission which takes place while we are relaxed in sleep reveals the sickness that lies hidden in our souls. Because of this the Doctor of our souls has also placed the remedy in the hidden regions of the soul, recognizing that the cause of our sickness lies there when He says: 'Whoever looks at a woman with lust has already committed adultery with her in his heart' (Matt. 5:28). He seeks to correct not so much our inquisitive and unchaste eyes as the soul which has its seat within and makes bad use of the eyes which God gave it for good purposes. That is why the Book of Proverbs in its wisdom does not say: 'Guard your eyes with all diligence' but 'Guard your heart with all diligence' (Prov. 4:23), imposing the remedy of diligence in the first instance upon that which makes use of the eyes for whatever purpose it desires.

The way to keep guard over our heart is immediately to expel from the mind every demon-inspired recollection of women – even of mother or sister or any other devout woman – lest by dwelling on it for too long the mind is thrown headlong by the deceiver into debased and pernicious thoughts. The commandment given by God to the first man, Adam, told him to keep watch over the head of the serpent (cf. Gen. 3:15. LXX), that is, over the first inklings of the pernicious thoughts by means of which the serpent tries to creep into our souls. If we do not admit the serpent's head, which is the provocation of the thought, we will not admit the rest of its body – that is, the assent* to the sensual pleasure which the thought suggests – and so debase the mind towards the illicit act itself.

As it is written, we should 'early in the morning destroy all the wicked of the earth' (Ps. 101:8), distinguishing in the light of divine knowledge our sinful thoughts and then eradicating them completely from the earth – our hearts – in accordance with the teaching of the Lord. While the children of Babylon – by which I mean our wicked thoughts – are still young, we should dash them to the ground and crush them against the rock, which is Christ (cf. Ps. 137:9; 1 Cor. 10:4). If these thoughts grow stronger because we assent to them, we will not be able to overcome them without much pain and labour.

It is good to remember the sayings of the Fathers as well as the passages from Holy Scripture cited above. For example, St Basil, Bishop of Caesarea in Cappadocia, said: 'I have not known a woman and yet I am not a virgin.' He recognized that the gift of virginity is achieved not so much by abstaining from intercourse with woman as by holiness and purity of soul, which in its turn is achieved through fear of God. The Fathers also say that we cannot fully acquire the virtue of purity unless we have first acquired real humility of heart. And we will not be granted true spiritual knowledge so long as the passion of unchastity lies hidden in the depths of our souls.

To bring this section of our treatise to a close, let us recall one of the Apostle's sayings which further illustrates his teaching on how to acquire self-restraint. He says: 'Pursue peace with all men and the holiness without which no one will see the Lord' (Heb. 12:14). It is clear that he is talking about self-restraint from what follows: 'Lest there be any unchaste or profane person, such as Esau' (Heb. 12:16). The more heavenly and angelic the degree of holiness, the heavier are the enemies' attacks to which it is subjected. We should therefore try to achieve not only bodily control, but also contrition of heart with frequent prayers of repentance, so that with the dew of the Holy Spirit we may extinguish the furnace of our flesh, kindled daily by the king of Babylon with the bellows of desire (cf. Dan. 3:19). In addition, a great weapon has been given us in the form of sacred vigils; for just as the watch we keep over our thoughts by day brings us holiness at night, so vigil at night brings purity to the soul by day.

ON AVARICE

Our third struggle is against the demon of avarice, a demon clearly foreign to our nature, who only gains entry into a monk because he is lacking in faith. The other passions, such as anger and desire, seem to be occasioned by the body and in some sense implanted in us at birth. Hence they are conquered only after a long time. The sickness of avarice, on the contrary, can with diligence and attention be cut off more readily, because it enters from outside. If neglected, however, it becomes even harder to get rid of and more destructive than the other passions, for according to the Apostle it is 'the root of all evil' (1 Tim. 6:10).

Let us look at it in this fashion. Movement occurs in the sexual organs not only of young children who cannot yet distinguish between good and evil, but also of the smallest infants still at their mother's breast. The latter, although quite ignorant of sensual pleasure, nevertheless manifest such natural movements in the flesh. Similarly, the incensive power exists in infants, as we can see when they are roused against anyone hurting them. I say this not to accuse nature of being the cause of sin – heaven forbid! – but to show that the incensive power and desire, even if implanted in man by the Creator for a good purpose, appear to change through neglect from being natural in the body into something that is unnatural. Movement in the sexual organs was given to us by the Creator for procreation and the continuation of the species, not for unchastity; while incensive power was planted in us for our salvation, so that we could manifest it against wickedness, but not so that we could act like wild beasts towards our fellow men. Even if we make bad use of these passions, nature itself is not therefore sinful, nor should we blame the Creator. A man who gives someone a knife for some necessary and useful purpose is not to blame if that person uses it to commit murder.

This has been said to make it clear that avarice is a passion deriving, not from our nature, but solely from an evil and perverted use of our free will. When this sickness finds the soul lukewarm and lacking in faith at the start of the ascetic path, it suggests to us various apparently justifiable and sensible reasons for keeping back something of what we possess. It conjures up in a monk's mind a picture of a lengthy old age and bodily illness; and it persuades him that the necessities of life provided by the monastery are insufficient to sustain a healthy man, much less an ill one; that in the monastery the sick, instead of receiving proper attention, are hardly cared for at all; and that unless he has some money tucked away, he will die a miserable death. Finally, it convinces him that he will not be able to remain long in the monastery because of the load of his work and the strictness of the abbot. When with thoughts like these it has seduced his mind with the idea of concealing any sum, however trifling, it persuades him to learn, unknown to the abbot, some handicraft through which he can increase his cherished hoardings. Then it deceives the wretched monk with secret expectations, making him imagine what he will earn from his handicraft, and the comfort and security which will result from it. Now completely given over to the thought of gain, he notices none of the evil passions which attack him: his raging fury when he happens to sustain a loss, his gloom and dejection when he falls short of the gain he hoped for. Just as for other people the belly is a god, so for him is money. That is why the Apostle, knowing this, calls avarice not only 'the root of all evil' but 'idolatry' as well (Col. 3 : 5).

How is it that this sickness can so pervert a man that he ends up as an idolater? It is because he now fixes his intellect on the love, not of God, but of the images of men stamped on gold. A monk darkened by such thoughts and launched on the downward path can no longer be obedient. He is irritable and resentful, and grumbles about every task. He answers back and, having lost his sense of respect, behaves like a stubborn, uncontrollable horse. He is not satisfied with the day's ration of food and complains that he cannot put up with such conditions for ever. Neither God's presence, he says, nor the possibility of his own salvation is confined to the monastery; and, he concludes, he will perish if he does not leave it. He is so excited and encouraged in these perverse thoughts by his secret hoardings that he even plans to quit the monastery. Then he replies proudly and harshly no matter what he is told to do, and pays no heed if he sees something in the monastery that needs to be set right, considering himself a stranger and outsider and finding fault with all that takes place. Then he seeks excuses for being angry or injured, so that he will not appear to be leaving the monastery frivolously and without cause. He does not even shrink from trying through gossip and idle talk to seduce someone else into leaving with him, wishing to have an accomplice in his sinful action.

Because the avaricious monk is so fired with desire for private wealth he will never be able to live at peace in a monastery or under a rule. When like a wolf the demon has snatched him from the fold and separated him from the flock, he makes ready to devour him; he sets him to work day and night in his cell on the very tasks which he complained of doing at fixed times in the monastery. But the demon does not allow him to keep the regular prayers or norms of fasting or orders of vigil. Having bound him fast in the madness of avarice, he persuades him to devote all his effort to his handicraft.

There are three forms of this sickness, all of which are equally condemned by the Holy Scriptures and the teaching of the Fathers. The first induces those who were poor to acquire and save the goods they lacked in the world. The second compels those who have renounced worldly goods by offering them to God, to have regrets and to seek after them again. A third infects a monk from the start with lack of faith and ardour, so preventing his complete detachment from worldly things, producing in him a fear of poverty and distrust in God's providence and leading him to break the promises he made when he renounced the world.

Examples of these three forms of avarice are, as I have said, condemned in Holy Scripture. Gehazi wanted to acquire property which he did not previously possess, and therefore never received the prophetic grace which his teacher had wished to leave him in the place of an inheritance. Because of the prophet's curse he inherited incurable leprosy instead of a blessing (cf. 2 Kgs. 5:27). And Judas, who wished to acquire money which he had previously abandoned on following Christ, not only lapsed so far as to betray the Master and lose his place in the circle of the apostles; he also put an end to his life in the flesh through a violent death (cf. Matt. 27:5). Thirdly, Ananias and Sapphira were condemned to death by the Apostle's word when they kept back something of what they had acquired (cf. Acts 5:1–10). Again, in Deuteronomy Moses is indirectly exhorting those who promise to renounce the world, and who then retain their earthly possessions because of the fear that comes from lack of faith, when he says: 'What man is there that is fearful and faint-hearted? He shall not go out to do battle; let him return to his house, lest his brethren's heart faint as well as his heart' (cf. Deut. 20:8). Could anything be clearer or more certain than this testimony? Should not we who have left the world learn from these examples to renounce it completely and in this state go forth to do battle? We should not turn others from the perfection taught in the Gospels and make them cowardly because of our own hesitant and feeble start.

Some, impelled by their own deceit and avarice, distort the

meaning of the scriptural statement, 'It is more blessed to give than to receive' (Acts 20:35). They do the same with the Lord's words when He says, 'If you want to be perfect, go and sell all you have and give to the poor, and you will have treasure in heaven; and come and follow Me' (Matt. 19:21). They judge that it is more blessed to have control over one's personal wealth, and to give from this to those in need, than to possess nothing at all. They should know, however, that they have not yet renounced the world or achieved monastic perfection so long as they are ashamed to accept for Christ's sake the poverty of the Apostle and to provide for themselves and the needy through the labour of their hands (cf. Acts 20:34); for only in this way will they fulfil the monastic profession and be glorified with the Apostle. Having distributed their former wealth, let them fight the good fight with Paul 'in hunger and thirst . . . in cold and nakedness' (2 Cor. 11:27). Had the Apostle thought that the possession of one's former wealth was more necessary for perfection, he would not have despised his official status as a Roman citizen (cf. Acts 22:25). Nor would those in Jerusalem have sold their houses and fields and given the money they got from them to the apostles (cf. Acts 4:34–35), had they felt that the apostles considered it more blessed to live off one's own possessions than from one's labour and the offerings of the Gentiles.

The Apostle gives us a clear lesson in this matter when he writes to the Romans in the passage beginning, 'But now I go to Jerusalem to minister to the saints', and ending: 'They were pleased to do it, and indeed they are in debt to them' (Rom. 15:25–27). He himself was often in chains, in prison or on fatiguing travel, and so was usually prevented from providing for himself with his own hands. He tells us that he accepted the necessities of life from the brethren who came to him from Macedonia (cf. 2 Cor. 11:9); and writing to the Philippians he says: 'Now you Philippians know also that . . . when I departed from Macedonia no church except you helped me with gifts of money. For even in Thessalonica you sent me help, not once but twice' (Phil. 4:15–16). Are, then, the avaricious right and are these men more blessed than the Apostle himself, because they satisfied his wants from their own resources? Surely no one would be so foolish as to say this.

If we want to follow the gospel commandment and the practice of the whole Church as it was founded initially upon the apostles, we should not follow our own notions or give wrong meanings to things rightly said. We must discard faint-hearted, faithless opinion and recover the strictness of the Gospel. In this way we shall be able to follow also in the footsteps of the Fathers, adhering to the discipline of the cenobitic life and truly renouncing this world.

It is good here to recall the words of St Basil, Bishop of Caesarea in Cappadocia. He is reported once to have said to a senator, who had renounced the world in a half-hearted manner and was keeping back some of his personal fortune: 'You have lost the senator and failed to make a monk.' We should therefore make every effort to cut out from our souls this root of all evils, avarice, in the certain knowledge that if the root remains the branches will sprout freely.

This uprooting is difficult to achieve unless we are living in a monastery, for in a monastery we cease to worry about even our most basic needs. With the fate of Ananias and Sapphira in mind, we should shudder at the thought of keeping to ourselves anything of our former possessions. Similarly, frightened by the example of Gehazi who was afflicted with incurable leprosy because of his avarice, let us guard against piling up money which we did not have while in the world. Finally, recalling Judas' death by hanging, let us beware of acquiring again any of the things which we have already renounced. In all this we should remember how uncertain is the hour of our death, so that our Lord does not come unexpectedly and, finding our conscience soiled with avarice, say to us what God says to the rich man in the Gospel: 'You fool, this night your soul will be required of you: who then will be the owner of what you have stored up?' (Luke 12:20).

ON ANGER

Our fourth struggle is against the demon of anger. We must, with God's help, eradicate his deadly poison from the depths of our souls. So long as he dwells in our hearts and blinds the eyes of the heart with his sombre disorders, we can neither discriminate what is for our good, nor achieve spiritual knowledge, nor fulfil our good intentions, nor participate in true life; and our intellect will remain impervious to the contemplation of the true, divine light; for it is written, 'For my eye is troubled because of anger' (Ps. 6:7. LXX).

Nor will we share in divine wisdom even though we are deemed wise by all men, for it is written: 'Anger lodges in the bosom of fools' (Eccles. 7:9). Nor can we discriminate in decisions affecting our salvation even though we are thought by our fellow men to have good sense, for it is written: 'Anger destroys even men of good sense' (Prov. 15:1. LXX). Nor will we be able to keep our lives in righteousness with a watchful heart, for it is written: 'Man's anger does not bring about the righteousness of God' (Jas. 1:20). Nor will we be able to acquire the decorum and dignity praised by all, for it is written: 'An angry man is not dignified' (Prov. 11:25. LXX).

If, therefore, you desire to attain perfection and rightly to pursue the spiritual way, you should make yourself a stranger to all sinful anger and wrath. Listen to what St Paul enjoins: 'Rid yourselves of all bitterness, wrath, anger, clamour, evil speaking and all malice' (Eph. 4:31). In saying 'all' he leaves no excuse for regarding any anger as necessary or reasonable. If you want to correct your brother when he is doing wrong or to punish him, you must try to keep yourself calm; otherwise you yourself may catch the sickness you are seeking to cure and you may find that the words of the Gospel now apply to you: 'Physician, heal yourself' (Luke 4:23), or 'Why do you look at the speck of dust in your brother's eye, and not notice the rafter in your own eye?' (Matt. 7:3).

No matter what provokes it, anger blinds the soul's eyes, preventing it from seeing the Sun of righteousness. Leaves, whether of gold or lead, placed over the eyes, obstruct the sight equally, for the value of the gold does not affect the blindness it produces. Similarly, anger, whether reasonable or unreasonable, obstructs our spiritual vision. Our incensive power can be used in a way that is according to nature only when turned against our own impassioned or self-indulgent thoughts. This is what the Prophet teaches us when he says: 'Be angry, and do not sin' (Ps. 4:4. LXX) – that is, be angry with your own passions and with your malicious thoughts, and do not sin by carrying out their suggestions. What follows clearly confirms this interpretation: 'As you lie in bed, repent of what you say in your heart' (Ps. 4:4. LXX) – that is, when malicious thoughts enter your heart, expel them with anger, and then turn to compunction and repentance as if your soul were resting in a bed of stillness.

St Paul agrees with this when he cites this passage and then adds:

'Do not let the sun go down upon your anger: and do not make room for the devil' (Eph. 4:26–27), by which he means: 'Do not make Christ, the Sun of righteousness, set in your hearts by angering him through your assent to evil thoughts, thereby allowing the devil to find room in you because of Christ's departure.' God has spoken of this Sun in the words of His prophet: 'But upon you that fear My name shall the Sun of righteousness arise with healing in His wings' (Mal. 4:2). If we take Paul's saying literally, it does not permit us to keep our anger even until sunset. What then shall we say about those who, because of the harshness and fury of their impassioned state, not only maintain their anger until the setting of this day's sun, but prolong it for many days? Or about others who do not express their anger, but keep silent and increase the poison of their rancour to their own destruction? They are unaware that we must avoid anger not only in what we do but also in our thoughts; otherwise our intellect will be darkened by our rancour, cut off from the light of spiritual knowledge and discrimination, and deprived of the indwelling of the Holy Spirit.

It is for this reason that the Lord commands us to leave our offering before the altar and be reconciled with our brother (cf. Matt. 5:23–24), since our offering will not be acceptable so long as anger and rancour are bottled up within us. The Apostle teaches us the same thing when he tells us to 'pray without ceasing' (1 Thess. 5:17), and to 'pray every where, lifting up holy hands without anger and without quarrelling' (1 Tim. 2:8). We are thus left with the choice either of never praying, and so of disobeying the Apostle's commandment, or of trying earnestly to fulfil his commandment by praying without anger or rancour.

We are often indifferent to our brethren who are distressed or upset, on the grounds that they are in this state through no fault of ours. The Doctor of souls, however, wishing to root out the soul's excuses from the heart, tells us to leave our gift and to be reconciled not only if we happen to be upset by our brother, but also if he is upset by us, whether justly or unjustly; only when we have healed the breach through our apology should we offer our gift.

We may find the same teaching in the Old Testament as well. As though in complete agreement with the Gospels, it says: 'Do not hate your brother in your heart' (Lev. 19:17); and: 'The way of the rancorous leads to death' (Prov. 12:28. LXX). These passages, then, not only forbid anger in what we do but also angry thought. If therefore we are to follow the divine laws, we must struggle with all our strength against the demon of anger and against the sickness which lies hidden within us. When we are angry with others we should not seek solitude on the grounds that there, at least, no one will provoke us to anger, and that in solitude the virtue of long-suffering can easily be acquired. Our desire to leave our brethren is because of our pride, and because we do not wish to blame ourselves and ascribe to our own laxity the cause of our unruliness. So long as we assign the causes for our weaknesses to others, we cannot attain perfection in long-suffering.

Self-reform and peace are not achieved through the patience which others show us, but through our own long-suffering towards our neighbour. When we try to escape the struggle for long-suffering by retreating into solitude, those unhealed passions we take there with us are merely hidden, not erased; for unless our passions are first purged, solitude and withdrawal from the world not only foster them but also keep them concealed, no longer allowing us to perceive what passion it is that enslaves us. On the contrary, they impose on us an illusion of virtue and persuade us to believe that we have achieved long-suffering and humility, because there is no one present to provoke and test us. But as soon as something happens which does arouse and challenge us, our hidden and previously unnoticed passions immediately break out like uncontrolled horses that have long been kept unexercised and idle, dragging their driver all the more violently and wildly to destruction. Our passions grow fiercer when left idle through lack of contact with other people. Even that shadow of patience and long-suffering which we thought we possessed while we mixed with our brethren is lost in our isolation through not being exercised. Poisonous creatures that live quietly in their lairs in the desert display their fury only when they detect someone approaching; and likewise passion-filled men, who live quietly not because of their virtuous disposition but because of their solitude, spit forth their venom whenever someone approaches and provokes them. This is why those seeking perfect gentleness must make every effort to avoid anger not only towards men, but also towards animals and even inanimate objects.

I can remember how, when I lived in the desert, I became angry with the rushes because they were either too thick or too thin; or with a piece of wood, when I wished to cut it quickly and could not; or with a flint, when I was in a hurry to light a fire and the spark would not come. So all-embracing was my anger that it was aroused even against inanimate objects.

If then we wish to receive the Lord's blessing we should restrain not only the outward expression of anger, but also angry thoughts. More beneficial than controlling our tongue in a moment of anger and refraining from angry words is purifying our heart from rancour and not harbouring malicious thoughts against our brethren. The Gospel teaches us to cut off the roots of our sins and not merely their fruits. When we have dug the root of anger out of our heart, we will no longer act with hatred or envy. 'Whoever hates his brother is a murderer' (1 John 3:15), for he kills him with the hatred in his mind. The blood of a man who has been slain by the sword can be seen by men, but blood shed by the hatred in the mind is seen by God, who rewards each man with punishment or a crown not only for his acts but for his thoughts and intentions as well. As God Himself says through the Prophet: 'Behold, I am coming to reward them according to their actions and their thoughts' (cf. Ecclus. 35:19); and the Apostle says: 'And their thoughts accuse or else excuse them in the day when God shall judge the secrets of men' (Rom. 2:15–16). The Lord Himself teaches us to put aside all anger when He says: 'Whoever is angry with his brother shall be in danger of judgment' (Matt. 5:22). This is the text of the best manuscripts; for it is clear from the purpose of Scripture in this context that the words 'without a cause' were added later. The Lord's intention is that we should remove the root of anger, its spark, so to speak, in whatever way we can, and not keep even a single pretext for anger in our hearts. Otherwise we will be stirred to anger initially for what appears to be a good reason and then find that our incensive power is totally out of control.

The final cure for this sickness is to realize that we must not become angry for any reason whatsoever, whether just or unjust. When the demon of anger has darkened our mind, we are left with neither the light of discrimination, nor the assurance of true judgment, nor the guidance of righteousness, and our soul cannot become the temple of the Holy Spirit. Finally, we should always bear in mind our ignorance of the time of our death, keeping ourselves from anger and recognizing that neither self-restraint nor the renunciation of all material things, nor fasting and vigils, are of any benefit if we are found guilty at the last judgment because we are the slaves of anger and hatred.

ON DEJECTION

Our fifth struggle is against the demon of dejection, who obscures the soul's capacity for spiritual contemplation and keeps it from all good works. When this malicious demon seizes our soul and darkens it completely, he prevents us from praying gladly, from reading Holy Scripture with profit and perseverance, and from being gentle and compassionate towards our brethren. He instils a hatred of every kind of work and even of the monastic profession itself. Undermining all the soul's salutary resolutions, weakening its persistence and constancy, he leaves it senseless and paralysed, tied and bound by its despairing thoughts.

If our purpose is to fight the spiritual fight and to defeat, with God's help, the demons of malice, we should take every care to guard our heart from the demon of dejection. Just as a moth devours clothing and a worm devours wood, so dejection devours a man's soul. It persuades him to shun every helpful encounter and stops him accepting advice from his true friends or giving them a courteous and peaceful reply. Seizing the entire soul, it fills it with bitterness and listlessness. Then it suggests to the soul that we should go away from other people, since they are the cause of its agitation. It does not allow the soul to understand that its sickness does not come from without, but lies hidden within, only manifesting itself when temptations attack the soul because of our ascetic efforts.

A man can be harmed by another only through the causes of the passions which lie within himself. It is for this reason that God, the Creator of all and the Doctor of men's souls, who alone has accurate knowledge of the soul's wounds, does not tell us to forsake the company of men; He tells us to root out the causes of evil within us and to recognize that the soul's health is achieved not by a man's separating himself from his fellows, but by his living the ascetic life in the company of holy men. When we abandon our brothers for some apparently good reason, we do not eradicate the motives for dejection but merely exchange them, since the sickness which lies hidden within us will show itself again in other circumstances.

Thus it is clear that our whole fight is against the passions within. Once these have been extirpated from our heart by the grace and help of God, we will readily be able to live not simply with other men, but even with wild beasts. Job confirms this when he says: 'And the beasts of the field shall be at peace with you' (Job 5:23). But first we must struggle with the demon of dejection who casts the soul into despair. We must drive him from our heart. It was this demon that did not allow Cain to repent after he had killed his brother, or Judas after he had betrayed his Master. The only form of dejection we should cultivate is the sorrow which goes with repentance for sin and is accompanied by hope in God. It was of this form of dejection that the Apostle said: 'Godly sorrow produces a saving repentance which is not to be repented of' (2 Cor. 7:10). This 'godly sorrow' nourishes the soul through the hope engendered by repentance, and it is mingled with joy. That is why it makes us obedient and eager for every good work: accessible, humble, gentle, forbearing and patient in enduring all the suffering or tribulation God may send us. Possession of these qualities shows that a man enjoys the fruits of the Holy Spirit: love, joy, peace, long-suffering, goodness, faith, self-control (cf. Gal. 5:22). But from the other kind of dejection we come to know the fruits of the evil spirit: listlessness, impatience, anger, hatred, contentiousness, despair, sluggishness in praying. So we should shun this second form of dejection as we would unchastity, avarice, anger and the rest of the passions. It can be healed by prayer, hope in God, meditation on Holy Scripture, and by living with godly people.

ON LISTLESSNESS

Our sixth struggle is against the demon of listlessness, who works hand in hand with the demon of dejection. This is a harsh, terrible demon, always attacking the monk, falling upon him at the sixth hour (mid-day), making him slack and full of fear, inspiring him with hatred for his monastery, his fellow monks, for work of any kind, and even for the reading of Holy Scripture. He suggests to the monk that he should go elsewhere and that, if he does not, all his effort and time will be wasted. In addition to all this, he produces in him at around the sixth hour a hunger such as he would not normally have after fasting for three days, or after a long journey or the heaviest labour. Then he makes him think that he will not be able to rid himself of this grievous sickness, except by sallying forth frequently to visit his brethren, ostensibly to help them and to tend them if they are unwell. When he cannot lead him astray in this manner, he puts him into the deepest sleep. In short, his attacks become stronger and more violent, and he cannot be beaten off except through prayer, through avoiding useless speech, through the study of the Holy Scriptures and through patience in the face of temptation. If he finds a monk unprotected by these weapons, he strikes him down with his arrows, making him a wayward and lazy wanderer, who roams idly from monastery to monastery, thinking only of where he can get something to eat and drink. The mind of someone affected by listlessness is filled with nothing but vain distraction. Finally he is ensnared in wordly things and gradually becomes so grievously caught up in them that he abandons the monastic life altogether.

The Apostle, who knows that this sickness is indeed serious, and wishes to eradicate it from our soul, indicates its main causes and says: 'Now we command you, brethren, in the name of our Lord Jesus Christ, to withdraw yourselves from every brother who lives in an unruly manner and not according to the tradition which you have received from us. For you yourselves know how you ought to imitate us: for we ourselves did not behave in an unruly manner when among you, nor did we eat any man's bread as a free gift; but we toiled strenuously night and day so that we might not be a burden to any of you: not because we do not have the right, but so as to give you an example to imitate. For even when we were with you, we gave you instructions that if anyone refuses to work he should have nothing to eat. For we hear that there are some among you who live in an unruly manner, not working at all, but simply being busybodies. Now we instruct such people and exhort them by our Lord Jesus Christ to work quietly and to eat their own bread' (2 Thess. 3 : 6–12). We should note how clearly the Apostle describes the causes of listlessness. Those who do not work he calls unruly, expressing a multiplicity of faults in this one word. For the unruly man is lacking in reverence, impulsive in speech, quick to abuse, and so

unfit for stillness. He is a slave to listlessness. Paul therefore tells us
to avoid such a person, that is, to isolate ourselves from him as from
a plague. With the words 'and not according to the tradition which
you have received from us' he makes it clear that they are arrogant
and that they destroy the apostolic traditions. Again he says: 'nor
did we eat any man's bread as a free gift; but we toiled strenuously
night and day'. The teacher of the nations, the herald of the Gospel,
who was raised to the third heaven, who says that the Lord ordained
that 'those who preach the Gospel should live by the Gospel' (1 Cor.
9 : 14) – this same man works night and day 'so that we might not be
a burden to any of you'. What then can be said of us, who are listless
about our work and physically lazy – we who have not been entrusted
with the proclamation of the Gospel or the care of the churches, but
merely with looking after our own soul? Next Paul shows more
clearly the harm born of laziness by adding: 'not working at all, but
simply being busybodies'; for from laziness comes inquisitiveness,
and from inquisitiveness, unruliness, and from unruliness, every
kind of evil. He provides a remedy, however, with the words:
'Now we instruct such people . . . to work quietly and to eat their
own bread.' But with even greater emphasis, he says: 'if anyone
refuses to work, he should have nothing to eat'.

The holy fathers of Egypt, who were brought up on the basis of
these apostolic commandments, do not allow monks to be without
work at any time, especially while they are young. They know that
by persevering in work monks dispel listlessness, provide for their
own sustenance and help those who are in need. They not only work
for their own requirements, but from their labour they also minister
to their guests, to the poor and to those in prison, believing that
such charity is a holy sacrifice acceptable to God. The fathers also
say that as a rule someone who works is attacked and afflicted by but
a single demon, while someone who does not work is taken prisoner
by a thousand evil spirits.

It is also good to recall what Abba Moses, one of the most
experienced of the fathers, told me. I had not been living long in the
desert when I was troubled by listlessness. So I went to him and said:
'Yesterday I was greatly troubled and weakened by listlessness, and
I was not able to free myself from it until I went to see Abba Paul.'
Abba Moses replied to me by saying: 'So far from freeing yourself
from it, you have surrendered to it completely and become its slave.

You must realize that it will attack all the more severely because you have deserted your post, unless from now on you strive to subdue it through patience, prayer and manual labour.'

ON SELF-ESTEEM

Our seventh struggle is against the demon of self-esteem, a multiform and subtle passion which is not readily perceived even by the person whom it tempts. The provocations of the other passions are more apparent and it is therefore somewhat easier to do battle with them, for the soul recognizes its enemy and can repulse him at once by rebutting him and by prayer. The vice of self-esteem, however, is difficult to fight against, because it has many forms and appears in all our activities – in our way of speaking, in what we say and in our silences, at work, in vigils and fasts, in prayer and reading, in stillness and long-suffering. Through all these it seeks to strike down the soldier of Christ. When it cannot seduce a man with extravagant clothes, it tries to tempt him by means of shabby ones. When it cannot flatter him with honour, it inflates him by causing him to endure what seems to be dishonour. When it cannot persuade him to feel proud of his display of eloquence, it entices him through silence into thinking he has achieved stillness. When it cannot puff him up with the thought of his luxurious table, it lures him into fasting for the sake of praise.

In short, every task, every activity, gives this malicious demon a chance for battle. He even prompts us to imagine we are priests. I remember a certain elder who, while I was staying in Sketis, went to visit a brother in his cell. When he approached his door, he heard him speaking inside; thinking that he was studying the Scriptures, he stood outside listening, only to realize that self-esteem had driven the man out of his mind and that he was ordaining himself deacon and dismissing the catechumens. When the elder heard this, he pushed open the door and went in. The brother came to greet him, bowed as is the custom, and asked him if he had been standing at the door for a long time. The elder replied with a smile: 'I arrived a moment ago, just when you were finishing the dismissal of the catechumens.' When the brother heard this, he fell at the feet of the elder and begged him to pray for him so that he would be freed from this delusion. I have recalled this incident because I want to show to what depths of stupidity this demon can bring us.

The person who wants to engage fully in spiritual combat and to win the crown of righteousness must try by every means to overcome this beast that assumes such varied forms. He should always keep in mind the words of David: 'The Lord has scattered the bones of those who please men' (Ps. 53:5. LXX). He should not do anything with a view to being praised by other people, but should seek God's reward only, always rejecting the thoughts of self-praise that enter his heart, and always regarding himself as nothing before God. In this way he will be freed, with God's help, from the demon of self-esteem.

ON PRIDE

Our eighth struggle is against the demon of pride, a most sinister demon, fiercer than all that have been discussed up till now. He attacks the perfect above all and seeks to destroy those who have mounted almost to the heights of holiness. Just as a deadly plague destroys not just one member of the body, but the whole of it, so pride corrupts the whole soul, not just part of it. Each of the other passions that trouble the soul attacks and tries to overcome the single virtue which is opposed to it, and so it darkens and troubles the soul only partially. But the passion of pride darkens the soul completely and leads to its utter downfall.

In order to understand more fully what is meant by this, we should look at the problem in the following way. Gluttony tries to destroy self-control; unchastity, moderation; avarice, voluntary poverty; anger, gentleness; and the other forms of vice, their corresponding virtues. But when the vice of pride has become master of our wretched soul, it acts like some harsh tyrant who has gained control of a great city, and destroys it completely, razing it to its foundations. The angel who fell from heaven because of his pride bears witness to this. He had been created by God and adorned with every virtue and all wisdom, but he did not want to ascribe this to the grace of the Lord. He ascribed it to his own nature and as a result regarded himself as equal to God. The prophet rebukes this claim when he says: 'You have said in your heart: "I will sit on a high mountain; I will place my throne upon the clouds and I will be like the Most

High." Yet you are a man, and not God' (cf. Isa. 14:13–14). And again, another prophet says, 'Why do you boast of your wickedness, O mighty man?' and he continues in this same vein (Ps. 52:1). Since we are aware of this we should feel fear and guard our hearts with extreme care from the deadly spirit of pride. When we have attained some degree of holiness we should always repeat to ourselves the words of the Apostle: 'Yet not I, but the grace of God which was with me' (1 Cor. 15:10), as well as what was said by the Lord: 'Without Me you can do nothing' (John 15:5). We should also bear in mind what the prophet said: 'Unless the Lord builds the house, they labour in vain that build it' (Ps. 127:1), and finally: 'It does not depend on man's will or effort, but on God's mercy' (Rom. 9:16).

Even if someone is sedulous, serious and resolute, he cannot, so long as he is bound to flesh and blood, approach perfection except through the mercy and grace of Christ. James himself says that 'every good gift is from above' (Jas. 1:17), while the Apostle Paul asks: 'What do you have which you did not receive? Now if you received it, why do you boast, as if you had not received it?' (1 Cor. 4:7). What right, then, has man to be proud as though he could achieve perfection through his own efforts?

The thief who received the kingdom of heaven, though not as the reward of virtue, is a true witness to the fact that salvation is ours through the grace and mercy of God. All of our holy fathers knew this and all with one accord teach that perfection in holiness can be achieved only through humility. Humility, in its turn, can be achieved only through faith, fear of God, gentleness and the shedding of all possessions. It is by means of these that we attain perfect love, through the grace and compassion of our Lord Jesus Christ, to whom be glory through all the ages. Amen.

On the Holy Fathers of Sketis
and on Discrimination
WRITTEN FOR ABBA LEONTIOS

The promise I made to the blessed Bishop Kastor to give an account of the way of life and the teaching of the holy fathers has been fulfilled in part by the writings I sent him entitled 'On Coenobitic Institutions' and 'On the Eight Vices'; and I now propose to fulfil it completely. But having heard that Bishop Kastor has left us to dwell with Christ, I felt I should send the remaining portion of my treatise to you, most holy Leontios, who have inherited both his virtuous qualities and the guardianship, with God's help, of his monastery.

I and my spiritual friend, the holy Germanos, whom I had known since my youth at school, in the army and in monastic life, were staying in the desert of Sketis, the centre of the most experienced monks. It was there that we saw Abba Moses, a saintly man, outstanding not only in the practice of the virtues but in spiritual contemplation as well. We begged him with tears, therefore, to tell us how we might approach perfection.

After much entreaty on our part, he said: 'Children, all virtues and all pursuits have a certain immediate purpose; and those who look to this purpose and adapt themselves accordingly will reach the ultimate goal to which they aspire. The farmer willingly works the earth, enduring now the sun's heat and now the winter's cold, his immediate purpose being to clear it of thorns and weeds, while his ultimate goal is the enjoyment of its fruits. The merchant, ignoring dangers on land and sea, willingly gives himself to his business with the purpose of making a profit, while his goal is enjoyment of this profit. The soldier, too, ignores the dangers of war and the miseries of service abroad. His purpose is to gain a higher rank by using his ability and skill, while his goal is to enjoy the advantages of this rank.

'Now our profession also has its own immediate purpose and its own ultimate goal, for the sake of which we willingly endure all manner of toil and suffering. Because of this, fasts do not cast us down, the hardship of vigils delights us; the reading and study of Scripture are readily undertaken; and physical work, obedience, stripping oneself of everything earthly, and the life here in this desert are carried out with pleasure.

'You have given up your country, your families, everything worldly in order to embrace a life in a foreign land among rude and uncultured people like us. Tell me, what was your purpose and what goal did you set before yourselves in doing all this?'

We replied: 'We did it for the kingdom of heaven.' In response Abba Moses said: 'As for the goal, you have answered well; but what is the purpose which we set before us and which we pursue unwaveringly so as to reach the kingdom of heaven? This you have not told me.'

When we confessed that we did not know, the old man replied: 'The goal of our profession, as we have said, is the kingdom of God. Its immediate purpose, however, is purity of heart, for without this we cannot reach our goal. We should therefore always have this purpose in mind; and, should it ever happen that for a short time our heart turns aside from the direct path, we must bring it back again at once, guiding our lives with reference to our purpose as if it were a carpenter's rule.

'The Apostle Paul knew this when he said: "Forgetting what lies behind, and reaching forward to what lies in front, I pursue my purpose, aiming at the prize of the high calling of God" (Phil. 3. 13–14). We, too, do everything for the sake of this immediate purpose. We give up country, family, possessions and everything worldly in order to acquire purity of heart. If we forget this purpose we cannot avoid frequently stumbling and losing our way, for we will be walking in the dark and straying from the proper path. This has happened to many men who at the start of their ascetic life gave up all wealth, possessions and everything worldly, but who later flew into a rage over a fork, a needle, a rush or a book. This would not have happened to them had they borne in mind the purpose for which they gave up everything. It is for the love of our neighbour that we scorn wealth, lest by fighting over it and stimulating our disposition to anger, we fall away from love. When we show this disposition to anger towards our brother even in small things, we have lapsed from our purpose and our renunciation of the world is useless. The blessed Apostle was aware of this and said: "Though I give my body to be burned, and have no love, it profits me nothing" (1 Cor. 13 : 3). From this we learn that perfection does not follow immediately upon renunciation and withdrawal from the world. It comes after the attainment of love which, as the Apostle said, "is not jealous or puffed up, does not grow angry, bears no grudge, is not arrogant, thinks no evil" (cf. 1 Cor. 13 : 4–5). All these things establish purity of heart; and it is for this that we should do everything, scorning possessions, enduring fasts and vigils gladly, engaging in spiritual reading and psalmody. If, however, some necessary task pleasing to God should keep us from our normal fasting and reading, we should not on this account neglect purity of heart. For what we gain by fasting is not so great as the damage done by anger; nor is the profit from reading as great as the harm done when we scorn or grieve a brother.

'Fasts and vigils, the study of Scripture, renouncing possessions and everything worldly are not in themselves perfection, as we have said; they are its tools. For perfection is not to be found in them; it is acquired through them. It is useless, therefore, to boast of our fasting, vigils, poverty, and reading of Scripture when we have not achieved the love of God and our fellow men. Whoever has achieved love has God within himself and his intellect is always with God.'

To this Germanos rejoined: 'What man, while in the flesh, can so fix his intellect on God that he thinks of nothing else, not even of visiting the sick, of entertaining guests, of his handicraft, or of the other unavoidable bodily needs? Above all, since God is invisible and incomprehensible, how can a man's mind always look upon Him and be inseparable from Him?'

Abba Moses replied: 'To look upon God at all times and to be inseparable from Him, in the manner which you envisage, is impossible for a man still in the flesh and enslaved to weakness. In another way, however, it is possible to look upon God, for the manner of contemplating God may be conceived and understood in many ways. God is not only to be known in His blessed and incomprehensible being, for this is something which is reserved for His saints in the age to come. He is also to be known from the grandeur and beauty of His creatures, from His providence which governs the world day by day, from His righteousness and from the wonders which He shows to His saints in each generation. When we reflect on the measurelessness of His power and His unsleeping eye which looks upon the hidden things of the heart and which nothing can escape, we are filled with the deepest awe, marvelling at Him and adoring Him. When we consider that He numbers the raindrops, the sand of the sea and the stars of heaven, we are amazed at the grandeur of His nature and His wisdom. When we think of His ineffable and inexplicable wisdom, His love for mankind, and His limitless long-suffering at man's innumerable sins, we glorify Him. When we consider His great love for us, in that though we had done nothing good He, being God, deigned to become man in order to save us from delusion, we are roused to longing for Him. When we reflect that He Himself has vanquished in us our adversary, the devil, and that He has given us eternal life if only we would choose and turn towards His goodness, then we venerate Him. There are many similar ways of seeing and apprehending God, which grow in us according to our labour and to the degree of our purification.'

Germanos then asked: 'How does it happen that even against our will many ideas and wicked thoughts trouble us, entering by stealth and undetected to steal our attention? Not only are we unable to prevent them from entering, but it is extremely difficult even to recognize them. Is it possible for the mind to be completely free of them and not be troubled by them at all?'

Abba Moses replied: 'It is impossible for the mind not to be troubled by these thoughts. But if we exert ourselves it is within our power either to accept them and give them our attention, or to expel them. Their coming is not within our power to control, but their expulsion is. The amending of our mind is also within the power of our choice and effort. When we meditate wisely and continually on the law of God, study psalms and canticles, engage in fasting and vigils, and always bear in mind what is to come – the kingdom of heaven, the Gehenna of fire and all God's works – our wicked thoughts diminish and find no place. But when we devote our time to worldly concerns and to matters of the flesh, to pointless and useless conversation, then these base thoughts multiply in us. Just as it is impossible to stop a watermill from turning, although the miller has power to choose between grinding either wheat or tares, so it is impossible to stop our mind, which is ever-moving, from having thoughts, although it is within our power to feed it either with spiritual meditation or with worldly concerns.'

When the old man saw us marvelling at this and still longing to hear more, he was silent for a short while and then said: 'Your longing has made me speak at length, and yet you are still eager for more; and from this I see that you are truly thirsty to be taught about perfection. So I would like to talk to you about the special virtue of discrimination. This is a kind of acropolis or queen among the virtues; and I will show you its excellence and value, not only in my own words, but also through the venerable teachings of the fathers; for the Lord fills His teachers with grace according to the quality and longing of those who listen.

'Discrimination, then, is no small virtue, but one of the most important gifts of the Holy Spirit. Concerning these gifts the Apostle says: "To one is given by the Spirit the principle of wisdom; to another the principle of spiritual knowledge by the same Spirit; to another faith by the same Spirit; to another the gifts of healing . . . to another discrimination of spirits" (1 Cor. 12 : 8–10). Then, having completed his catalogue of spiritual gifts, he adds: "But all these are energized by the one and selfsame Spirit" (1 Cor. 12 : 11). You can see, therefore, that the gift of discrimination is nothing worldly or insignificant. It is the greatest gift of God's grace. A monk must seek this gift with all his strength and diligence, and acquire the ability to discriminate between the spirits that enter him and to assess them accurately. Otherwise he will not only fall into the foulest pits of wickedness as he wanders about in the dark, but even stumble when his path is smooth and straight.

'I remember how in my youth, when I was in the Thebaid, where the blessed Antony used to live, some elders came to see him, to enquire with him into the question of perfection in virtue. They asked him: "Which is the greatest of all virtues – we mean the virtue capable of keeping a monk from being harmed by the nets of the devil and his deceit?" Each one then gave his opinion according to his understanding. Some said that fasting and the keeping of vigils make it easier to come near to God, because these refine and purify the mind. Others said that voluntary poverty and detachment from personal possessions make it easier, since through these the mind is released from the intricate threads of worldly care. Others judged acts of compassion to be the most important, since in the Gospel the Lord says: "Come, you whom my Father has blessed, inherit the kingdom prepared for you from the foundation of the world; for I was hungry and you gave Me food" and so on (Matt. 25:34–36). The best part of the night was passed in this manner, taken up with a discussion in which each expressed his opinion as to which virtue makes it easiest for a man to come near to God.

'Last of all the blessed Antony gave his reply: "All that you have said is both necessary and helpful for those who are searching for God and wish to come to Him. But we cannot award the first place to any of these virtues; for there are many among us who have endured fasting and vigils, or have withdrawn into the desert, or have practised poverty to such an extent that they have not left themselves enough for their daily sustenance, or have performed acts of compassion so generously that they no longer have anything to give; and yet these same monks, having done all this, have nevertheless fallen away miserably from virtue and slipped into vice.

' "What was it, then, that made them stray from the straight path? In my opinion it was simply that they did not possess the grace of discrimination; for it is this virtue that teaches a man to walk along the royal road, swerving neither to the right through immoderate self-control, nor to the left through indifference and laxity. Discrimination is a kind of eye and lantern of the soul, as is said in the gospel passage: 'The light of the body is the eye; if therefore your eye is pure, your whole body will be full of light. But if your eye is evil, your whole body will be full of darkness' (Matt. 6:22–3). And this is just what we find; for the power of discrimination, scrutinizing all the thoughts and actions of a man, distinguishes and sets aside everything that is base and not pleasing to God, and keeps him free from delusion.

' "We can see this in what is said in the Holy Scriptures. Saul, the first to be entrusted with the kingship of Israel, did not have the eye of discrimination; so his mind was darkened and he was unable to perceive that it was more pleasing to God that he should obey the commandment of Samuel than that he should offer sacrifices. He gave offence through the very things with which he thought to serve God, and because of them he was deposed. This would not have happened had he possessed the light of discrimination (cf. 1 Sam. 13:8–9).

' "The Apostle calls this virtue 'the sun', as we can see from his saying: 'Do not let the sun go down upon your anger' (Eph. 4:26). It is also called 'the guidance' of our lives, as when it is written: 'Those who have no guidance fall like leaves' (Prov. 11:14. LXX). Scripture also refers to it as the 'discernment' without which we must do nothing – not even drink the spiritual wine that 'makes glad the heart of man' (Ps. 104:15. LXX); for it is said: 'Drink with discernment' (Prov. 31:3. LXX); and: 'He that does not do all things with discernment is like a city that is broken down and without walls' (Prov. 25:28. LXX). Wisdom, intellection and perceptiveness are united in discrimination: and without these our inner house cannot be built, nor can we gather spiritual wealth; for it is written: 'Through wisdom a house is built, through understanding it is established, and through good judgment its storehouses will be filled with wealth' (Prov. 24:3–4. LXX). Discrimination is also called the 'solid food' that 'is suitable for those who have their organs of perception trained by practice to discriminate between good and evil' (Heb. 5:14). These passages show very clearly that without the gift of discrimination no virtue can stand or remain firm to the end, for it is the mother of all the virtues and their guardian."

'This was Antony's statement, and it was approved by the other fathers. But in order to confirm what St Antony said by means of fresh examples from our own times, we should recall Abba Hiron and how a few days ago, as we ourselves saw, he was thrown down from the height of the ascetic state to the depths of death by the deception of the devil. We know how he spent some fifty years in the nearby desert, following a life of great severity and the strictest self-control, seeking out and living in parts of the desert wilder than those inhabited by any of the other monks there. This same man cast all the fathers and brothers of the nearby desert into inconsolable grief because, after so many labours and struggles, he was deceived by the devil and suffered such a disastrous fall. This would not have happened to him had he been armed with the virtue of discrimination, which would have taught him to trust, not his own judgment, but rather the advice of his fathers and brethren. Following his own judgment he fasted and isolated himself to such a degree that he did not even come to church for the Holy Pascha, lest by meeting the fathers and brethren and feeding with them he would be obliged to eat lentils or whatever else was brought to the table, thereby appearing to fall short of the target which he had set himself.

'He had already for long been deceived in this way by his own wilfulness when, coming upon an angel of Satan, he bowed before him as if he were an angel of light. The angel commanded him to hurl himself, around midnight, into a very deep well so that he might then know by experience, because of his great virtue and ascetic efforts, that he would never again be subject to any danger. His darkened mind failed to discern who was suggesting this to him, and he hurled himself into the well during the night. Soon afterwards the brethren, discovering what had happened, were only just able to pull him up half dead. He lived for two more days and died on the third, plunging his brethren and the priest Paphnoutios into great grief. The latter, moved by feelings of compassion and remembering Hiron's numerous labours and the many years during which he had persevered in the desert, mentioned his name in the oblation for the dead so that he should not be numbered among those who have taken their own lives.

'And what am I to say about those two brethren who lived beyond the desert of the Thebaid, where the blessed Antony once lived? Impelled by a thought the real nature of which they could not discern, they decided to go into the vast, uncultivated inner desert; and they even made up their minds to refuse food offered them by man, and to accept only what the Lord would give them in a miraculous fashion. Finally they were seen in the distance wandering about the desert, weak with hunger, by the Mazikes who, though fiercer and wilder than almost all other savage peoples, now providentially exchanged their natural wildness for humane feelings and went to meet them carrying loaves of bread. One of the two brethren accepted the bread with joy and thanksgiving, since his power of discrimination had returned and he realized that such wild and fierce men, who normally rejoice at the sight of blood, would not have felt sympathy with them in their exhaustion and brought them food if God had not moved them to it. The other, however, refused the food on the grounds that it was offered him by men and, persisting in his undiscriminating judgment, he died from the weakness brought on by his hunger.

'Both monks at first showed total lack of judgment and made a senseless and destructive plan. One of them, however, when his power of discrimination returned, corrected the decision he had made so recklessly. But the other, persisting in his stupid and undiscriminating plan, brought upon himself the death which the Lord had wanted to avert.

'What am I to say about another monk whose name I do not wish to mention because he is still alive? He frequently entertained a demon as if he were an angel and received revelations from him, often seeing what looked like the light of a lamp in his cell. Later, he was ordered by this demon to offer his son as a sacrifice to God – his son was staying with him in the monastery – on the grounds that he would as a result be deemed worthy of the honour accorded to the patriarch Abraham. He was so led astray by the demon's advice that he would have carried out the sacrifice of his son, had the latter not seen him, contrary to his normal practice, sharpening a knife and preparing the bonds with which he was going to tie him up like a burnt offering. This enabled the son to make his escape.

'It would take me a long time to give an account of the deception of that Mesopotamian monk who, having shown great self-control, shutting himself up in his cell for many years and surpassing all monks in those regions in asceticism and virtue, was then so deluded by demonic dreams and revelations that he reverted to Judaism and circumcision. In order to deceive him, the devil often showed him dreams that turned out to be true, in this way making him more ready to accept his final act of deception. One night he showed him the Christian people with the apostles and martyrs, downcast and filled with shame, wasting away with dejection and grief, while on the other side he showed him the Jewish people, with Moses and the prophets, surrounded by light and living in joy and gladness. The deceiver then advised him to be circumcised if he wanted to share in the blessedness and joy of the Jewish people. He was deceived and followed this advice. From all this it is clear that none of these people would have been deluded in this pathetic and miserable fashion had they possessed the gift of discrimination.'

In reply to this Germanos said: 'By means of these recent examples and the statements of the fathers of old, you have made it clear that discrimination is the source, root, crown and common bond of all the virtues. But we would like very much to know how we can acquire it, and how we can recognize the true kind of discrimination which comes from God and distinguish it from the false and fictitious kind that comes from the devil.'

Abba Moses then said: 'True discrimination comes to us only as a result of true humility, and this in turn is shown by our revealing to our spiritual fathers not only what we do but also what we think, by never trusting our own thoughts, and by following in all things the words of our elders, regarding as good what they have judged to be so. In this way not only does the monk remain unharmed through true discrimination and by following the correct path, but he is also kept safe from all the snares of the devil. It is impossible for anyone who orders his life on the basis of the judgment and knowledge of the spiritually mature to fall because of the wiles of the demons. In fact, even before someone is granted the gift of discrimination, the act of revealing his base thoughts openly to the fathers weakens and withers them. For just as a snake which is brought from its dark hole into the light makes every effort to escape and hide itself, so the malicious thoughts that a person brings out into the open by sincere confession seek to depart from him.

'In order to give you a more accurate understanding of this virtue by means of an example, I shall tell you of something that Abba Serapion once did and which he used to speak about to those who came to him for help. He used to say: "When I was a young man I lived with my spiritual father, and at mealtimes, prompted by the devil, I would steal a rusk as I got up from the table and eat it without my father's knowledge. Because I persisted in this habit, I was utterly overcome by it and was unable to conquer it. Though I was condemned by my own conscience, I was ashamed to speak of it to my father. But through God's love it happened that certain brethren came to the old man for advice and asked him about their thoughts. The elder replied that nothing so harms a monk and brings such joy to the demons as the hiding of one's thoughts from one's spiritual father. He also spoke to them about self-control. As this was being said I came to myself and, thinking that God had revealed my past mistakes to the elder, I was pricked with compunction and began to cry, throwing from my pocket the rusk which I had stolen as usual. Casting myself to the ground I begged his forgiveness for my past faults and his prayers for my future safety. Then the old man said: 'My child, your confession has freed you, although I was silent. You have slain the demon that was wounding you because of your silence, by expressing openly what you were keeping to yourself. Until this moment you ensured that he would be your master by not opposing or rebuking him. From now on, however, he will no longer find room in you, since he has been brought out of your heart into the open.' The old man had not finished speaking when the energy of the demon could be seen coming out of my breast like the flame of a lamp. It filled the room with a nasty smell, so that those present thought that a lump of sulphur was burning. Then the elder said: 'Look, through this sign the Lord has borne witness to my words and to your deliverance.' Thus, as the result of my confession, the passion of gluttony and the demonic energy left me and I never again felt any such desire."

'From what Abba Serapion said, we can learn that we shall be granted the gift of true discrimination when we trust, no longer in the judgments of our own mind, but in the teaching and rule of our fathers. The devil brings the monk to the brink of destruction more effectively through persuading him to disregard the admonitions of the fathers and follow his own judgment and desire, than he does through any other fault. We should learn from examples provided by human arts and sciences. If we cannot accomplish anything in them by ourselves – in spite of the fact that they deal with things we can touch with our hands, see with our eyes and hear with our ears – but still need someone who will instruct us well and guide us, how can it be anything but foolish to think that the spiritual art, the most difficult of all the arts, has no need of a teacher? It is an invisible, hidden art which is understood only through purity of heart, and failure in it brings, not temporary loss, but the soul's destruction and eternal death.'

Germanos then said: 'Certain fathers who have listened to the thoughts of the brethren have often not only failed to heal them, but have even condemned them and driven them to despair. This has provided us with an excuse for shameful and harmful caution; for we ourselves know of cases of this kind in the region of Syria. A certain brother revealed his private thoughts to one of the elders living in those parts, unashamedly laying bare the hidden things of his heart with complete simplicity and truth. When the elder heard these things, however, he at once began to be angry with the brother and to attack him, rebuking him for having such base thoughts. As a result, many who heard of this were ashamed to tell their thoughts to the elders.'

Abba Moses said: 'It is a good thing, as I said, not to hide your thoughts from the fathers. But you should not tell them to just anyone; you should confess them to spiritual masters who have discrimination, not simply to those whose hair has grown white with age. Many who have looked to age as a guide, and then revealed their thoughts, have not only remained unhealed but have been driven to despair because of the inexperience of those to whom they confessed. There was once a very zealous brother who was greatly troubled by the demon of unchastity. He went to a certain father and confessed his private thoughts to him; but this father, being inexperienced, became angry when he heard about them and told the brother that he was contemptible and unworthy of the monastic habit for having entertained thoughts such as these. When the brother heard this, he lost heart, left his cell and set off back to the world. Through God's providence, however, Abba Apollos, one of the most experienced of the elders, chanced to meet him and, seeing him over-wrought and very despondent, asked him why he was in this state. At first the brother did not reply because he was so depressed but, after the elder had pleaded with him, he told him what was wrong, saying: "Because I was often troubled by evil thoughts, I went to tell them to the elder; and as he said I have no hope of salvation, I have given up and am now on my way back to the world."

'When Abba Apollos heard this, he comforted and encouraged him, saying: "Do not be surprised, my child, and do not lose hope. I too, old and grey as I am, am still much troubled by these thoughts. Do not be discouraged by this burning desire, which is healed not so much by human effort as by God's compassion. Please do this for me: go back to your cell just for today." This the brother did; and Apollos, after leaving him, went to the cell of the elder who had caused his despair. Standing outside he implored God with tears and said: "O Lord, who puts us to the test for our own benefit, let this elder be given the brother's battle, so that in old age he may learn through experience what he has not been taught over these many years: how to feel sympathy with those who are under attack by the demons." As he finished his prayer, he saw a dark figure standing near the cell shooting arrows at the elder. Wounded by the arrows, the elder at once began to stumble back and forth as though drunk. Unable to withstand the attack, he finally left his cell and set off for the world by the same road that the young monk had taken.

'Seeing what had happened, Abba Apollos confronted him, and asked him where he was going and why he was so troubled. Although he realized that the holy man knew what was wrong with him, he was too ashamed to say anything. Abba Apollos then said to him: "Return to your cell, and in the future recognize your own weakness. The devil has either not noticed or has despised you, and so not thought you worth fighting. Not that there has been any question of a fight: you could not stand up to his provocation even for a day! This has happened to you because, when you received a younger brother who was being attacked by our common enemy, you drove him to despair instead of preparing him for battle. You did not recall that wise precept: 'Deliver them that are being led away to death; and redeem them that are appointed to be slain' (Prov. 24:11. LXX). You did not even remember the parable of our Saviour, which teaches us not to break a bruised reed or quench smoking flax (cf. Matt. 12:20). None of us could endure the plots of the enemy, or allay the fiery turmoil of our nature, if God's grace did not protect our human weakness. Seeing, then, that God has had this compassion for us, let us pray to Him together and ask Him to withdraw the whip with which He has lashed you. 'For He wounds but binds up; He strikes but His hands heal' (Job 5:18). 'The Lord kills and gives life; he brings down to the grave and raises again. . . . He brings low and lifts up' (1 Sam. 2:6–7)." After Abba Apollos had said this and had prayed, the attack which had been launched against the elder was at once suspended. Finally, Abba Apollos advised him to ask God to give him "the tongue of the learned" so as to know "how to speak a word in season" (Isa. 50:4).

'From all that has been said, we may conclude that nothing leads so surely to salvation as to confess our private thoughts to those fathers most graced with the power of discrimination, and in our pursuit of holiness to be guided by them rather than by our own thoughts and judgment. Nor should the fact that we may encounter an elder who is somewhat simple-minded or lacking in experience either prevent us from confessing to the fathers who are truly qualified, or make us despise our ancestral traditions. Many texts from the divine Scriptures make it clear that the fathers did not say these things according to their own lights, but were inspired by God Himself and by the Scriptures to hand down to their successors the tradition of asking advice from those who had travelled far along the spiritual path. This is borne out especially by the story of the holy Samuel, who from infancy was dedicated by his mother to God and was granted communion with Him. He still did not trust his own thoughts, and in spite of having been called three times by God, he went to the elder, Eli, and was instructed and guided by him about how he should answer God (cf. 1 Sam. 3:9-10). Although God called him personally, none the less He wanted Samuel to receive the guidance and discipline of the elder, so that by means of this example we too might be led towards humility.

'When Christ Himself spoke to Paul and called him, He could have opened his eyes at once and made known to him the way of perfection; instead He sent him to Ananias and told him to learn from him the way of truth, saying: "Arise and go into the city, and there you will be told what you must do" (Acts 9:6). In this manner He teaches us to be guided by those who are advanced on the way, so that the vision rightly given to Paul should not be wrongly interpreted; otherwise it might lead later generations presumptuously to suppose that each individual must be initiated into the truth directly by God, as Paul was, and not by the fathers.

'That this is the correct interpretation of these incidents can be seen not only from what is said here, but also from St Paul's own actions. He writes that he went up to Jerusalem to see Peter and James, and "laid before them the gospel I preach . . . in case I was running or had run in vain" (Gal. 2:2); and he did this even though the grace of the Holy Spirit was already with him, as can be seen from the miracles which he performed. Who, then, can be so proud and boastful as to be satisfied with his own judgment or opinion, when St Paul himself admits that he needs the advice of those who were apostles before him? All this shows with complete clarity that the Lord reveals the way of perfection only to those guided to it by their spiritual fathers. This accords with what He Himself has said through the Prophet: "Ask your father, and he will show you; your elders, and they will tell you" (Deut. 32:7).

'We should therefore make every effort to acquire for ourselves that gift of discrimination which is able to keep us from excess in either direction. For, as the fathers have said, all extremes are equally harmful. It is as dangerous to fast too much as it is to overfill the stomach; to stay awake too long as to sleep too much; and so on. I myself have known monks who were not defeated by gluttony, but were undermined by immoderate fasting and lapsed into gluttony because of the weakness caused by this fasting. Indeed, I can remember having experienced this once myself. I had kept such strict control over my food that I forgot what it meant to be hungry, remaining without food for two or three days and still feeling no desire for it whatsoever, unless prompted by others. Then, through the wiles of the devil, I was so tormented by insomnia that, having remained awake for many nights, I begged God to grant me a little sleep. Thus I was in greater danger because of my immoderate fasting and insomnia than I was from gluttony and too much sleep.'

Abba Moses so cheered us with teaching of this kind that we could not help glorifying the Lord who grants such great wisdom to those who fear Him; for to Him belong honour and power through all the ages. Amen.

ST MARK THE ASCETIC

Introductory Note

Little can be affirmed with confidence about the life of St Mark the Ascetic, also known as Mark the Monk or Mark the Hermit. St Nikodimos dates him to the early fifth century, and this seems to be correct; according to another but less probable view, he lived at the beginning of the sixth century. Like his contemporary St Neilos, he may have been a disciple of St John Chrysostom, but this is not certain. As the *Letter to Nicolas the Solitary* indicates, Mark was living at one stage of his life as a hermit in the desert, although we cannot be sure where this was; both Palestine and Egypt have been suggested. Prior to this he may have been superior of a community near Ankyra (Ankara), in Asia Minor. In addition to the three works included in the *Philokalia*, Mark wrote at least six other treatises, the most important being those on baptism, on repentance, and against Nestorios. In his spiritual teaching, which is directed particularly against the heretical Syrian movement of Messalianism, he lays great emphasis upon the role played by baptismal grace and provides a detailed analysis of the nature of temptation.[1]

In addition to the Greek text provided by St Nikodimos, we have had before us the variant readings found in the earliest Greek manuscripts of Mark's writings; we have indicated in the footnotes when we depart from the text of the printed Greek *Philokalia*. In our translation of the treatises *On the Spiritual Law* and *On Those who Think that They are Made Righteous by Works*, the numbering of sections follows that in the Greek *Philokalia*. In Migne, *Patrologia Graeca*, lxv, the numbering is slightly different.

In the Orthodox Church Mark is commemorated as a saint on 5 March.

[1] See I. Hausherr, 'L'erreur fondamentale et la logique de Messalianisme', in *Orientalia Christiana Periodica*, i (1935), pp. 328–60, reprinted in I. Hausherr, *Études de spiritualité orientale* (*Orientalia Christiana Analecta*, 183, Rome, 1969), pp. 64–96; and Kallistos Ware, 'The Sacrament of Baptism and the Ascetic Life in the Teaching of Mark the Monk', in *Studia Patristica*, x (*Texte und Untersuchungen*, 107, Berlin, 1970), pp. 441–52.

On the Spiritual Law:
Two Hundred Texts

1. Because you have often asked what the Apostle means when he says that 'the law is spiritual' (Rom. 7:14), and what kind of spiritual knowledge and action characterizes those who wish to observe it, we shall speak of this as far as we can.

2. First of all, we know that God is the beginning, middle and end of everything good; and it is impossible for us to have faith in anything good or to carry it into effect except in Christ Jesus and the Holy Spirit.

3. Everything good is given by the Lord providentially; and he who has faith that this is so will not lose what he has been given.

4. Steadfast faith is a strong tower; and for one who has faith Christ comes to be all.

5. May He who inaugurates every good thing inaugurate all that you undertake, so that it may be done with His blessing.

6. When reading the Holy Scriptures, he who is humble and engaged in spiritual work will apply everything to himself and not to someone else.

7. Call upon God to open the eyes of your heart, so that you may see the value of prayer and of spiritual reading when understood and applied.

8. If a man has some spiritual gift and feels compassion for those who do not have it, he preserves the gift because of his compassion. But a boastful man will lose it through succumbing to the temptations of boastfulness.

9. The mouth of a humble man speaks the truth; but he who speaks against the truth is like the servant who struck the Lord on the face (cf. Mark 14:65).

10. Do not become a disciple of one who praises himself, in case you learn pride instead of humility.

11. Do not grow conceited about your interpretations of Scripture, lest your intellect fall victim to blasphemy.

12. Do not attempt to explain something difficult with contentiousness, but in the way which the spiritual law enjoins: with patience, prayer and unwavering hope.

13. Blind is the man crying out and saying: 'Son of David, have mercy on me' (Luke 18:38). He prays with the body alone, and not yet with spiritual knowledge.

14. When the man once blind received his sight and saw the Lord, he acknowledged Him no longer as Son of David but as Son of God, and worshipped Him (cf. John 9:38).

15. Do not grow conceited if you shed tears when you pray. For it is Christ who has touched your eyes and given you spiritual sight.

16. He who, like the blind man, casts away his garment and draws near to the Lord, becomes His disciple and a preacher of true doctrine (cf. Mark 10:50).

17. To brood on evil makes the heart brazen; but to destroy evil through self-restraint and hope breaks the heart.

18. There is a breaking of the heart which is gentle and makes it deeply penitent, and there is a breaking which is violent and harmful, shattering it completely.

19. Vigils, prayer and patient acceptance of what comes constitute a breaking that does not harm but benefits the heart, provided we do not destroy the balance between them through excess. He who perseveres in them will be helped in other ways as well; but he who is slack and negligent will suffer intolerably on leaving this life.

20. A self-indulgent heart becomes a prison and chain for the soul when it leaves this life; whereas an assiduous heart is an open door.

21. 'The iron gate that leads into the city' is a hard heart (Acts 12:10); but to one who suffers hardship and affliction the gate will open of its own accord, as it did to Peter.

22. There are many differing methods of prayer. No method is harmful; if it were, it would be not prayer but the activity of Satan.

23. A man wanted to do evil, but first prayed as usual; and finding himself prevented by God, he was then extremely thankful.

24. When David wanted to kill Nabal the Carmelite, but was

reminded of the divine retribution and abandoned his intention, he was extremely thankful. Again, we know what he did when he forgot God, and how he did not stop until Nathan the Prophet reminded him (cf. 1 Sam. 25; 2 Sam. 12).

25. At the times when you remember God, increase your prayers, so that when you forget Him, the Lord may remind you.

26. When you read Holy Scripture, perceive its hidden meanings. 'For whatever was written in past times was written for our instruction' (Rom. 15:4).

27. Scripture speaks of faith as 'the substance of things hoped for' (Heb. 11:1), and describes as 'worthless' those who do not know the indwelling of Jesus (cf. 2 Cor. 13:5).

28. Just as a thought is made manifest through actions and words, so is our future reward through the impulses of the heart.

29. Thus a merciful heart will receive mercy, while a merciless heart will receive the opposite.

30. The law of freedom teaches the whole truth. Many read about it in a theoretical way, but few really understand it, and these only in the degree to which they practise the commandments.

31. Do not seek the perfection of this law in human virtues, for it is not found perfect in them. Its perfection is hidden in the Cross of Christ.

32. The law of freedom is studied by means of true knowledge, it is understood through the practice of the commandments, and is fulfilled through the mercy of Christ.

33. When we are compelled by our conscience to accomplish all the commandments of God, then we shall understand that the law of the Lord is faultless (cf. Ps. 19:8. LXX). It is performed through our good actions, but cannot be perfected by men without God's mercy.

34. Those who do not consider themselves under obligation to perform all Christ's commandments study the law of God in a literal manner, 'understanding neither what they say nor what they affirm' (1 Tim. 1:7). Therefore they think that they can fulfil it by their own works.

35. There are acts which appear to be good, but the motive of the person who does them is not good; and there are other acts which appear to be bad, while the motive of the doer is good. The same is true of some statements. This discrepancy is due sometimes to

inexperience or ignorance, sometimes to evil intention, and sometimes to good intention.

36. When a man outwardly praises someone, while accusing and
disparaging him in his heart, it is hard for the simple to detect this.
Similarly a person may be outwardly humble but inwardly arrogant.
For a long time such men present falsehood as truth, but later they
are exposed and condemned.

37. One man does something apparently good, in defence of his
neighbour; another, by not doing it, gains in understanding.

38. Rebukes may be given in malice and self-defence, or out of
fear of God and respect for truth.

39. Cease rebuking a man who has stopped sinning and who has
repented. If you say that you are rebuking him in God's name, first
reveal the evils in yourself.

40. God is the source of every virtue, as the sun is of daylight.

41. When you have done something good, remember the words
'without Me you can do nothing' (John 15:5).

42. Afflictions bring blessing to man; self-esteem and sensual
pleasure, evil.

43. He who suffers injustice escapes sin, finding help in proportion
to his affliction.

44. The greater a man's faith that Christ will reward him, the
greater his readiness to endure every injustice.

45. By praying for those who wrong us we overthrow the devil;
opposing them we are wounded by him.

46. Better a human than a demonic sin. Through performing
the Lord's will we overcome both.

47. Every blessing comes from the Lord providentially. But this
fact escapes the notice of the ungrateful and the idle.

48. Every vice leads in the end to forbidden pleasure; and every
virtue to spiritual blessing. Each arouses what is akin to it.

49. Censure from men afflicts the heart; but if patiently accepted
it generates purity.

50. Ignorance makes us reject what is beneficial; and when it
becomes brazen it strengthens the hold of evil.

51. Even when nothing is going wrong, be ready for affliction;
and since you will have to give an account, do not make extortionate
demands.

52. Having sinned secretly, do not try to hide. For 'all things are

naked and open to the eyes of Him to whom we have to give an account' (Heb. 4:13).

53. Reveal yourself to the Lord in your mind. 'For man looks at the outward appearance, but the Lord looks at the heart' (1 Sam. 16:7).

54. Think nothing and do nothing without a purpose directed to God. For to journey without direction is wasted effort.

55. Because God's justice is inexorable, it is hard to obtain forgiveness for sins committed with complete deliberation.

56. Distress reminds the wise of God, but crushes those who forget Him.

57. Let all involuntary suffering teach you to remember God, and you will not lack occasion for repentance.

58. Forgetfulness as such has no power, but acquires it in proportion to our negligence.

59. Do not say: 'What can I do? I don't want to be forgetful but it happens.' For when you did remember, you cheated over what you owed.

60. Do good when you remember, and what you forget will be revealed to you; and do not surrender your mind to blind forgetfulness.

61. Scripture says: 'Hell and perdition are manifest to the Lord' (Prov. 15:11. LXX). This refers to ignorance of heart and forgetfulness.

62. Hell is ignorance, for both are dark; and perdition is forgetfulness, for both involve extinction.

63. Concern yourself with your own sins and not with those of your neighbour; then the workplace of your intellect will not be robbed.

64. Failure to do the good that is within your power is hard to forgive. But mercy and prayer reclaim the negligent.

65. To accept an affliction for God's sake is a genuine act of holiness; for true love is tested by adversities.

66. Do not claim to have acquired virtue unless you have suffered affliction, for without affliction virtue has not been tested.

67. Consider the outcome of every involuntary affliction, and you will find it has been the destruction of sin.

68. Neighbours are very free with advice, but our own judgment is best.

69. If you want spiritual health, listen to your conscience, do all it tells you, and you will benefit.

70. God and our conscience know our secrets. Let them correct us.

70a. He who toils unwillingly grows poor in every way, while he who presses ahead in hope is doubly rich.

71. Man acts so far as he can in accordance with his own wishes; but God decides the outcome in accordance with justice.

72. If you wish not to incur guilt when men praise you, first welcome reproof for your sins.

73. Each time someone accepts humiliation for the sake of Christ's truth he will be glorified a hundredfold by other men. But it is better always to do good for the sake of blessings in the life to come.

74. When one man helps another by word or deed, let them both recognize in this the grace of God. He who does not understand this will come under the power of him who does.

75. Anyone who praises his neighbour out of hypocrisy will later abuse him and bring disgrace upon himself.

76. He who is ignorant of the enemy's ambush is easily slain; and he who does not know the causes of the passions is soon brought low.

77. Knowledge of what is good for him has been given to everyone by God; but self-indulgence leads to negligence, and negligence to forgetfulness.

78. A man advises his neighbour according to his own understanding; but in the one who listens to such advice, God acts in proportion to his faith.

79. I have seen unlearned men who were truly humble, and they became wiser than the wise.

80. Another unlearned man, upon hearing them praised, instead of imitating their humility, prided himself on being unlearned and so fell into arrogance.

81. He who despises understanding and boasts of ignorance is unlearned not only in speech but also in knowledge (cf. 2 Cor. 11:6).

82. Just as wisdom in speech is one thing and sound judgment another, so lack of learning in speech is one thing and folly another.

83. Ignorance of words will do no harm to the truly devout, nor will wisdom in speaking harm the humble.

84. Do not say: 'I do not know what is right, therefore I am not

to blame when I fail to do it.' For if you did all the good about which you do know, what you should do next would then become clear to you, as if you were passing through a house from one room to another. It is not helpful to know what comes later before you have done what comes first. For knowledge without action 'puffs up', but 'love edifies', because it 'patiently accepts all things' (1 Cor. 8:1; 13:7).

85. Understand the words of Holy Scripture by putting them into practice, and do not fill yourself with conceit by expatiating on theoretical ideas.

86. He who neglects action and depends on theoretical knowledge holds a staff of reed instead of a double-edged sword; and when he confronts his enemies in time of war, 'it will go into his hand, and pierce it' (2 Kgs. 18:21), injecting its natural poison.

87. Every thought has its weight and measure in God's sight. For it is possible to think about the same thing either passionately or objectively.

88. After fulfilling a commandment expect to be tempted: for love of Christ is tested by adversity.

89. Never belittle the significance of your thoughts, for not one escapes God's notice.

90. When you observe some thought suggesting that you seek human fame, you can be sure it will bring you disgrace.

91. The enemy, understanding how the justice of the spiritual law is applied, seeks only the assent of our mind. Having secured this, he will either oblige us to undergo the labours of repentance or, if we do not repent, will torment us with misfortunes beyond our control. Sometimes he encourages us to resist these misfortunes so as to increase our torment, and then, at our death, he will point to this impatient resistance as proof of our lack of faith.

92. Many have fought in various ways against circumstances; but without prayer and repentance no one has escaped evil.

93. Evils reinforce each other; so do virtues, thus encouraging us to still greater efforts.

94. The devil belittles small sins; otherwise he cannot lead us into greater ones.

95. Praise from others engenders sinful desire, while their condemnation of vice, if not only heard but accepted, engenders self-restraint.

96. A self-indulgent monk has achieved nothing through his renunciation. For what he once did through possessions he still does though possessing nothing.

97. Moreover, the self-controlled man, if he clings to possessions, is a brother in spirit of this kind of monk; because they both feel inward enjoyment they have the same mother – though not the same father, since each has a different passion.

98. Sometimes a man cuts off a passion in order to indulge himself more fully, and he is praised by those unaware of his aim. He may even be unaware of it himself, and so his action is self-defeating.

99. All vice is caused by self-esteem and sensual pleasure; you cannot overcome passion without hating them.

100. 'Avarice is the root of all evil' (1 Tim. 6:10); but avarice is clearly a product of these two components.

101. The intellect is made blind by these three passions: avarice, self-esteem and sensual pleasure.

102. Scripture calls these three the daughters of the horseleech, dearly loved by their mother folly (cf. Prov. 30:15. LXX).

103. These three passions on their own dull spiritual knowledge and faith, the foster-brothers of our nature.

104. It is because of them that wrath, anger, war, murder and all other evils have such power over mankind.

105. We must hate avarice, self-esteem and sensual pleasure, as mothers of the vices and stepmothers of the virtues.

106. Because of them we are commanded not to love 'the world' and 'the things that are in the world' (1 John 2:15); not so that we should hate God's creation through lack of discernment, but so that we should eliminate the occasions for these three passions.

107. 'The soldier going to war', it is said, 'does not entangle himself in the affairs of this world' (2 Tim. 2:4). For he who entangles himself with the passions while trying to overcome them is like a man who tries to put out a fire with straw.

108. If one becomes angry with one's neighbour on account of riches, fame or pleasure, one does not yet realize that God orders all things with justice.

109. When you hear the Lord saying that if someone does not renounce all that he has he 'is not worthy of Me' (Matt. 10:37), apply this not only to money but to all forms of vice.

110. He who does not know the truth cannot truly have faith; for by nature knowledge precedes faith.

111. Just as God assigns to everything visible what is appropriate, so He does also to human thoughts, whether we wish it or not.

112. If some obvious sinner who does not repent has suffered nothing before his death, you may be sure that judgment in his case will be merciless.

113. He who prays with understanding patiently accepts circumstances, whereas he who resents them has not yet attained pure prayer.

114. When harmed, insulted or persecuted by someone, do not think of the present but wait for the future, and you will find he has brought you much good, not only in this life but also in the life to come.

115. Just as the bitterness of absinth helps a poor appetite, so misfortunes help a bad character. For the first benefits the physical condition, and the second leads to repentance.

116. If you do not want to suffer evil, do not inflict it, since the suffering of it inevitably follows its infliction. 'For whatever a man sows he will also reap' (Gal. 6:7).

117. Reaping unwillingly the wickedness we deliberately sow, we should marvel at God's justice.

118. Because an interval of time elapses between sowing and reaping, we begin to think there will be no requital.

119. When you sin, blame your thought, not your action. For had your intellect not run ahead, your body would not have followed.

120. The secret sinner is worse than those who do evil openly; and so he receives a worse punishment.

121. The trickster who works mischief in secret is a snake 'lying in wait on the road and biting the horse's heel' (Gen. 49:17. LXX).

122. If you praise your neighbour to one man and criticize him to another, you are the slave of self-esteem and jealousy. Through praise you try to hide your jealousy, through criticism to appear better than your neighbour.

123. Just as sheep and wolves cannot feed together, so a man cannot receive mercy if he tricks his neighbour.

124. He who secretly mingles his own wishes with spiritual counsel is an adulterer, as the Book of Proverbs indicates (cf. Prov. 6:32–33); and because of his stupidity he suffers pain and dishonour.

125. Just as water and fire cannot be combined, so self-justification and humility exclude one another.

126. He who seeks forgiveness of his sins loves humility, but if he condemns another he seals his own wickedness.

127. Do not leave unobliterated any fault, however small, for it may lead you on to greater sins.

128. If you wish to be saved, welcome words of truth, and never reject criticism uncritically.

129. Words of truth converted the 'progeny of vipers' and warned them 'to flee from the anger to come' (Matt. 3:7).

130. To accept words of truth is to accept the divine Word; for He says: 'He that receives you receives me' (matt. 10:40).

131. The paralytic let down through the roof (cf. Mark 2:4) signifies a sinner reproved in God's name by the faithful and receiving forgiveness because of their faith.

132. It is better to pray devoutly for your neighbour than to rebuke him every time he sins.

133. The truly repentant is derided by the foolish – which is a sign that God has accepted his repentance.

134. Those engaged in spiritual warfare practise self-control in everything, and do not desist until the Lord destroys all 'seed from Babylon' (Jer. 27:16. LXX).

135. Suppose that there are twelve shameful passions. Indulging in any one of them is equivalent to indulging in them all.

136. Sin is a blazing fire. The less fuel you give it, the faster it dies down; the more you feed it, the more it burns.

137. When elated by praise, be sure disgrace will follow; for it is said: 'Whoever exalts himself will be abased' (Luke 14:11).

138. When we have freed ourselves from every voluntary sin of the mind, we should then fight against the passions which result from prepossession.*

139. Prepossession is the involuntary presence of former sins in the memory. At the stage of active warfare we try to prevent it from developing into a passion; after victory it is repulsed while still but a provocation.

140. A provocation is an image-free stimulation in the heart. Like a mountain-pass, the experienced take control of it ahead of the enemy.

141. Once our thoughts are accompanied by images we have

already given them our assent; for a provocation does not involve us in guilt so long as it is not accompanied by images. Some people flee away from these thoughts like 'a brand plucked out of the fire' (Zech. 3:2); but others dally with them, and so get burnt.

142. Do not say: 'I don't want it, but it happens.' For even though you may not want the thing itself, yet you welcome what causes it.

143. He who seeks praise is involved in passion; he who laments afflictions is attached to sensual pleasure.

144. The thoughts of a self-indulgent man vacillate, as though on scales; sometimes he laments and weeps for his sins, and sometimes he fights and contradicts his neighbour, justifying his own sensual pleasures.

145. He who tests all things and 'holds fast that which is good' (1 Thess. 5:21) will in consequence refrain from all evil.

146. 'A patient man abounds in understanding' (Prov. 14:29); and so does he who listens to words of wisdom.

147. Without remembrance of God, there can be no true knowledge but only that which is false.

148. Deeper spiritual knowledge helps the hard-hearted man: for unless he has fear, he refuses to accept the labour of repentance.

149. Unquestioning acceptance of tradition is helpful for a gentle person, for then he will not try God's patience or often fall into sin.

150. Do not rebuke a forceful man for arrogance, but point out to him the danger of dishonour; if he has any sense he will accept this kind of rebuke.

151. If you hate rebuke, it shows that the passion in which you are involved is due to your own free choice. But if you welcome rebuke, the passion is due to prepossession.

152. Do not listen to talk about other people's sins. For through such listening the form of these sins is imprinted on you.

153. When you delight in hearing evil talk, be angry with yourself and not with the speaker. For listening in a sinful way makes the messenger seem sinful.

154. If you come across people gossiping idly, consider yourself responsible for their talk – if not on account of some recent fault of your own, then because of an old debt.

155. If someone praises you hypocritically, be sure that in due course he will vilify you.

156. Accept present afflictions for the sake of future blessings; then you will never weaken in your struggle.

157. When someone supplies your bodily needs and you praise him as good in his own right apart from God, he will later seem to you to be evil.

158. All good things come from God providentially, and those who bring them are the servants of what is good.

159. Accept with equanimity the intermingling of good and evil, and then God will resolve all inequity.

160. It is the uneven quality of our thoughts that produces changes in our condition. For God assigns to our voluntary thoughts consequences which are appropriate but not necessarily of our choice.

161. The sensible derives from the intelligible, by God's decree providing what is needed.

162. From a pleasure-loving heart arise unhealthy thoughts and words; and from the smoke of a fire we recognize the fuel.

163. Guard your mind, and you will not be harassed by temptations. But if you fail to guard it, accept patiently whatever trial comes.

164. Pray that temptation may not come to you; but when it comes, accept it as your due and not undeserved.

165. Reject all thoughts of greed, and you will be able to see the devil's tricks.

166. He who says he knows all the devil's tricks falls unknowingly into his trap.

167. The more the intellect withdraws from bodily cares, the more clearly it sees the craftiness of the enemy.

168. A man who is carried away by his thoughts is blinded by them; and while he can see the actual working of sin, he cannot see its causes.

169. It can happen that someone may in appearance be fulfilling a commandment but is in reality serving a passion, and through evil thoughts he destroys the goodness of the action.

170. When you first become involved in something evil, don't say: 'It will not overpower me.' For to the extent that you are involved you have already been overpowered by it.

171. Everything that happens has a small beginning, and grows the more it is nourished.

172. Wickedness is an intricate net; and if someone is careless when partially entangled, he gets completely enmeshed.

173. Do not desire to hear about the misfortunes of your enemies. For those who like listening to such things will themselves suffer what they wish for others.

174. Do not think that every affliction is a consequence of sin. For there are some who do God's will and yet are tested. Thus it is written that the ungodly and wicked shall be persecuted (cf. Ps. 37:28), but also that those who 'seek to live a holy life in Christ Jesus will suffer persecution' (2 Tim. 3:12).

175. At a time of affliction, expect a provocation to sensual pleasure; for because it relieves the affliction it is readily welcomed.

176. Some call men intelligent because they have the power of discernment on the sensible plane. But the really intelligent people are those who control their own desires.

177. Until you have eradicated evil, do not obey your heart; for it will seek more of what it already contains within itself.

178. Just as some snakes live in glens and others in houses, so there are some passions which take shape in our thoughts while others express themselves in action. It is possible, however, for them to change from one type to the other.

179. When you find that some thought is disturbing you deeply in yourself and is breaking the stillness of your intellect with passion, you may be sure that it was your intellect which, taking the initiative, first activated this thought and placed it in your heart.

180. No cloud is formed without a breath of wind; and no passion is born without a thought.

181. If we no longer fulfil the desires of the flesh, then with the Lord's help the evils within us will easily be eliminated.

182. Images already established in our intellect are more pernicious and stubborn than those which arise while we are thinking. The latter precede the former and are their cause.

183. One kind of evil dwells in the heart through long-continued prepossession; another kind attacks our thoughts through the medium of everyday things.

184. God assesses our action according to our intention; for it is

said that the Lord will 'reward you according to your heart' (Ps. 20:4).

185. He who does not persevere in examining his conscience will not endure bodily suffering for God's sake.

186. The conscience is nature's book. He who applies what he reads there experiences God's help.

187. He who does not choose to suffer for the sake of truth will be chastened more painfully by suffering he has not chosen.

188. He who knows God's will, and performs it according to his power, escapes more severe suffering by suffering a little.

189. If a man tries to overcome temptations without prayer and patient endurance, he will become more entangled in them instead of driving them away.

190. The Lord is hidden in His own commandments, and He is to be found there in the measure that He is sought.

191. Do not say: 'I have fulfilled the commandments, but have not found the Lord'. For you have often found 'spiritual knowledge with righteousness', as Scripture says, 'and those who rightly seek Him shall find peace' (Prov. 16:8. LXX).

192. Peace is deliverance from the passions, and is not found except through the action of the Holy Spirit.

193. Fulfilling a commandment is one thing, and virtue is another, although each promotes the other.

194. Fulfilling a commandment means doing what we are enjoined to do; but virtue is to do it in a manner that conforms to the truth.

195. All material wealth is the same, but is acquired in many different ways; similarly, virtue is one, but is many-sided in its operations.

196. If someone makes a display of wisdom and instead of applying it talks at length, he has a spurious wealth and his labours 'come into the houses of strangers' (Prov. 5:10. LXX).

197. It is said that gold rules everything; but spiritual things are ruled by the grace of God.

198. A good conscience is found through prayer, and pure prayer through the conscience. Each by nature needs the other.

199. Jacob made for Joseph a coat of many colours (cf. Gen. 37:3), and the Lord gives knowledge of truth to the gentle; as

it is written, 'He will teach the gentle His ways' (Ps. 25:9. LXX).

200. Always do as much good as you can, and at a time of greater good do not turn to a lesser. For it is said that no man who turns back 'is fit for the kingdom of heaven' (cf. Luke 9:62).

On Those who Think that
They are Made Righteous by Works:
Two Hundred and Twenty-Six Texts

1. In the texts which follow, the beliefs of those in error will be refuted by those whose faith is well founded and who know the truth.

2. Wishing to show that to fulfil every commandment is a duty, whereas sonship is a gift given to men through His own Blood, the Lord said: 'When you have done all that is commanded you, say: "We are useless servants: we have only done what was our duty" ' (Luke 17:10). Thus the kingdom of heaven is not a reward for works, but a gift of grace prepared by the Master for his faithful servants.

3. A slave does not demand his freedom as a reward; but he gives satisfaction as one who is in debt, and he receives freedom as a gift.

4. 'Christ died on account of our sins in accordance with the Scriptures' (1 Cor. 15:3); and to those who serve Him well He gives freedom. 'Well done, good and faithful servant,' He says, 'you have been faithful over a few things, I will make you ruler over many things: enter into the joy of your Lord' (Matt. 25:21).

5. He who relies on theoretical knowledge alone is not yet a faithful servant: a faithful servant is one who expresses his faith in Christ through obedience to His commandments.

6. He who honours the Lord does what the Lord bids. When he sins or is disobedient, he patiently accepts what comes as something he deserves.

7. If you love true knowledge, devote yourself to the ascetic life; for mere theoretical knowledge puffs a man up (cf. 1 Cor. 8:1).

8. Unexpected trials are sent by God to teach us to practise the

ascetic life; and they lead us to repentance even when we are reluctant.

9. Afflictions that come to us are the result of our own sins. But if we accept them patiently through prayer, we shall again find blessings.

10. Some people when praised for their virtue are delighted, and attribute this pleasurable feeling of self-esteem to grace. Others when reproved for their sins are pained, and they mistake this beneficial pain for the action of sin.

11. Those who, because of the rigour of their own ascetic practice, despise the less zealous, think that they are made righteous by physical works. But we are even more foolish if we rely on theoretical knowledge and disparage the ignorant.

12. Even though knowledge is true, it is still not firmly established if unaccompanied by works. For everything is established by being put into practice.

13. Often our knowledge becomes darkened because we fail to put things into practice. For when we have totally neglected to practise something, our memory of it will gradually disappear.

14. For this reason Scripture urges us to acquire the knowledge of God, so that through our works we may serve Him rightly.

15. When we fulfil the commandments in our outward actions, we receive from the Lord what is appropriate; but any real benefit we gain depends on our inward intention.

16. If we want to do something but cannot, then before God, who knows our hearts, it is as if we have done it. This is true whether the intended action is good or bad.

17. The intellect does many good and bad things without the body, whereas the body can do neither good nor evil without the intellect. This is because the law of freedom applies to what happens before we act.

18. Some without fulfilling the commandments think that they possess true faith. Others fulfil the commandments and then expect the kingdom as a reward due to them. Both are mistaken.

19. A master is under no obligation to reward his slaves; on the other hand, those who do not serve him well are not given their freedom.

20. If 'Christ died on our account in accordance with the Scriptures' (Rom. 5:8; 1 Cor. 15:3), and we do not 'live for

ourselves', but 'for Him who died and rose' on our account (2 Cor. 5:15), it is clear that we are debtors to Christ to serve Him till our death. How then can we regard sonship as something which is our due?

21. Christ is Master by virtue of His own essence and Master by virtue of His incarnate life. For He creates man from nothing, and through His own Blood redeems him when dead in sin; and to those who believe in Him He has given His grace.

22. When Scripture says 'He will reward every man according to his works' (Matt. 16:27), do not imagine that works in themselves merit either hell or the kingdom. On the contrary, Christ rewards each man according to whether his works are done with faith or without faith in Himself; and He is not a dealer bound by contract, but God our Creator and Redeemer.

23. We who have received baptism offer good works, not by way of repayment, but to preserve the purity given to us.

24. Every good work which we perform through our own natural powers causes us to refrain from the corresponding sin; but without grace it cannot contribute to our sanctification.

25. The self-controlled refrain from gluttony; those who have renounced possessions, from greed; the tranquil, from loquacity; the pure, from self-indulgence; the modest, from unchastity; the self-dependent, from avarice; the gentle, from agitation; the humble, from self-esteem; the obedient, from quarrelling; the self-critical, from hypocrisy. Similarly, those who pray are protected from despair; the poor, from having many possessions; confessors of the faith, from its denial; martyrs, from idolatry. Do you see how every virtue that is performed even to the point of death is nothing other than refraining from sin? Now to refrain from sin is a work within our own natural powers, but not something that buys us the kingdom.

26. While man can scarcely keep what belongs to him by nature, Christ gives the grace of sonship through the Cross.

27. Certain commandments are specific, and others are comprehensive. Thus Christ enjoins us specifically to 'share with him who has none' (Luke 3:11); and He gives us a comprehensive command to forsake all that we have (cf. Luke 14:33).

28. There is an energy of grace not understood by beginners, and there is also an energy of evil which resembles the truth. It is

advisable not to scrutinize these energies too closely, because one may be led astray, and not to condemn them out of hand, because they may contain some truth; but we should lay everything before God in hope, for He knows what is of value in both of them.

29. He who wants to cross the spiritual sea is long-suffering, humble, vigilant and self-controlled. If he impetuously embarks on it without these four virtues, he agitates his heart, but cannot cross.

30. Stillness helps us by making evil inoperative.[1] If it also takes to itself these four virtues in prayer, it is the most direct support in attaining dispassion.

31. The intellect cannot be still unless the body is still also; and the wall between them cannot be demolished without stillness and prayer.

32. The flesh with its desire is opposed to the spirit, and the spirit opposed to the flesh, and those who live in the spirit will not carry out the desire of the flesh (cf. Gal. 5:15-17).

33. There is no perfect prayer unless the intellect invokes God; and when our thought cries aloud without distraction, the Lord will listen.

34. When the intellect prays without distraction it afflicts the heart; and 'a broken and a contrite heart, O God, Thou wilt not despise' (Ps. 51:17).

35. Prayer is called a virtue, but in reality it is the mother of the virtues: for it gives birth to them through union with Christ.

36. Whatever we do without prayer and without hope in God turns out afterwards to be harmful and defective.

37. Christ's words that the 'first will be last, and the last will be first' (Matt. 19:30) refer to those who participate in the virtues and those who participate in love. For love is the last of the virtues to be born in the heart, but it is the first in value, so that those born before it turn out to be 'the last'.

38. If you are listless when you pray or afflicted by various forms of evil, call to mind your death and the torments of hell. But it is better to cleave to God through hope and prayer than to think about external things, even though such thoughts may be helpful.

39. No single virtue by itself opens the door of our nature; but all the virtues must be linked together in the correct sequence.

[1] We have followed here the reading of the early manuscripts.

40. He whose mind teems with thoughts lacks self-control; and even when they are beneficial, hope is more so.

41. There is a sin which is always 'unto death' (1 John 5:16): the sin for which we do not repent. For this sin even a saint's prayers will not be heard.

42. He who repents rightly does not imagine that it is his own effort which cancels his former sins; but through this effort he makes his peace with God.

43. If we are under an obligation to perform daily all the good actions of which our nature is capable, what do we have left over to give to God in repayment for our past sins?

44. However great our virtuous actions of today, they do not requite but condemn our past negligence.

45. He who suffers affliction in his intellect but relaxes physically is like one who suffers affliction in his body while allowing his intellect to be dispersed.

46. Voluntary affliction in one of these parts of our nature benefits the other: to suffer affliction with the mind benefits the flesh, and to suffer it with the flesh benefits the mind. When our mind and flesh are not in union,[1] our state deteriorates.

47. It is a great virtue to accept patiently whatever comes and, as the Lord enjoins, to love a neighbour who hates you.

48. The sign of sincere love is to forgive wrongs done to us. It was with such love that the Lord loved the world.

49. We cannot with all our heart forgive someone who does us wrong unless we possess real knowledge. For this knowledge shows us that we deserve all we experience.

50. You will lose nothing of what you have renounced for the Lord's sake. For in its own time it will return to you greatly multiplied.

51. When the intellect forgets the purpose of true devotion, then external works of virtue bring no profit.

52. If poor judgment is harmful to everyone, it is particularly so to those who live with great strictness.

53. Philosophize through your works about man's will and God's retribution. For your words are only as wise and as profitable as your works.

54. Those who suffer for the sake of true devotion receive help.

[1] Reading *asyntheton* in accordance with most manuscripts.

This must be learnt through obeying God's law and our own conscience.

55. One man received a thought and accepted it without examination. Another received a thought and tested its truth. Which of them acted with greater reverence?

56. Real knowledge is patiently to accept affliction and not to blame others for our own misfortunes.

57. He who does something good and expects a reward is serving not God but his own will.

58. A sinner cannot escape retribution except through repentance appropriate to his offence.

59. There are those who claim that we cannot do good unless we actively receive the grace of the Spirit.

60. Those who always by choice incline to sensual pleasures refrain from doing what lies within their power on the grounds that they lack help.

61. Grace has been given mystically to those who have been baptized into Christ; and it becomes active within them to the extent that they actively observe the commandments. Grace never ceases to help us secretly; but to do good – as far as lies in our power – depends on us.

62. Initially grace arouses the conscience in a divine manner. That is how even sinners have come to repent and so to conform to God's will.

63. Again, grace may be hidden in advice given by a neighbour. Sometimes it also accompanies our understanding during reading, and as a natural result teaches our intellect the truth about itself. If, then, we do not hide the talent given to us in this way, we shall enter actively into the joy of the Lord.

64. He who seeks the energies of the Spirit, before he has actively observed the commandments, is like someone who sells himself into slavery and who, as soon as he is bought, asks to be given his freedom while still keeping his purchase-money.

65. When you have found that external events come to you through God's justice, then in your search for the Lord you have found 'spiritual knowledge and justice' (cf. Prov. 16:8. LXX).

66. Once you recognize that the Lord's judgments 'are in all the earth' (1 Chr. 16:14), then everything that happens to you will teach you knowledge of God.

67. Everyone receives what he deserves in accordance with his inner state. But only God understands the many different ways in which this happens.

68. When you suffer some dishonour from men, recognize at once the glory that will be given you by God. Then you will not be saddened or upset by the dishonour; and when you receive the glory you will remain steadfast and innocent.

69. When God allows you to be praised, do not become boastful on account of this divine providence, lest you then fall into dishonour.

70. A seed will not grow without earth and water; and a man will not develop without voluntary suffering and divine help.

71. Rain cannot fall without a cloud, and we cannot please God without a good conscience.

72. Do not refuse to learn, even though you may be very intelligent. For what God provides has more value than our own intelligence.

73. When through some sensual pleasure the heart is deflected from the ascetic way, it becomes difficult to control, like a heavy stone dislodged on steep ground.

74. Like a young calf which, in its search for grazing, finds itself on a ledge surrounded by precipices, the soul is gradually led astray by its thoughts.

75. When the intellect, having grown to full maturity in the Lord, wrenches the soul from long-continued prepossession, the heart suffers torments as if on the rack, since intellect and passion drag it in opposite directions.

76. Just as sailors, in the hope of gain, gladly endure the burning heat of the sun, so those who hate wickedness gladly accept reproof. For the former contend with the winds, the latter with passions.

77. Just as flight in winter or on the sabbath day (cf. Matt. 24:20) brings suffering to the flesh and defilement to the soul, so too does resurgence of the passions in an aged body and a consecrated soul.

78. No one is as good and merciful as the Lord. But even He does not forgive the unrepentant.

79. Many of us feel remorse for our sins, yet we gladly accept their causes.

80. A mole burrowing in the earth is blind and cannot see the stars; and he who does not trust God in temporal things will not trust Him in eternal things.

81. Real knowledge has been given to men by God as a grace preceding the fulness of grace; it teaches those who partake of it to believe above all in the Giver.

82. When a sinful soul does not accept the afflictions that come to it, the angels say: 'We would have healed Babylon, but she was not healed' (Jer. 51:9)

83. When an intellect forgets real knowledge, it fights with men for harmful things as though they were helpful.

84. Fire cannot last long in water, nor can a shameful thought in a heart that loves God. For every man who loves God suffers gladly, and voluntary suffering is by nature the enemy of sensual pleasure.

85. A passion which we allow to grow active within us through our own choice afterwards forces itself upon us against our will.

86. We have a love for the causes of involuntary thoughts, and that is why they come. In the case of voluntary thoughts we clearly have a love not only for the causes but also for the objects with which they are concerned.

87. Presumption and boastfulness are causes of blasphemy. Avarice and self-esteem are causes of cruelty and hypocrisy.

88. When the devil sees that our intellect has prayed from the heart, he makes a powerful attack with subtle temptations; but he does not bother to destroy the lesser virtues by such powerful attacks.

89. When a thought lingers within a man, this indicates his attachment to it; but when it is quickly destroyed, this signifies his opposition and hostility to it.

90. The intellect changes from one to another of three different noetic states: that according to nature, above nature, and contrary to nature. When it enters the state according to nature, it finds that it is itself the cause of evil thoughts, and confesses its sins to God, clearly understanding the causes of the passions. When it is in the state contrary to nature, it forgets God's justice and fights with men, believing itself unjustly treated. But when it is raised to the state above nature, it finds the fruits of the Holy Spirit: love, joy, peace and the other fruits of which the Apostle speaks (cf. Gal. 5:22); and it knows that if it gives priority to bodily cares it cannot remain in this state. An intellect that departs from this state falls into sin and all the terrible consequences of sin – if not immediately, then in due time, as God's justice shall decide.

91. Each man's knowledge is genuine to the extent that it is confirmed by gentleness, humility and love.

92. Everyone baptized in the orthodox manner has received mystically the fulness of grace; but he becomes conscious of this grace only to the extent that he actively observes the commandments.

93. If we fulfil Christ's commandments according to our conscience, we are spiritually refreshed to the extent that we suffer in our heart. But each thing comes to us at the right time.

94. Pray persistently about everything, and then you will never do anything without God's help.

95. Nothing is stronger than prayer in its action, nothing more effective in winning God's favour.

96. Prayer comprises the complete fulfilment of the commandments; for there is nothing higher than love for God.

97. Undistracted prayer is a sign of love for God; but careless or distracted prayer is a sign of love for pleasure.

98. He who can without strain keep vigil, be long-suffering and pray is manifestly a partaker of the Holy Spirit. But he who feels strain while doing these things, yet willingly endures it, also quickly receives help.

99. One commandment is higher than another; consequently one level of faith is more firmly founded than another.

100. There is faith 'that comes by hearing' (Rom. 10:17) and there is faith that 'is the substance of things hoped for' (Heb. 11:1).

101. It is good to help enquirers with words; but it is better to co-operate with them through prayer and the practice of virtue. For he who through these offers himself to God, helps his neighbour through helping himself.

102. If you want with a few words to benefit one who is eager to learn, speak to him about prayer, right faith, and the patient acceptance of what comes. For all else that is good is found through these.

103. Once we have entrusted our hope about something to God, we no longer quarrel with our neighbour over it.

104. If, as Scripture teaches, everything involuntary has its cause in what is voluntary, man has no greater enemy than himself.

105. The first among all evils is ignorance; next comes lack of faith.

106. Escape from temptation through patience and prayer. If

you oppose temptation without these, it only attacks you more strongly.

107. He who is gentle in God's sight is wiser than the wise; and he who is humble in heart is stronger than the strong. For they bear the yoke of Christ with spiritual knowledge.

108. Everything we say or do without prayer afterwards turns out to be unreliable or harmful, and so shows us up without our realizing it.

109. One alone is righteous in works, words and thoughts. But many are made righteous[1] in faith, grace and repentance.

110. One who is repentant cannot be haughty, just as one who sins deliberately cannot be humble-minded.

111. Humility consists, not in condemning our conscience, but in recognizing God's grace and compassion.

112. What a house is to the air, the spiritual intellect is to divine grace. The more you get rid of materiality, the more the air and grace will come in of their own accord; and the more you increase materiality, the more they will go away.

113. Materiality in the case of a house consists of furnishings and food. Materiality in the case of the intellect is self-esteem and sensual pleasure.

114. Ample room in the heart denotes hope in God; congestion denotes bodily care.

115. The grace of the Spirit is one and unchanging, but energizes in each one of us as He wills (cf. 1 Cor. 12:11).

116. When rain falls upon the earth, it gives life to the quality inherent in each plant: sweetness in the sweet, astringency in the astringent; similarly, when grace falls upon the hearts of the faithful, it gives to each the energies appropriate to the different virtues without itself changing.

117. To him who hungers after Christ grace is food; to him who is thirsty, a reviving drink; to him who is cold, a garment; to him who is weary, rest; to him who prays, assurance; to him who mourns, consolation.

118. When you hear Scripture saying of the Holy Spirit that He 'rested upon each' of the Apostles (Acts 2:3), or 'came upon' the Prophet (1 Sam. 11:6), or 'energizes' (1 Cor. 12:11), or is 'grieved' (Eph. 4:30), or is 'quenched' (1 Thess. 5:19), or is

---

[1] Reading *dikaiountai* in accordance with the early manuscripts.

'vexed' (Isa. 63:10), and again, that some 'have the firstfruits' (Rom. 8:23), and that others are 'filled with the Holy Spirit' (Acts 2:4), do not suppose that the Spirit is subject to some kind of division, variation or change; but be sure that, in the way we have described, He is unvarying, unchanging and all-powerful. Therefore in all His energies He remains what He is, and in a divine manner He gives to each person what is needful. On those who have been baptized He pours Himself out in His fulness like the sun. Each of us is illumined by Him to the extent to which we hate the passions that darken us and get rid of them. But in so far as we have a love for them and dwell on them, we remain in darkness.

119. He who hates the passions gets rid of their causes. But he who is attracted by their causes is attacked by the passions even though he does not wish it.

120. When evil thoughts become active within us, we should blame ourselves and not ancestral sin.

121. The roots of evil thoughts are the obvious vices, which we keep trying to justify in our words and actions.

122. We cannot entertain a passion in our mind unless we have a love for its causes.

123. For what man, who cares nothing about being put to shame, entertains thoughts of self-esteem? Or who welcomes contempt and yet is disturbed by dishonour? And who has 'a broken and a contrite heart' (Ps. 51:17) and yet indulges in carnal pleasure? Or who puts his trust in Christ and yet worries or quarrels about transitory things?

124. If a man is treated with contempt by someone and yet does not react with anger in either word or thought, it shows he has acquired real knowledge and firm faith in the Lord.

125. 'The sons of men are false, and cheat with their scales' (Ps. 62:9. LXX), but God assigns to each what is just.

126. If the criminal will not keep his gains for ever and his victim will not always suffer want, 'surely man passes like a shadow and troubles himself in vain' (Ps. 39:6. LXX).

127. When you see someone suffering great dishonour, you may be sure that he was carried away by thoughts of self-esteem and is now reaping, much to his disgust, the harvest from the seeds which he sowed in his heart.

128. He who enjoys bodily pleasures beyond the proper limit will pay for the excess a hundredfold in sufferings.

129. A man exercising authority should tell his subordinate his duty; and, if disobeyed, should warn him of the evil consequences.

130. He who suffers wrong and does not demand any reparation from the man who wronged him, trusts in Christ to make good the loss; and he is rewarded a hundredfold in this world and inherits eternal life (cf. Mark 10:30).

131. The remembrance of God is suffering of heart endured in a spirit of devotion. But he who forgets God becomes self-indulgent and insensitive.

132. Do not say that a dispassionate man cannot suffer affliction; for even if he does not suffer on his own account, he is under a liability to do so for his neighbour.

133. When the enemy has booked against a man many forgotten sins, he forces his debtor to recall them in memory, taking full advantage of 'the law of sin' (cf. Rom. 8:2).

134. If you wish to remember God unceasingly, do not reject as undeserved what happens to you, but patiently accept it as your due. For patient acceptance of whatever happens kindles the remembrance of God, whereas refusal to accept weakens the spiritual purpose of the heart and so makes it forgetful.

135. If you want your sins to be 'covered' by the Lord (cf. Ps. 32:1), do not display your virtues to others. For whatever we do with our virtues, God will also do with our sins.

136. Having hidden your virtue, do not be filled with pride, imagining you have achieved righteousness. For righteousness is not only to hide your good actions, but also never to think forbidden thoughts.

137. Rejoice, not when you do good to someone, but when you endure without rancour the hostility that follows. For just as night follows day, so acts of malice follow acts of kindness.

138. Acts of kindness and generosity are spoilt by self-esteem, meanness and pleasure, unless these have first been destroyed by fear of God.

139. The mercy of God is hidden in sufferings not of our choice; and if we accept such sufferings patiently, they bring us to repentance and deliver us from everlasting punishment.

140. Some, when they actively observe the commandments, expect this to outweigh their sins; others, who observe the commandments without this presumption, gain the grace of Him who

died on account of our sins. We should consider which of these is right.

141. Fear of hell and love for God's kingdom enable us patiently to accept affliction; and this they do, not by themselves, but through Him who knows our thoughts.

142. He who believes in the blessings of the world to come abstains of his own accord from the pleasures of this present world. But he who lacks such faith becomes pleasure-loving and insensitive.

143. Do not ask how a poor man can be self-indulgent when he lacks the material means. For it is possible to be self-indulgent in a yet more despicable way through one's thoughts.

144. Knowledge of created beings is one thing, and knowledge of the divine truth is another. The second surpasses the first just as the sun outshines the moon.

145. Knowledge of created beings increases the more we observe the commandments actively; but knowledge of the truth grows the more we hope in Christ.

146. If you wish to be saved and 'to come unto the knowledge of the truth' (1 Tim. 2:4), endeavour always to transcend sensible things, and through hope alone to cleave to God. Then you will find principalities and powers fighting against you (cf. Eph. 6:12), deflecting you against your will and provoking you to sin. But if you prevail over them through prayer and maintain your hope, you will receive God's grace, and this will deliver you from the wrath to come.

147. If you understand what is said in a mystical sense by St Paul, that 'we wrestle . . . against spiritual wickedness' (Eph. 6:12), you will also understand the parable of the Lord, which He spoke 'to this end, that men ought always to pray, and not to lose heart' (Luke 18:1).

148. The Law figuratively commands men to work for six days and on the seventh to rest (cf. Exod. 20:9–10). The term 'work' when applied to the soul signifies acts of kindness and generosity by means of our possessions – that is, through material things. But the soul's rest and repose is to sell everything and 'give to the poor' (Matt. 19:21), as Christ Himself said; so through its lack of possessions it will rest from its work and devote itself to spiritual hope. Such is the rest into which Paul also exhorts us to enter, saying: 'Let us strive therefore to enter into that rest' (Heb. 4:11).

149. In saying this we are not forgetting the blessings of the life to come or limiting the universal reward to the present life. We are simply affirming that it is necessary in the first place to have the grace of the Holy Spirit energizing the heart and so, in proportion to this energizing, to enter into the kingdom of heaven. The Lord made this clear in saying: 'The kingdom of heaven is within you' (cf. Luke 17:21). The Apostle, too, said the same: 'Faith is the substance of things hoped for' (Heb. 11:1); 'Run, that you may reach your goal' (1 Cor. 9:24); 'Examine yourselves whether you are in the faith. . . . Do you not know . . . that Jesus Christ is in you unless you are worthless' (2 Cor. 13:5).

150. He who has come to know the truth does not oppose the afflictions that befall him, for he knows that they lead him to the fear of God.

151. To recall past sins in detail inflicts injury on the man who hopes in God. For when such recollection brings remorse it deprives him of hope; but if he pictures the sins to himself without remorse, they pollute him again with the old defilement.

152. When the intellect through rejection of the passions attains to unwavering hope, then the enemy makes it visualize its past sins on the pretext of confessing them to God. Thus he tries to rekindle passions which by God's grace have been forgotten, and so secretly to inflict injury. Then, even though someone is illumined and hates the passions, he will inevitably be filled with darkness and confusion at the memory of what he has done. But if he is still befogged and self-indulgent, he will certainly dally with the enemy's provocations and entertain them under the influence of passion, so that this re-collection will prove to be a prepossession and not a confession.

153. If you wish to make a blameless confession to God do not go over your failings in detail, but firmly resist their renewed attacks.

154. Trials come upon us because of our former sins, bringing what is appropriate to each offence.

155. The man who possesses spiritual knowledge and understands the truth confesses to God, not by recalling what he has done, but by accepting patiently what comes.

156. If you refuse to accept suffering and dishonour, do not claim to be in a state of repentance because of your other virtues. For self-esteem and insensitivity can serve sin even under the cover of virtue.

157. Just as suffering and dishonour usually give birth to virtues, so pleasure and self-esteem usually give birth to vices.

158. All bodily pleasure results from previous laxity, and laxity results from lack of faith.

159. He who is under the power of sin cannot by himself prevail over the will of the flesh, because he suffers continual stimulation in all his members.

160. Those who are under the sway of passions must pray and be obedient. For even when they receive help, they can only just manage to fight against their preposessions.

161. He who tries to conquer his own will by means of obedience and prayer is following a wise ascetic method. His renunciation of external things indicates his inward struggle.

162. He who does not make his will agree with God is tripped up by his own schemes and falls into the hands of his enemies.

163. When you see two evil men befriending one another, you may be sure that each is co-operating with the other's desires.

164. The haughty and the conceited gladly agree together; for the haughty man praises the conceited man who fawns on him in a servile manner, while the conceited man extols the haughty man who continually praises him.

165. The man who loves God benefits from both praise and blame: if commended for his good actions he grows more zealous, and if reproved for his sins he is brought to repentance. Our outward life should accord with our inner progress, and our prayers to God with our life.

166. It is good to hold fast to the principal commandment, and not to be anxious about particular things or to pray for them specifically, but to seek only the kingdom and the word of God (cf. Matt. 6:25–33). If, however, we are still anxious about our particular needs, we should also pray for each of them. He who does or plans anything without prayer will not succeed in the end. And this is what the Lord meant when He said: 'Without Me you can do nothing' (John 15:5).

167. If a man disregards the commandment about prayer, he then commits worse acts of disobedience, each one handing him over to the next like a prisoner.

168. He who accepts present afflictions in the expectation of

future blessings has found knowledge of the truth; and he will easily be freed from anger and remorse.

169. He who chooses maltreatment and dishonour for the sake of truth is walking on the apostolic path; he has taken up the cross and is bound in chains (cf. Matt. 16:24; Acts 28:20). But when he tries to concentrate his attention on the heart without accepting these two, his intellect wanders from the path and he falls into the temptations and snares of the devil.

170. In our ascetic warfare we can neither rid ourselves of evil thoughts apart from their causes, nor of their causes without ridding ourselves of the thoughts. For if we reject the one without the other, before long the other will involve us in them both at once.

171. He who fights against others out of fear of hardship or reproach will either suffer more harshly through what befalls him in this life, or will be punished mercilessly in the life to come.

172. He who wishes to be spared all misfortunes should associate God with everything through prayer; with his intellect he should set his hope in Him, putting aside, so far as possible, all concern about things of the senses.

173. When the devil finds someone preoccupied needlessly with bodily things, he first deprives him of the hard-won fruits of spiritual knowledge, and then cuts off his hope in God.

174. If you should ever reach the stronghold of pure prayer, do not accept the knowledge of created things which is presented to you at that moment by the enemy, lest you lose what is greater. For it is better to shoot at him from above with the arrows of prayer, cooped up as he is down below, then to parley with him as he offers us the knowledge he has plundered,[1] and tries to tear us away from this prayer which defeats him.

175. Knowledge of created things helps a man at a time of temptation and listlessness; but at a time of pure prayer it is usually harmful.

176. If it is your task to give spiritual instruction and you are disobeyed, grieve inwardly but do not be outwardly upset. For if you grieve, you will not share the guilt of the person who disobeys you; but if you are upset you will be tested by the same temptations as he is.

177. When you are explaining things, do not conceal what is

---

[1] Reading *skyla* in accordance with the early manuscripts.

relevant to the needs of those present. You should discuss explicitly whatever is seemly, but refer less explicitly to what is hard to accept.

178. If someone is not under obedience to you, do not rebuke him to his face for his faults. For that would imply you have authority over him, and are not just giving advice.

179. What is said without explicit reference to individuals is helpful to all, for each applies it to himself according to his own conscience.

180. He who speaks rightly should recognize that he receives the words from God. For the truth belongs not to him who speaks, but to God who is energizing him.

181. Do not argue with people not under obedience to you when they oppose the truth; otherwise you may arouse their hatred.

182. If you give way when someone who is under obedience to you wrongly contradicts you, you lead him astray over the point at issue and also encourage him to repudiate his promise of obedience.

183. He who with fear of God admonishes or corrects a man who has sinned, gains the virtue that is opposite to that sin. But he who reproaches him out of rancour and ill will becomes subject to a similar passion, according to the spiritual law.

184. He who has learned the law properly fears the Lawgiver and, fearing Him, he turns away from every evil.

185. Do not be double-tongued, saying one thing when your conscience says another. For Scripture places such people under a curse (cf. Ecclus. 28:13).

186. One man speaks the truth and is hated for it by the foolish; another speaks hypocritically and for this reason is loved. But in in both cases their reward is not long delayed, for at the appropriate moment the Lord renders to each his due.

187. He who wishes to avoid future troubles should endure his present troubles gladly. For in this way, balancing the one against the other, through small sufferings he will avoid those which are great.

188. Guard your speech from boasting and your thoughts from presumption; otherwise you may be abandoned by God and fall into sin. For man cannot do anything good without the help of God, who sees everything.

189. God, who sees everything, rewards at their proper value not only our actions but also our voluntary thoughts and purposes.

190. Involuntary thoughts arise from previous sin; voluntary ones from our free will. Thus the latter are the cause of the former.

191. Evil thoughts which arise against our will are accompanied by remorse, and so they soon disappear; but when they are freely chosen, they are accompanied by pleasure, and so they are hard to get rid of.

192. The self-indulgent are distressed by criticism and hardship; those who love God by praise and luxury.

193. He who does not understand God's judgments walks on a ridge like a knife-edge and is easily unbalanced by every puff of wind. When praised, he exults; when criticized, he feels bitter. When he feasts, he makes a pig of himself; and when he suffers hardship, he moans and groans. When he understands, he shows off; and when he does not understand, he pretends that he does. When rich, he is boastful; and when in poverty, he plays the hypocrite. Gorged, he grows brazen; and when he fasts, he becomes arrogant. He quarrels with those who reprove him; and those who forgive him he regards as fools.

194. Unless a man acquires, through the grace of Christ, knowledge of the truth and fear of God, he is gravely wounded not only by the passions but also by the things that happen to him.

195. When you want to resolve a complex problem, seek God's will in the matter, and you will find a constructive solution.

196. When something accords with God's will, all creation aids it. But when God rejects something, creation too opposes it.

197. He who opposes unpleasant events opposes the command of God unwittingly. But when someone accepts them with real knowledge, he 'waits patiently for the Lord' (Ps. 27:14).

198. When tested by some trial you should try to find out not why or through whom it came, but only how to endure it gratefully, without distress or rancour.

199. Another man's sin does not increase our own, unless we ourselves embrace it by means of evil thoughts.

200. If it is not easy to find anyone conforming to God's will who has not been put to the test, we ought to thank God for everything that happens to us.

201. If Peter had not failed to catch anything during the night's fishing (cf. Luke 5:5), he would not have caught anything during the day. And if Paul had not suffered physical blindness (cf. Acts

9:8), he would not have been given spiritual sight. And if Stephen had not been slandered as a blasphemer, he would not have seen the heavens opened and have looked on God (cf. Acts 6:15; 7:56).

202. As work according to God is called virtue, so unexpected affliction is called a test.

203. God 'tested Abraham' (cf. Gen. 22:1–14), that is, God afflicted him for his own benefit, not in order to learn what kind of man Abraham was – for He knew him, since He knows all things before they come into existence – but in order to provide him with opportunities for showing perfect faith.

204. Every affliction tests our will, showing whether it is inclined to good or evil. This is why an unforeseen affliction is called a test, because it enables a man to test his hidden desires.

205. The fear of God compels us to fight against evil; and when we fight against evil, the grace of God destroys it.

206. Wisdom is not only to perceive the natural consequence of things, but also to accept as our due the malice of those who wrong us. People who go no further than the first kind of wisdom become proud, whereas those who attain the second become humble.

207. If you do not want evil thoughts to be active within you, accept humiliation of soul and affliction of the flesh; and this not just on particular occasions, but always, everywhere and in all things.

208. He who willingly accepts chastening by affliction is not dominated by evil thoughts against his will; whereas he who does not accept affliction is taken prisoner by evil thoughts, even though he resists them.

209. When you are wronged and your heart and feelings are hardened, do not be distressed, for this has happened providentially; but be glad and reject the thoughts that arise within you, knowing that if they are destroyed at the stage when they are only provocations, their evil consequences will be cut off; whereas if the thoughts persist the evil may be expected to develop.

210. Without contrition of the heart it is altogether impossible to rid ourselves of evil. Now the heart is made contrite by threefold self-control: in sleep, in food and in bodily relaxation. For excess of these three things leads to self-indulgence; and this in turn makes us accept evil thoughts, and is opposed to prayer and to appropriate work.

211. If it is your duty to give orders to your brethren, be mindful

of your role and, when they contradict you, do not fail to tell them what is necessary. When they obey you, you will be rewarded because of their virtue; but when they disobey you, you will none the less forgive them, and will equally be rewarded by Him who said: 'Forgive and it shall be forgiven you' (cf. Matt. 6:14).

212. Every event is like a bazaar. He who knows how to bargain makes a good profit, he who does not makes a loss.

213. If someone does not obey you when you have told him once, do not argue and try to compel him; but take for yourself the profit which he has thrown away. For forbearance will benefit you more than correcting him.

214. When the evil conduct of one person begins to affect others, you should not show long-suffering; and instead of your own advantage you should seek that of the others, so that they may be saved. For virtue involving many people is more valuable than virtue involving only one.

215. If a man falls into some sin and does not feel remorse for his offence as he should, he will easily fall into the same net again.

216. Just as a lioness does not make friends with a calf, so impudence does not gladly admit the remorse that accords with God's will.

217. Just as a sheep does not mate with a wolf, so suffering of the heart does not couple with satiety for the conception of virtues.

218. No one can experience suffering and remorse in a way that accords with God's will, unless he first loves what causes them.

219. Fear of God and reproof induce remorse; hardship and vigils make us intimate with suffering.

220. He who does not learn from the commandments and warnings of Scripture will be driven by 'the horse's whip' and 'the ass's goad' (cf. Prov. 26:3. LXX). And if he refuses to obey these as well, his 'mouth must be controlled with bit and bridle' (Ps. 32:9).

221. He who is easily overcome by the lesser will inevitably be enslaved by the greater. But he who is superior to the lesser will also with the Lord's help resist the greater.

222. When someone boasts about his virtues, do not try to help him by reproving him. For a man cannot love showing off and at the same time love the truth.

223. Every word of Christ shows us God's mercy, justice and wisdom and, if we listen gladly, their power enters into us. That is

why the unmerciful and the unjust, listening to Christ with repug-
nance, were not able to understand the wisdom of God, but even
crucified Him for teaching it. So we, too, should ask ourselves
whether we listen to Him gladly. For He said: 'He who loves Me
will keep My commandments, and he will be loved by My Father,
and I will love him, and will manifest Myself to him' (cf. John
14:21). Do you see how He has hidden His manifestation in the
commandments? Of all the commandments, therefore, the most
comprehensive is to love God and our neighbour. This love is made
firm through abstaining from material things, and through stillness of
thoughts.

224. Knowing this, the Lord enjoins us 'not to be anxious about
the morrow' (Matt. 6:34); and rightly so. For if a man has not
freed himself from material things and from concern about them,
how can he be freed from evil thoughts? And if he is beset by evil
thoughts, how can he see the reality of the sin concealed behind
them? This sin wraps the soul in darkness and obscurity, and increases its hold upon us through our evil thoughts and actions. The
devil initiates the whole process by testing a man with a provocation
which he is not compelled to accept; but the man, urged on by
self-indulgence and self-esteem, begins to entertain this provocation
with enjoyment. Even if his discrimination tells him to reject it, yet
in practice he takes pleasure in it and accepts it. If someone has not
perceived this general process of sinning, when will he pray about it
and be cleansed from it? And if he has not been cleansed, how will he
find purity of nature? And if he has not found this, how will he
behold the inner dwelling-place of Christ? For we are a dwelling-
place of God, according to the words of Prophet, Gospel and
Apostle (cf. Zech. 2:10; John 14:23; 1 Cor. 3:16; Heb. 3:6).

225. Following the sequence just described, we should try to
find the dwelling-place and knock with persistent prayer, so that
either in this life or at our death the Master may open to us and not
say because of our negligence: 'I do not know where you come from'
(Luke 13:25). Not only ought we to ask and receive, but we should
also keep safely what is given; for some people lose what they have
received. A theoretical knowledge or chance experience of these
things may perhaps be gained by those who have begun to learn late
in life or who are still young; but the constant and patient practice of
these things is barely to be acquired even by devout and deeply

experienced elders, who have repeatedly lost it through lack of attention and then through voluntary suffering have searched for and found it again. So let us constantly imitate them in this, until we, too, have acquired this practice irremovably.

226. Out of the many ordinances of the spiritual law we have come to understand these few. The great Psalmist again and again urges us to learn and practise them as we ceaselessly praise the Lord Jesus. To Him are due glory, power and worship, both now and through all the ages. Amen.

Letter to Nicolas the Solitary

Since you have recently become much concerned about your salvation, and have been asking yourself how you can live a life according to God, you have consulted us and told us about yourself: how with great labour and burning desire you wished to cleave to God through a strict way of life, through self-control and much hardship, through vigils and intense prayer. You spoke of the conflicts and the swarm of carnal passions stirred up in our bodily nature and aroused against the soul by the law of sin that fights against the law of our intellect (cf. Rom. 7:23). You deplored the fact that you are especially troubled by the passions of anger and desire, and you asked for some method and words of advice indicating what ascetic practices you should adopt to overcome these two destructive passions. At that time we talked with you directly and suggested, as far as we could, various ideas to help you, explaining how the soul should engage in ascetic efforts with understanding and spiritual knowledge, in accordance with the Gospel; and how, living by faith and helped by grace, it can overcome the evils that spring up in the heart, and especially the two passions just mentioned. Our soul should fight most vigorously and continually against those passions to which it is especially liable through prepossession and habit, until it has subdued the non-spiritual and uncontrolled operations of vice to which up till now it has been subject; for the soul is carried away captive through its inward assent to the thoughts with which it is constantly and sinfully occupied.

We are now physically separated from you 'for a short time, in presence but not in heart' (1 Thess. 2:17), for we have gone to live in the desert with the true ascetics of Christ. It is our hope that we, too, may to some small extent pursue the spiritual way in company with our brethren, who are fighting against the hostile energies and bravely resisting the passions. We are trying to shake off sloth and laxity, to free ourselves from negligence, and to make every effort to conform to God's will. So we have decided to write you a few words of advice for the benefit of your soul. In this modest letter you will find some of the things we mentioned to you in our talk; we ask you to read it carefully, as though we were ourselves present, so that it may help you spiritually.

This, my son, is how you should begin your life according to God. You should continually and unceasingly call to mind all the blessings which God in His love has bestowed upon you in the past, and still bestows for the salvation of your soul. You must not let forgetfulness of evil or laziness make you grow unmindful of these many and great blessings, and so pass the rest of your life uselessly and ungratefully. For this kind of continual recollection, pricking the heart like a spur, moves it constantly to confession and humility, to thanksgiving with a contrite soul, and to all forms of sincere effort, repaying God through its virtue and holiness. In this way the heart meditates constantly and conscientiously on the words from the Psalms: 'What shall I give to the Lord in return for all His benefits towards me?' (Ps. 116:12).

Thus the soul recalls the blessings of God's love which it has received from the moment it came into existence: how it has often been delivered from dangers; how in spite of having often fallen by its own free choice into great evils and sins, it was not justly given up to destruction and death at the hands of the spirits of deception; and how God with long-suffering overlooked its offences and protected it, awaiting its return. It also recalls that although through the passions it had become the willing servant of hostile and malicious spirits, He sustained it, guarding it and in all ways providing for it; and finally that He guided it with a clear sign to the path of salvation, and inspired it with the love of the ascetic life. So He gave it the strength gladly to abandon the world and all the deceitfulness of worldly pleasure, adorning it with the angelic habit of the monastic order, and providing for it to be received by holy men in an organized brotherhood.

Can any man consciously call these things to mind and not be moved always to contrition of heart? Having so many pledges from past blessings, will he not always have firm hope, in spite of the fact that he himself has so far done nothing good? He will say to himself: 'Though I have done nothing good and have committed many sins before Him, living in uncleanness of the flesh and indulging in many other vices, yet He did not deal with me according to my sins, or reward me according to my iniquities (cf. Ps. 103:10), but gave me all these gifts of grace for my salvation. If, then, from now onwards I give myself completely to His service, living in all purity and acquiring the virtues, how many holy and spiritual gifts will He not grant me, strengthening me in every good work, guiding and leading me aright.' If a man always thinks in this way and does not forget God's blessings, he encourages and urges himself on to the practice of every virtue and of every righteous work, always ready, always eager to do the will of God.

Therefore, my dear son, since through the grace of Christ you possess natural understanding, continue always to occupy your mind with such meditation. Do not let yourself be overcome by destructive forgetfulness or by the laziness which paralyzes the intellect and turns it away from life; do not allow ignorance, the cause of all evils, to darken your thinking; do not be lured by the corrosive vice of negligence; do not be seduced by sensual pleasure or defeated by gluttony; do not let your intellect be taken prisoner by lust through assenting to sexual thoughts, defiling yourself inwardly; do not be overcome by the anger which causes you to hate your brother and for some pathetic reason to inflict and suffer pain, leading you to store up malicious thoughts against your neighbour and to turn away from pure prayer. Anger enslaves the intellect, and makes you regard your brother with bestial cruelty; it fetters the conscience with uncontrolled impulses of the flesh, and surrenders you for a time to be chastised by the evil spirits to whom you have yielded.

Eventually your intellect, at a loss where to turn, is overwhelmed by dejection and laziness and forfeits all its spiritual progress. Then in deep humility it sets out once more on the path of salvation. Labouring much in prayer and all-night vigils, it uproots the causes of evil within itself through humility and confession before God and our neighbour. In this way it begins to regain the state of watchfulness and, illumined with divine grace and understanding of the Gospels, it perceives that no one can become a true Christian unless he gives himself up completely to the cross in a spirit of humility and self-denial, and makes himself lower than all, letting himself be trampled underfoot, insulted, despised, wronged, ridiculed and mocked; and all this he must endure joyfully for the Lord's sake, not claiming for himself in return any human advantages: glory, honour or praise, or the pleasures of food, drink or clothes.

Such are the contests and such the prizes that lie before us. How long, then, shall we mock ourselves by pretending to be devout, serving the Lord with hypocrisy, being thought one thing by men but clearly seen to be quite different by Him who knows our secrets? Other people regard us as saintly, but we are still savage. Although we have indeed an outward form of godliness, we do not possess its power before God (cf. 2 Tim. 3:5). Other people regard us as virginal and chaste, but in the sight of Him who knows our secrets, we are inwardly defiled by our assent to thoughts of unchastity, and made filthy by the activity of the passions. In spite of this, thanks to our seeming asceticism, we attract men's praises and are bowled over and blinded in our intellect.

How long shall we continue in this manner, our intellect reduced to futility, failing to make the spirit of the Gospel our own, not knowing what it means to live according to our conscience, making no serious effort to keep it pure? Lacking real knowledge, we still trust solely in the apparent righteousness of our outward way of life, and so lead ourselves astray, trying to please men, pursuing the glory, honour and praise which they offer. But the Judge who cannot be deceived will certainly come, and 'will bring to light the things now hidden in darkness, and reveal the purposes of hearts' (1 Cor. 4:5). He neither respects the wealthy nor pities the poor, but strips away the outward appearance and reveals the truth hidden within. In the presence of the angels and before His own Father, He crowns those who have truly pursued the spiritual way and lived according to their conscience; and in the presence of the heavenly Church of the saints and of all the celestial hosts, He exposes those who possessed merely an outward pretence of devotion, which they displayed to men, vainly relying on it and deceiving themselves; and He banishes them in shame to outer darkness.

Such people are like the foolish virgins (cf. Matt. 25:1–12), who did indeed preserve their outer virginity, yet in spite of this were not admitted to the marriage-feast; they also had some oil in their vessels, that is, they possessed some virtues and external achievements and some gifts of grace, so that their lamps remained alight for a certain time. But because of negligence, ignorance and laziness they were not provident, and did not pay careful attention to the hidden swarm of passions energized within them by the evil spirits. Their thoughts were corrupted by these hostile energies, while they themselves assented to this demonic activity and shared in it. They were secretly enticed and overcome by malicious envy, by jealousy that hates everything good, by strife, quarrelling, hatred, anger, bitterness, rancour, hypocrisy, wrath, pride, self-esteem, love of popularity, self-satisfaction, avarice, listlessness, by sensual desire which provokes images of self-indulgence, by unbelief, irreverence, cowardice, dejection, contentiousness, sluggishness, sleep, presumption, self-justification, pomposity, boastfulness, insatiateness, profligacy, greed, by despair which is the most dangerous of all, and by the subtle workings of vice. Even the good acts which they performed and their life of chastity were all for the sake of being seen and praised by men; and though they had a share in some gifts of grace, this they sold to the spirits of self-esteem and popularity. Because of their involvement with the other passions, they mixed their virtues with sinful and worldly thoughts, so rendering them unacceptable and impure, like Cain's sacrifice (cf. Gen. 4:5). Thus they were deprived of the joy of the Bridegroom and shut out from the heavenly bridal chamber.

Pondering, assessing and testing all this, let us realize our situation and correct our way of life while we still have time for repentance and conversion. Let us perform our good actions with purity, so that they are really good and not mixed with worldly thoughts; otherwise they will be rejected, like a blemished sacrifice, because of our irreverence, negligence and want of real knowledge. Let us be careful not to waste our days, lest we undergo all the effort of the life of virginity – practising self-control, keeping vigil, fasting, showing hospitality – only to find at the end that, because of the passions we have mentioned, our apparent righteousness, like the blemished sacrifice, proves unacceptable to the heavenly Priest, Christ our God.

Therefore, my son, he who wishes to take up the cross and follow Christ must first acquire spiritual knowledge and understanding through constantly examining his thoughts, showing the utmost concern for his salvation, and seeking God with all his strength. He should question other servants of God who are of the same mind and engaged in the same ascetic struggle, so that he does not travel in the dark without a light, not knowing how or where to walk. For the

man who goes his own way, travelling without understanding of the
Gospels and without any guidance, often stumbles and falls into
many pits and snares of the devil; he frequently goes astray and
exposes himself to many dangers, not knowing where he is going.
For many have endured great ascetic labours, much hardship and
toil for God's sake; but because they relied on their own judgment,
lacked discrimination, and failed to accept help from their neighbour,
their many efforts proved useless and vain.

So then, my beloved son, follow the advice I gave you at the beginning of this letter, and do not let yourself be dragged down
unwittingly by vice and laziness, so that you forget the gifts you have
received through God's love. Bring before your eyes the blessings,
whether physical or spiritual, conferred on you from the beginning
of your life down to the present, and call them repeatedly to mind
in accordance with the words: 'Forget not all His benefits' (Ps.
103:2). Then your heart will readily be moved to the fear and love
of God, so that you repay Him, as far as you can, by your strict life,
virtuous conduct, devout conscience, wise speech, true faith and
humility – in short, by dedicating your whole self to God. When
you are moved by the recollection of all these blessings which you
have received through God's loving goodness, your heart will be
spontaneously wounded with longing and love through this recollection or, rather, with the help of divine grace; for He has not done
for others who are much better than yourself such miraculous things
as in His ineffable love He has done for you.

Try, then, to remember unceasingly all the blessings that have
been given to you by God. In particular, always keep in mind that
miraculous grace which you told us He conferred on you when you
were sailing with your mother from the Holy Land to Constantinople.
Recall the terrifying and uncontrollable violence of the storm that
broke on you during the night, and how everyone in the ship,
including the crew and your mother herself, perished in the sea;
and how by an incredible act of divine power you and two others
alone were thrown clear of the wreck and escaped. Remember how
you came providentially to Ankyra, and how, with fatherly compassion, you were given hospitality by a certain freeman, and
became friends with his devout son Epiphanios. Then both of you,
under the guidance of a holy man, entered on the path of salvation,
and were received as true sons by the servants of God.

What repayment for all these blessings can you possibly make to Him who has called your soul to eternal life? It is only right, then, that you should live no longer for yourself, but for Christ, who died for your sake and rose again. In your struggle to acquire every virtue and to fulfil every commandment, always seek 'the good, acceptable and perfect will of God' (Rom. 12 : 2), endeavouring with all your strength to pursue it.

Submit your youth to the word of God, my son, and, as this word commands, present your body as 'a living sacrifice, holy, acceptable to God, for this is your spiritual worship' (Rom. 12 : 1). Cool and dry up all the moisture of sensual desire by being content with little, drinking little, and keeping all-night vigils, so that you can say in all sincerity: 'I am become like a wineskin in the frost; yet I have not forgotten Thy ordinances' (Ps. 119 : 83. LXX). Knowing that you are Christ's, crucify your flesh together with its affections and desires (cf. Gal. 5 : 24). 'Put to death whatever is earthly in you' (Col. 3 : 5), avoiding not only external acts of unchastity, but also the impurity stimulated in your flesh by evil spirits.

Yet he who hopes to achieve true, undefiled and complete virginity does not stop here. Following the Apostle's teaching, he struggles to put to death every trace and stirring of passion itself. Even so, he is still not entirely satisfied but he longs intensely for angelic and undefiled virginity to establish itself in his body. He prays for the disappearance even of the mere thought of lust, occurring as a momentary disturbance of the intellect, without any movement and working of bodily passion. A person can achieve this only through the help and power of the Holy Spirit – if indeed there is anyone who is counted worthy of this grace.

Thus he who hopes to achieve pure, spiritual and undefiled virginity crucifies the flesh through ascetic labours and puts to death whatever is earthly in him through intense and persistent self-control. He erodes the outer man, refining him, stripping him down to the bone, so that through faith, ascetic effort and the energy of grace the inner man may be 'renewed day by day' (2 Cor. 4 : 16), advancing to a higher state. He grows in love, is adorned with gentleness, rejoices greatly in spirit, is ruled by the peace of Christ, led by kindness, guarded by goodness, protected by the fear of God, enlightened by understanding and knowledge, illumined by wisdom, guided by humility. The intellect, renewed by the Spirit through these and similar virtues, discovers within itself the imprint of the divine image, and perceives the spiritual and ineffable beauty of the divine likeness; and so, learning from itself, it attains the rich wisdom of the inner law.

Therefore, my son, refine the youthful impulses of your flesh, and through the virtues we have described strengthen your immortal soul and renew your intellect with the help of the Spirit. For the flesh of youth, gorged with food and wine, is like a pig ready for slaughter. The flames of sensual pleasure kill the soul, while the intellect is made a prisoner by the fierce heat of evil desire and cannot then resist such pleasure. For when the blood is heated the spirit is cooled.

Young people should particularly avoid drinking wine, and even getting the smell of it. Otherwise the inward action of passion and the wine poured in from outside will produce a double conflagration; the combination of the two will bring the flesh's sensual pleasure to boiling point, driving away the spiritual pleasure that accompanies the pain of contrition, and producing confusion and hardness of heart. Indeed, their spiritual desire should prevent the young from drinking their fill even of water, for this is a great help towards self-restraint. If you try this for yourself, experience will show you that it really is so. For in recommending this rule we do not wish to impose on you a yoke of compulsion; but with love we advise it, as an aid in attaining true virginity and strict self-restraint, leaving it to your own free choice to do as you wish.

Now let us say something about the senseless passion of anger, which ravages, confuses and darkens every soul and, when it is active, makes those in whom it is easily and quickly aroused behave like beasts. This passion is strengthened particularly by pride, and so long as it is so strengthened it cannot be destroyed. While the diabolical tree of bitterness, anger and wrath has its roots kept moist by the foul water of pride, it blossoms and thrives and produces quantities of rotten fruit. Thus the structure of evil in the soul is impossible to destroy so long as it is rooted firmly in pride.

Do you want this tree of disorder – I mean the passion of bitterness, anger and wrath – to dry up within you and become barren, so that with the axe of the Spirit it may be 'hewn down and cast into the fire' together with every other vice (Matt. 3 : 10)? Do you want the destruction of this house of evil which the devil builds

in your soul by continually using as stones various plausible or
senseless pretexts, whether material or mental, and by constructing
its foundations out of thoughts of pride? If this is what you really
want, keep the humility of the Lord in your heart and never forget it.

Call to mind who He is, and what He became for our sakes.
Reflect first on the sublime light of His Divinity revealed to the
essences above (in so far as they can receive it) and glorified in the
heavens by all spiritual beings: angels, archangels, thrones, do-
minions, principalities, authorities, cherubim and seraphim, and the
spiritual powers whose names we do not know, as the Apostle hints
(cf. Eph. 1 : 21). Then think to what depth of human humiliation
He descended in His ineffable goodness, becoming in all respects
like us who were dwelling in darkness and the shadow of death (cf.
Isa. 9 : 2 ; Matt. 4 : 16), captives through the transgression of Adam
and dominated by the enemy through the activity of the passions.
When we were in this harsh captivity, ruled by invisible and bitter
death, the Master of all visible and invisible creation was not ashamed
to humble Himself and to take upon Himself our human nature,
subject as it was to the passions of shame and desire and condemned
by divine judgment; and He became like us in all things except that
He was without sin (cf. Heb. 4 : 15), that is, without ignoble
passions. All the penalties imposed by divine judgment upon man for
the sin of the first transgression – death, toil, hunger, thirst and the
like – He took upon Himself, becoming what we are, so that we
might become what He is. The Logos became man, so that man
might become Logos. Being rich, He became poor for our sakes, so
that through His poverty we might become rich (cf. 2 Cor. 8 : 9). In
His great love for man He became like us, so that through every
virtue we might become like Him.

From the time that Christ came to dwell with us, man created
according to God's image and likeness is truly renewed through the
grace and power of the Spirit, attaining to the perfect love which
'casts out fear' (1 John 4 : 18) – the love which is no longer able to
fail, for 'love never fails' (1 Cor. 13 : 8). Love, says John, is God;
and 'he who dwells in love dwells in God' (1 John 4 : 16). The
apostles were granted this love, and so were those who practised
virtue as they did, offering themselves completely to the Lord, and
following Christ with all their heart throughout their lifetime.

So you should continually keep in mind the great humiliation which the Lord took upon Himself in His ineffable love for us: how the divine Logos dwelt in a womb; how He took human nature upon Himself; His birth from a woman; His gradual bodily growth; the shame He suffered, the insults, vilification, ridicule and abuse; how He was scourged and spat upon, derided and mocked; the scarlet robe, the crown of thorns; His condemnation by those in power; the outcry of the unruly Jews, men of His own race, against Him: 'Away with him, away with him, crucify him' (John 19:15); the cross, the nails, the lance, the drink of vinegar and gall; the scorn of the Gentiles; the derision of the passers-by who said: 'If you are the Son of God, come down from the cross and we will believe you' (cf. Matt. 27:39–42); and the rest of the sufferings which He patiently accepted for us: crucifixion; death; the three-day burial; the descent into hell. Then keep in mind all that has come from these sufferings: the resurrection from the dead; the liberation from hell and from death of those who were raised with the Lord; the ascension to the heavens; the enthronement at the right hand of the Father; the honour and glory that is 'far above every principality and power . . . and above every name that is named' (Eph. 1:21); the veneration of the Firstborn from the dead by all the angels, because of the sufferings He had undergone. As the Apostle says: 'Let this mind be in you, which was also in Christ Jesus. Though He is in the form of God, He did not insist on clinging to His equality with God; but He emptied Himself and took upon Himself the form of a servant, and was made in the likeness of man. Being in this likeness, He humbled Himself and became obedient to death, even the death of the cross. Therefore God has highly exalted Him and given Him a name which is above every name, so that at the name of Jesus every knee should bow, of things in heaven, things on earth and things under the earth' (Phil. 2:5–10). See to what a height of glory the Lord's human nature was raised up by God's justice through these sufferings and humiliations.

If, therefore, you continually recall this with all your heart, the passion of bitterness, anger and wrath will not master you. For when the foundations constructed of the passion of pride are sapped through this recalling of Christ's humiliation, the whole perverse edifice of anger, wrath and resentment automatically collapses. For can anyone keep perpetually in mind the humiliation that the Divinity of the only-begotten Son accepted for our sake, and all the sufferings that we have mentioned, and yet be so hard and stony-hearted as not to be shattered, humbled and filled with remorse? Will he not willingly become dust and ashes, trampled underfoot by all men?

So, when we are humbled and shattered, and keep in mind Christ's humiliation, what anger, wrath or bitterness can take possession of us? But when forgetfulness of these life-creating truths is accompanied by the sister vices of laziness and ignorance, then these three oppressive and deep-seated passions of the soul, hard to discover and correct, overlay and darken us with a terrible futility. They prepare the way for the rest of the evil passions to become active and nest in the soul, stifling its sense of awe, making it neglect what is good, and providing easy access and free scope for every passion.

For when the soul has been overlaid by pernicious forgetfulness, by destructive laziness, and by ignorance, the mother and nurse of every vice, the afflicted intellect in its blindness is readily enchained by everything that is seen, thought or heard. For instance, when we see a beautiful woman, our intellect is at once wounded by sensual desire. Then we recall what we have seen, heard, or touched with impassioned pleasure in the past, and so our memory forms sinful images within us. These defile the intellect that is still impassioned and afflicted through the activity of the demons of unchastity. Then the flesh, too, if it is well fed, full of youthful spirit, or flabby, is easily roused to passion by such memories, and moved to lust; and it performs acts of uncleanness either in sleep or awake, even though it does not have intercourse physically with a woman. Although such a man is regarded by others as chaste, pure and virgin, and may even have the reputation of being a saint, yet he is condemned as defiled, dissolute and adulterous by Him who sees into the secrets of men's hearts. At the Last Day he will justly be condemned, unless he first laments and mourns and offers to God worthy repentance, refining his flesh in fasting, vigils and unceasing prayers, healing and correcting his intellect by meditating on holy themes and on the word of God, in whose sight he conceived or did these evil things. For God says truly to each one of us: 'But I say to you that whoever looks at a woman with lust has already committed adultery with her in his heart' (Matt. 5:28).

This is why, if possible, it is very helpful for young monks not to meet women at all, even though these women are considered saintly. And if they can live in seclusion, the warfare becomes easier and they can see their own progress more clearly, especially if they confine their attention strictly to themselves, pursuing their spiritual struggle through abstemiousness, drinking but little water and being greatly vigilant in prayer. They should make every effort to seek the company of experienced spiritual fathers and to be guided by them. For it is dangerous to isolate oneself completely, relying on one's own judgment with no one else as witness; and it is equally dangerous to live with those who are inexperienced in spiritual warfare. For then we become involved in battles of other kinds, because the enemy has many hidden ways of attacking us and sets his snares around us on every side. Thus a man should try to live with those who possess spiritual knowledge, or at least to consult them continually, so that even if he is still spiritually immature and childish and does not himself possess a lamp of true knowledge, he can travel in company with someone who does. Then he will not be walking in the dark, in danger from snares and traps; and he will not fall prey to the demons who prowl like beasts in the dark, seizing and destroying those who grope there without the spiritual lamp of God's word.

If then, my son, you wish to acquire within yourself your own lamp of spiritual light and knowledge, so as to walk without stumbling in the dark night of this age; and if you wish your steps to be ordered by the Lord, delighting in the way of the Gospel – that is, desiring with ardent faith to hold fast to the most perfect gospel commandments, and to share in the sufferings of the Lord through aspirations and prayer – then I will show you a wonderful spiritual method to help you achieve this. It does not call for bodily exertion, but requires effort of the soul, control of the intellect, and an attentive understanding, assisted by fear and love of God. Through this method you can easily put to flight the hordes of the enemy, like the blessed David, who through his faith and trust in God destroyed Goliath, the giant of the Philistines (cf. 1 Sam. 17:45), and with the help of his own people easily put to flight the great host of the enemy.

Imagine that there are three powerful and mighty giants of the Philistines, upon whom depends the whole hostile army of the demonic Holofernes (cf. Judith 2:4). When these three have been overthrown and slain, all the power of the demons is fatally weakened.

These three giants are the vices already mentioned: ignorance, the source of all evils; forgetfulness, its close relation and helper; and laziness, which weaves the dark shroud enveloping the soul in murk. This third vice supports and strengthens the other two, consolidating them so that evil becomes deep-rooted and persistent in the negligent soul. Laziness, forgetfulness and ignorance in their turn support and strengthen the other passions. Helping each other, and unable to hold their position apart from one another, they are the mainstay and the chief leaders of the devil's army. Through them the whole of this army infiltrates into the soul and is enabled to achieve its objectives, which otherwise it could not do.

If then you wish to conquer these three passions and easily to put to flight the hordes of the demonic Philistines, enter within yourself through prayer and with the help of God. Descend into the depths of the heart, and search out these three powerful giants of the devil – forgetfulness, laziness and ignorance, the support of the demonic Philistines – which enable the rest of the evil passions to infiltrate and be active, to live and prevail in the hearts of the self-indulgent and in the souls of the uninstructed. Then through strict attention and control of the intellect, together with help from above, you will track down these evil passions, about which most men are ignorant, not even suspecting their existence, but which are more destructive than all the rest. Take up the weapons of righteousness that are directly opposed to them: mindfulness of God, for this is the cause of all blessings; the light of spiritual knowledge, through which the soul awakens from its slumber and drives out of itself the darkness of ignorance; and true ardour, which makes the soul eager for salvation.

So, through the power of the Holy Spirit, with all prayer and entreaty, you will contend bravely against the three giants of the demonic Philistines. Through mindfulness of God, you will always reflect on 'whatever is true, whatever is modest, whatever is just, whatever is pure, whatever is lovely, whatever is of good report, whatever is holy and deserving of praise' (Phil. 4:8); and in this way you will banish from yourself the pernicious evil of forgetfulness. Through the light of spiritual knowledge you will expel the destructive darkness of ignorance; and through your true ardour for all that is good you will drive out the godless laziness that enables evil to root itself in the soul. When by deep attentiveness and prayer you have acquired these virtues, not only through your own personal choice, but also through the power of God and with the help of the Holy Spirit, you will be able to deliver yourself from the three powerful giants of the devil. For when real knowledge, mindfulness of God's word and true ardour are firmly established in the soul through active grace and are carefully guarded, the combination of these three expels from the soul and obliterates every trace of forgetfulness, ignorance, and laziness, and henceforth grace reigns within it, through Christ Jesus our Lord. May He be glorified through all the ages. Amen.

ST HESYCHIOS THE PRIEST

Introductory Note

St Nikodimos identifies the writer of the work that follows, *On Watchfulness and Holiness*, with Hesychios of Jerusalem, author of many Biblical commentaries, who lived in the first half of the fifth century. But it is today accepted that *On Watchfulness and Holiness* is the work of an entirely different Hesychios, who was abbot of the Monastery of the Mother of God of the Burning Bush (Vatos) at Sinai. Hesychios of Sinai's date is uncertain. He is probably later than St John Klimakos (sixth or seventh century), with whose book *The Ladder of Divine Ascent* he seems to be familiar; possibly he lived in the eighth or ninth century. As well as drawing upon Klimakos, he incorporates in his work passages from St Mark the Ascetic and St Maximos the Confessor.[1]

St Nikodimos commends the work of St Hesychios especially for its teaching on watchfulness, inner attentiveness and the guarding of the heart. Hesychios has a warm devotion to the Holy Name of Jesus, and this makes his treatise of particular value to all who use the Jesus Prayer.*

We have followed the numbering of sections as given in the Greek *Philokalia*, which differs from that in Migne, *Patrologia Graeca*, xciii.

---

[1] For further details, see the footnotes to our translation; and compare J. Kirchmeyer, 'Hésychius le Sinaïte et ses Centuries', in *Le Millénaire du Mont Athos 963-1963. Études et Mélanges*, i (Chevetogne, 1963), pp. 319-29.

On Watchfulness and Holiness
WRITTEN FOR THEODOULOS

1. Watchfulness is a spiritual method which, if sedulously practised over a long period, completely frees us with God's help from impassioned thoughts, impassioned words and evil actions. It leads, in so far as this is possible, to a sure knowledge of the inapprehensible God, and helps us to penetrate the divine and hidden mysteries. It enables us to fulfil every divine commandment in the Old and New Testaments and bestows upon us every blessing of the age to come. It is, in the true sense, purity of heart, a state blessed by Christ when He says: 'Blessed are the pure in heart, for they shall see God' (Matt. 5:8); and one which, because of its spiritual nobility and beauty – or, rather, because of our negligence – is now extremely rare among monks. Because this is its nature, watchfulness is to be bought only at a great price. But once established in us, it guides us to a true and holy way of life. It teaches us how to activate the three aspects of our soul correctly, and how to keep a firm guard over the senses. It promotes the daily growth of the four principal virtues, and is the basis of our contemplation.

2. The great lawgiver Moses – or, rather, the Holy Spirit – indicates the pure, comprehensive and ennobling character of this virtue, and teaches us how to acquire and perfect it, when he says: 'Be attentive to yourself, lest there arise in your heart a secret thing which is an iniquity' (Deut. 15:9. LXX). Here the phrase 'a secret thing' refers to the first appearance of an evil thought. This the Fathers call a provocation introduced into the heart by the devil. As soon as this thought appears in our intellect, our own thoughts chase after it and enter into impassioned intercourse with it.

3. Watchfulness is a way embracing every virtue, every com-

mandment. It is the heart's stillness and, when free from mental images, it is the guarding of the intellect.

4. Just as a man blind from birth does not see the sun's light, so one who fails to pursue watchfulness does not see the rich radiance of divine grace. He cannot free himself from evil thoughts, words and actions, and because of these thoughts and actions he will not be able freely to pass the lords of hell when he dies.

5. Attentiveness is the heart's stillness, unbroken by any thought. In this stillness the heart breathes and invokes, endlessly and without ceasing, only Jesus Christ who is the Son of God and Himself God. It confesses Him who alone has power to forgive our sins, and with His aid it courageously faces its enemies. Through this invocation enfolded continually in Christ, who secretly divines all hearts, the soul does everything it can to keep its sweetness and its inner struggle hidden from men, so that the devil, coming upon it surreptitiously, does not lead it into evil and destroy its precious work.

6. Watchfulness is a continual fixing and halting of thought at the entrance to the heart. In this way predatory and murderous thoughts are marked down as they approach and what they say and do is noted; and we can see in what specious and delusive form the demons are trying to deceive the intellect. If we are conscientious in this, we can gain much experience and knowledge of spiritual warfare.

7. In one who is attempting to dam up the source of evil thoughts and actions, continuity of watchful attention in the intellect is produced by fear of hell and fear of God, by God's withdrawals from the soul, and by the advent of trials which chasten and instruct. For these withdrawals and unexpected trials help us to correct our life, especially when, having once experienced the tranquillity of watchfulness, we neglect it. Continuity of attention produces inner stability; inner stability produces a natural intensification of watchfulness; and this intensification gradually and in due measure gives contemplative insight into spiritual warfare. This in its turn is succeeded by persistence in the Jesus Prayer and by the state that Jesus confers, in which the intellect, free from all images, enjoys complete quietude.

8. When the mind, taking refuge in Christ and calling upon Him, stands firm and repels its unseen enemies, like a wild beast facing a pack of hounds from a good position of defence, then it inwardly

anticipates their inner ambuscades well in advance. Through continually invoking Jesus the peacemaker against them, it remains invulnerable.

9. If you are an adept, initiated into the mysteries and standing before God at dawn (cf. Ps. 5:3), you will divine the meaning of my words. Otherwise be watchful and you will discover it.

10. Much water makes up the sea. But extreme watchfulness and the Prayer of Jesus Christ, undistracted by thoughts, are the necessary basis for inner vigilance and unfathomable stillness of soul, for the deeps of secret and singular contemplation, for the humility that knows and assesses, for rectitude and love. This watchfulness and this Prayer must be intense, concentrated and unremitting.

11. It is written: 'Not everyone who says to Me: "Lord, Lord" shall enter into the kingdom of heaven; but he that does the will of My Father' (Matt. 7:21). The will of the Father is indicated in the words: 'You who love the Lord, hate evil' (Ps. 97:10). Hence we should both pray the Prayer of Jesus Christ and hate our evil thoughts. In this way we do God's will.

12. Through His incarnation God gave us the model for a holy life and recalled us from our ancient fall. In addition to many other things, He taught us, feeble as we are, that we should fight against the demons with humility, fasting, prayer and watchfulness. For when, after His baptism, He went into the desert and the devil came up to Him as though He were merely a man, He began His spiritual warfare by fasting and won the battle by this means – though, being God, and God of gods, He had no need of any such means at all.

13. I shall now tell you in plain, straightforward language what I consider to be the types of watchfulness which gradually cleanse the intellect from impassioned thoughts. In these times of spiritual warfare I have no wish to conceal beneath words whatever in this treatise may be of use, especially to more simple people. As St Paul puts it: 'Pay attention, my child Timothy, to what you read' (cf. 1 Tim. 4:13).

14. One type of watchfulness consists in closely scrutinizing every mental image or provocation; for only by means of a mental image can Satan fabricate an evil thought and insinuate this into the intellect in order to lead it astray.

15. A second type of watchfulness consists in freeing the heart from all thoughts, keeping it profoundly silent and still, and in praying.

16. A third type consists in continually and humbly calling upon the Lord Jesus Christ for help.

17. A fourth type is always to have the thought of death in one's mind.

18. These types of watchfulness, my child, act like doorkeepers and bar entry to evil thoughts. Elsewhere, if God gives me words, I shall deal more fully with a further type which, along with the others, is also effective: this is to fix one's gaze on heaven and to pay no attention to anything material.

19. When we have to some extent cut off the causes of the passions, we should devote our time to spiritual contemplation; for if we fail to do this we shall easily revert to the fleshly passions, and so achieve nothing but the complete darkening of our intellect and its reversion to material things.

20. The man engaged in spiritual warfare should simultaneously possess humility, perfect attentiveness, the power of rebuttal, and prayer. He should possess humility because, as his fight is against the arrogant demons, he will then have the help of Christ in his heart, for 'the Lord hates the arrogant' (cf. Prov. 3 : 34. LXX). He should possess attentiveness in order always to keep his heart clear of all thoughts, even of those that appear to be good. He should possess the power of rebuttal so that, whenever he recognizes the devil, he may at once repulse him angrily; for it is written: 'And I shall reply to those who vilify me; will not my soul be subject to God?' (Pss. 119 : 42 ; 62 : 1. LXX). He should possess prayer so that as soon as he has rebutted the devil he may call to Christ with 'cries that cannot be uttered' (Rom. 8 : 26). Then he will see the devil broken and routed by the venerable name of Jesus – will see him and his dissimulation scattered like dust or smoke before the wind.

21. If we have not attained prayer that is free from thoughts, we have no weapon to fight with. By this prayer I mean the prayer which is ever active in the inner shrine of the soul, and which by invoking Christ scourges and sears our secret enemy.

22. The glance of your intellect should be quick and keen, able to perceive the invading demons. When you perceive one, you should at once rebut it, crushing it like the head of a serpent. At the same time, call imploringly to Christ, and you will experience God's unseen help. Then you will clearly discern the heart's rectitude.

23. Just as someone in the midst of a crowd, holding a mirror

and looking at it, sees not only his own face but also the faces of those looking in the mirror with him, so someone who looks into his own heart sees in it not only his own state, but also the black faces of the demons.

24. The intellect cannot conquer a demonic fantasy by its own unaided powers, and should never attempt to do so. The demons are a sly lot: they pretend to be overcome and then trip us up by filling us with self-esteem. But when we call upon Jesus Christ, they do not dare to play their tricks with us even for a second.

25. Do not become conceited like the ancient Israelites, and so betray yourself into the hands of your spiritual enemies. For the Israelites, liberated from the Egyptians by the God of all, devised a molten idol to help them (cf. Exod. 32:4).

26. The molten idol denotes our crippled intellect. So long as the intellect invokes Jesus Christ against the demons, it easily routs them, putting their invisible forces to flight with the skill born of knowledge. But when it stupidly places all its confidence in itself, it falls headlong like a hawk. For it is written: 'My heart has trusted in God and I am helped; and my flesh flowers again' (Ps. 28:7. LXX); and 'Who but the Lord will rise up for me and stand with me against the host of wicked thoughts?' (cf. Ps. 94:16). Whoever places his confidence in himself and not in God will indeed fall headlong.

27. If you wish to engage in spiritual warfare, let that little animal, the spider, always be your example for stillness of heart; otherwise you will not be as still in your intellect as you should be. The spider hunts small flies; but you will continually slay 'the children of Babylon' (cf. Ps. 137:9) if during your struggle you are as still in your soul as is the spider; and, in the course of this slaughter, you will be blessed by the Holy Spirit.

28. It is impossible to find the Red Sea among the stars or to walk this earth without breathing air; so too it is impossible to cleanse our heart from impassioned thoughts and to expel its spiritual enemies without the frequent invocation of Jesus Christ.

29. Be watchful as you travel each day the narrow but joyous and exhilarating road of the mind, keeping your attention humbly in your heart, reproaching yourself, ready to rebut your enemies, thinking of your death and invoking Jesus Christ. You will then attain a vision of the Holy of Holies and be illumined by Christ with deep mysteries. For in Christ 'the treasures of wisdom and know-

ledge' are hidden, and in Him 'the fulness of the Godhead dwells bodily' (Col. 2:3, 9). In the presence of Christ you will feel the Holy Spirit spring up within your soul. It is the Spirit who initiates man's intellect, so that it can see with 'unveiled face' (2 Cor. 3:18). For 'no one can say "Lord Jesus" except in the Holy Spirit' (1 Cor. 12:3). In other words, it is the Spirit who mystically confirms Christ's presence in us.

30. Those who love true knowledge should also be aware that the demons in their jealousy sometimes hide themselves and cease from open spiritual battle. Begrudging us the benefit, knowledge and progress towards God that we derive from the battle, they try to make us careless so that they can suddenly capture our intellect and again reduce our mind to inattention. Their unremitting purpose is to prevent the heart from being attentive, for they know how greatly such attentiveness enriches the soul. We on the contrary, through remembrance of our Lord Jesus Christ, should redouble our efforts to achieve spiritual contemplation; and then the intellect again finds itself engaged in battle. Let all we do be done with great humility and only, if I may put it like this, with the will of the Lord Himself.

31. We who live in coenobitic monasteries should of our own free choice gladly cut off our whole will through obedience to the abbot. In this way, with God's help, we shall become to some degree tractable and free from self-will. It is good to acquire this art, for then our bile will not be aroused and we shall not excite our incensive power unnaturally and uncontrollably, and so be deprived of communion with God in our unseen warfare. If we do not voluntarily cut off our self-will, it will become enraged with those who try to compel us to cut it off; and then our incensive power will become abusively aggressive and so destroy that knowledge of the warfare which we have gained only after great effort. The incensive power by nature is prone to be destructive. If it is turned against demonic thoughts it destroys them; but if it is roused against people it then destroys the good thoughts that are in us. In other words, the incensive power, although God-given as a weapon or a bow against evil thoughts, can be turned the other way and used to destroy good thoughts as well, for it destroys whatever it is directed against. I have seen a spirited dog destroying equally both wolves and sheep.

32. We should shun loose speech like an asp's venom and too

much company like a 'progeny of vipers' (Matt. 3:7), for it can plunge us into total forgetfulness of the inner struggle and bring the soul down from the heights of the joy that purity of heart gives us. This accursed forgetfulness is as opposed to attentiveness as water to fire, and forcibly fights against it all the time. Forgetfulness leads to negligence, and negligence to indifference, laziness and unnatural desire. In this way we return to where we started, like a dog to his own vomit (cf. 2 Pet. 2:22). So let us shun loose speech like deadly poison. As for forgetfulness and all its consequences, they can be cured by the most strict guarding of the intellect and by the constant invocation of our Lord Jesus Christ. For without Him, we can do nothing (cf. John 15:5).

33. One cannot befriend a snake and carry it about in one's shirt, or attain holiness while pampering and cherishing the body above its needs. It is the snake's nature to bite whoever tends it, and the body's to defile with sensual pleasure whoever indulges it. When it offends, the body should be whipped mercilessly like a drunken runaway slave; it should taste the Lord's scourge. Slavish nocturnal thing of perishable clay that it is, there must be no dallying allowed it; it must be made to recognize its true and imperishable mistress. Until you leave this world, do not trust the flesh. 'The will of the flesh,' it is said, 'is hostile to God; for it is not subject to the law of God. The flesh desires against the Spirit. They that are in the flesh cannot conform to God's will; but we are not in the flesh, but in the Spirit' (cf. Rom. 8:7-9; Gal. 5:17).

34. The task of moral judgment is always to prompt the soul's incensive power to engage in inner warfare and to make us self-critical. The task of wisdom is to prompt the intelligence to strict watchfulness, constancy, and spiritual contemplation. The task of righteousness is to direct the appetitive aspect of the soul towards holiness and towards God. Fortitude's task is to govern the five senses and to keep them always under control, so that through them neither our inner self, the heart, nor our outer self, the body, is defiled.

35. 'His majesty is upon Israel' (Ps. 68:34. LXX) – that is, upon the intellect that beholds, so far as this is possible, the beauty of the glory of God Himself. 'And His strength is in the clouds' (ibid.), that is, in radiant souls that gaze towards the dawn. In such souls it reveals the Beloved, He who sits at the right hand of God

and floods them with light as the sun's rays flood the white clouds.

36. A single sinner, says the Holy Scripture, destroys much righteousness (cf. Eccles. 9:18); while an intellect that sins loses its heavenly food and drink (cf. Eccles. 9:7).

37. We are not mightier than Samson, wiser than Solomon, more knowledgeable about God than David, and we do not love God better than did Peter, prince of the apostles. So let us not have confidence in ourselves; for he who has confidence in himself will fall headlong.

38. Let us learn humility from Christ, humiliation from David, and from Peter to shed tears over what has happened; but let us also learn to avoid the despair of Samson, Judas, and that wisest of men, Solomon.

39. The devil, with all his powers, 'walks about like a roaring lion, seeking whom he may devour' (1 Pet. 5:8). So you must never relax your attentiveness of heart, your watchfulness, your power of rebuttal or your prayer to Jesus Christ our God. You will not find a greater help than Jesus in all your life, for He alone, as God, knows the deceitful ways of the demons, their subtlety and their guile.

40. Let your soul, then, trust in Christ, let it call on Him and never fear; for it fights, not alone, but with the aid of a mighty King, Jesus Christ, Creator of all that is, both bodiless and embodied, visible and invisible.

41. The more the rain falls on the earth, the softer it makes it; similarly, Christ's holy name gladdens the earth of our heart the more we call upon it.

42. Those who lack experience should know that it is only through the unceasing watchfulness of our intellect and the constant invocation of Jesus Christ, our Creator and God, that we, coarse and cloddish in mind and body as we are, can overcome our bodiless and invisible enemies; for not only are they subtle, swift, malevolent and skilled in malice, but they have an experience in warfare gained over all the years since Adam. The inexperienced have as weapons the Jesus Prayer and the impulse to test and discern what is from God. The experienced have the best method and teacher of all: the activity, discernment and peace of God Himself.

43. Just as a child, young and guileless, delights in seeing a

conjuror and in his innocence follows him about, so our soul, simple and good because created thus by its Master, delights in the delusive provocations of the devil. Once deceived it pursues something sinister as though it were good, just as a dove is lured away by the enemy of her children. In this way its thoughts become entwined in the fantasy provoked by the devil, whether this happens to be the face of a beautiful woman or some other thing forbidden by the commandments of Christ. Then, seeking to contrive some means through which it can actually attain what attracts it, the soul assents to the provocation and, to its own condemnation, turns this unlawful mental fantasy into a concrete action by means of the body.

44. Such is the cunning of the evil one, and with these arrows he poisons every soul. It is therefore not safe to allow these thoughts to enter the heart in order to increase the intellect's experience of warfare, especially to start with, when the soul still greatly enjoys these demonic provocations and delights in pursuing them. But as soon as we perceive them, we should counter-attack and repulse them. Once the intellect has matured in this excellent activity, it is disciplined and perceptive. From then on it is unceasingly engaged in the battle of perceiving in their true light these 'little foxes', as the Prophet calls them (S. of S. 2 : 1 5), and it easily lays hold of them. Only when we have such knowledge and experience should we admit them and censure them.

45. Just as it is impossible for fire and water to pass through the same pipe together, so it is impossible for sin to enter the heart without first knocking at its door in the form of a fantasy provoked by the devil.

46. The provocation comes first, then our coupling* with it, or the mingling of our thoughts with those of the wicked demons. Third comes our assent to the provocation, with both sets of intermingling thoughts contriving how to commit the sin in practice. Fourth comes the concrete action – that is, the sin itself. If, however, the intellect is attentive and watchful, and at once repulses the provocation by counter-attacking and gainsaying it and invoking the Lord Jesus, its consequences remain inoperative; for the devil, being a bodiless intellect, can deceive our souls only by means of fantasies and thoughts. David was speaking about these provocations of the devil when he said: 'Early in the morning I destroyed all the wicked of the earth, that I might cut off all evildoers

from the city of the Lord' (Ps. 101:8. LXX); and Moses was referring to the act of assent to a provocation in his words: 'You shall make no covenant with them, nor with their gods' (Exod. 23:32).

47. Intellect is invisibly interlocked in battle with intellect, the demonic intellect with our own. So from the depths of our heart we must at each instant call on Christ to drive the demonic intellect away from us and in His compassion give us the victory.

48. Let your model for stillness of heart be the man who holds a mirror into which he looks. Then you will see both good and evil imprinted on your heart.

49. See that you never have a single thought in your heart, whether senseless or sensible; then you can easily recognize that alien tribe, the firstborn sons of the Egyptians.

50. Watchfulness is a graceful and radiant virtue when guided by Thee, Christ our God, and accompanied by the alertness and deep humility of the human intellect. Its branches reach to the seas and to deep abysses of contemplation, its shoots to the rivers of the beauteous and divine mysteries (cf. Ps. 80:11). Again, it cleanses the intellect consumed in ungodliness by the brine of demonic thoughts and the hostile will of the flesh, which is death (cf. Rom. 8:6–8).

51. Watchfulness is like Jacob's ladder: God is at the top while the angels climb it. It rids us of everything bad, cuts out loose chatter, abuse, backbiting, and all other evil practices of this kind. Yet in doing this, not for an instant does it lose its own sweetness.

52. We should zealously cultivate watchfulness, my brethren; and when – our mind purified in Christ Jesus – we are exalted by the vision it confers, we should review our sins and our former life, so that shattered and humbled at the thought of them we may never lose the help of Jesus Christ our God in the invisible battle. If because of pride, self-esteem or self-love we are deprived of Jesus' help, we shall lose that purity of heart through which God is known to man. For, as the Beatitude states, purity of heart is the ground for the vision of God (cf. Matt. 5:8).

53. An intellect that does not neglect its inner struggle will find that – along with the other blessings which come from always keeping a guard on the heart – the five bodily senses, too, are freed from all external evil influences. For while the intellect is wholly

attentive to its own virtue and watchfulness and longs to enjoy holy thoughts, it does not allow itself to be plundered and carried away when vain material thoughts approach it through the senses. On the contrary, recognizing the wiliness of these thoughts, it withdraws the senses almost completely into itself.

54. Guard your mind and you will not be harassed by temptations. But if you fail to guard it, accept patiently whatever trial comes.[1]

55. Just as the bitterness of absinth helps a poor appetite, so misfortunes help a bad character.

56. If you do not want to suffer evil, do not inflict it, since the suffering of it inevitably follows its infliction. 'For whatever a man sows he will also reap' (Gal. 6:7). Reaping unwillingly the wickedness we deliberately sow, we should marvel at God's justice.

57. The intellect is made blind by these three passions: avarice, self-esteem and sensual pleasure.

58. These three passions on their own dull spiritual knowledge and faith, the foster-brothers of our nature.

59. It is because of them that wrath, anger, war, murder and all other evils have such power over mankind.

60. He who does not know the truth cannot truly have faith; for by nature knowledge precedes faith. What is said in Scripture is said not solely for us to understand, but also for us to act upon.

61. We should therefore set about our task, for by doing so and advancing steadily we will find that hope in God, sure faith, inner knowledge, release from temptations, gifts of grace, heart-felt confession and prolonged tears come to the faithful through prayer. For not only these blessings, but the patient acceptance of affliction, sincere forgiveness of our neighbour, knowledge of the spiritual law, the discovery of God's justice, frequent visitations of the Holy Spirit, the giving of spiritual treasures and all that God has promised to bestow to men of faith now and in the future age – in short, the manifestation of the soul in accordance with the image of God – can come only through God's grace and man's faith when he guards his mind with great humility and undistracted prayer.

---

[1] §§ 54–60 are identical with St Mark the Ascetic, *On the Spiritual Law*, §§ 163, 115–17, 101, 103–4 and 110 (see above, pp. 121, 118 117). Hesychios, § 61, is also identical with a passage in one of Mark's writings not found in the *Philokalia: Dispute with a Lawyer*, § 8 (Migne, *Patrologia Graeca*, LXV, 1081D–1084A).

62. We have learned from experience that for one who wishes to purify his heart it is a truly great blessing constantly to invoke the name of the Lord Jesus against his intelligible enemies. Notice how what I speak of from experience concurs with the testimony of Scripture. It is written: 'Prepare yourself, O Israel, to call upon the name of the Lord your God' (cf. Amos. 4:12. LXX); and the Apostle says: 'Pray without ceasing' (1 Thess. 5:17). Our Lord Himself says: 'Without Me you can do nothing. If a man dwells in Me, and I in him, then he brings forth much fruit'; and again: 'If a man does not dwell in Me, he is cast out as a branch' (John 15:5–6). Prayer is a great blessing, and it embraces all blessings, for it purifies the heart, in which God is seen by the believer.

63. Because humility is by nature something that exalts, something loved by God which destroys in us almost all that is evil and hateful to Him, for this reason it is difficult to attain. Even if you can easily find someone who to some extent practises a number of virtues, you will hardly find the odour of humility in him, however you search for it. It is something that can be acquired only with much diligence. Indeed, Scripture refers to the devil as 'unclean' because from the beginning he rejected humility and espoused arrogance. As a result he is called an unclean spirit throughout the Scriptures. For what bodily uncleanliness could one who is completely without body, fleshless and weightless, bring about in himself so as to be called 'unclean' as a result? Clearly he was called unclean because of his arrogance, defiling himself thus after having been a pure and radiant angel. 'Everyone that is arrogant is unclean before the Lord' (Prov. 16:5. LXX), for it is written that the first sin was arrogance (cf. Ecclus. 10:13). And it was in arrogance that Pharaoh said: 'I do not know the Lord, neither will I let Israel go' (Exod. 5:2).

64. If we are concerned with our salvation, there are many things the intellect can do in order to secure for us the blessed gift of humility. For example, it can recollect the sins we have committed in word, action and thought; and there are many other things which, reviewed in contemplation, contribute to our humility. True humility is also brought about by meditating daily on the achievements of our brethren, by extolling their natural superiorities and by comparing our gifts with theirs. When the intellect sees in this way how worthless we are and how far we fall short of the perfection

of our brethren, we will regard ourselves as dust and ashes, and not as men but as some kind of cur, more defective in every respect and lower than all men on earth.

65. St Basil the Great, mouthpiece of Christ and pillar of the Church, says that a great help towards not sinning and not committing daily the same faults is for us to review in our conscience at the end of each day what we have done wrong and what we have done right.[1] Job did this with regard both to himself and to his children (cf. Job 1 : 5). These daily reckonings illumine a man's hour by hour behaviour.

66. Someone else wise in the things of God has said that as the fruit begins with the flower, so the practice of the ascetic life begins with self-control.[2] Let us then learn to control ourselves with due measure and judgment, as the Fathers teach us. Let us pass all the hours of the day in the guarding of the intellect, for by doing this we shall with God's help and with a certain forcefulness be able to quell and reduce the evil in us. For the spiritual life, through which the kingdom of heaven is given, does indeed require a certain forcefulness (cf. Matt. 11 : 12).

67. Dispassion and humility lead to spiritual knowledge. Without them, no one can see God.[3]

68. He who always concentrates on the inner life will acquire self-restraint. He will also be able to contemplate, theologize and pray. This is what the Apostle meant when he said: 'Walk in the Spirit, and you will not fulfil the desire of the flesh' (Gal. 5 : 16).

69. One ignorant of the spiritual path is not on his guard against his impassioned thoughts, but devotes himself entirely to the flesh. He is either a glutton, or dissipated, or full of resentment, anger and rancour. As a result, he darkens his intellect, or he practises excessive asceticism and so confuses his mind.

70. He who has renounced such things as marriage, possessions and other worldly pursuits is outwardly a monk, but may not yet be a monk inwardly. Only he who has renounced the impassioned thoughts of his inner self, which is the intellect, is a true monk. It is

---

[1] See St Basil, 'An Ascetic Discourse' (323CD), in W. K. Lowther Clarke, *The Ascetic Works of Saint Basil* (London, 1925), p. 139.

[2] A quotation from a work by Neilos (or possibly by Evagrios), *On the Eight Spirits of Wickedness* (Migne, *Patrologia Graeca*, lxxix, 1145A).

[3] §§ 67–75 are identical with St Maximos the Confessor, *Fourth Century on Love*, §§ 58, 64, 65, 50–52, 63; *Second Century*, § 40; *First Century*, § 76; *Fourth Century*, § 72.

easy to be a monk in one's outer self if one wants to be; but no small struggle is required to be a monk in one's inner self.

71. Who in this generation is completely free from impassioned thoughts and has been granted uninterrupted, pure, and spiritual prayer? Yet this is the mark of the inner monk.

72. Many passions are hidden in the soul; they can be checked only when their causes are revealed.

73. Do not devote all your time to your body but apply to it a measure of asceticism appropriate to its strength and then turn all your intellect to what is within. 'Bodily asceticism has only a limited use, but true devotion is useful in all things' (1 Tim. 4:8).

74. We grow proud when the passions cease to be active in us, and this whether they are inactive because their causes have been eradicated or because the demons have deliberately withdrawn in order to deceive us.

75. Humility and ascetic hardship free a man from all sin, for the one cuts out the passions of the soul, the other those of the body. It is for this reason that the Lord says: 'Blessed are the pure in heart, for they shall see God' (Matt. 5:8). They shall see God and the riches that are in Him when they have purified themselves through love and self-control; and the greater their purity, the more they will see.

76. David's watchman prefigures the circumcision of the heart; for the guarding of the intellect is a watchtower commanding a view over our whole spiritual life (cf. 2 Sam. 18:24).

77. Just as in the world of the senses we are harmed when we see something harmful, so in the world of the intellect the same is true.

78. Just as someone who wounds the heart of a plant withers it completely, so too sin, when it wounds a man's heart, withers it completely. We must watch for such moments, because brigands are always at work.

79. Wishing to show that to fulfil every commandment is a duty, whereas sonship is a gift given to men through His own Blood, the Lord said, 'When you have done all that is commanded you, say: "We are useless servants: we have only done what was our duty"' (Luke 17:10). Thus the kingdom of heaven is not a reward for works, but a gift of grace prepared by the Master for His faithful servants. A slave does not demand his freedom as a reward: but he

gives thanks as one who is in debt, and he receives freedom as a gift.[1]

80. 'Christ died on account of our sins in accordance with the Scriptures' (1 Cor. 15:3); and to those who serve Him well He gives freedom. 'Well done, good and faithful servant,' He says, 'you have been faithful over a few things, I will make you ruler over many things: enter into the joy of your Lord' (Matt. 25:21). He who relies on theoretical knowledge alone is not yet a faithful servant: a faithful servant is one who expresses his faith in Christ through obedience to His commandments.

81. He who honours the Lord does what the Lord bids. When he sins or is disobedient, he patiently accepts what comes as something he deserves. If you love true knowledge, devote yourself to the ascetic life; for mere theoretical knowledge puffs a man up (cf. 1 Cor. 8:1).

82. Unexpected trials are sent by God to teach us to practise the ascetic life.

83. Light is the property of a star, as simplicity and humility are the property of a holy and God-fearing man. Nothing distinguishes more clearly the disciples of Christ than a humble spirit and a simple way of life. The four Gospels shout this aloud. Whoever has not lived in this humble manner is deprived of his share in Him who 'humbled Himself . . . to death, even the death of the cross' (Phil. 2:8), the actual Lawgiver of the divine Gospels.

84. It is said that those who thirst should go to the waters (cf. Isa. 55:1). Those who thirst for God should go in purity of mind. But he who through such purity soars aloft should also keep an eye on the earth of his own lowliness and simplicity, for no one is more exalted than he who is humble. Just as when light is absent, all things are dark and gloomy, so when humility is absent, all our efforts to please God are vain and pointless.

85. 'Let us hear the conclusion of the whole matter: fear God and keep His commandments' (Eccles. 12:13), both where the intellect and where the senses are concerned. If you force yourself to keep the commandments on the plane of the intellect, you will seldom need great effort to keep those that refer to the senses. In the words of David the Prophet, 'I wished to carry out Thy will and Thy law in my inward parts' (cf. Ps. 40:8. LXX).

---

[1] §§ 79–82 are identical with St Mark the Ascetic, *On Those who Think that They are Made Righteous by Works*, §§ 2–8 (see above, pp. 125–6).

86. If a man does not carry out the will and law of God 'in his inward parts', that is, in his heart, he will not be able to carry them out easily in the outward sphere of the senses either. The careless and unwatchful man will say to God: 'I do not want to know Thy ways' (Job 21 : 14. LXX), obviously because he lacks divine illumination. But he who participates in that light will be confident and steadfast in matters that concern God.

87. Just as salt seasons our bread and other food and keeps certain meats from spoiling for quite a time, so the spiritual sweetness and marvellous working which result from the guarding of the intellect effect something similar. For in a divine manner they season and sweeten both the inner and the outer self, driving away the stench of evil thoughts and keeping us continually in communion with good thoughts.

88. Many of our thoughts come from demonic provocation, and from these derive our evil outward actions. If with the help of Jesus we instantly quell the thought, we will avoid its corresponding outward action. We will enrich ourselves with the sweetness of divine knowledge and so will find God, who is everywhere. Holding the mirror of the intellect firmly towards God, we will be illumined constantly as pure glass is by the sun. Then the intellect, having reached the term of its desires, will in Him cease from all other contemplation.

89. Because every thought enters the heart in the form of a mental image of some sensible object, the blessed light of the Divinity will illumine the heart only when the heart is completely empty of everything and so free from all form. Indeed, this light reveals itself to the pure intellect in the measure to which the intellect is purged of all concepts.

90. The more closely attentive you are to your mind, the greater the longing with which you will pray to Jesus; and the more carelessly you examine your mind, the further you will separate yourself from Him. Just as close attentiveness brilliantly illumines the mind, so the lapse from watchfulness and from the sweet invocation of Jesus will darken it completely. All this happens naturally, not in any other way; and you will experience it if you test it out in practice. For there is no virtue – least of all this blessed light-generating activity – which cannot be learnt from experience.

91. To invoke Jesus continually with a sweet longing is to fill

the heart in its great attentiveness with joy and tranquillity. But it is Jesus Christ, the Son of God and Himself God, cause and creator of all blessings, who completely purifies the heart; for it is written: 'I am God who makes peace' (cf. Isa. 45:7).

92. The soul that is being given blessings and sweetness by Jesus repays her Benefactor by offering thanks to Him with a certain exultation and love; joyfully and gratefully she calls upon Him who gives her peace, and with the eyes of the intellect she sees Him within herself destroying the demonic fantasies.

93. 'My spiritual eyes have looked upon my spiritual enemies,' says David the Prophet, 'and my ear shall hear those who in their wickedness rise up against me' (cf. Ps. 92:11. LXX). And again: 'I have seen God's requital of sinners take place within me' (cf. Ps. 91:8). When there are no fantasies or mental images in the heart, the intellect is established in its true nature, ready to contemplate whatever is full of delight, spiritual and close to God.

94. Watchfulness and the Jesus Prayer, as I have said, mutually reinforce one another; for close attentiveness goes with constant prayer, while prayer goes with close watchfulness and attentiveness of intellect.

95. The unremitting remembrance of death is a powerful trainer of body and soul. Vaulting over all that lies between ourselves and death, we should always visualize it, and even the very bed on which we shall breathe our last, and everything else connected with it.

96. If you want never to be wounded, do not succumb to sleep. There are only two choices: to fall and be destroyed, stripped of all virtue; or, armed with the intellect, to stand firm through everything. For the enemy and his host stand always ready for battle.

97. A certain God-given equilibrium is produced in our intellect through the constant remembrance and invocation of our Lord Jesus Christ, provided that we do not neglect this constant spiritual entreaty or our close watchfulness and diligence. Indeed, our true task is always the same and is always accomplished in the same way: to call upon our Lord Jesus Christ with a burning heart so that His holy name intercedes for us. In virtue as in vice, constancy is the mother of habit; once acquired, it rules us like nature. When the intellect is in such a state of equilibrium, it searches out its enemies like a hound searching for a hare in a thicket. But the hound searches in order to get food, the intellect in order to destroy.

98. Whenever we are filled with evil thoughts, we should throw the invocation of our Lord Jesus Christ into their midst. Then, as experience has taught us, we shall see them instantly dispersed like smoke in the air. Once the intellect is left to itself again, we can renew our constant attentiveness and our invocation. Whenever we are distracted, we should act in this way.

99. Just as it is impossible to fight battles without weapons, or to swim a great sea with clothes on, or to live without breathing, so without humility and the constant prayer to Christ it is impossible to master the art of inward spiritual warfare or to set about it and pursue it skilfully.

100. That great spiritual master David said to the Lord: 'I shall preserve my strength through Thee' (cf. Ps. 59:9. LXX). So the strength of the heart's stillness, mother of all the virtues, is preserved in us through our being helped by the Lord. For He has given us the commandments, and when we call upon Him constantly He expels from us that foul forgetfulness which destroys the heart's stillness as water destroys fire. Therefore, monk, do not 'sleep unto death' (Ps. 13:3. LXX) because of your negligence; but lash the enemy with the name of Jesus and, as a certain wise man has said, let the name of Jesus adhere to your breath, and then you will know the blessings of stillness.[1]

101. When in fear, trembling and unworthiness we are yet permitted to receive the divine, undefiled Mysteries of Christ, our King and our God, we should then display even greater watchfulness, strictness and guard over our hearts, so that the divine fire, the body of our Lord Jesus Christ, may consume our sins and stains, great and small. For when that fire enters into us, it at once drives the evil spirits from our heart and remits the sins we have previously committed, leaving the intellect free from the turbulence of wicked thoughts. And if after this, standing at the entrance to our heart, we keep strict watch over the intellect, when we are again permitted to receive those Mysteries the divine body will illumine our intellect still more and make it shine like a star.

102. Forgetfulness can extinguish our guard over our intellect as water extinguishes fire; but the continuous repetition of the

---

[1] See St John Klimakos, *The Ladder of Divine Ascent*, § 27 (Migne, *Patrologia Graeca*, lxxxviii, 1112C; English translation by Archimandrite Lazarus Moore, London, 1959, p. 246).

Jesus Prayer combined with strict watchfulness uproots it from our heart. The Jesus Prayer requires watchfulness as a lantern requires a candle.

103. We should strive to preserve the precious gifts which preserve us from all evil, whether on the plane of the senses or on that of the intellect. These gifts are the guarding of the intellect with the invocation of Jesus Christ, continuous insight into the heart's depths, stillness of mind unbroken even by thoughts which appear to be good, and the capacity to be empty of all thought. In this way the demons will not steal in undetected; and if we suffer pain through remaining centred in the heart, consolation is at hand.

104. The heart which is constantly guarded, and is not allowed to receive the forms, images and fantasies of the dark and evil spirits, is conditioned by nature to give birth from within itself to thoughts filled with light. For just as coal engenders a flame, or a flame lights a candle, so will God, who from our baptism dwells in our heart, kindle our mind to contemplation when He finds it free from the winds of evil and protected by the guarding of the intellect.

105. The name of Jesus should be repeated over and over in the heart as flashes of lightning are repeated over and over in the sky before rain. Those who have experience of the intellect and of inner warfare know this very well. We should wage this spiritual warfare with a precise sequence: first, with attentiveness; then, when we perceive the hostile thought attacking, we should strike at it angrily in the heart, cursing it as we do so; thirdly, we should direct our prayer against it, concentrating the heart through the invocation of Jesus Christ, so that the demonic fantasy may be dispersed at once, the intellect no longer pursuing it like a child deceived by some conjuror.

106. Let us exert ourselves like David, crying out 'Lord Jesus Christ' until our throats are sore; and let our spiritual eyes never cease to give us hope in the Lord our God (cf. Ps. 69:3).

107. If we constantly bear in mind the parable of the unjust judge, which the Lord related in order to show us that we ought always to pray and not to lose heart, we shall both profit and be vindicated (cf. Luke 18:1-8).

108. Just as he who looks at the sun cannot but fill his eyes with light, so he who always gazes intently into his heart cannot fail to be illumined.

109. Just as it is impossible to live this present life without eating or drinking, so it is impossible for the soul to achieve anything spiritual and in accordance with God's will, or to be free from mental sin, without that guarding of the intellect and purity of heart truly described as watchfulness; and this is so even if one forces oneself not to sin through the fear of punishment.

110. Nevertheless, those who force themselves to refrain from active sin are blessed by God, angels and men; for they take the kingdom of God by force (cf. Matt. 11:12).

111. The intellect's great gain from stillness is this: all the sins which formerly beat upon the intellect as thoughts and which, once admitted by the mind, were turned into outward acts of sin, are now cut off by mental watchfulness. For, with the help of our Lord Jesus Christ, this watchfulness does not allow these sins to enter our inner self and so to burgeon into outward acts of evil.

112. The Old Testament is an ikon of outward bodily asceticism. The Holy Gospel, or New Testament, is an ikon of attentiveness, that is, of purity of heart. For the Old Testament did not perfect or fulfil the relationship of the inner self to God – 'the law made no one perfect', as the Apostle says (cf. Heb. 7:19) – it simply forbade bodily sins. But to cut off evil thoughts from the heart, as the Gospel commands, contributes much more to purity of soul than an injunction against putting out a neighbour's eye or knocking out his teeth. Similarly, it contributes more than other bodily discipline and ascetic practice, such as fasting and self-control, sleeping on the ground, standing, vigils and the rest, which are related to the body and stop that aspect of the body which is vulnerable to passion from committing sinful acts. Like the Old Testament itself, these things are also good, for they train the outer self and are guard against the workings of passion; but they are not a defence against and they do not prevent mental sins, so as to free us, with God's help, from jealousy, anger, and so on.

113. If we preserve, as we should, that purity of heart or watch and guard of the intellect whose image is the New Testament, this will not only uproot all passions and evils from our hearts; it will also introduce joy, hopefulness, compunction, sorrow, tears, an understanding of ourselves and of our sins, mindfulness of death, true humility, unlimited love of God and man, and an intense and heartfelt longing for the divine.

114. Just as it is impossible when walking not to part the air, so it is impossible for a man's heart not to be assailed continually by demons or be secretly energized by them, however great his bodily asceticism.

115. If you wish to be 'in the Lord', do not just *seem* to be a monk, and good, and gentle, and always at one with God; decide to *be* such a person in truth. With all your strength pursue the virtue of attentiveness – that guard and watch of the intellect, that perfect stillness of heart and blessed state of the soul when free from images, which is all too rarely found in man.

116. This is the path of true spiritual wisdom. In great watchfulness and fervent desire travel along it with the Jesus Prayer, with humility and concentration, keeping the lips of both the senses and the intellect silent, self-controlled in food and drink and in all things of a seductive nature; travel along it with a mind trained in understanding, and with God's help it will teach you things you had not hoped for; it will give you knowledge, enlightenment and instruction of a kind to which your intellect was impervious while you were still walking in the murk of passions and dark deeds, sunk in forgetfulness and in the confusion of chaos.

117. Just as valleys produce copious wheat, so this wisdom produces copious blessings in the heart – or, rather, our Lord Jesus Christ produces them, for without Him we can do nothing (cf. John 15:5). At first, you will find that it is a ladder; then, a book to be read; then, as you advance, you will find that it is the heavenly city of Jerusalem, and you will have a clear spiritual vision of Christ, King of the hosts of Israel, together with His co-essential Father and the Holy Spirit, adored in our worship.

118. The demons always lead us into sin by means of deceitful fantasies. Through the fantasy of gaining wealth they led the wretched Judas to betray the Lord and God of all; through the deceit of worthless bodily comfort and of esteem, gain and glory they put the noose around his neck and brought him to age-long death. The scoundrels requited him with precisely the opposite of what their fantasy, or provocation, had suggested to him.

119. Do you see how the enemies of our salvation make us fall by means of their fantasies, deceits and empty promises? Satan himself was cast down like lightning from the heights because he fancied himself to be the equal of God (cf. Luke 10:18); and he sundered

Adam from God by making him fancy that he could be of divine rank (cf. Gen. 3:5). In the same way the lying and crafty enemy deceives all who fall into sin.

120. We embitter the heart with the poison of evil thoughts when we are led by forgetfulness to long neglect of inner attention and the Jesus Prayer. But we sweeten it with the sense of blessed delight when in intense desire for God we practise this attention and prayer resolutely, keenly and diligently in the mind's workshop. Then we are eager to pursue stillness of heart simply for the sweetness and delight it produces in the soul.

121. The science of sciences and art of arts is the mastery of evil thoughts. The best way to master them is to see with spiritual vision the fantasy in which the demonic provocation is concealed and to protect the mind from it. It is just the same as the way in which we protect our bodily eyes, looking sharply about us and doing all we can to prevent anything, however small, from striking them.

122. Just as snow will not produce a flame, or water a fire, or the thorn-bush a fig, so a person's heart will not be freed from demonic thoughts, words and actions until it has first purified itself inwardly, uniting watchfulness with the Jesus Prayer, attaining humility and stillness of soul, and eagerly pressing forward on its path. But in its lack of spiritual understanding, the inattentive soul will be devoid of every good and perfect thought, and barren and stupid as the mule. The soul's true peace lies in the gentle name of Jesus and in its emptying itself of impassioned thoughts.

123. When the soul conspires with the body in wickedness, then together they build a city of vanity and a tower of pride, and they people them with unholy thoughts. But the Lord disrupts and destroys their concord through the fear of hell (cf. Gen. 11:1–9), forcing the soul, our ruling part, to think and say things opposed to the body. Out of this fear there arises a division, 'because the will of the flesh is hostile to God, for it is not subject to the law of God' (Rom. 8:7).

124. Each hour of the day we should note and weigh our actions and in the evening we should do what we can to free ourselves from the burden of them by means of repentance – if, that is, we wish, with Christ's help, to overcome wickedness. We should also make sure that we perform all our outward tasks in a manner that accords

with God's will, before God and for God alone, so that we are not mindlessly seduced by the senses.

125. For if with God's help we make progress daily by means of our watchfulness, we should not behave indiscriminately and damage ourselves through a host of random meetings and conversations. On the contrary, we should scorn all vanities for the sake of the beauty and blessings of holiness.

126. We should use the three aspects of the soul fittingly and in accordance with nature, as created by God. We should use our incensive power against our outer self and against Satan. 'Be incensed', it is written, 'against sin' (cf. Ps. 4:4), that is, be incensed with yourselves and the devil, so that you will not sin against God. Our desire should be directed towards God and towards holiness. Our intelligence should control our incensive power and our desire with wisdom and skill, regulating them, admonishing them, correcting them and ruling them as a king rules over his subjects. Then, even should they rebel against it, our inmost intelligence will direct the passions in a way that accords with God's will, for we shall have set it in charge of them. The brother of the Lord declares: 'He who does not lapse in his inmost intelligence is a perfect man, able also to bridle the whole body' (Jas. 3:2). For the truth is that every sin and transgression is brought about through these three aspects of the soul, just as every virtue and good action is also produced through them.

127. Our intellect is darkened and remains fruitless whenever we speak words of worldly import or, entertaining such words in our mind, begin to give them our attention, or whenever the body and the intellect waste their time in some outward matter, or whenever we give ourselves over to vanities. For then we immediately lose our fervour, our sense of compunction, and our intimacy with God and knowledge of Him. So long as we concentrate our attention on the intellect, we are enlightened; but when we are not attentive to it we are in darkness.

128. Whoever aspires day and night to peace and stillness of intellect finds it easy to be indifferent to all material matters and so does not labour in vain. But if he scorns or cheats his own conscience, he will sleep bitterly the death of forgetfulness. This is the death that David prayed not to sleep (cf. Ps. 13:3); and the Apostle says: 'To know how to do good and yet not to do it is sin' (Jas. 4:17).

129. If we give attention to the intellect and assiduously re-establish its activity, it will stop being neglectful and will regain its proper state and its watchfulness.

130. A donkey going round and round in a mill cannot step out of the circle to which it is tethered; nor can the intellect which is not inwardly chastened advance in the path of holiness. With its inner eyes blinded, it cannot perceive holiness or the radiant light of Jesus.

131. A proud and spirited horse steps out delightedly once the rider is in the saddle. But the delighted intellect delights in the light of the Lord when, free from concepts, it enters into the dawn of spiritual knowledge. By continually denying itself, it advances from the wisdom necessary for the practice of the virtues to an ineffable vision in which it contemplates holy and ineffable things. Then the heart is filled with perceptions of infinite and divine realities and sees the God of gods in its own depths, so far as this is possible. Astounded, the intellect lovingly glorifies God, the Seer and the Seen, and the Saviour of those who contemplate Him in this way.

132. When the heart has acquired stillness it will perceive the heights and depths of knowledge; and the ear of the still intellect will be made to hear marvellous things from God.

133. A traveller setting out on a long, difficult and arduous journey and foreseeing that he may lose his way when he comes back, will put up signs and guideposts along his path in order to make his return simpler. The watchful man, foreseeing this same thing, will use sacred texts to guide him.

134. For the traveller it is a source of joy to return to where he started. But for the watchful man to turn back is the death of his deiform soul and the sign of his apostasy from thoughts, words and actions that accord with God's will. In the lethal sleep of his soul he will have thoughts stirring him up like goads with remembrance of the heavy torpor and indolence that is his because of his negligence.

135. When we are in trouble or despair or have lost hope, we should do what David did: pour out our hearts to God and tell Him of our needs and troubles, just as they are (cf. Ps. 142:2). It is because He can deal with us wisely that we confess to God: He can make our troubles easy to bear, if this is for our benefit, and can save us from the dejection which destroys and corrupts.

136. The incensive power roused in an unnatural fashion against

men, sorrow that does not accord with God's will and listlessness are all equally destructive of holy thoughts and spiritual knowledge. If we confess these things the Lord will rid us of them and fill us with joy.

137. When combined with watchfulness and deep understanding, the Jesus Prayer will erase from our heart even those thoughts rooted there against our will.

138. When under the pressure of stupid thoughts, we will find relief and joy by rebuking ourselves truthfully and unemotionally, or by confessing everything to the Lord as to a human being. In both these ways we will always find tranquillity, whatever troubles us.

139. The Fathers regard Moses the Lawgiver as an ikon of the intellect. He saw God in the burning bush (cf. Exod. 3:2–4:17); his face shone with glory (cf. Exod. 34:30); he was made a god to Pharaoh by the God of gods (cf. Exod. 7:1); he flayed Egypt with a scourge; he led Israel out of bondage and gave laws. These happenings, when seen metaphorically and spiritually, are activities and privileges of the intellect.

140. Aaron, the brother of Moses, is an ikon of the outer self. On this account we too should bring angry accusations against our outer self as Moses did against Aaron when he sinned: 'In what way did Israel do you wrong, that you should hasten to turn them from the Lord, the living God and Ruler of all?' (cf. Exod. 32:21).

141. Among many other good things, the Lord showed us, when He was about to raise Lazarus from the dead (cf. John 11:33), that we should reject with angry indignation all that is womanish and unstable in our soul; we should strive after firmness of character, for this is able to free our self-reproach from arrogance, pride and self-love.

142. Just as it is impossible to cross the sea without a boat, so it is impossible to repulse the provocation of an evil thought without invoking Jesus Christ.

143. Rebuttal bridles evil thoughts, but the invocation of Jesus Christ drives them from the heart. Now when the provocation has taken the form of a mental image of a sensory object, the evil thought behind it can be identified. For instance, if the image is of the face of someone who has angered us, or of a beautiful woman, or of gold or silver, it can at once be shewn that it is the thought of rancour, or of unchastity, or of avarice that fills our heart with fantasies. And if our

intellect is experienced, well-trained and used to guarding itself and to examining clearly and openly the seductive fantasies and deceits of the demons, it will instantly 'quench the fiery darts of the devil' (cf. Eph. 6: 16), counter-attacking by means of its power of rebuttal and the Jesus Prayer. It will not allow the impassioned fantasy to consort with it or allow our thoughts passionately to conform themselves to the fantasy, or to become intimate with it, or be distracted by it, or give assent to it. If anything like this happens, then evil actions will follow as surely as night follows day.

144. If our intellect is inexperienced in the art of watchfulness, it at once begins to entertain whatever impassioned fantasy appears in it, and plies it with illicit questions and responds to it illicitly. Then our own thoughts are conjoined to the demonic fantasy, which waxes and burgeons until it appears lovely and delectable to the welcoming and despoiled intellect. The intellect then is deceived in much the same way as lambs when a stray dog comes into the field in which they happen to be: in their innocence they often run towards the dog as though it were their mother, and their only profit in coming near it is that they pick up something of its stench and foulness. In the same way our thoughts run ignorantly after demonic fantasies that appear in our intellect and, as I said, the two join together and one can see them plotting to destroy the city of Troy like Agamemnon and Menelaus. For they plot together the course of action they must take in order to bring about, in practice and by means of the body, that purpose which the demons have persuaded them is sweet and delectable. In this way sins are produced in the soul: and hence the need to bring out into the open what is in our hearts.

145. The intellect, being good-natured and innocent, readily goes in pursuit of lawless fantasies; and it can be restrained only on condition that its intelligence, the ruler of the passions, always bridles it and holds it back.

146. Contemplation and spiritual knowledge are indeed the guides and agents of the ascetic life; for when the mind is raised up by them it becomes indifferent to sensual pleasures and to other material attractions, regarding them as worthless.

147. The life of attentiveness, brought to fruition in Christ Jesus, is the father of contemplation and spiritual knowledge. Linked to humility, it engenders divine exaltation and thoughts of the

wisest kind. As the prophet Isaiah says: 'They that wait upon the Lord shall renew their strength; they shall mount up with wings and soar aloft through the power of the Lord' (cf. Isa. 40:31).

148. To human beings it seems hard and difficult to still the mind so that it rests from all thought. Indeed, to enclose what is bodiless within the limits of the body does demand toil and struggle, not only from the uninitiated but also from those experienced in inner immaterial warfare. But he who through unceasing prayer holds the Lord Jesus within his breast will not tire in following Him, as the Prophet says (cf. Jer. 17:16. LXX). Because of Jesus' beauty and sweetness he will not desire what is merely mortal. Nor will he be disgraced by his enemies, the wicked demons that walk on every side; for he confronts them at the entrance to his heart and, with Jesus' help, drives them away.

149. If the soul has Christ with it, it will not be disgraced by its enemies even at death, when it rises to heaven's entrance; but then, as now, it will boldly confront them. But let it not tire in calling upon the Lord Jesus Christ, the Son of God, day and night until the time of its departure from this mortal life, and He will speedily avenge it in accordance with the promise which He Himself made when speaking of the unjust judge (cf. Luke 18:1–8). Indeed, He will avenge it both in this present life and after its departure from its body.

150. As you sail across the sea of the intellect, put your trust in Jesus, for secretly in your heart He says: 'Fear not, my child Jacob, the least of Israel; fear not, you worm Israel, I will protect you' (cf. Isa. 41:13–14). If God is for us, what evil one is against us (cf. Rom. 8:31)? For He has blessed the pure of heart and given the commandments; and so Jesus, who alone is truly pure, in a divine way readily enters into hearts that are pure and dwells in them. Therefore, as Paul counsels, let us ceaselessly exercise our intellect in devotion (cf. 1 Tim. 4:7). For devotion uproots the seeds sown by the devil, and is the path of the intelligence.

151. David's words, 'He will delight himself in the abundance of peace' (cf. Ps. 37:11), apply to him who is not taken in by the appearance of man and who judges injustice in his heart. That is to say, they apply to one who is not taken in by the forms of the demons and who is not led to meditate sin because of these forms, judging unjustly in the land of his heart and giving over to sin what is

righteous. For the great gnostic Fathers in some of their writings call the demons 'men' because demons too are endowed with intelligence. For example, in the gospel passage the Lord says: 'An evil man has done this, and mixed tares among the wheat' (cf. Matt. 13:24–30). Those who commit evil lack the power swiftly to rebut their evil thoughts. Hence they are consumed and destroyed by them.

152. We will travel the road of repentance correctly if, as we begin to give attention to the intellect, we combine humility with watchfulness, and prayer with the power to rebut evil thoughts. In this way we will adorn the chamber of our heart with the holy and venerable name of Jesus Christ as with a lighted lamp, and will sweep our heart clean of wickedness, purifying and embellishing it. But if we trust only in our own watchfulness and attentiveness, we shall quickly be pushed aside by our enemies. We shall be overturned and cast down by their extreme craftiness. We will become ever more fully entangled in their nets of evil thought, and will readily be slaughtered by them, lacking as we do the powerful sword of the name of Jesus Christ. For only this sword, swifty turning in the undivided heart, is able to cut them down, to burn and obliterate them as fire the reed.

153. It is the task of unceasing watchfulness – and one of great benefit and help to the soul – to see the mental images of evil thoughts as soon as they are formed in the intellect. The task of rebuttal is to counter and expose such thoughts when they attempt to infiltrate our intellect in the form of an image of some material thing. What instantly extinguishes and destroys every demonic concept, thought, fantasy, illusion and idol is the invocation of the Lord. And in our intellect we ourselves can observe how our great God, Jesus, triumphs over them all, and how He avenges us, poor, base and useless as we are.

154. Most of us do not realize that all evil thoughts are but images of material and worldly things. Yet if we persist in watchful prayer, this will rid our mind of all such images; it will also make it conscious both of the devices of our enemies and of the great benefit of prayer and watchfulness. 'With your eyes you will see how spiritual sinners are recompensed; you yourself will see spiritually and understand', says David the divine poet (cf. Ps. 91:8).

155. Whenever possible, we should always remember death, for this displaces all cares and vanities, allowing us to guard our intellect

and giving us unceasing prayer, detachment from our body and hatred of sin. Indeed, it is a source of almost every virtue. We should therefore, if possible, use it as we use our own breathing.

156. A heart that has been completely emptied of mental images gives birth to divine, mysterious intellections that sport within it like fish and dolphins in a calm sea. The sea is fanned by a soft wind, the heart's depth by the Holy Spirit. 'And because you are sons, God has sent forth the Spirit of his Son into your hearts, crying: "Abba, Father" ' (Gal. 4:6).

157. Every monk will be uncertain about his spiritual work until he has achieved watchfulness of intellect. Either he will be ignorant of the beauty of this watchfulness or, if he is aware of it, he will fail to achieve it because of his negligence. He will resolve his uncertainty only when he has learnt to guard his intellect. This guarding is rightly called mental philosophy or the practical wisdom of the intellect. Through it one finds the way of Him who said, 'I am the way, the resurrection and the life' (cf. John 11:25; 14:6).

158. Again, every monk will be at a loss when he sees the abyss of his evil thoughts and the swarming children of Babylon. But again Christ will resolve this doubt if we always base our mind firmly on Him. By dashing them against this rock we can repulse all the children of Babylon (cf. Ps. 137:9), thus doing what we want with them, in accordance with the sayings: 'Whoever keeps the commandment will know no evil thing' (Eccles. 8:5. LXX), and 'Without Me you can do nothing' (John 15:5).

159. A true monk is one who has achieved watchfulness; and he who is truly watchful is a monk in his heart.

160. Human life extends cyclically through years, months, weeks, days and nights, hours and minutes. Through these periods we should extend our ascetic labours – our watchfulness, our prayer, our sweetness of heart, our diligent stillness – until our departure from this life.

161. The hour of death will come upon us, it will come, and we shall not escape it. May the prince of this world and of the air (cf. John 14:30; Eph. 2:2) find our misdeeds few and petty when he comes, so that he will not have good grounds for convicting us. Otherwise we shall weep in vain. 'For that servant who knew his lord's will and did not do it as a servant, shall be beaten with many stripes' (cf. Luke 12:47).

162. 'Woe to those who have lost their heart; what will they do at the visitation of the Lord?' (cf. Ecclus. 2:14. LXX). Therefore, brethren, we should labour in earnest.

163. Impassioned thoughts follow hard upon thoughts that appear to be innocent and dispassionate: the latter open the way for the former. This we have found through years of experience and observation.

164. We should indeed be cut in two by a wise decision of our own free will; we should be our own worst enemy. If we want to fulfil the first and greatest commandment – by which I mean the Christ-like way of life, blessed humility, the life of the incarnate God – we should have the same feelings toward ourselves as a person might have toward someone who had time and again grievously injured him and treated him unjustly. Indeed, we should have even stronger feelings than these. Hence the Apostle says: 'Who shall deliver me from the body of this death? . . . For it is not subject to the law of God' (Rom. 7:24; 8:7). Here he shows that to subject the body to the will of God is something within our own power. 'For if we would judge ourselves, we should not be judged; but when we are judged, we are chastened by the Lord' (1 Cor. 11:31–32).

165. The fruit starts in the flower; and the guarding of the intellect begins with self-control in food and drink, the rejection of all evil thoughts and abstention from them, and stillness of heart.

166. While we are being strengthened in Christ Jesus and beginning to move forward in steadfast watchfulness, He at first appears in our intellect like a torch which, carried in the hand of the intellect, guides us along the tracks of the mind; then He appears like a full moon, circling the heart's firmament; then He appears to us like the sun, radiating justice, clearly revealing Himself in the full light of spiritual vision.

167. Jesus mystically reveals these things to the intellect that perseveres in the commandment: 'Circumcise the foreskin of your heart' (Deut. 10:16). As has been said, the assiduous practice of watchfulness teaches a man marvellous thoughts. 'For God is impartial' (Rom. 2:11); and therefore the Lord says: 'Hear Me and understand: for to him who has, more shall be given and he shall have in abundance; and from him who has not, shall be taken even what he thinks he has' (cf. Luke 8:18). 'All things work together for

good to them that love God' (Rom. 8:28); how much the more, then, will the virtues work together in the case of such people?

168. A ship does not go far without water; and there is no progress whatsoever in the guarding of the intellect without watchfulness, humility and the Jesus Prayer.

169. Stones form the foundation of a house; but the foundation of sanctity – and its roof – is the holy and venerable name of our Lord Jesus Christ. A foolish captain can easily wreck his ship during a storm, dismissing the sailors, throwing the sails and oars into the sea, and going to sleep himself; but the soul can be sent to the bottom even more swiftly by the demons if it neglects watchfulness and does not call upon the name of Jesus Christ when they begin their provocations.

170. We write of what we know; and for those who want to understand what we say, we bear witness to all that we have seen as we journeyed on our path. He Himself has declared: 'If a man does not abide in Me, he is cast out as a branch; and men gather it, and cast it into the fire, and it is burned. If he abides in Me, I abide in him' (cf. John 15:5–6). The sun cannot shine without light; nor can the heart be cleansed of the stain of destructive thoughts without invoking in prayer the name of Jesus. This being the case, we should use that name as we do our own breath. For that name is light, while evil thoughts are darkness; it is God and Master, while evil thoughts are slaves and demons.

171. The guarding of the intellect may appropriately be called 'light-producing', 'lightning-producing', 'light-giving' and 'fire-bearing', for truly it surpasses endless virtues, bodily and other. Because of this, and because of the glorious light to which it gives birth, one must honour this virtue with worthy epithets. Those who are seized by love for this virtue, from being worthless sinners, ignorant, profane, uncomprehending and unjust, are enabled to become just, responsive, pure, holy, and wise through Jesus Christ. Not only this, but they are able to contemplate mystically and to theologize; and when they have become contemplatives, they bathe in a sea of pure and infinite light, touching it ineffably and living and dwelling in it. They have tasted that the Lord is good (cf. Ps. 34:8), and in these harbingers are fulfilled the words of David: 'Surely the righteous shall give thanks unto Thy name; and the upright shall dwell in Thy presence' (Ps. 140:13). Such men alone

truly call upon God and give thanks to Him, and in their love for Him continually speak with Him.

172. Woe to what is within from what is without! For the inner self suffers great distress from the outer senses, and when it suffers in this way it scourges the outer senses. He who has experienced this knows already what it means.

173. According to the Fathers, if our inner self is watchful it can protect the outer self. But we and the demons combine in committing sins. The demons work through evil thoughts alone by forming in the intellect what fanciful pictures they wish; while we sin both inwardly through evil thoughts and outwardly through our actions. Lacking the density of physical bodies, the demons through deceitfulness and guile are purveyors of torment, both to themselves and to us, by means of evil thoughts alone. If they did not lack the density of physical bodies, they would always be sinning through outward actions as well, for their will is always disposed to ungodliness.

174. The single-phrased Jesus Prayer destroys and consumes the deceits of the demons. For when we invoke Jesus, God and Son of God, constantly and tirelessly, He does not allow them to project in the mind's mirror even the first hint of their infiltration – that is to say, their provocation – or any form, nor does He allow them to have any converse with the heart. If no demonic form enters the heart, it will be empty of evil thoughts, as we have said; for it is the demons' habit to converse with the soul by means of evil thoughts and so deceitfully to pervert it.

175. It is through unceasing prayer that the mind is cleansed of the dark clouds, the tempests of the demons. And when it is cleansed, the divine light of Jesus cannot but shine in it, unless we are puffed up with self-esteem and delusion and a love of ostentation, and elevate ourselves towards the unattainable, and so are deprived of Jesus' help. For Christ, the paradigm of humility, loathes all such self-inflation.

176. Let us hold fast, therefore, to prayer and humility, for together with watchfulness they act like a burning sword against the demons. If we do this, we shall daily and hourly be able to celebrate a secret festival of joy within our hearts.

177. Every evil thought is subsumed in the eight principal evil thoughts and all take their origin from these eight, much as every

accursed demon-god of the Greeks derives from Hera and Zeus according to their myths. These eight approach the heart's entrance and, if they find the intellect unguarded, one by one they enter, each in its own time. Whichever of the eight enters the heart introduces a swarm of other evil thoughts as well; and having thus darkened the intellect, it stimulates the body and provokes it to sinful actions.

178. Whoever, then, watches out for the head of the serpent, and strikes it vehemently with all his power of rebuttal, will ward off the fight. By crushing the serpent's head he repulses a host of evil thoughts and actions. The mind then remains undisturbed, God approving its vigilance over its thoughts. In return it is given the ability to know how to overcome its adversaries, and how little by little to purify the heart from thoughts that defile the inner self. As the Lord Jesus said, 'Out of the heart proceed evil thoughts, adulteries, fornications, and these are the things which defile a man' (cf. Matt. 15:19–20).

179. In this way the soul can attain in the Lord that state of beauty, loveliness and integrity in which it was created by God in the beginning. As Antony, the great servant of God, said, 'Holiness is achieved when the intellect is in its natural state.' And again he said: 'The soul realizes its integrity when its intellect is in that state in which it was created.' And shortly after this he adds: 'Let us purify our mind, for I believe that when the mind is completely pure and is in its natural state, it gains penetrating insight, and it sees more clearly and further than the demons, since the Lord reveals things to it.' So spoke the renowned Antony, according to the *Life of Antony* by Athanasios the Great.[1]

180. Every evil thought produces in the intellect the image of some material thing; for since the devil is an intellect he cannot deceive us except by making use of things we are in the habit of perceiving by means of the senses.

181. Since we are human beings, it is not in our nature to pursue birds through the air or to fly as they do. Similarly, without watchful and frequent prayer we cannot prevail over bodiless, demonic thoughts, or fix the eye of the intellect fully and intently upon God. Without such prayer, we merely hunt after earthly things.

182. If you really wish to cover your evil thoughts with shame,

[1] See Athanasios, *Life of Antony*, §§ 20, 34.

to be still and calm, and to watch over your heart without hindrance, let the Jesus Prayer cleave to your breath, and in a few days you will find that this is possible.

183. Letters cannot be written on air; they have to be inscribed on some material if they are to have any permanence. Similarly, we should weld our hard-won watchfulness to the Jesus Prayer, so that this watchfulness may always be attached to Him and may through Him remain with us for ever.

184. Bring your works to the Lord, and you will find grace. Then the words of the Prophet will not be spoken of you: 'Thou art near in their mouth, O Lord, and far from their reins '(cf. Jer. 12:2). None but Jesus Christ Himself, unifier of what is disunited, can give your heart lasting peace from passions.

185. Both mental converse with evil thoughts and external encounters and chatter alike darken the soul. If we are not to injure the intellect, we must not spare either of these chatterboxes, whether they be our own thoughts or other people. And we must not spare them for a most cogent reason: because otherwise our intellect will be darkened and we will lose our watchfulness. If we are darkened by forgetfulness, we destroy the intellect.

186. He who with all diligence keeps his purity of heart will have Christ, establisher of that purity, as his teacher, and Christ will secretly communicate His will to him. 'I will hear what God the Lord will speak within me', says David, giving expression to this (Ps. 85:8. LXX). Speaking of the intellect's investigation of itself in the course of the unseen war, and of the help given by God, he says: 'And a man will say, Is there a reward for the righteous?' Then, giving the solution to this problem, he says: 'Truly, he is a God that judges those in the earth' (Ps. 58:11. LXX) – that is to say, judges the wicked demons in the earth of the heart. And elsewhere he says: 'A man shall approach, and the heart is deep, and God shall be exalted' (Ps. 64:6–7. LXX). Then we will regard the attacks of the demons as stones thrown by infants.

187. Let us live every moment in 'applying our hearts to wisdom' (Ps. 90:12), as the Psalmist says, continually breathing Jesus Christ, the power of God the Father and the wisdom of God (cf. 1 Cor. 1:24). If, however, we are distracted by some circumstance or other and grow slack in our spiritual effort, the following morning let us again gird up the loins of our intellect and once more set to

work forcefully. There is no excuse for us if, knowing what is to be done, we do not do it.

188. Noxious foods give trouble when taken into the body; but as soon as he feels the pain, the person who has eaten them can quickly take some emetic and so be unharmed. Similarly, once the intellect that has imbibed evil thoughts senses their bitterness, it can easily expel them and get rid of them completely by means of the Jesus Prayer uttered from the depths of the heart. This lesson, and the experience corresponding to it, have by God's grace conveyed understanding to those who practise watchfulness.

189. With your breathing combine watchfulness and the name of Jesus, or humility and the unremitting study of death. Both may confer great blessing.

190. The Lord said: 'Learn from Me; for I am gentle and humble in heart, and you will find rest for your souls' (Matt. 11:29).

191. The Lord said: 'Whoever humbles himself as this little child will be exalted; and whoever exalts himself will be abased' (cf. Matt. 18:4; 23:12). 'Learn from Me', He said. Do you see how this learning means humility? For His commandment is eternal life (cf. John 12:50), and this in turn is humility. Thus he who is not humble has lost life and obviously will be found with its opposite.

192. If every virtue comes into being through soul and body, and soul and body are the creation of God, how shall we not be utterly mad if we boast of accidental adornments of soul or body, and puff ourselves up, supported by our vanity as by a flimsy staff? Worst of all, how, through our extreme wickedness and folly, shall we not rouse against us God who transcends us so infinitely? 'For God ranges Himself against the proud' (Jas. 4:6). Because of our arrogance and vanity, instead of imitating the Lord in humility, we embrace His enemy, the demon of pride. It was with reference to this that the Apostle said: 'For what do you have which you did not receive?' (1 Cor. 4:7). Did you create yourself? And if you received from God both soul and body, from which and in which and through which every virtue comes into being, 'why do you boast as if you had not received?' (1 Cor. 4:7). For it is the Lord who has given you these things.

193. Purification of heart, through which we acquire humility and every blessing that comes from above, consists simply in our not letting evil thoughts enter the soul.

194. If with God's help and for His sake alone we manage to guard the intellect for some time, it acquires a certain good sense in pursuing the spiritual battle. This good sense in its turn gives us, in no small measure, the ability to arrange our work and regulate our words with a judgment that accords with God's will.

195. The high priest's emblems in the Old Testament are models for purity of heart. They teach us so to give attention to the gold disc of the heart (cf. Exod. 28:22. LXX) that, should we tarnish it through sin, we should cleanse it with tears, repentance and prayer. For the intellect is very receptive and hard to hold back from illicit thoughts. It pursues with equal readiness both good and evil images.

196. Truly blessed is the man whose mind and heart are as closely attached to the Jesus Prayer and to the ceaseless invocation of His name as air to the body or flame to the wax. The sun rising over the earth creates the daylight; and the venerable and holy name of the Lord Jesus, shining continually in the mind, gives birth to countless intellections radiant as the sun.

197. When clouds are scattered the air is clear; and when the fantasies of passion are scattered by Jesus Christ, the sun of righteousness, bright and star-like intellections are born in the heart, for the heart is then illumined by Jesus. Solomon says: 'They that trust in the Lord shall understand truth, and the faithful in love shall abide with Him' (Wisd. 3:9).

198. One of the saints has said: 'Let the rancorous man vent his rancour on the demons, and let the belligerent man turn his hostility once and for all against his own body. The flesh is a treacherous friend, and the more it is coddled the more it fights back.' And again: 'Be hostile to your body, and fight against your stomach.'

199. In the paragraphs up to this point – those comprising the first and second centuries – we have set down how to learn the difficult art of stilling the intellect. These paragraphs are the fruit not of our mind alone, but also of what the holy Fathers teach us about purity of intellect. Now, after a few words indicating the value of guarding the intellect, we shall draw to a close.

200. Come, then, you who long in spirit to see days of blessing, follow me towards that union attained through the guarding of the intellect; and I, in the Lord, will instruct you in your task on earth and the angelic life. For neither the angels nor the intellect rivalling them in purity will ever be sated with praising the Creator. And

just as the angels, being immaterial, do not concern themselves with food, so neither do material beings when once they have entered the heaven of the intellect's stillness and have themselves become angelic.

201. Just as the angels do not concern themselves with property and money, so those who have purified the soul's vision and who have attained the state of holiness are not troubled by the evil ploys of the demons. And just as the richness that comes from moving closer to God is evident in the angels, so love and intense longing for God is evident in those who have become angelic and gaze upwards towards the divine. Moreover, because the taste of the divine and the ecstasy* of desire make their longing ever more intense and insatiable as they ascend, they do not stop until they reach the Seraphim; nor do they rest from their watchfulness of intellect and the intense longing of their aspiration until they have become angels in Christ Jesus our Lord.

202. There is no venom more poisonous than that of the asp or cobra, and there is no evil greater than that of self-love. The winged children of self-love are self-praise, self-satisfaction, gluttony, unchastity, self-esteem, jealousy and the crown of all these, pride. Pride can drag down not men alone, but even angels from heaven, and surround them with darkness instead of light.

203. This, then, Theodoulos, comes to you from Hesychios, who bears the name of stillness even if he belies it in practice. Yet perhaps it is not from us, but has been given by God, who is praised and glorified in the Father, the Son and the Holy Spirit by every spiritual being, men and angels, and by all creation fashioned by the Holy Trinity, the one God. May we, too, reach His glorious kingdom through the prayers of the most pure Mother of God and of our holy Fathers. To the unattainable God be everlasting glory. Amen.

ST NEILOS THE ASCETIC

Introductory Note

St Neilos the Ascetic was abbot of a monastery near Ankyra (Ankara) in the early decades of the fifth century, and seems to have died around the year 430. Possibly he was a disciple of St John Chrysostom. According to the traditional biography of Neilos – accepted as authentic by St Nikodimos, but now considered legendary – he was originally from Constantinople, and after serving as prefect of the city during the reign of Theodosios the Great (379–95) he became a hermit near Sinai. There seems in fact to be no good reason for connecting him with the Sinaite peninsula.

The *Ascetic Discourse* of Neilos contains a valuable section on the relationship between the spiritual father and his disciples. In other of his writings, although not in this work, St Neilos refers to the invocation of the name of Jesus. Along with St Diadochos of Photiki, his younger contemporary, Neilos is the earliest writer to refer explicitly to the Jesus Prayer.[1]

---

[1] See Neilos, *Letters*, ii, 140, 214; iii, 273, 278 (Migne, *Patrologia Graeca*, lxxix, 260A, 261D, 312C, 520C, 521BC). Compare I. Hausherr, *Noms du Christ et voies d'oraison* (*Orientalia Christiana Analecta*, 157, Rome, 1960), pp. 195–6.

Ascetic Discourse

Many Greeks and not a few Jews attempted to philosophize; but only the disciples of Christ have pursued true wisdom, because they alone have Wisdom as their teacher, showing them by His example the way of life they should follow. [For the Greeks, like actors on a stage, put on false masks; they were philosophers in name alone, but lacked true philosophy.] They displayed their philosophic calling by their cloak, beard and staff, but indulged the body and kept their desires as mistresses. They were slaves of gluttony and lust, accepting this as something natural. They were subject to anger and excited by glory, and they gulped down rich food like dogs. They did not realize that the philosopher must be above all a free man, and not a slave of the passions who can be bought or sold. A man of upright life can be the slave of others and yet suffer no harm; but to be enslaved to the passions and pleasures brings a man into disgrace and great ridicule.

Some of the Greeks imagined themselves to be engaged in metaphysics, but they neglected the practice of the virtues altogether. Some were star-gazers, explaining the inexplicable, and claiming to know the size of the heavens, the dimensions of the sun and the movement of the stars. At times they even tried to theologize, although here the truth lies beyond man's unaided grasp, and speculation is dangerous; yet in their way of life they were more degraded than swine wallowing in the mud. And when some of them did try to apply their principles in practice, they became worse than those who only theorized, for they sold their labours for glory and praise. Usually their only object was to show off, and they endured hardships simply to gain cheap applause. Moreover, what can be more stupid than to keep silent continually, live on vegetables, cover oneself with ragged garments of hair and spend one's days in a barrel, if one expects no recompense after death? If the rewards of virtue are restricted to this present life, then one is engaged in a contest where no prizes are ever offered, wrestling all one's life for no return but the toil and the sweat.

Those of the Jews, on the other hand, who hold philosophy in honour – the Rechabites, the descendants of Jonadab (cf. Jer. 35:6) – do indeed encourage their disciples to follow an appropriate way of life. They always live in tents, abstaining from wine and all luxuries; their fare is frugal and provision for their bodily needs is moderate. While devoting full attention to the practice of the virtues, they also attach great importance to contemplation, as their name 'Essene' indicates. In short, they pursue the goal of philosophy while avoiding the things that conflict with their calling. But what do they gain from their arduous ascetic contest, since they deny Christ, who acts as judge and gives the award? So they, too, fail to gain from their labours, falling short of the true goal of philosophy.

For philosophy is a state of moral integrity combined with a doctrine of true knowledge concerning reality. Both Jews and Greeks fell short of this, for they rejected the Wisdom that is from heaven and tried to philosophize without Christ, who alone has revealed the true philosophy in both His life and His teaching. For by the purity of His life He was the first to establish the way of true philosophy. He always held His soul above the passions of the body, and in the end, when His death was required by His design for man's salvation, He laid down even His soul. In this He taught us that the true philosopher must renounce all life's pleasures, mastering pains and passions, and paying scant attention to the body: he must not overvalue even his soul, but must readily lay it down when holiness demands.

The Apostles received this way of life from Christ and made it their own, renouncing the world in response to His call, disregarding fatherland, relatives and possessions. At once they adopted a harsh and strenuous way of life, facing every kind of adversity, afflicted, tormented, harassed, naked, lacking even necessities; and finally they met death boldly, imitating their Teacher faithfully in all things. Thus through their actions they left behind a true image of the highest way of life.

Although all Christians should have modelled their own life on this image, most of them either lacked the will to do so or else made

only feeble efforts. There were, however, a few who had the strength
to rise above the turmoil of the world and to flee from the agitation
of cities. Having escaped from this turbulence, they embraced the
monastic life and reproduced in themselves the pattern of apostolic
virtue. They preferred voluntary poverty to possessions, because this
freed them from distraction; and so as to control the passions, they
satisfied their bodily needs with food that was readily available and
simply prepared, rather than with richly dressed dishes. Soft and
unnecessary clothing they rejected as an invention of human luxury,
and they wore only such plain garments as are required for the body.
It seemed to them a betrayal of philosophy to turn their attention
from heavenly things to earthly concerns more appropriate to animals. They ignored the world, being above human passions.

They did not seek excessive gain by exploiting each other; nor
did they bring lawsuits against one another, for each had his own
conscience as an impartial judge. One was not rich while another was
destitute, nor did one overeat while another starved. The generosity
of those who were well off made good what others lacked, this
willingness to share eliminating every anomaly and establishing
equality and fairness – though even then inequality still existed,
produced not as it is now by the mad struggle for social status, but
by a great desire to live more humbly than others. Envy, malice,
arrogance and haughtiness were banished, along with all that leads
to discord. Some were impervious or dead to the coarser passions;
they had so firmly repudiated all traces of them from the start that
now, through daily asceticism and perseverance, they had acquired
inner stability and did not even have fantasies of them in their
dreams. In short, they were lights shining in darkness; they were
fixed stars illuminating the jet-black night of life; they were harbour
walls unshaken by storms. They showed everyone how simple it is to
escape unharmed from the provocations of the passions.

But this strict and angelic way of life has suffered the fate of a
portrait many times recopied by careless hands, until gradually all
likeness to the original has been lost. Though we are crucified to the
world, though we have renounced this transitory life and our
purely human limitations, aspiring to the state of the angels by
sharing their dispassion, yet we have relapsed and fallen back.
Because of our material concerns and shameful acquisitiveness, we
have blunted the edge of true asceticism; and by our negligence we

discredit even those who through their genuine sanctity truly deserve to be honoured. Wearing the monastic habit, we have 'put our hand to the plough'; yet we look back, forgetting and even strongly rejecting our duties, and so do not become 'fit for the kingdom of heaven' (cf. Luke 9:62).

So we no longer pursue plainness and simplicity of life. We no longer value stillness, which helps to free us from past defilement, but prefer a whole host of things which distract us uselessly from our true goal. Rivalry over material possessions has made us forget the counsel of the Lord, who urged us to take no thought for earthly things, but to seek only the kingdom of heaven (cf. Matt. 6:33). Deliberately doing the opposite, we have disregarded the Lord's commandment, trusting in ourselves and not in His protection. For He says: 'Behold the fowls of the air: for they do not sow or reap or gather into barns; yet your heavenly Father feeds them' (Matt. 6:26); and again: 'Consider the lilies of the field, how they grow; they do not toil or spin' (Matt. 6:28). When He sent the apostles out to declare the good news to their fellow men, He even forbade them to carry wallet, purse or staff, and told them to be content with His promise: 'The workman is worthy of his food' (Matt. 10:10). This promise is to be trusted far more than our own resources.

Despite all this we go on accumulating as much land as we can, and we buy up flocks of sheep, fine oxen and fat donkeys – the sheep to supply us with wool, the oxen to plough and provide food for us and fodder for themselves and for the other animals, the donkeys to transport from foreign lands the goods and luxuries which our own country lacks. We also select the crafts which give the highest return, even though they absorb all our attention and leave no time for the remembrance of God. It is as if we accused God of being incapable of providing for us, or ourselves of being unable to fulfil the commitments of our calling. Even if we do not admit this openly, our actions condemn us; for we show approval of the ways of worldly men by engaging in the same pursuits, and perhaps working at them even harder than they do.

Thus, like so many others, we look on the ascetic way as a means of gain, and follow the once unworldly life of blessedness merely in order to avoid hard work through a feigned piety, and to gain greater scope for indulging in illusory pleasures. We shamelessly revile those who live simply, and sometimes even our own superiors, as though we thought the spiritual life was a matter of aggressiveness, not of humility and gentleness. As a result, instead of being respected, we are regarded as a useless crowd, involved in buying and selling just as much as the man in the street. Nothing marks us out as it should from others, and we distinguish ourselves merely by the habit that we wear, not by our way of life. We reject all ascetic effort, but madly desire a reputation for asceticism. We have debased the truth into play-acting.

Today, a person wears the monastic habit without washing away the stains on his soul, or erasing the marks which past sins have stamped upon his mind; indeed, he may still take lustful pleasure in the fantasies these sins suggest. He has not yet trained his character so as to fit his vocation, nor does he grasp the purpose of the divine philosophy. Already he has developed a Pharisaic superciliousness, being filled with conceit by his robes. He goes about carrying various tools the use of which he does not understand. By virtue of his outward dress he lays claim to a knowledge which in reality he has not tasted even with the tip of his tongue. He is a reef, not a harbour; a whited sepulchre, not a temple; a wolf, not a sheep; the ruin of those decoyed by his appearance.

Unable to endure the strictness of life in their monastery, such monks run away and swarm into a city like a party of revellers. Then, when they get hungry, they begin to deceive others with an outward show of piety, and are ready to do anything to satisfy their needs; for nothing is more compelling and inventive than the demands of the body, especially when one is idle. Their techniques get more and more cunning and ingenious. They hang about the doors of the wealthy like parasites, and like slaves they dance attendance on them through the streets, shoving people out of the way and clearing a path for them. All this they do for the sake of a meal, never having learnt to control their gluttony. Nor do they obey Moses and carry on their girdle a trowel for covering their excrement (cf. Deut. 23 : 13. LXX). They do not realize that indulgence in gluttony leads only to further hunger, and that they should satisfy the needs of the body only with whatever food is at hand, thus quelling their shameful and disordered appetites.

This is why the name of God is blasphemed, and the ascetic way of life, instead of inspiring men, fills them with disgust. The attainments of genuine ascetics are dismissed as trickery. Cities are full of vagabonds, and people are pestered at home, revolted by the very sight of these monks, seeing them standing at their doors more shamelessly than beggars. Many have even been admitted into people's homes, where for a little while they make a pretence of piety, deceitfully concealing their wicked plans; then they rob their hosts and make off, thus bringing the whole monastic life into disrepute. Once the monks taught self-restraint; now they are banished from cities as a corrupting influence, and shunned like lepers. People would rather trust thieves and burglars than those who follow the monastic life, thinking straightforward criminals easier to guard against than plausible tricksters.

These monks have not so much as begun the ascetic life, far less learnt the value of stillness. Perhaps they came to the monastic life because of some pressure, not realizing what is involved; so they regard it merely as a way of earning their living. This attitude might change to something more spiritual, if only they would stop knocking on every door and if, shamed by their monastic habit into restraining their gross acquisitiveness, they were willing to impose a much-needed curb on their body. But, being self-indulgent, they do not realize how their soft living constantly breeds new and extravagant desires.

It is difficult to treat those who suffer from chronic diseases. For how can you explain the value of health to people who have never enjoyed it, but have been sickly from birth? Because this is their customary state, they regard it as a misfortune of nature, and even as perfectly normal. It is useless to offer advice to those who have no intention of taking it, but continue regardless on the downward path. In particular, those with a lust for any kind of gain, however shameful, are completely deaf to advice.

As for ourselves, who claim to have renounced worldly life and its desires in our longing for holiness, and who profess to follow Christ, why do we entangle ourselves once more in worldly distractions? Why do we wrongly build again what we have rightly torn down? Why do we share in the folly of those who are disloyal to their vocation? Why in our pursuit of empty trivialities do we kindle the appetites of our weaker brethren and fill them with greed? The Lord has commanded us to watch over those who are easily misled, not inciting them to evil, and preferring their advantage to our pleasure. In this way, by not following our own unconsidered impulses, we help many of our simpler brethren to be more careful, and set them an example by our attitude to worldly concerns.

Why do we attach such value to material things, seeing that we have been taught to despise them? Why do we cling to money and possessions, and disperse our intellect among a host of useless cares? Our preoccupation with such things diverts us from what is more important and makes us neglect the well-being of the soul, leading us to perdition. For we who profess to be philosophers and pride ourselves on being superior to pleasure are seen to pursue material gain with more zest than anyone else. Nothing brings such severe punishment on us as our persuasion of others to imitate our own evil ways.

Let no one despise these words. Either correct your evil conduct, which brings disgrace upon the divine philosophy, leading others to indifference, or else give up all claim to be a philosopher. For the true philosopher possessions are superfluous, since he detaches himself from bodily concerns for the sake of the soul's purity. If your aim is material riches and pleasure, why pretend to honour philosophy while you act in a manner which entirely conflicts with it, cloaking your conduct under fine words?

So great is our preoccupation with material things that we feel no shame when, on breaking the Saviour's commandments, we are rebuked even by those whom we despise because they still live 'in the world'; for they now teach us instead of us teaching them. When we are quarrelling, they remind us that 'the servant of Christ must not engage in strife, but be gentle to all men' (2 Tim. 2:24); when we are disputing about money and possessions, they quote to us the text, 'If anyone . . . takes away your coat, let him have your cloak also' (Matt. 5:40). They ridicule and deride us because of the incongruity between our actions and our vocation. Indeed, is it ever right to engage in disputes in order to protect our property? Suppose that someone destroys the boundary of our vineyard and adds it to his own land: someone else lets his animal loose in it; and someone else diverts the water supply from our garden. Must we then lose all self-control in such situations, and become worse than madmen? But in that case our intellect, which should be engaged in the contemplation of created beings, must now give its attention to lawsuits, turning its contemplative power to worldly cunning, so as to defend a quantity of unnecessary possessions.

Why do we try to make other people's property our own, weighing ourselves down with material fetters, and paying no attention to the prophet's imprecation: 'Woe to him who gathers what is not his own, and heavily loads his yoke' (cf. Hab. 2 : 6. LXX). Those who pursue us are, as Jeremiah says, 'swifter than the eagles of heaven' (Lam. 4 : 19); but we weigh ourselves down with worldly things, move slowly along the road and so are easily overtaken by our pursuer, covetousness, which Paul taught us to flee (cf. Col. 3 : 5). Even if we are not heavily laden, we must still run as fast as we can, or else the enemy will overtake us.

Attachment to worldly things is a grave obstacle to those who are striving after holiness, and often brings ruin to both soul and body. For what destroyed Naboth the Israelite? Was not his vineyard the cause of his death, because it roused the jealousy of his neighbour Ahab (cf. 1 Kgs. 21 : 1–16)? What made the two and a half tribes stay outside the promised land, but their huge herds and flocks (cf. Num. 34 : 15)? What divided Lot and Abraham? Was it not also their huge herds and flocks which caused continual quarrels among the herdsmen, and in the end forced them to part (cf. Gen. 13 : 5–11)?

So possessions arouse feelings of jealousy against their owners, cut off their owners from men better than themselves, divide families, and make friends hate one another. Possessions, moreover, have no place in the life to come, and even in this present life have no great use. Why, then, do we abandon the service of God and devote ourselves entirely to empty trivialities? For it is God who supplies us with all that we need. Human efforts inevitably fail unless God helps us; while God in His providence bestows every blessing without man's assistance. What benefits were gained from their efforts by those to whom God said: 'You sowed much and gathered little, and I blew it away out of your hands' (cf. Hag. 1 : 9)? And what did the righteous lack, though they gave no thought at all for their needs? Were not the Israelites fed in the desert for forty years, without cultivating the land? They always had enough to eat, for in a strange and miraculous way quails came in from the sea and manna fell from the sky (cf. Exod. 16), and a dry rock, when struck, gushed water (cf. Exod. 17 : 6); and throughout the whole forty years their clothes and shoes never wore out (cf. Deut. 8:4). What land was tilled beside the brook Kerith where Elijah hid? Did not the ravens bring him food (cf. 1 Kgs. 17:6)? And when he came to Sarepta, did not the widow, despite her desperate need, give him bread, snatching it from the mouth of her own children (cf. 1 Kgs. 17:10–16)? All this shows that we should seek holiness, not clothing, food and drink.

Strange though all these things may seem, they are by no means impossible. A man can live without eating if God so wills. For how did Elijah complete a journey of forty days with the strength received from a single meal (cf. 1 Kgs. 19:8)? And how did Moses remain on the mountain in communion with God for eighty days without tasting human food? After forty days he came down and, enraged by the image of the calf which the Israelites had made, immediately he broke the tablets of stone engraved with the Law and went back up the mountain, remaining there for another forty days; and only then, after receiving two further tablets of stone, did he go down again to the people (cf. Exod. 24:12–18; 31:18–34:35). How can the human mind explain this miracle? How did his bodily nature survive without anything to replenish its daily loss of strength? This enigma is solved by the divine Logos, when He says: 'Man shall not live by bread alone, but by every word that proceeds out of the mouth of God' (Matt. 4:4).

Why, then, do we drag the monastic way of life down from heaven to earth, burying ourselves in material anxieties? Why do we who once were 'brought up in scarlet' now 'embrace dunghills', as Jeremiah says in his Lamentations (Lam. 4:5)? For when we are refreshed with radiant and fiery thoughts, we are 'brought up in scarlet'; but when we leave this state and involve ourselves in material things, we 'embrace dunghills'. Why do we abandon hope in God and rely on the strength of our own arm, ascribing the gifts of God's providence to the work of our hands? Job considered that his greatest sin was to raise his hand to his mouth and kiss it (cf. Job 31:27), but we feel no qualms in doing this. For many people are accustomed to kiss their hands, saying that it is their hands which bring them prosperity. The Law refers to such people symbolically when it says: 'Whatever goes upon its paws is unclean', and 'whatever goes upon all fours or has many feet is always unclean' (cf. Lev. 11:27, 42). Now the phrase 'goes upon its paws'

indicates someone who relies on his own hands and places all his
hope in them, while to 'go on all fours' is to trust in sensory
things and continually to seduce one's intellect into worrying
about them; and to have 'many feet' signifies clinging to material
objects.

This is why the author of Proverbs, speaking figuratively, does
not wish the perfect man to have even two feet, but only one, and
this one seldom involving him in material things; for he says:
'Seldom set your foot within your friend's house, lest he grow weary
of you, and so hate you' (Prov. 25:17. LXX). 'You are my friends',
says the Saviour to His disciples (John 15:14); and if we try not to
worry our friends about our bodily needs, then we should only
seldom trouble Christ about such matters; for if we keep worrying
our friends they will come to hate us. What will our fate be, and
how shall we escape condemnation, if we are constantly occupied
with these bodily needs, and never stand upright or straighten our
legs, so as to raise ourselves from the ground? For our two legs
together carry the whole mass of the body, and by crouching a little
we are able to spring upwards; and in the same way our faculty of
discrimination, after stooping to attend to the needs of the body,
can once more look upwards unimpeded, separating itself from all
worldly thoughts.

Standing upright, then, is characteristic of men who do not
constantly indulge their lower impulses; it is also characteristic of
the angelic powers, because they have no need of physical things
and feel no longing for them. That is what Ezekiel meant when he
said: 'Their legs were straight and their feet were winged' (Ezek.
1:7. LXX). This signifies the unbending steadfastness of their
outlook and the swiftness of their movement towards spiritual
things. Men, on the other hand, have been given legs that bend: in
this way they can descend sometimes to fulfil the needs of the
body, and at other times ascend to fulfil those of the soul. Because
of the soul's kinship with the heavenly powers, we should for the
most part dwell with them on high; as regards the body, we should
turn our attention to material things only in so far as some necessity
forces us to do so. But always to be creeping on the ground in
search of pleasure is defiling and degrading for someone with
experience of spiritual knowledge.

Strictly speaking, we should call someone unclean, not because he goes on all fours, but only if he does so continually; for God allows those who are in a body to attend from time to time to their bodily needs. Thus Jonathan, when fighting Nahash the Ammonite, gained the victory over him by moving on all fours (cf. 1 Sam. 14:13); but he did this solely because he had to. When fighting the snake that creeps on its belly – for this is what the name Nahash means – he was forced for a short time to do the same by going on all fours; and then, standing up again in the usual way, he easily defeated his opponent.

The story of Ish-bosheth also teaches us not to be over-anxious about bodily things, and not to rely on the senses to protect us. He was a king who went to rest in his chamber, leaving a woman as door-keeper. When the men of Rechab came, they found her dozing off as she was winnowing wheat; so, escaping her notice, they slipped in and slew Ish-bosheth while he was asleep (cf. 2 Sam. 4:5–8). Now when bodily concerns predominate, everything in man is asleep: the intellect, the soul and the senses. For the woman at the door winnowing wheat indicates the state of one whose reason is closely absorbed in physical things and trying with persistent efforts to purify them. It is clear that this story in Scripture should not be taken literally. For how could a king have a woman as door-keeper, when he ought properly to be guarded by a troop of soldiers, and to have round him a large body of attendants? Or how could he be so poor as to use her to winnow the wheat? But improbable details are often included in a story because of the deeper truth they signify. Thus the intellect in each of us resides within like a king, while the reason acts as door-keeper of the senses. When the reason occupies itself with bodily things – and to winnow wheat is something bodily – the enemy without difficulty slips past unnoticed and slays the intellect. This is why Abraham did not entrust the guarding of the door to a woman, knowing that the senses are easily deceived; for they take pleasure in the sight of sensory things, and so divide the intellect and persuade it to share in sensual delights, although this is clearly dangerous. But Abraham himself sat by the door (cf. Gen. 18:1), allowing free entry to divine thoughts, while barring the way to worldly cares.

What advantage do we gain in life from all our useless toil over worldly things? 'Is not all man's labour for the sake of his mouth' (Eccles. 6:7)? Now, according to the Apostle (1 Tim. 6:8), 'food and raiment' are all we need to maintain our humble flesh. Why, then, as Solomon asks, do we labour endlessly 'for the wind' (Eccles. 5:16)? Through our anxiety about worldly things we hinder the soul from enjoying divine blessings and we bestow on the flesh greater care and comfort than are good for it. We nourish it with what is harmful and thus make it an adversary, so that it not only wavers in battle but, because of over-indulgence, it fights vigorously against the soul, seeking honours and rewards. What in fact are the basic needs of the body that we use as a pretext when indulging an endless succession of desires? Simply bread and water. Well, do not the springs provide running water in abundance, while bread is easily earned by those who have hands? In this way we can satisfy the needs of the body, while suffering little or no distraction. And does our clothing call for much care? Again, no – if we reject a stupid conformity to fashion, and consider only our actual needs. For what fine-spun clothing, what linen or purple or silk did the first man wear? Did not the Creator command him to wear a coat of skins and to eat herbs (cf. Gen. 3:18, 21)? Such were the limits He set to the needs of the body – far different from the civilized shamelessness of today.

I am not arguing here that He who feeds the birds of the air and clothes the lilies of the field with such glory will certainly provide also for us if we pursue holiness; for those who are still far from real faith in God cannot as yet be persuaded by this argument. But who, when asked, will refuse to give what is needful to one who lives a holy life? The barbarous Babylonians who took Jerusalem by force showed respect for the holiness of Jeremiah (cf. Jer. 40:4–5), and provided him abundantly with all his bodily requirements, giving him not only food but the vessels with which it was the custom to serve guests. Surely, then, our own fellow-countrymen, since they are not totally barbarous, will appreciate goodness and admire what is holy, and so will show respect for our ascetic life. Even if they themselves cannot follow the ascetic way owing to the weakness of their nature, at least they hold this way in honour and venerate those who pursue it. What persuaded the Shunammite woman to build a chamber for Elisha, and to put there a table, bed and candle-stick (cf. 2 Kgs. 4:10)? Was it not Elisha's holiness? And what made the widow, when the whole country was ravaged by famine, place the needs of the Prophet before her own (cf. 1 Kgs. 17:10–16)?

Had she not been amazed by Elijah's spiritual wisdom, she would not have deprived herself and her children of what small material solace still remained to them, and given it to him. She expected in any case to die before long, but in her generosity to the stranger she was ready to do so even before the time came.

Men such as Elijah and Elisha became what they were through their courage, perseverance and indifference to the things of this life. They practised frugality; by being content with little they reached a state in which they wanted nothing, and so came to resemble the bodiless angels. As a result, though outwardly insignificant and unnoticed, they became stronger than the greatest of earthly rulers; they spoke more boldly to crowned monarchs than any king does to his own subjects. In what weapons or strength did Elijah trust when he rebuked Ahab, saying: 'It is not I who have troubled Israel, but you and your father's house' (1 Kgs. 18:18)? How was Moses able to withstand Pharaoh when he had nothing but holiness to give him courage (cf. Exod. 5)? When the armies of the kings of Israel and Judah were gathered for war, how did Elisha dare to say to Jehoram: 'As the Lord of hosts lives, before whom I stand, surely, were it not that I regard the presence of Jehoshaphat the king of Judah, I would not look toward you, nor see you' (2 Kgs. 3:14)? He was afraid neither of the assembled troops nor of the king's anger, which was likely to flare up for no good reason in time of war, when his mind was confused and anxious. Can any king achieve what holiness achieves? What robe of royal purple divided a river, as did the mantle of Elijah (cf. 2 Kgs. 2:8)? And what royal crown cured diseases, as did the handkerchiefs of the apostles (cf. Acts 19:12)? A solitary prophet once censured a king for his unlawful acts, when the king had his whole army with him. Incensed by the criticisms, the king stretched out his hand to seize the prophet; yet not only did he fail to catch hold of him, but he was unable to draw his hand back again, for it had withered (cf. 1 Kgs. 13:4). Here was a contest between holiness and a king's power; and victory went to holiness. The prophet did not fight; it was holiness that routed the enemy. The combatant himself did nothing while his faith acted. The king's allies stood by as judges of the contest; and the king's hand stuck fast, showing that holiness had won.

These holy men achieved such things because they had resolved to live for the soul alone, turning away from the body and its wants. The fact of needing nothing made them superior to all men. They chose to forsake the body and to free themselves from life in the flesh, rather than to betray the cause of holiness and, because of their bodily needs, to flatter the wealthy. But, as for us, when we lack something, instead of struggling courageously against our difficulties, we come fawning to the rich, like puppies wagging their tails in the hope of being tossed a bare bone or some crumbs. To get what we want, we call them benefactors and protectors of Christians, attributing every virtue to them, even though they may be utterly wicked. We do not investigate how the saints lived, although supposedly it is our aim to imitate their holiness.

Naaman, the commander of the Syrian army, came to Elisha with many gifts. And what did the prophet do? Did he go out to meet him? Did he run towards him? No, he sent a lad to find out why Naaman had come, and did not even admit him to his presence. This was to prevent anyone thinking that he had cured Naaman in return for the gifts that he brought (cf. 2 Kgs. 5:8–16). This story, without teaching us to be arrogant, shows us that we should not flatter, because of our needs, those who value highly the very things it is our vocation to despise.

Why do we forsake the pursuit of spiritual wisdom, and engage in agriculture and commerce? What can be better than to entrust our anxieties to God, so that He may help us with the farming? The soil is tilled and the seeds are sown by human effort; then God sends the rain, watering the seeds in the soft womb of the earth and enabling them to develop roots. He makes the sun rise, warming the soil, and with this warmth He stimulates the growth of the plants. He sends winds tempered to their development. When young shoots begin to come up, He fans them with gentle breezes, so that the crop is not scorched by hot streams of air. Then with steady winds He ripens the milky substance of the grains inside the husks. At threshing-time He provides fiery heat; for winnowing, suitable breezes. If one of these factors is missing, all our human toil is wasted; our efforts achieve nothing when they are not sealed by God's gifts. Often, even when all these factors are present, a violent and untimely storm of rain spoils the grain as it is being threshed or when it has been heaped up clean. Sometimes, again, it is destroyed by worms in the granary: the table, as it were, is already laid and then the food is suddenly snatched from our very mouths. What, then, is the use of relying on our own efforts, since God controls the helm and directs all things as He wills?

We are apt to say that in sickness the body needs some relief. But is it not much better to die rather than do something unworthy of our vocation? In any case, if God wishes us to go on living, either He will give our body enough strength to bear the pain of the illness, and will reward us for our courage; or else He will find some way to relieve the pain, for the Fountain of Wisdom never lacks a remedy.

What we need to do above all else is to return to the blessed way of life followed by the first monks. This way can easily be attained by all who wish. And then, if any suffering comes, it will not be fruitless; for there is this consolation: that it corrects our faults and enables us to make progress. Such suffering also confers great benefit on those who have embarked on the spiritual path but then abandoned it, in that it makes them return to this path once more.

Let us avoid staying in towns and villages; it is better for their inhabitants to come and visit us. Let us seek the wilderness and so draw after us the people who now shun us. For Scripture praises those who 'leave the cities and dwell in the rocks, and are like the dove' (cf. Jer. 48:28). John the Baptist lived in the wilderness and the population of entire towns came out to him. Men dressed in garments of silk hastened to see his leather girdle; those who lived in houses with gilded ceilings chose to endure hardship in the open air; and rather than sleep on beds adorned with jewels they preferred to lie on the sand. All this they endured, although it was contrary to their usual habits; for in their desire to see John the Baptist and in their wonder at his holiness they did not notice the hardships and discomfort. For holiness is held in higher honour than wealth; and the life of stillness wins greater fame than a large fortune. How many rich men there were at that time, proud of their glory, and yet today they are quite forgotten; whereas the miraculous life of this humble desert-dweller is acclaimed until this day, and his memory is greatly revered by all. For the renown of holiness is eternal, and its intrinsic virtues proclaim its value.

Let us give up our flocks and herds, and so become real shepherds. Let us abandon sordid commerce, and so acquire the 'pearl of great price' (Matt. 13:46). Let us stop tilling the earth which 'brings forth thorns and thistles' (Gen. 3:18), and so become cultivators and keepers of paradise. Let us give up everything and choose the life of stillness, and so put to silence those who now reproach us for owning possessions. The best way to abash our critics is discreetly to correct in ourselves the faults for which they revile us; for such a change in those reproached puts their reproachers to shame.

There is another thing which in my opinion is truly disgraceful, and for which with good reason we are ridiculed by all. When someone has just entered the monastic life and has learnt merely about the outward practices of asceticism – how and when monks pray, what they eat and how they dress – at once he claims to teach others concerning things he has not mastered himself. He goes about with a bevy of disciples, although himself still needing instruction; he thinks it easy to be a spiritual guide, not realizing that the care of other men's souls is of all things the most difficult. For men must first be purified from old defilements, and then with close attention must learn about holiness. But when a person imagines that there is nothing beyond bodily ascetic practice, how will he correct the moral character of his pupils? How will he refashion those enslaved to evil habits? How will he help those attacked by the passions, when he knows nothing about mental warfare? How will he heal the wounds they receive when fighting, since he himself lies wounded and is in need of aid?

To master any art requires time and much instruction; can the art of arts alone be mastered without being learnt? No one without experience would go in for farming; nor would someone who has never been taught medicine try to practise as a doctor. The first would be condemned for making good farmland barren and weed-infested; the second, for making the sick worse instead of better. The only art which the uninstructed dare to practise, because they think it the simplest of all, is that of the spiritual way. What is difficult the majority regard as easy; and what Paul says he has not yet apprehended (cf. Phil. 3 : 12), they claim to know through and through, although they do not know even this: that they are totally ignorant.

This is why the monastic life has come to be treated with contempt, and those who follow it are mocked by everyone. For who would not laugh when he sees someone who yesterday served in a tavern, posing today as a teacher of virtue, surrounded by pupils? Or when he sees a man who has just left a life of civic dishonesty now swaggering all over the market-place with a crowd of disciples? If such people realized clearly how much painful toil is required to guide others on the spiritual way, and if they knew the risks involved, they would certainly abandon the task as beyond their powers. But because they remain ignorant of this and regard it as a glory to be the guide of others, they will when the moment comes tumble headlong into the pit. They think nothing of leaping into a burning furnace. They provoke laughter in those who know their previous life, and arouse God's anger by their foolhardiness. Because Eli failed to correct his children, nothing could avert God's wrath from him – neither his venerable old age, nor his past freedom of communion with God, nor the honour due to his priesthood (cf. 1 Sam. 2:12, 29; 4:18). How, then, will they escape His wrath whose previous actions have not commended them to God, who understand neither the workings of sin nor how to correct it, and who embark on this dangerous task without experience, incited by love for glory?

At first sight it seems that the only teachers our Lord had in mind were the Pharisees when He said: 'Woe to you, scribes and Pharisees, hypocrites! for you scour sea and land to gain one proselyte, and when he is gained, you make him twice as much the child of hell as yourselves' (Matt. 23:15). But in reality, by rebuking the Pharisees in this way, He was warning those who in the future would fall into the same mistake; so that, heeding His words 'Woe to you . . .', from fear of His condemnation they would restrain their improper desire for human glory. They should also recall the example of Job, and either care for their disciples as he cared for his children, or else renounce all claim to give spiritual direction. Wishing his sons to be free from sins in their mind, Job offered sacrifices every day on their behalf in case, as he said, 'my sons have thought evil in their minds against God' (Job 1:5. LXX). But these men cannot discern even outward sins, because their intelligence is still obscured by dust from the battle which they are waging against the passions. How, then, do they rashly take upon themselves the direction and cure of others, when as yet they have not cured their own passions, and when they cannot lead others to victory, since they have not yet gained the victory for themselves? First we must struggle against our own passions, watching and keeping in mind the course of the battle; and then on the basis of personal experience we can advise others about this warfare, and render victory easier for them by describing the tactics beforehand.

There are some who gain control over their passions by practising great austerities; but, as happens in skirmishes by night, they do not know how victory was won, and have no clear idea of the snares laid against them by the enemy. This is indicated symbolically by what Joshua did: while his army was crossing the Jordan at night, he ordered his men to take stones out of the river, set them up on the bank, and then cover them with whitewash and write on them how they had passed over the Jordan (cf. Josh. 4:2–9). By this he signified that the hidden thoughts underlying our passionate behaviour should be brought into the open and pilloried, and that we should not mind sharing this knowledge with others. In this way, not only will the one who has crossed know how he did it, but others who wish to do the same will cross more easily because they have been instructed. Through such experience the first teaches others.

But these self-appointed teachers lack personal experience, and do not even listen when others speak to them. Relying solely on their own self-assurance, they order their brethren to wait on them like slaves. They glory in this one thing: to have many disciples. Their main objective is to ensure that, when they go about in public, their retinue of followers is no smaller than those of their rivals. They behave like mountebanks rather than teachers. They think nothing of giving orders, however burdensome, but they fail to teach others by their own conduct. Thus they make their purpose obvious to all: they have insinuated themselves into a position of leadership, not for the benefit of their disciples, but to promote their own pleasure.

They should learn from Abimelech and Gideon that it is not words but actions that inspire people to follow a leader. Abimelech prepared a load of wood, then laid it on his own shoulders, saying: 'Make haste, and do what you have seen me do' (Judg. 9:48). Gideon also shared tasks with his men and by his own example showed them what to do, saying: 'Look at me, and do the same' (Judg. 7:17). Similarly, the Apostle said: 'These hands have ministered to my necessities, and to those who were with me' (Acts 20:34), while the Lord Himself first acted and then taught. All this proves that it is more convincing to teach through actions than through words.

But false teachers are blind to such examples, and arrogantly tell men what to do. Imagining that they know something about these matters at second hand, they are like the inexperienced shepherds who were rebuked by the prophet for carrying a sword on their arm: 'The sword is on their arm . . . and their right eye will be blinded' (cf. Zech. 11:17. LXX). For in their foolishness they have neglected right action, and so they have extinguished the light of contemplation. Yet as shepherds they are harsh and inhuman whenever they can inflict punishment. So their contemplative understanding is immediately destroyed, and then their actions, deprived of this understanding, prove misguided; for those who do not gird their sword to their thigh but carry it on their arm can neither do nor see anything. To 'gird the sword to the thigh' means to use the incisive power of the intelligence to cut off one's own passions, while to bear it 'on the arm' means to have punishment ready for the sinful acts of others. Thus Nahash the Ammonite, whose name means 'snake', threatened the Israelites gifted with contemplative insight, that he would put out all their right eyes (cf. 1 Sam. 11:2), thus depriving them of any right understanding to lead them to right action. He knew that when people proceed from contemplation to action, this right understanding enables them to make great progress. The action is good because it has first been contemplated by the clear-sighted eyes of spiritual knowledge.

Experience shows that the task of guiding others should be undertaken by someone who is equable and has no personal advantage in view. For such a person, having tasted stillness and contemplation, and begun in some measure to be inwardly at peace, will not choose to entangle his intellect with bodily cares; he will not want to turn it away from knowledge and drag it down from the spiritual to the material. This point is underlined in the well-known parable which Jotham told the men of Shechem: 'Once upon a time the trees went out to anoint a king over them; and they said . . . to the vine, "Come and reign over us." And the vine said to them: "Should I leave my wine, which cheers God and man, and go to be promoted over the trees?"' Similarly, the fig-tree declined because of its sweetness, and the olive because of its own good qualitites. Then a bramble, a barren plant full of thorns, accepted the sovereignty which they offered, though it possessed neither a special good quality of its own, nor those of the trees that were to be subject to it (cf. Judg.

9 : 7–15). Now in this parable the trees which sought a ruler were not cultivated but wild. The vine, the fig-tree and the olive refused to rule over the wild trees, preferring to bear their own fruits rather than to occupy a position of authority. Likewise, those who perceive in themselves some fruit of virtue and feel its benefit, refuse to assume leadership even when pressed by others, because they prefer this benefit to receiving honour from men.

The curse which befell the trees in the parable also falls on these people who act in a similar way. 'Let fire come out of the bramble,' it says, 'and devour the trees of the forest; or let it come out of the trees and devour the bramble.' For when these people make a harmful agreement, inevitably it proves dangerous not only to those who place themselves under an inexperienced teacher, but equally to the teacher who assumes authority over inattentive disciples. The teacher's ineptitude destroys the disciples, and the disciples' negligence endangers the teacher, especially when, because of his ineptitude, they grow lazy. For it is the teacher's duty to notice and correct all his disciples' faults, and it is the disciples' duty to obey all his instructions. It is a serious and dangerous thing both for them to commit sins and for him to overlook them.

Let no one imagine that to be a spiritual guide is an excuse for ease and self-indulgence, for nothing is so demanding as the charge of souls. Those who have charge of horses and other animals keep them under control, and so they generally achieve their purpose. But to govern men is harder, because of the variety of their characters and their deliberate cunning. Anyone undertaking this task must prepare himself for a severe struggle. He must treat the faults of all with great forbearance, and patiently teach them things of which in their ignorance they are not aware.

This is the reason why, in the temple, oxen support the basin for washing (cf. 1 Kgs. 7 : 25); and why the whole candlestick was made of solid enchased gold (cf. Exod. 25 : 31). Now the candlestick signifies that whoever intends to enlighten others must be altogether solid and firmly based, and have nothing about him empty or hollow; everything in him which is superfluous and cannot serve others as an example of holiness must be cut away. And the oxen supporting the basin signify that anyone undertaking this work should not avoid what comes to him, but ought to bear the burdens and the defilement of those weaker than himself, so long as it is safe for him to do so.

For if he is going to purify the actions of those who come to him, he must to some degree himself share their defilement, just as a basin of water, while cleaning the hands of those who wash, itself receives their dirt. For one who speaks about the passions and wipes others clean of their stain cannot escape undefiled, since the act of discussing them inevitably defiles the mind of the speaker. And even though he does not depict the sins in vivid colours, yet by speaking about them he stains the surface of his intellect.

The spiritual director must also possess knowledge of all the devices of the enemy, so that he can forewarn those under his charge about snares of which they are unaware, thus enabling them to gain victory without difficulty. Such a person is rare and not easily found. It is true that Paul says of himself: 'We are not ignorant of Satan's devices' (2 Cor. 2:11); but Job asks in perplexity: 'Who will reveal the face of his garment? and who can enter within the folds of his breastplate? Who will open the doors of his face?' (Job 41:13–14 [41:4–5. LXX]). What he means is something like this: Satan has no visible face, for he conceals his cunning beneath many garments. He deceitfully entices men with his outward appearance, while lying in wait secretly and devising their destruction. And Job, to show that he himself is not ignorant of Satan's ways, speaks clearly about his sinister powers, saying: 'His eyes are like the morning star, but his inward parts are asps' (Job 41:18 [41:10, 6. LXX]). All this he says to expose the devil's wickedness. For Satan entices men by simulating the beauty of the morning star, and when they draw near, he schemes to kill them with the asps inside him.

There is a proverb which emphasizes the hazards involved in undertaking spiritual direction: 'He who chops wood is in danger if the head of the axe flies off' (Eccles. 10:9–10. LXX). For when someone makes distinctions between things that are generally thought to be the same, trying to show the fundamental difference between what is apparently and what is really good, he runs a grave risk: if he makes a mistake, he will lead his hearers into error. Remember how one of Elisha's followers was cutting wood by the Jordan, and the head of his axe flew off and fell into the river. Realizing that he was in trouble – for the axe had been borrowed – he cried out to his teacher: 'Alas, master!' (2 Kgs. 6:5). The same thing happens to those who try to teach on the basis of what they have wrongly understood from others, and who cannot complete the task because they do not speak from personal experience. Half-way through they are discovered to be contradicting themselves; and then they admit their ignorance, finding themselves in trouble because their teaching is merely borrowed.

In the Biblical story Elisha then threw a stick into the Jordan and brought to the surface the axe-head his disciple had lost (cf. 2 Kgs. 6:6); that is to say, he revealed a thought which his disciple believed to be hidden deep within him and he exposed it to the view of those present. Here the Jordan signifies speaking about repentance, for it was in the Jordan that John performed the baptism of repentance. Now if someone does not speak accurately about repentance, but makes his listeners despise it by failing to communicate its hidden power, he lets the axe-head fall into the Jordan. But then a stick – and this signifies the Cross – brings the axe-head up from the depths to the surface. For prior to the Cross the full meaning of repentance was hidden, and anyone who tried to say something about it could easily be convicted of speaking rashly and inadequately. After the Crucifixion, however, the meaning of repentance became clear to all, for it had been revealed at the appointed time through the wood of the Cross.

My aim in saying all this is not to discourage people from assuming the spiritual direction of beginners, but to urge them first to acquire the inward state needed for so great a task, and not to undertake it without adequate preparation. They should not think of the pleasures they will enjoy – disciples to wait on them, praise from outsiders – and so overlook the dangers involved. Before peace has been established, they should not turn the weapons of war into tools for cultivation. When a man has subdued all the passions, is no longer troubled by warfare, and is not forced to use weapons in self-defence, then he may properly undertake the direction of others. But so long as the passions oppress us and we are involved in carnal war against the will of the flesh, we should constantly keep hold of our weapons; otherwise our enemies will take advantage of our relaxation and overpower us without a fight.

In order to encourage those who have struggled successfully to attain holiness, but who in their great humility think that they are not yet victorious, Scripture says: 'Beat your swords into plough-shares, and your spears into pruning hooks' (cf. Isa. 2:4). This means that they should stop worrying pointlessly about their defeated enemies, and should for the benefit of others re-equip the powers of their soul, diverting them from warfare to the cultivation of those still rank with the weeds of wickedness. But Scripture gives the opposite advice to those who, before reaching this stage, through inexperience or foolishness undertake what lies beyond their power; for to them it says: 'Beat your ploughshares into swords, and your pruning-hooks into spears' (Joel 3:10). For what is the use of farming when there is war in the land, and the produce will be enjoyed by the enemy, not by those who did the work? This is probably why the Israelites, so long as they were fighting various nations in the desert, were not permitted to take up farming, since this would have hindered them as soldiers. But once they had made peace with the enemy, they were allowed to engage in farming; for they had been told that until they entered the promised land they should do no planting. Understandably, the entry must precede the planting; for when a man has not yet reached perfection and lacks stability, the qualities he tries to implant in others will not take root.

In the spiritual life, more than anywhere else, the proper order and sequence must be observed from the start. Guests at a dinner may not like the introductory dishes and may feel more attracted by what comes later, but they are forced to comply with the order of the courses. Likewise Jacob despised Leah's ugly eyes and was more attracted by Rachel's beauty; but first he had to serve seven years to gain Leah (cf. Gen. 29:15–28). To become a true monk a man should not work backwards from the end to the beginning, but start at the beginning and so advance towards perfection. In this way he will himself gain what he seeks, and will also be able to guide his disciples to holiness.

Most people, however, without exerting any effort or making any real progress, small or great, in the practice of virtue, simply chase after the status of spiritual director, not realizing how dangerous this is. When others urge them to undertake the work of teaching, they do not refuse; indeed, they even wander about the back streets, recruiting anyone they find, and they promise all kinds of perquisites, as if making a contract with servants about food and clothing. Spiritual directors of this kind like to appear in public supported by a large crowd of attendants, and to have all the outward pomp of an abbot, as if playing a part on the stage. So as not to lose the services of their disciples, they are forced to keep on gratifying their whims. They are like a charioteer who drops the reins and lets his horses go where they like. Their disciples are allowed to run wild: carried away by their desires, they fall over precipices or stumble at every obstacle in their path, because there is no one to stop them or to restrain their disordered impulses.

Such teachers should note how Ezekiel condemns those who indulge the pleasures of others. In giving way to everyone's wishes they are treasuring up future punishment for themselves. 'Woe to the women that sew patches on every elbow,' says Ezekiel, 'and put veils on the heads of people of every age . . . so as to slay souls for a handful of barley and a piece of bread' (Ezek. 13:18–19. LXX). These false teachers are acting similarly, for they supply their bodily needs from the contributions of their disciples and wear clothes sewn together as it were from rags. By making others put veils on their heads they bring shame upon them, for men ought to pray or prophesy with their heads uncovered (cf. 1 Cor. 11:4); they render them effeminate and destroy souls that ought not to die.

Instead of doing this they ought to obey the true teacher Christ, and to refuse, as far as possible, to assume the direction of others. For He says to His disciples: 'Do not be called Rabbi' (Matt. 23:8). And if He admonished Peter and John and the rest of the apostles to avoid such work and to consider themselves unworthy of such a position, how can anyone imagine himself superior to them and claim for himself the office from which they were debarred? For in saying 'Do not be called Rabbi', He does not mean that we are free to assume the office so long as we avoid the title.

But what if someone, not from any choice of his own, is obliged to accept one or two disciples, and so to become the spiritual director of others as well? First, let him examine himself carefully, to see whether he can teach them through his actions rather than his words, setting his own life before them as a model of holiness. He must take care that, through copying him, they do not obscure the beauty of holiness with the ugliness of sin. He should also realize that he ought to work as hard for his disciples' salvation as he does for his own; for, having once accepted responsibility for them, he will be accountable to God for them as well as for himself. That is why the saints tried to leave behind them disciples whose

holiness was no less than their own, and to change these disciples
from their original condition to a better state. Thus Paul the Apostle
changed Onesimus from a runaway slave into a martyr (cf. Philem.
10–19); Elijah turned Elisha from a ploughman into a prophet (cf.
1 Kgs. 19:19); Moses transmitted special gifts to Joshua, though he
was younger than all the rest (cf. Deut. 31:7–8); and Eli made
Samuel greater than himself (cf. 1 Sam. 3:19–20). In each of these
cases the disciple was helped by his own efforts, but the chief cause
of his progress was the fact that he had found a teacher capable of
fanning the smouldering spark of his zeal and of kindling it into
flame. So these teachers became God's spokesmen, communicating
His will to others; for God says: 'If you bring forth the precious
from the vile, you shall be as My mouth' (Jer. 15:19).

God also showed Ezekiel what the teacher's attitude should be,
and what kind of change he should bring about in his disciples: 'Son
of man,' He says, 'take a tile, and lay it before you, and portray
upon it the city, even Jerusalem' (Ezek. 4:1). This means that the
teacher should transform his disciple from clay into a holy temple.
The words 'and lay it before you' are particularly significant, for the
disciple will quickly improve if he is continually in the sight of his
teacher. The constant influence of a good example marks other souls
with its own impress, so long as they are not completely stubborn and
insensitive. The reason Gehazi and Judas succumbed, the first to
theft and the second to treachery, was that they withdrew from the
sight of their teachers: had they remained under the restraining
influence of their teacher's eye, they would not have sinned.

God likewise indicates that the disciples' negligence endangers
the teacher himself, when He says: 'And you shall set a frying-pan
between yourself and the tile; and it shall be a wall between the
tile and you' (cf. Ezek. 4:3). For if the teacher wishes to avoid the
punishment suffered by a lazy disciple whom he has changed from
clay into a city, he should tell this disciple of the chastisement that
awaits those who relapse; and then his words of warning will serve
as a wall, separating the innocent from the guilty. That is what God
means when He says to Ezekiel: 'Son of man, I have set you as a
watchman over the house of Israel; and if you see the sword threatening one of them and do not give him warning, and he dies, I will
require his soul at your hand' (cf. Ezek. 3:17–18).

Moses made such a wall for himself when he said to the Israelites:

'Watch yourselves, so that you do not try to follow them after they have been destroyed before you' (Deut. 12 : 30. LXX). For if some-one does not watch his mind attentively, he will find that, after he has cut down the passions, the images of past fantasies begin to emerge again like young shoots. If he constantly allows these images to force their way into his intellect and does not bar their entry, the passions will once more establish themselves within him; despite his previous victory, he will have to struggle against them again. For, after being tamed and taught to graze like cattle, the passions can become savage once more through our negligence and regain the ferocity of wild beasts. It is to prevent this that Scripture says: 'Do not try to follow them after they have been destroyed before you'; that is, we must not allow our soul to form the habit of taking pleasure in fantasies of this kind, and so to relapse into its previous wickedness.

Realizing this, Jacob hid the images of the strange gods at Shechem, and 'destroyed them up to the present day' (Gen. 35:4. LXX); for he knew that to look at such things and constantly to think about them harms the mind by impressing upon it clear and distinct images of shameful fantasies. Our struggle against the passions should hide and destroy them, not just for a short time, but 'up to the present day', that is, for all time; since 'the present day' is co-extensive with every age, always referring to the present moment. Now Shechem means 'to shoulder', thus signifying the struggle against the passions. Joseph was sent to Shechem and fought an arduous battle there against the passions (cf. Gen. 37:12–28). Like-wise Jacob said that he took Shechem by sword and bow (cf. Gen. 34:26), meaning that he subdued the passions after a hard struggle, hiding them in the earth at Shechem.

Now there is evidently a difference between hiding gods at Shechem and placing an idol in a secret place. The first action is praised while the second is condemned, for Scripture says: 'Cursed is he who puts an idol in a secret place' (cf. Deut. 27:15). To hide something completely in the earth is not the same as putting it in a secret place; for what is hidden in the earth and no longer per-ceived by the senses is in time erased even from the memory, whereas what is put in a secret place may escape the attention of others, but it is constantly seen by whoever put it there, and so the memory of it is kept fresh, since it is carried about secretly as an

image in the mind. Every shameful thought formed in the mind is a
secret idol. If it is disgraceful to disclose such thoughts to others,
it is also dangerous to set them as an idol in a secret place; and it is
even more dangerous to search for images that have already been
made to disappear, since our mind readily inclines towards a passion
that we have previously expelled, and we are drawn towards it by
sensual pleasure.

From this we may understand that virtue is a thing most delicately
balanced, and that if neglected it quickly turns into its opposite.
Scripture seems to refer to this symbolically, saying: 'The land into
which you go so as to inherit it is a land subject to change through the
movement of the peoples' (Ezra 9 : 11. LXX). For as soon as someone
who has attained the state of virtue inclines towards its opposite, his
virtue is thereby altered, being 'a land subject to change'. So from
the moment that harmful fantasies appear we should deny them
entry into our mind. We should not allow it to 'go down into
Egypt', for from there it is led away into captivity by the Assyrians
(cf. Jer. 42 : 19; 43 : 2–3). For when the mind descends into the
darkness of impure thoughts – and that is what Egypt means – then
the passions drag it forcibly and against its will into their service.

This is why the Lawgiver, symbolically commanding us to deny
entry to sensual pleasure, told us to watch the head of the serpent,
because it is watching our heel (cf. Gen. 3 : 15). Its aim is to bite
our heel and so to poison us; whereas our aim is to crush every
provocation to sensual pleasure, for when the provocation is
crushed, sensuality has little power over us. Samson surely would
not have been able to burn the Philistines' crops unless he had
first turned the foxes' heads in opposite directions, tied their tails
together, and put a burning torch between them (cf. Judg. 15:4).
This means that we should learn to detect the attack of deceitful
thoughts from premonitory signs and to watch their first beginnings,
which they contrive to make attractive in appearance so as to attain
their end; then we can expose the wickedness of these thoughts by
comparing their first beginnings with the final results. This is to tie
the tails together and to set between them a torch, thus showing
things up for what they are.

To clarify what has been said, let us take two examples. Often
the vice of unchastity has its first beginning in self-esteem; the
gateway at the entrance appears attractive, but hidden behind it lies

the destructive path that leads the mindless into the realm of death. Under the influence of self-esteem, a man may perhaps enter the priesthood or the life of monastic perfection; and because many come to him for help, his self-esteem makes him think highly of himself thanks to what he says and does. So, by beguiling him with such thoughts, self-esteem draws him far away from the inner watchfulness that he should possess. Then it suggests to him that he should meet a woman of supposedly holy life, and so leads him to assent to an act of carnal lust, depriving his conscience of its intimate communion with God and plunging it into abject disgrace. To 'tie tail to tail' like Sampson, let us reflect how this man's thought began and where it led him; and let us consider how he was punished for his self-esteem by falling into a shameful act of unchastity. Then we we shall see clearly the contrast between the beginning and the end, and the way they are linked together.

To take a second example: the vice of gluttony can lead to that of unchastity; and this in turn can lead to the vice of dejection. For as soon as one who has been overcome by the vice of unchastity regains the state of inner watchfulness, he is filled with despondency and dejection. When pursuing the spiritual way, therefore, we should not be influenced by the pleasures of eating or the allurements of sensuality, but should consider where they both end up. And when we find that they lead to dejection, we have 'tied tail to tail' and, by showing things up for what they are, we have set the crops of the Philistines on fire with a burning torch.

Since warfare against the passions requires such knowledge and experience, anyone who assumes the task of spiritual direction should realize how much he needs to know in order to lead those under his charge to 'the prize of the high calling' (Phil. 3:14), and to teach them clearly all that this warfare entails. He should not pretend to gain the victory by shadow-boxing, but must engage in a real battle with the enemy and inflict deadly wounds upon him. This struggle is far harder than any gymnastic contest. When an athlete's body is thrown to the ground, he can easily get up; but in the spiritual warfare it is men's souls that fall, and then it is very difficult for them to rise once more.

If a man, while still battling against the passions and stained with blood, tries to build a temple of God out of souls made in the divine image, he should listen to these words: 'You shall not build Me a temple, because you are a man of blood' (cf. 1 Chr. 22:8). To build a temple for God one must be in a state of peace. Moses took the tabernacle and pitched it outside the camp (cf. Exod. 33:7): this shows that the teacher must be far removed from the tumult of war and the confusion of the camp, and must have attained a peaceful and unwarlike state.

But even when such teachers have been found, they require disciples who have renounced themselves and their own will, so as to become exactly like dead bodies or the raw material in the craftsman's hand. Just as the soul acts as it wishes in the body, without the body offering any opposition, and just as the raw material does not resist the craftsman when he demonstrates his skill by working upon it, so disciples should be obedient to their teacher when he is guiding them to holiness, and should not contradict him in any way. If they become over-curious about the manner in which he is performing his task and start questioning his instructions, they hinder their own progress.

What seems reasonable and convincing to the inexperienced is not necessarily correct. The skilled craftsman judges things quite differently from the unskilled man, for the first is guided by precise knowledge, the second by what seems to him probable. Now probability relies on guesswork and is usually wrong, for it is closely related to error. For example, when a ship is sailing close to the wind, the helmsman tells the people on board to do what seems the more improbable: to leave the side of the ship which has risen up out of the water and against which the wind is exerting greater pressure, and to sit on the side which is dipping down into the waves. Considerations of probability would lead us to expect exactly the opposite advice. Nevertheless, those who are in the ship obey the helmsman rather than their own ideas; of necessity they defer to the skill of the man in charge, however questionable his instructions may appear. Surely, then, those who have entrusted their salvation to others should abandon all notions of probability and submit to the skill of the expert, judging his knowledge more trustworthy than their own opinions.

Those who renounce the world should in the first place make sure that they keep back nothing. They should fear the terrible example of Ananias, who thought that no one would notice if he kept back something for himself, and who was condemned by God for stealing (cf. Acts 5:1–10). They should renounce not only themselves but everything they have, knowing that whatever they retain will form an object of continuing attraction to their minds, and so will draw them away from higher things and eventually cut them off altogether from the brotherhood. Let us recall the lives of the men of old, written by the Holy Spirit: here appropriate examples can be found to bring each man to the truth, whatever his way of life. When Elisha placed himself under his teacher, how did he renounce the world? Scripture says that he was ploughing with twelve pairs of oxen before him, and that he killed the cattle, made a fire of their harness, and roasted them (cf. 1 Kgs. 19:19, 21). This gives us some idea how eager he was. He did not say, 'I shall sell the harness and distribute the money appropriately'; he did not calculate that the things would do more good if sold. Entirely absorbed by his desire to join his teacher, he despised all visible things and sought to get rid of them, because they would distract him from his intention; and he knew that delay often leads to a change of mind. And why did the Lord, when He spoke to the rich man about the life of perfection ordained by God, instruct him to sell his possessions and give the money to the poor, keeping back nothing for himself (cf. Matt. 19:21)? Was it not because He knew that anything kept back would give rise to all kinds of distractions? And I think that when Moses requires those who wish to sanctify themselves through intense prayer to shave their entire body, he is likewise demanding the complete renunciation of possessions (cf. Num. 8:7).

In the second place, those embracing the monastic life should forget their relatives and friends to such an extent that they are never troubled at all by memories of them. When the Ark was being pulled in a cart by two cows, it made them forget their own nature. Their calves had been taken from them and shut up at home, and there was no one driving the cows; yet they finished the journey without making a mistake, turning aside to neither right nor left (cf. 1 Sam. 6:12). Though distressed by the separation from their calves, they did not moo; though labouring under the weight of the Ark and subject to the tyranny of their natural instincts, they kept to the direct route as though walking along a straight line, so overwhelming was their reverence for the Ark that was in the cart. If cows acted in this manner, should not equal reverence be shown by those who have undertaken to carry the spiritual Ark? Indeed, their reverence should be far greater; otherwise human nature formed in God's image would be surpassed by the beasts, for men would be failing to do by conscious choice what animals did by necessity.

Perhaps the reason why Joseph wandered in the desert was because he sought to attain perfection without renouncing the bonds of kinship (cf. Gen. 37:15–16). Thus the man who asked him the reason for his wandering gathered from his answer that it was his attachment to his relatives, and not the fact that he was a shepherd; for he said: 'I seek my brethren; tell me, I pray you, where they feed their flocks.' But had he possessed a true understanding of the shepherd's art, he would have said 'tend' and not 'feed'. The man answered: 'They have gone away; for I heard them say, Let us go to Dothan' (Gen. 37:17). Now Dothan means 'sufficient detachment'; and so the man's answer teaches one who is still wandering because of attachment to his relatives that it is not possible to attain perfection unless one has fully abandoned all such attachment. It is not enough to depart from Haran (cf. Gen. 29:4), a name which means 'caves', and so signifies the senses. Again, it is not enough to go out from the valley of Hebron (cf. Gen. 37:14), that is, of humble works, and to leave the desert in which those who seek perfection are still wandering. For unless we reach Dothan – that is, attain sufficient detachment – we gain nothing from our efforts; if bonds of kinship still hold us under their spell, we shall fail to attain perfection. Indeed, the Lord himself strongly urged us to abandon bonds of kinship; for He rebuked Mary the Mother of God because she sought Him among His relatives (cf. Luke 2:49), and He said that whoever loves father and mother more than Him is unworthy of Him (cf. Matt. 10:37).

After they have succeeded in these two things, those who have only recently escaped from the agitation of the world should be advised to practise stillness; otherwise, by frequently going out, they will reopen the wounds inflicted on their mind through the senses. They should take care not to add new images to their old fantasies. Those who have only just renounced the world find stillness hard to practise, for memory now has time to stir up all the filth that is within them, whereas previously it had no chance to do this because of their many preoccupations. But, though hard to practise, stillness will in time free the intellect from being disturbed by impure thoughts. Since the aim is to cleanse the soul and purify it

from all defilement, such people should avoid everything that makes
it unclean. They should keep their intelligence in a state of profound
calm, far from all that irritates it, and should refrain from talking
with men of frivolous character. They should embrace solitude, the
mother of wisdom.

If these people mix freely with the confusion of the outside world,
it is easy for them to be caught again in the snares from which they
thought they had escaped. When one is aiming at holiness it is useless
to indulge in the very things one has condemned and run away
from. But such is the force of habit that they are in danger of losing
the stillness which they have acquired with so much effort, and of
reverting to their shameful ways, reviving memories of forgotten
sins. The intellect of someone who has lately withdrawn from sin is
like a body that has begun to recover from a protracted illness:
when the physical organism is in this state, something quite trivial
is enough to cause a relapse, since it has not yet fully regained its
strength. Likewise, when a man has only just embarked on the
monastic life, the sinews of his intellect are weak and flabby and
there is a danger that his passions will return, for they are naturally
aroused by contact with the tumult of the world outside. That is
why Moses ordered those who wished to escape the destroying angel
to stay indoors, saying: 'None of you shall go out of the door of his
house, lest the destroyer touch him' (cf. Exod. 12:22–23).
Jeremiah, too, seems to give the same advice: 'Do not go out into
the field, or walk by the way, for the sword of the enemy . . . is on
every side' (Jer. 6:25).

A veteran of tested courage goes out to engage the enemy at
close quarters, but anyone incapable of fighting should stay at home
out of harm's way, keeping safe from danger by remaining quiet
and in stillness. Joshua, the son of Nun, acted in this way; for it is
written: 'His servant Joshua, a young man, did not go out of the
tabernacle' (Exod. 33:11). He knew from the story of Abel that
those who go out into the battlefield and engage prematurely in the
fight are killed by their relatives and friends (cf. Gen. 4:8). The
same lesson may be learnt from the story of Dinah (cf. Gen. 34:1ff).
It is the mark of a girlish mind for one to attempt things beyond
one's power, and falsely to imagine that one's own resources are
adequate. If Dinah had not rashly gone to see what was going on in
the neighbourhood, supposing herself strong enough to resist its

attractions, her soul's judgment would not have been seduced by sensory things and corrupted before growing to maturity; for her lawful husband, the spiritual power of the intelligence, was not yet known to her. Wishing to uproot this passion of presumption that has established itself within man, God said to Moses: 'Fill the children of Israel with a spirit of reverence' (Lev. 15:31. LXX). For rashly to undertake tasks beyond one's power is contrary to the spirit of reverence.

Before we are properly trained, then, we should avoid the agitation of city life and keep our minds far from all distracting noise. It is no great gain to renounce things, and then to listen all the time to gossip about them – to leave the city and its activities, and yet to sit at the gate like Lot (cf. Gen. 19:1) and be filled with the tumult that comes from inside. But like Moses we should abandon the city altogether, avoiding not only its activities but also any talk about them. 'When I depart from the city', says Moses, 'and stretch out my hands, the sounds will cease' (Exod. 9:29. LXX).

When we not only refrain from worldly actions but no longer call them to mind, we have attained true tranquillity. This gives the soul the opportunity to look at the impressions previously stamped on the mind, and to struggle against each one and eliminate it. So long as we go on receiving new impressions, our intelligence is occupied with them and so it is not possible to erase the earlier ones. In consequence our struggle to eradicate the passions is inevitably far harder, since these passions have become strong through being allowed to increase gradually; and now, like a river in full flood, they drown the soul's discernment with one fantasy after another.

If we want to make a river-bed dry, perhaps to investigate something of interest, it is no use drawing off the water in the particular place where we imagine the thing to be, since more water keeps flowing down. But if we cut off the flow from above, the river-bed becomes dry without any further effort on our part: the water automatically runs away, and so we can examine what interests us. Likewise, as soon as the senses are no longer supplying material from outside, it becomes easy to empty our mind of the impressions that produce the passions. But when the senses keep conveying a constant stream of impressions, it is not just difficult but completely impossible to free the intellect from this inundation.

Now when we are continually meeting other people, we are not consciously troubled by the passions, because they lack the opportunity to become active; yet they persist unnoticed within us, and the longer they remain, the stronger they grow. If the ground is constantly trodden underfoot, the weeds, though present in it, do not rise above the surface; but they thrust vigorous and thriving roots deep into the earth, and then, as soon as they get the chance, they shoot up above ground. Similarly, if we are always meeting other people, the passions are prevented from emerging into the open; nevertheless they grow steadily more powerful and then, taking advantage of the life of stillness which we have begun to pursue, they attack us with great force. Our struggle with them is hard and dangerous because we failed to fight against them when they first occurred.

That is why the prophet commanded the Israelites to 'destroy the seed from Babylon' (Jer. 50:16 [27:16. LXX]), meaning that we should erase sense-impressions before they penetrate into the mind. For if we let them enter the earth of our mind and grow, and if we allow them to be watered with violent rains by repeatedly thinking about them, they will produce a plentiful crop of evil. The Psalms praise those who do not wait for the passions to grow to full strength but kill them in infancy: 'Blessed is he who seizes your little ones and dashes them against the rock' (Ps. 137:9). Perhaps Job, too, is hinting at some such thing when, reflecting on the course of his life, he says that the rush and the flag flourish in the river, but wither when deprived of water (cf. Job. 8:11). And his statement that the 'ant-lion[1] has perished for lack of food' (Job 4:11. LXX) would seem to have a similar significance. Wishing to show how the passions ensnare us, he coined this composite name from the boldest of all creatures, the lion, and the most trivial, the ant. For the provocations of the passions begin with trivial fantasies, creeping up unnoticed like an ant; but eventually the passions grow to an enormous size and their attack is as dangerous as a lion's. One who is pursuing the spiritual way should therefore fight the passions when they approach like ants, hoping to deceive him by their trivial appearance. For if they are allowed to gain a lion's strength, it is hard to resist them and to refuse them the food they demand.

Now the food of the passions, as we have already stated many

---

[1] This imaginary creature is not to be confused with the insect of the same name.

times, consists of sense-impressions. They nourish the passions by
attacking the soul with a succession of mental fantasies or idols.
This is why Moses put screens of latticework round the altar in the
tabernacle (cf. Exod. 27:4), signifying that if we wish to keep our
mind pure like a tabernacle we should do the same. Just as the
lattices round the altar prevented anything unclean from entering,
so we should weave a mental barrier against the senses by reflecting
on the terrors of the coming judgment, and so bar the entry to
unclean impressions. Ahaziah became ill because he fell from a
lattice-window (cf. 2 Kgs. 1:2); and to fall from a lattice-window
means to succumb to sensual pleasure because, when tempted, we
did not reflect seriously about the future retribution. And what
can be worse than this kind of illness? For the body falls ill when the
balance of its constituent elements is impaired, because one of them
has come to predominate in a manner contrary to nature. But the
soul falls ill when its right judgment is impaired and it is overcome
by the passions which cause disease.

Solomon wove such lattices for the eyes of all those capable of
understanding his meaning when he said: 'When your eyes see a
strange woman, your mouth will speak crooked things' (Prov.
23:33. LXX). By 'crooked things' he means the answer which, after
sinning, we shall give at the time of retribution; but when we judge
things in the right way, this prevents any dangerous gazing with our
eyes and saves us from the confusion we should otherwise be in at
that time. Solomon continues: 'Be like someone who lies down in
the midst of the sea, and like a pilot in a great storm' (Prov.
23:34. LXX). Now if someone at the actual moment of temptation
resists the sight which is tempting him, he is struggling to escape
future punishment like a man battling in a storm at sea. Then he
easily overcomes his assailants, not noticing the wounds they inflict,
and he is able to say: 'They struck me, but I felt no pain; they
mocked me, but I paid no attention' (Prov. 23:35. LXX). 'They
struck me,' he is saying, 'and thought they had made a fool of me;
yet I did not notice the wounds – for they were like children's
arrows – and I paid no attention to their tricks, but behaved as if
they were not there.' David also despised such adversaries, for he
said: 'When the evil one turned away from me, I did not notice'
(Ps. 101:4. LXX). By this he means: 'I perceived them neither
when they approached nor when they withdrew.'

Many of us, however, do not even realize that through the senses
we enter into close association with sensory objects, and that such
association leads easily to deception. We do not suspect the harm
that results from this, but are unguardedly carried away by these
sense-impressions. How, then, at the moment when we are being
deceived will we recognize the trap that has been laid for us, since
we have not been trained to discern such things? The war fought
by the Assyrians against the men of Sodom (cf. Gen. 14: 1–2) shows
how the senses fight against sensory objects, and how the latter
exact tribute from the senses when these are defeated. The Scriptural narrative records the agreement, truce and peace-offerings
made at the Dead Sea by the four kings of the Assyrians and the five
kings of the regions round Sodom; then the bondage of the five
kings for twelve years; then their revolt in the thirteenth year, and
the war that ensued in the fourteenth year when the four kings
attacked the five and took them captive.

Such was the external course of events. Now this story teaches us
something about ourselves and about the warfare of our senses
against sensory objects. The five kings represent the five senses and
the four kings the objects of sense-perception. All of us, from birth
up to the age of twelve, uncritically allow our senses to be controlled by the objects of sense-perception, because our power of
discrimination has not yet been purified. We let our senses obey
sensory objects as if they were the masters; our sense of sight is
controlled by things visible, our hearing by sounds, our taste by
flavours, our sense of smell by odours, and our sense of touch by
physical objects. Because we are children, we cannot discriminate
between the various things we perceive or offer any opposition to
them. But when our judgment starts to mature and we become
aware of the harm we are suffering, we at once begin to think of
rebelling against this slavery and escaping from it. And if we continue firm in this resolve, we can escape from these cruel masters
and remain for ever free. But if we waver in our decision, we betray
our senses into captivity once more: they are overcome by the
power of sensory objects, and from then on they endure a tyrannical
servitude without any hope of escape. This is why the five kings in
the story, after being defeated by the four, were driven to wells of
pitch (cf. Gen. 14: 10. LXX); in other words those who are overcome by sensory things turn with each of their senses to the objects

proper to that sense, as if to pits and wells. Henceforth they think about nothing except visible objects, because they have fixed their desire upon what is earthly and are more attached to the things of this world than to those of the intellect.

Similarly, when a slave has come to love his master and his own wife and children, he may reject true freedom because of his bonds of physical kinship; and so he becomes a slave for ever, allowing his ear to be pierced through with an awl (cf. Exod. 21:6). He will never hear the word that can set him free, but will remain perpetually a slave in his love for present things. This is why the Law commanded that a woman's hand should be cut off if she seized hold of the genitals of a man who was fighting with another (cf. Deut. 25:11); in other words, when there was a battle between her thoughts, whether to choose worldly or heavenly blessings, she failed to choose the heavenly and grasped those which are subject to generation and corruption – for by the genitals the Law signifies the things which belong to the realm of change.

We gain nothing, therefore, by our decision to renounce earthly things if we do not abide by it, but continue to be attracted by such things and allow ourselves to keep thinking about them. By constantly looking back like Lot's wife towards what we have renounced, we make clear our attachment to it. For she looked back and was turned into a pillar of salt, remaining to this day an example to the disobedient (cf. Gen. 19:26). She symbolizes the force of habit, which draws us back again after we have tried to make a definitive act of renunciation.

What does the Law mean when it commands anyone entering the temple not to return, after finishing his prayers, by the door through which he entered, but to go straight out through the opposite door without changing direction? It means that we should keep to the path that leads straight to holiness, not allowing any doubts to make us turn back. By habitually thinking about what we have left behind, we undermine our determination to advance and we are pulled in the opposite direction, returning to our old sins. It is a terrible thing when the force of habit holds us fast, not allowing us to rise to the state of virtue which we possessed initially. For habit leads to a set disposition, and this in turn becomes what may be called 'second nature'; and it is hard to shift and alter nature. For though it may yield a little to pressure, it quickly reasserts itself. It may be shaken and forced to give way, but it is not permanently changed, unless through prolonged effort we retrace our steps, abandoning our bad habits and returning to the state of virtue we possessed when we first made our renunciation.

The soul that succumbs to past habits and gives all its attention to material things, which lack true reality, is like Rachel sitting on Laban's idols; it does not listen to the teaching which would raise it up to higher things, but says like Rachel: 'I cannot rise up before you, for the custom of women is upon me' (Gen. 31 : 35). For the soul which has long been brooding on the things of this life is indeed 'sitting on idols'. Insubstantial in themselves, these idols are given substance by human artifice. Wealth, fame and the other things of this life all lack substance, for there is nothing clear and distinct about them. They possess a specious resemblance to reality, but change from day to day. We ourselves give them substance when in our thoughts we shape fantasies about things that serve no real purpose. With our fertile imagination we exceed the basic needs of the body to the point of impossible luxury; we lavish innumerable sauces on our food; to show off, we dress up in expensive and luxurious clothes; and when criticized for this useless extravagance we answer that we are merely doing what is fitting and proper. What else are we trying to do in all this but to give substance to what in itself lacks reality?

We rightly spoke of such a soul as 'sitting on idols'. For when the soul becomes firmly attached to these unreal objects, it is enslaved to habit instead of serving truth, and through habit it is defiling the real nature of things, as though with menstrual blood. Scripture uses the expression 'sitting' to signify both failure to do what is right and also love of pleasure. It has in mind failure to do what is right when it speaks of 'those that sit in darkness and the shadow of death, fettered by poverty and iron' (Isa. 9 : 2 ; Ps. 107 : 10. LXX), for darkness and fetters prevent us from taking action. And it has in mind love of pleasure when it speaks of those who in their hearts turned back toward Egypt and said one to another: 'We remembered how we sat by the flesh-pots and ate our fill of meat' (cf. Exod. 16 : 3). Those who love pleasure, keeping their appetites hot and humid, are indeed sitting by the flesh-pots; for gluttony engenders love of pleasure and many other passions as well. It is the root from which the rest of the passions spring up in vigorous growth, little by little developing as suckers alongside the mother tree, and putting out branches of evil that reach up to the sky.

Avarice, anger and dejection are all offshoots of gluttony. For the glutton needs money first of all, so as to satisfy his ever-present desire – even though it never can be satisfied. His anger is inevitably aroused against those who obstruct his acquisition of money, and in turn gives place to dejection when he proves too weak to get his way. He is like the snake which goes 'on its breast and belly' (Gen. 3 : 14. LXX). For when he possesses the material means for pleasure, he goes on his belly; but when he lacks these he goes on his breast, since this is where the incensive power has its seat. For those who love pleasure, when deprived of it, grow angry and embittered. Moses therefore made the priest wear a breastplate, intimating through this symbol that he should inwardly restrain every impulse to anger by means of the intelligence; for it is termed 'the breast-plate of judgment' (Exod. 28 : 15). Now the priest must control this passion by means of the intelligence, for he is imperfect. Moses, however, being perfect, totally removed from himself the impulse to anger; figuratively speaking, he does not wear a breastplate but removes, as it were, his own breast. Thus Scripture says: 'Moses removed the breast, and brought it as an offering before the Lord' (Lev. 8 : 29. LXX). There are others who neither eliminate anger completely nor control it with the intelligence, but who overcome it by laborious efforts. They are said to remove the breast 'with their arm', the arm being a symbol of toil and work. Similarly, to go 'on the belly' is a very apt symbol for the life of pleasure, since the belly is the cause of virtually all the pleasures: when the belly has been filled, our desires for other pleasures are intensified, but when it is not full they subside.

Here is another illustration of the difference between one who is perfect and one who is still making progress. Moses, completely rejecting the pleasures of food, 'washed the belly and the feet with water' (Lev. 8 : 21). Here 'belly' signifies pleasure, and 'feet' a man's ascent and progress. He who is still progressing, on the other hand, washes what is inside the belly, but not the belly as a whole. Note that in this passage it says 'he washed', not 'they shall wash'. The first represents something voluntary, while the second indicates an action performed in obedience to a command. He who is perfect does what is right, not because of any command, but by his own free choice; whereas he who is still progressing acts in obedience to his superior. With very great care he removes, as it were, the breast in its entirety, but he does not remove the belly – he only washes it. The wise man is able altogether to renounce and eradicate wrath, but he is unable to eliminate the belly, since nature compels even the most ascetic to eat a bare minimum of food.

When, however, the soul does not submit to the true and stable guidance of the intelligence, but has been corrupted by impure pleasures, the belly becomes distended; for even when the body is sated, desire is unsatisfied. And if the belly is swollen, the thigh will rot (cf. Num. 5:22); for when the belly is inflamed by luxurious foods, the mind loses all power to conceive what is good and is paralysed in its spiritual efforts. It is to these spiritual efforts that the Law is referring when it talks about the thigh.

The lover of pleasure, then, goes on his belly, wallowing in sensual indulgence. But one who is beginning to pursue the spiritual way gets rid of the fat round his belly by giving up rich food. One who has progressed further cleanses what is inside his belly, while he who is perfect washes the whole of the belly, entirely rejecting what is superfluous to his basic needs. Very appropriately, Scripture applies the word 'goes' (Gen. 3:14) to the man who has sunk down upon his chest and belly, for sensual pleasure is characteristic of those who are restless and full of agitation, not of those who are still and calm.

Sexual desire is even more closely related to gluttony than are the passions of anger and dejection mentioned above. Nature herself has indicated the intimate connection between the two by placing the organs of sexual intercourse immediately below the belly. If lust is weak, it is because the belly has been made to go in want; while if lust is easily excited, it is from the belly that it derives its strength.

As well as nursing and feeding these passions, gluttony also destroys everything good. Once it gains the upper hand, it drives out self-control, moderation, courage, fortitude and all the other virtues. This is what Jeremiah cryptically indicates when he says: 'And the chief cook of the Babylonians pulled down the wall of Jerusalem round about' (cf. 2 Kgs. 25:9–10; Jer. 52:14. LXX).[1] Here the 'chief cook' signifies the passion of gluttony; for a chef

[1] The Hebrew word here translated 'chief cook' also means 'captain of the guard'.

makes every effort to minister to the belly, devising innumerable ways of giving it pleasure, and gluttony does just the same. A great variety of different foods overthrows the fortress of the virtues and razes it to the ground. Sauces and condiments are the siege-engines that batter against virtue and overthrow it, even when it is already firmly established. And while over-indulgence destroys the virtues, frugality destroys the stronghold of vice. Just as the chief cook of the Babylonians pulled down the walls of Jerusalem (and Jerusalem means a soul that is at peace) by encouraging fleshly pleasures through the art of cooking, so in the dream the Israelite's cake of barley bread, rolling down the hill, knocked down the Midianite tent (cf. Judg. 7 : 13); for a frugal diet, steadily maintained – gathering impetus, as it were, from year to year – destroys the impulse to unchastity. The Midianites symbolize the passions of unchastity, because it was they who introduced this vice into Israel and deceived a great number of the young people (cf. Num. 31 : 9). Scripture aptly says that the Midianites had tents while Jerusalem had a wall; for all the things that contain virtue are wellfounded and firm, whereas those that contain vice are an external appearance – a tent – and are no different from fantasy.

In order to escape such vice, the saints fled from the towns and avoided meeting a large number of people, for they knew that the company of corrupt men is more destructive than a plague. This is why, indifferent to gain, they let their estates become sheep-pastures, so as to avoid distractions. This is why Elijah left Judaea and went to live on Mount Carmel (cf. 1 Kgs. 18 : 19), which was desolate and full of wild animals; and apart from what grew on trees and shrubs there was nothing to eat, so he kept himself alive on nuts and berries. Elisha followed the same mode of life, inheriting from his teacher, besides many other good things, a love of the wilderness (cf. 2 Kgs. 2 : 25). John, too, dwelt in the wilderness of Jordan, 'eating locusts and wild honey' (Mark 1 : 6); thus he showed us that our bodily needs can be satisfied without much trouble, and he reproached us for our elaborate pleasures. Possibly Moses was instituting a general law in this matter when he commanded the Israelites to gather daily no more than one day's supply of manna (cf. Exod. 16 : 16–17), thereby ordaining in a concealed fashion that men should live from day to day and not make preparations for the morrow. He thought it right that creatures made in the divine image should be content with whatever comes to hand and should trust God to supply the rest; otherwise, by making provision for the future, they seem to lack faith in God's gifts of grace and to be afraid that He will cease to bestow His continual blessings upon mankind.

In short, this is why all the saints, 'of whom the world was not worthy', left the inhabited regions and 'wandered in deserts and in mountains, and in dens and caves of the earth', going about 'in sheepskins, in goatskins, being destitute, afflicted, tormented' (Heb. 11:37–38). They fled from the sophisticated wickedness of men and from all the unnatural things of which the towns are full, not wishing to be swept off their feet and carried along with all the others into the whirlpool of confusion. They were glad to live with the wild beasts, judging them less harmful than their fellow men. They avoided men as being treacherous, while they trusted the animals as their friends; for animals do not teach us to sin, but revere and respect holiness. Thus men tried to kill Daniel but the lions saved him, preserving him when he had been unjustly condemned out of malice (cf. Dan. 6:16–23); and when human justice had miscarried, the animals proclaimed his innocence. Whereas Daniel's holiness gave rise to strife and envy among men, among the wild animals it evoked awe and veneration.

All of us, then, who long to make spiritual progress should strive to imitate the holiness of the saints. Let us rid ourselves of enslavement to the body's demands and pursue freedom. The wild ass was made by the Creator to run free in the wilderness: he does not hear the chiding of the driver and laughs to scorn the crowds in the town (cf. Job 39:5–7). But until this moment we have made him carry burdens, placing him under the yoke of passion and sin. Let us now loose him from his bonds, despite the objections of those who through long habit have acquired control over him, even though they are not his masters by nature. Certainly when they hear us say, not with our tongue alone but in all sincerity, 'The Lord has need of him' (Mark 11:3), they will at once release him. Then, covered with the apostles' garments, he will become the bearer of the divine Logos. Set loose in his original place of grazing, he will be able to 'search after every green thing' (Job 39:8) – which means he will seek the riches of Holy Scripture and so be led to the life of perfection, gaining nourishment and joy. But why, we ask, does the wild ass, created by God to live in the salt land of the desert, 'search after every green thing', since generally such land is not suitable for the growth of plants? The answer must be that, where the moisture of the passions has dried up and there is a desert, it is possible to seek the inner truth contained in Scripture.

Let us leave behind wordly things and raise ourselves towards the soul's true good. How long shall we continue with trivial playthings? Will we never assume a manly spirit? We are more feeble than tiny children, and unlike them we make no progress towards greater things. When they grow up, they abandon their games, readily relinquishing their attachment to the things they played with – nuts, knucklebones, balls and so on. They are attached to these and prize them so long as their understanding is immature; but when they grow up and become men, they drop such things and devote their full attention to the affairs of adult life. We, however, have remained children, enchanted by what really deserves mockery and derision. Abandoning all effort to attain higher things and to develop an adult intelligence, we are seduced by worldly amusements, making ourselves a laughing-stock to those who judge things at their true value. It is disgraceful for a grown man to be seen sitting and drawing pictures in the dust to amuse children; and it is equally disgraceful – indeed much more so – for those whose professed aim is the enjoyment of eternal blessings to be seen grovelling in the dust of worldly things, shaming their vocation by incongruous behaviour.

Probably the reason why we act like this is because we never think about anything superior to the visible objects around us. We do not appreciate how much better the blessings of the spiritual world are than the tawdry attractions of this present world, which dazzle us with their specious glory and draw all our desire to them. In the absence of what is better, what is worse will take its place and be held in honour. If only we had a deeper understanding of the realities of the divine world, we would not be taken in by the attractions of this world.

Let us begin, then, to withdraw from the things of this world. Let us despise possessions and money and all that swamps and drowns our intelligence. Let us cast overboard our cargo, so that our ship may float more buoyantly. Hard-pressed by the storm, let us jettison the greater part of our equipment; then our helmsman – the intellect, together with its thoughts – will be saved. Those who travel by sea, when overtaken by a storm, do not worry about their merchandise but throw it into the waters with their own hands, considering their property less important than their life. Why, then, do we not follow their example, and for the sake of the higher life despise whatever drags our soul down to the depths? Why is fear of God less powerful than fear of the sea? In their desire not to be deprived of this transitory life, they judge the loss of their goods no great disaster; but we, who claim to be seeking eternal life, do not look with detachment on even the most insignificant object, but prefer to perish with the cargo rather than be saved without it.

Let us strip ourselves of everything, since our adversary stands before us stripped. Do athletes compete with their clothes on? No, the rules require them to enter the stadium naked. Whether it is warm or cold, that is how they enter, leaving their clothes outside; and if anyone refuses to strip, he excludes himself from the contest. Now we too claim to be athletes, and we are struggling against opponents far more skilful than any that are visible. Yet, instead of stripping ourselves, we try to engage in the contest while carrying countless burdens on our shoulders, thus giving our opponents many chances of getting a grip on us. How can someone encumbered with material possessions contend against 'spiritual wickedness' (Eph. 6:12), since he is vulnerable from every angle? How can someone weighed down with wealth wrestle with the demon of avarice? How can someone clothed in worldly preoccupations race against demons stripped of every care? Holy Scripture says, 'The naked shall run swiftly in that day' (Amos 2:16. LXX) – the naked, not the one who is hindered in running by thoughts about money and material possessions.

A naked person is hard or even impossible to catch. If Joseph had been naked, the Egyptian woman would not have found anything to seize hold of, for the Scriptures say that 'she caught him by his garment, saying: "Lie with me" ' (Gen. 39:12). Now 'garments' are the physical things whereby sensual pleasure seizes hold of us and drags us about; for whoever is encumbered with such things will of necessity be dragged about by them against his will. When Joseph saw that, because of his body's need for clothes, he was being dragged into intimacy and union with sensual pleasure, he abandoned them and fled; he realized that, unless he was naked, the mistress of the house would seize him and hold him back by force. So when he left he was naked except for his virtue, like Adam in Paradise; for God allowed Adam to go about naked as a special privilege, but after the fall he needed to wear clothes. So long as Adam resisted the enemies who urged him to break God's commandment, he stood naked like an athlete in the arena; but once he had been defeated in the contest, it was appropriate for him to put on clothes. This is why the writer of Proverbs says to the intelligence, our trainer: 'Take away his garment, for he has entered' (Prov. 27:13. LXX). So long as someone does not compete but stays outside the arena, he will of course remain clothed, smothering beneath the garments of sensory things the manly strength required for the contest; but once he enters the contest, his garment is taken away, for he must compete naked.

Indeed, we must be not only naked but anointed with oil. Stripping prevents our opponent from getting a grasp on us, while oil enables us to slip away should he in fact seize hold of us. That is why a wrestler tries to cover his opponent's body with dust; this will counteract the slipperiness of the oil and make it easier for him to get a hold. Now what dust is in their case, worldly things are in the case of our own struggle; and what oil is in their case, detachment is in ours. In physical wrestling, someone anointed with oil easily breaks free from his opponent's grip, but if he is covered with dust he finds it hard to escape. Similarly, in our case it is difficult for the devil to seize hold of one who has no worldly attachments. But when a man is full of anxiety about material things the intellect, as though covered with dust, loses the agility which detachment confers upon it; and then it is hard for him to escape from the devil's grip.

Detachment is the mark of a perfect soul, whereas it is characteristic of an imperfect soul to be worn down with anxiety about material things. The perfect soul is called a 'lily among thorns' (S. of S. 2:2), meaning that it lives with detachment in the midst of those who are troubled by such anxiety. For in the Gospel the lily signifies the soul that is detached from worldly care: 'They do not toil or spin . . . yet even Solomon in all his glory was not arrayed like one of them' (Matt. 6:28–29). But of those who devote much anxious thought to bodily things, it is said: 'All the life of the ungodly is spent in anxiety' (Job 15:20. LXX). It is indeed ungodly to pass one's whole life worrying about bodily things and to give no thought to the blessings of the age to come – to spend all one's time on the body, though it does not need much attention, and not to devote even a passing moment to the soul, though the journey before it is so great that a whole lifetime is too short to bring it to perfection. Even if we do seem to allot a certain amount of time to it, we do this carelessly and lazily, for we are always being attracted by visible things.

We are like people enticed by ugly prostitutes who lack true beauty but conceal their ugliness with the help of cosmetics, producing a counterfeit beauty that ensnares those who see it. Having once been overcome by the vain things of this present life, we are unable to see the ugliness of matter, for we are fooled by our attachment to it. For this reason, we do not remain content with basic necessities, but become dependent on all sorts of possessions, ruining our lives by our greed. We do not see that our possessions should be limited according to our bodily needs, and that what exceeds these is in bad taste and unnecessary. A cloak measured to fit the body is both necessary and in good taste; while one which is too long, getting entangled in our feet and dragging on the ground, not only looks unsightly, but also proves a hindrance in every kind of work. Similarly, possessions superfluous to our bodily needs are an obstacle to virtue, and are strongly condemned by those capable of understanding the true nature of things.

We should therefore pay no attention to such as are deceived by sensory things, and should not uncritically follow those who remain attached to what is worldly because they have never given thought to spiritual realities. To rely upon such men, and to consider that they have made a wise choice in pursuing transitory pleasures, is to put our trust in those who lack any criterion for making a sound judgment; it is like using the blind as judges of colour or the deaf as music critics. For those whose intelligence is crippled are truly blind, since they lack the basic criterion whereby to distinguish between the important and the trivial. One such man was Achan, the son of Carmi, who confessed to Joshua that the stolen things were hidden in his tent, buried in the ground, with the silver underneath them (cf. Josh. 7:21). For he who assigns a higher position to the varied attractions of material things and buries his intelligence beneath them, is led astray like a fool, yielding to whatever takes his fancy, because he has deposed his intelligence from its royal throne and assigned it a place among those it should be ruling – or, rather, among condemned criminals. But if his intelligence were established in its proper position and entrusted with the judging of sensory matters, it would deliver a just and sound verdict, punishing the impulse that chases after deceptive things.

We should remain, then, within the limits imposed by our basic needs and strive with all our power not to exceed them. For once we are carried a little beyond these limits in our desire for the pleasures of this life, there is then no criterion by which to check our onward movement, since no bounds can be set to that which exceeds the necessary. Pointless effort and endless labour wasted on what is unnecessary only serve to increase our longing for it, adding more fuel to the flames. Once a man has passed beyond the limits of his natural needs, as he grows more materialistic he wants to put jam on his bread; and to water he adds first the modicum of wine required for his health, and then the most expensive vintages. He does not rest content with essential clothing, but starts to purchase clothes made from brightly-coloured wool of the very best quality; next he demands clothes made from a mixture of linen and wool; next he searches for silken clothes – at first just for plain silk, and then for silk embroidered with scenes of battles and hunting and the like. He acquires vessels of silver and gold, not just for banqueting but for animals to feed from and for use as chamber-pots. What need is there to say more about such absurd ostentation, extending as it does to the basest needs, so that even chamber-pots must be made of nothing less than silver? Such is the nature of sensual pleasure: it embraces even the lowliest things and leads us to invest the meanest of functions with material luxury.

All this is contrary to nature, for the Creator has ordained the same natural way of life for both us and the animals. 'Behold,' says God to man, 'I have given you every herb of the field, to serve as food for you and for the beasts' (cf. Gen. 1:29–30). Thus we have been given a common diet with the animals; but if we use our powers of invention to turn this into something extravagant, shall we not rightly be judged more unintelligent than they? The animals remain within the boundaries of nature, not altering in any way what God has ordained; but we, who have been honoured with the power of intelligence, have completely abandoned His original ordinance. Do animals demand a luxury diet? What chefs and pastry-cooks pander to their bellies? Do they not prefer the original simplicity, eating the herbs of the field, content with whatever is at hand, drinking water from springs – and this only infrequently? In this way they diminish sexual lust and do not inflame their desires with fatty foods. They become conscious of the difference between male and female only during the one season of the year ordained by the law of nature for them to mate in, so as to propagate and continue their species. The rest of the year they keep away from one another as if they had altogether forgotten any such appetite. In men, on the other hand, as a result of the richness of their food, an insatiable desire for sexual pleasure has grown up, producing in them frenzied appetites which never allow this passion to be still.

Since, then, possessions are the cause of great harm and, like a source of disease, they give rise to all the passions, we must eliminate this cause if we are really concerned for the well-being of our souls. Let us cure the passion of avarice through voluntary poverty. By embracing solitude let us avoid meeting those who do us no good, for the company of frivolous people is harmful and undermines our state of peace. Just as those who live in an unhealthy climate are generally ill, so those who spend their time with worthless men share in their vices.

What do those who have renounced the world still have in common with the world? 'In order to please the leader who has chosen him, the soldier going to war does not entangle himself in the affairs of this world' (2 Tim. 2:4). Preoccupation with business hinders military training; and if we are untrained, how can we stand our ground when fighting against experienced troops? Rather, to tell the truth, we fight so half heartedly that we do not withstand the enemy even when he is lying on the ground. We who stand upright are the prey of him who is fallen. We suffer the same miserable fate as those who, out of avarice, despoil corpses in wartime. After the battle has been won, they come up to someone who lies half-dead and start searching his body; and then, taken unawares, they receive a mortal blow from him, foolishly bringing disgrace upon themselves after their glorious victory. In the same way, when we have overthrown the enemy through our self-control and restraint – or rather, when we think we have overthrown him – we become attracted by his clothes, that is, by the different things men prize: wealth, power, good living, fame. We approach our fallen enemy in our longing to take his things; and so we are killed, having led ourselves to the slaughter. That was how the five virgins came to grief (cf. Matt. 25:1–13); through their purity they had destroyed the enemy, but because of their hardness of heart, which is engendered by avarice, they drove the enemy's sword through their own bodies, when he himself lay helpless.

Let us not seek anything that belongs to the enemy, lest in so doing we lose our own life. For even now he is urging us to take what is his, especially when he finds us ready to comply. He even urged the Lord himself in this way, saying: 'All these things will I give Thee, if Thou wilt fall down and worship me' (Matt. 4:9). So with the specious allurements of this life he tried to deceive the Son of God, who has no need of any such things. How, then, could he fail to think of deceiving men who are easily led astray and attracted to the enjoyment of sensory things?

Once we have learnt to train our body, let us also train our intellect in true devotion. For 'bodily asceticism has only a limited use', in this respect resembling elementary education; whereas 'true devotion is useful in all things' (1 Tim. 4:8), and brings well-being to the souls of those who seek to defeat their enemies, the passions. Children who are training for sports need to exercise their bodies, to move their limbs constantly, to make every effort to gain an athlete's strength, and to anoint themselves with oil in preparation for the sacred games. Likewise those who are beginning the life of holiness should try to hinder the activity of the passions. At this stage they are still driven frantic by the pleasures that accompany the passions, and habit forces them into sin, almost without any act of choice on their part; they have therefore done well if they can control the passions. But those in whom the practice of the virtues has become established can also direct their attention to the mind. They should make every effort to keep watch over their intelligence so that it does not get out of control and go astray. In short, beginners try to train their body, while the more advanced attempt to restrain the impulses of their intelligence, so that its workings may accord solely with the teachings of wisdom, and no worldly fantasy may distract it from thoughts about God.

One who is pursuing the spiritual way should direct all his desire towards the Lord whom he loves; then human thoughts will find no opportunity whatever to activate within him the corresponding passions. Each passion, when active within someone whom it controls, holds his intelligence in chains; why, then, cannot zeal for holiness keep our mind free from everything else? When an angry man fights in his imagination against the person who has offended him, is he conscious of anything external? Is not the same true of the man who desires material possessions, when he imagines ways of getting what he wants? And the lustful man, even when in the company of others, often becomes oblivious of his surroundings and sits like a block of stone, saying nothing, thinking only of the women he desires; turning in upon himself, he is completely absorbed by his own fantasies. Perhaps it is a soul such as this that the Law describes as 'sitting apart' (Lev. 15:33. LXX): sitting far from the senses, it concentrates all its activities within itself, totally unconscious of external things because of the shameful fantasy that dominates it.

Now if our attachment to such things gives them this power over our intelligence and stops the senses from functioning, how much more should the love of wisdom cause our intellect to renounce both sensory things and the senses themselves, lifting it up and concentrating it upon the contemplation of spiritual things? Just as someone who is cut or burnt can think of nothing else because of the intense pain, so a man who is thinking passionately about some object has no thoughts for anything else; the passion that dominates him affects his whole intelligence. Intense pain makes hard work impossible; sorrow excludes joy, and dejection mirth; hard work in its turn excludes sensual pleasure. Thus opposing passions are mutually exclusive and will never unite; co-operation between them is impossible, because of the implacable enmity and opposition that separates them by nature.

Do not, therefore, let the purity of your virtue be clouded by thoughts of worldly things: do not let the intensity of your contemplation be disturbed by bodily cares. Then true wisdom will stand revealed in its full beauty and it will no longer be maligned by insolent men because of our shortcomings, or mocked by those who know nothing about it; but it will be praised, if not by men, at any rate by the angelic powers and by Christ our Lord. It was His praise that was desired by the saints, such as David, who despised human glory but sought honour from God, saying: 'My praise shall be from Thee', and 'My soul shall be praised by the Lord' (Ps. 22:25;

34:2. LXX). From malice men often speak slanderously of what is good; but the tribunal on high gives judgment with impartiality, and delivers its verdict in accordance with the truth.

Let us, then, bring joy to this heavenly tribunal, which rejoices in our acts of righteousness. We need not worry about men's opinions, for men can neither reward those who have lived well nor punish those who have lived otherwise. If because of envy or worldly attachment they seek to discredit the way of holiness, they are defaming with deluded blasphemies the life honoured by God and the angels. At the time of judgment those who have lived rightly will be rewarded with eternal blessings, not on the basis of human opinion, but in accordance with the true nature of their life. May all of us attain these blessings through the grace and love of our Lord Jesus Christ, to whom be glory together with the Father and the Holy Spirit, now and ever and through all the ages. Amen.

ST DIADOCHOS OF PHOTIKI

Introductory Note

St Diadochos, who was born around 400 and died before 486, was bishop of Photiki in Epirus (North Greece); he wrote against the Monophysites and supported the Council of Chalcedon (451). In the work *On Spiritual Knowledge and Discrimination* he reveals, as St Nikodimos puts it, 'the deepest secrets of the virtue of prayer'. Written in a sensitive style of great beauty, the work is of basic importance for an understanding of Orthodox mystical theology. Diadochos' thought is of exceptional subtlety and precision, and his exact meaning is not easy to grasp.

St Diadochos borrows many of the Evagrian technical terms, but his work contains certain features not found in Evagrios: an emphasis, for instance, upon the primacy of love (see especially §§ 90–92), upon the sacraments, and upon the heart as well as the intellect (*nous*). His teaching on baptism (§§ 76–78) is closely parallel to that of St Mark the Ascetic; here, and in many other passages of the work, St Diadochos has particularly in view the errors of the Messalians. St Diadochos emphasizes the fundamental unity of man's body and soul: our present state of dividedness is the consequence of the fall (§§ 24 25). He attaches great importance to the continual remembrance and invocation of the Lord Jesus (§§ 31, 32, 33, 59, 61, 85, 88, 97).

In our translation we have used the critical Greek text of E. des Places, *Diadoque de Photicé: Oeuvres spirituelles* (*Sources chrétiennes* 4: 2nd edition, reprinted with additions, Paris, 1966).

Definitions

Faith: dispassionate understanding of God.

Hope: the flight of the intellect in love towards that for which it hopes.

Patience: with the eyes of the mind always to see the Invisible as visible.

Freedom from avarice: to desire not to have possessions with the same fervour as men generally desire to have possessions.

Knowledge: to lose awareness of oneself through going out to God in ecstasy.

Humility: attentive forgetfulness of what one has accomplished.

Freedom from anger: a real longing not to lose one's temper.

Purity: unwavering perception of God.

Love: growing affection for those who abuse us.

Total transformation: through delight in God, to look on the repulsiveness of death as a joy.

On Spiritual Knowledge and Discrimination:[1]
One Hundred Texts

1. All spiritual contemplation should be governed by faith, hope and love, but most of all by love. The first two teach us to be detached from visible delights, but love unites the soul with the excellence of God, searching out the Invisible by means of intellectual perception.

2. Only God is good by nature, but with God's help man can become good through careful attention to his way of life. He transforms himself into what he is not when his soul, by devoting its attention to true delight, unites itself to God, in so far as its energized power desires this. For it is written: 'Be good and merciful as is your Father in heaven' (cf. Luke 6:36; Matt. 5:48).

3. Evil does not exist by nature, nor is any man naturally evil, for God made nothing that was not good. When in the desire of his heart someone conceives and gives form to what in reality has no existence, then what he desires begins to exist. We should therefore turn our attention away from the inclination to evil and concentrate it on the remembrance of God; for good, which exists by nature, is more powerful than our inclination to evil. The one has existence while the other has not, except when we give it existence through our actions.

4. All men are made in God's image; but to be in His likeness is granted only to those who through great love have brought their own freedom into subjection to God. For only when we do not belong to ourselves do we become like Him who through love has reconciled us to Himself. No one achieves this unless he persuades his soul not to be distracted by the false glitter of this life.

[1] Most manuscripts continue: 'Explaining what kind of spiritual knowledge we need in order to reach, under the Lord's guidance, the perfection which He has revealed, so that each of us may apply to himself the parable of deliverance and bring to fruition the seed which is the Logos' (cf. Matt. 13:3–8).

5. Free will is the power of a deiform soul to direct itself by deliberate choice towards whatever it decides. Let us make sure that our soul directs itself deliberately only towards what is good, so that we always consume our remembrance of evil with good thoughts.

6. The light of true knowledge is the power to discriminate without error between good and evil. Then the path of righteousness leads the intellect upward towards the Sun of Righteousness and brings it into the boundless illumination of spiritual knowledge, so that henceforward it will grow more and more confident in its quest for love. With an incensive power free from anger we should snatch righteousness from the hands of those who dare to outrage it, since the aspiration for holiness triumphs not by hating others, but by convincing them of their faults.

7. Spiritual discourse fully satisfies our intellectual perception, because it comes from God through the energy of love. It is on account of this that the intellect continues undisturbed in its concentration on theology. It does not suffer then from the emptiness which produces a state of anxiety, since in its contemplation it is filled to the degree that the energy of love desires. So it is right always to wait, with a faith energized by love, for the illumination which will enable us to speak. For nothing is so destitute as a mind philosophizing about God when it is without Him.

8. The unilluminated should not embark on spiritual speculations nor, on the other hand, should anyone try to speak while the light of the Holy Spirit is shining richly upon him. For where there is emptiness, ignorance is also to be found, but where there is richness of the Spirit, no speech is possible. At such a time the soul is drunk with the love of God and, with voice silent, delights in His glory. We should therefore watch for the middle point between these two extremes before we begin to speak of God. This balance confers a certain harmony on our words glorifying God; as we speak and teach, our faith is nourished by the richness of the illumination and so, because of our love, we are the first to taste the fruits of knowledge. For it is written: 'The farmer who does the work should be the first to eat of the produce' (2 Tim. 2:6).

9. Wisdom and spiritual knowledge are both gifts of the one Holy Spirit, as are all the divine gifts of grace; but each has its own distinctive energy. For this reason the Apostle testifies that to one is

given wisdom, to another spiritual knowledge by the same Spirit (cf. 1 Cor. 12:8). Such knowledge unites man to God through experience, but does not move him to express outwardly what he knows. Some, then, of those who practise the solitary life are consciously illuminated by spiritual knowledge, yet do not speak about God. But when wisdom, with the fear of God, is given to someone at the same time as spiritual knowledge – and this seldom happens – it leads him to express outwardly the inner energies of this knowledge within him; for spiritual knowledge illuminates men through its inner energy while wisdom does so through being expressed outwardly. Spiritual knowledge comes through prayer, deep stillness and complete detachment, while wisdom comes through humble meditation on Holy Scripture and, above all, through grace given by God.

10. When the soul's incensive power is aroused against the passions, we should know that it is time for silence, as the hour of battle is at hand. But when this turbulence grows calm, whether through prayer or through acts of mercy, we may then be moved by a desire to proclaim God's mysteries, restraining the wings of our intellect with the cords of humility. For unless a man sets himself utterly at nought, he cannot speak of the majesty of God.

11. Spiritual discourse always keeps the soul free from self-esteem, for it gives every part of the soul a sense of light, so that it no longer needs the praise of men. In the same way, such discourse keeps the mind free from fantasy, transfusing it completely with the love of God. Discourse deriving from the wisdom of this world, on the other hand, always provokes self-esteem; because it is incapable of granting us the experience of spiritual perception, it inspires its adepts with a longing for praise, being nothing but the fabrication of conceited men. It follows, therefore, that we can know with certainty when we are in the proper state to speak about God, if during the hours when we do not speak we maintain a fervent remembrance of God in untroubled silence.

12. Whoever loves himself cannot love God; but if, because of 'the overflowing richness' of God's love, a man does not love himself, then he truly loves God (Eph. 2:7). Such a man never seeks his own glory, but seeks the glory of God. The man who loves himself seeks his own glory, whereas he who loves God loves the glory of his Creator. It is characteristic of the soul which consciously

senses the love of God always to seek God's glory in every commandment it performs, and to be happy in its low estate. For glory befits God because of His majesty, while lowliness befits man because it unites us with God. If we realize this, rejoicing in the glory of the Lord, we too, like St John the Baptist, will begin to say unceasingly, 'He must increase, but we must decrease' (cf. John 3 : 30).

13. I know a man who loves God with great intensity, and yet grieves because he does not love Him as much as he would wish. His soul is ceaselessly filled with burning desire that God should be glorified in him and that he himself should be as nothing. This man does not think of what he is, even when others praise him. In his great desire for humility he does not think of his priestly rank, but performs his ministry as the rules enjoin. In his extreme love for God, he strips himself of any thought of his own dignity; and with a spirit of humility he buries in the depths of divine love any pride to which his high position might give rise. Thus, out of desire to humble himself, he always sees himself in his own mind as a useless servant, extraneous to the rank he holds. We too should do the same, fleeing all honour and glory in the overflowing richness of our love for the Lord who loves us so greatly.

14. He who loves God consciously in his heart is known by God (cf. 1 Cor. 8 : 3), for to the degree that he receives the love of God consciously in his soul, he truly enters into God's love. From that time on, such a man never loses an intense longing for the illumination of spiritual knowledge, until he senses its strength in his bones and no longer knows himself, but is completely transformed by the love of God. He is both present in this life and not present in it; still dwelling in the body, he yet departs from it, as through love he ceaselessly journeys towards God in his soul. His heart now burns constantly with the fire of love and clings to God with an irresistible longing, since he has once and for all transcended self-love in his love for God. As St Paul writes: 'If we go out of ourselves, it is because of God; if we are restrained, it is for your sake' (2 Cor. 5 : 13).

15. When a man begins to perceive the love of God in all its richness, he begins also to love his neighbour with spiritual perception. This is the love of which all the scriptures speak. Friendship after the flesh is very easily destroyed on some slight pretext, since it is not held firm by spiritual perception. But when a person is

spiritually awakened, even if something irritates him, the bond of love is not dissolved; rekindling himself with the warmth of the love of God, he quickly recovers himself and with great joy seeks his neighbour's love, even though he has been gravely wronged or insulted by him. For the sweetness of God completely consumes the bitterness of the quarrel.

16. No one can love God consciously in his heart unless he has first feared Him with all his heart. Through the action of fear the soul is purified and, as it were, made malleable and so it becomes awakened to the action of love. No one, however, can come to fear God completely in the way described, unless he first transcends all worldly cares; for when the intellect reaches a state of deep stillness and detachment, then the fear of God begins to trouble it, purifying it with full perception from all gross and cloddish density, and thereby bringing it to a great love for God's goodness. Thus the fear which characterizes those who are still being purified is accompanied by a moderate measure of love. But perfect love is found in those who have already been purified and in whom there is no longer any fear, for 'perfect love casts out fear' (1 John 4 : 18). Fear and love are found together only in the righteous who achieve virtue through the energy of the Holy Spirit in them. For this reason Holy Scripture says in one place: 'O fear the Lord, all you who are His saints' (Ps. 34:9), and in another: 'O love the Lord, all you who are His saints' (Ps. 31:23). From this we see clearly that the righteous, who are still in the process of being purified, are characterized both by fear and by a moderate measure of love; perfect love, on the other hand, is found only in those who have already been purified and in whom there is no longer any thought of fear, but rather a constant burning and binding of the soul to God through the energy of the Holy Spirit. As it is written, 'My soul is bound to Thee: Thy right hand has upheld me' (Ps. 63:8. LXX).

17. If wounds in the body have been neglected and left unattended, they do not react to medicine when the doctors apply it to them; but if they have first been cleansed, then they respond to the action of the medicine and so are quickly healed. In the same way, if the soul is neglected and wholly covered with the leprosy of self-indulgence, it cannot experience the fear of God, however persistently it is warned of the terror and power of God's judgment. When, however, through great attentiveness the soul begins to be

purified, it also begins to experience the fear of God as a life-giving medicine which, through the reproaches it arouses in the conscience, burns the soul in the fire of dispassion. After this the soul is gradually cleansed until it is completely purified; its love increases as its fear diminishes, until it attains perfect love, in which there is no fear but only the complete dispassion which is energized by the glory of God. So let us rejoice endlessly in our fear of God and in the love which is the fulfilling of the law of perfection in Christ (cf. Rom. 13:10).

18. A person who is not detached from worldly cares can neither love God truly nor hate the devil as he should, for such cares are both a burden and a veil. His intellect cannot discern the tribunal which will judge him, neither can it foresee the verdict which will be given at his trial. For all these reasons, then, withdrawal from the world is invaluable.

19. The qualities of a pure soul are intelligence devoid of envy, ambition free from malice, and unceasing love for the Lord of glory. When the soul has these qualities, then the intellect can accurately assess how it will be judged, seeing itself appear before the most faultless of tribunals.

20. Faith without works and works without faith will both alike be condemned, for he who has faith must offer to the Lord the faith which shows itself in actions. Our father Abraham would not have been counted righteous because of his faith had he not offered its fruit, his son (cf. Jas. 2:21; Rom. 4:3).

21. He who loves God both believes truly and performs the works of faith reverently. But he who only believes and does not love, lacks even the faith he thinks he has; for he believes merely with a certain superficiality of intellect and is not energized by the full force of love's glory. The chief part of virtue, then, is faith energized by love.

22. The deep waters of faith seem turbulent when we peer into them too curiously; but when contemplated in a spirit of simplicity, they are calm. The depths of faith are like the waters of Lethe, making us forget all evil; they will not reveal themselves to the scrutiny of meddlesome reasoning. Let us therefore sail these waters with simplicity of mind, and so reach the harbour of God's will.

23. No one can either love truly or believe truly unless he has first brought accusation against himself. For so long as our conscience is troubled with self-reproach, the intellect is no longer able

to sense the perfume of heavenly blessings, but at once becomes divided and ambivalent. Because of the experience it once enjoyed it reaches out fervently towards faith, but can no longer perceive faith in the heart through love because of the pricks of an accusing conscience. But when we have purified ourselves by closer attentiveness, then with a fuller experience of God we shall attain what we desire.

24. Just as the senses of the body impel us almost violently towards what attracts them, so the perceptive faculty of the intellect, once it tastes the divine goodness, leads us towards invisible blessings. Everything longs for what is akin to itself: the soul, since it is bodiless, desires heavenly goods, while the body, being dust, seeks earthly nourishment. So we shall surely come to experience immaterial perception if by our labours we refine our material nature.

25. Divine knowledge, once it is awakened in us, teaches us that the perceptive faculty natural to our soul is single, but that it is split into two distinct modes of operation as a result of Adam's disobedience. This single and simple perceptive faculty is implanted in the soul by the Holy Spirit; but no one can realize this singleness of perception except those who have willingly abandoned the delights of this corruptible life in the hope of enjoying those of eternity, and who have caused every appetite of the bodily senses to wither away through self-control. Only in such men does the intellect, because of its freedom from worldly care, act with its full vigour so that it is capable of perceiving ineffably the goodness of God. Then, according to the measure of its own progress, the intellect communicates its joy to the body too, rejoicing endlessly in the song of love and praise: 'My heart has trusted in Him and I am helped; my flesh flowers again, and with all my being I will sing His praise' (Ps. 28:7. LXX). The joy which then fills both soul and body is a true recalling of the life without corruption.

26. Those pursuing the spiritual way must always keep the mind free from agitation in order that the intellect, as it discriminates among the thoughts that pass through the mind, may store in the treasuries of its memory those thoughts which are good and have been sent by God, while casting out those which are evil and come from the devil. When the sea is calm, fishermen can scan its depths and therefore hardly any creature moving in the water escapes their

notice. But when the sea is disturbed by the winds, it hides beneath its turbid and agitated waves what it was happy to reveal when it was smiling and calm; and then the fishermen's skill and cunning prove vain. The same thing happens with the contemplative power of the intellect, especially when it is unjust anger which disturbs the depths of the soul.

27. Very few men can accurately recognize all their own faults; indeed, only those can do this whose intellect is never torn away from the remembrance of God. Our bodily eyes, when healthy, can see everything, even gnats and mosquitoes flying about in the air; but when they are clouded by some discharge, they see large objects only indistinctly and small things not at all. Similarly if the soul, through attentiveness, reduces the blindness caused by the love of this world, it will consider its slightest faults to be very grave and will continually shed tears with deep thankfulness. For it is written, 'The righteous shall give thanks unto Thy name' (Ps. 140:13). But if the soul persists in its worldly disposition, even though it commits a murder or some other act deserving severe punishment, it takes little notice; and it is quite unable to discern its other faults, often considering them to be signs of progress, and in its wretchedness it is not ashamed to defend them heatedly.

28. Only the Holy Spirit can purify the intellect, for unless a greater power comes and overthrows the despoiler, what he has taken captive will never be set free (cf. Luke 11:21–22). In every way, therefore, and especially through peace of soul, we must make ourselves a dwelling-place for the Holy Spirit. Then we shall have the lamp of spiritual knowledge burning always within us; and when it is shining constantly in the inner shrine of the soul, not only will the intellect perceive all the dark and bitter attacks of the demons, but these attacks will be greatly weakened when exposed for what they are by that glorious and holy light. That is why the Apostle says: 'Do not quench the Spirit' (1 Thess. 5:19), meaning: 'Do not grieve the goodness of the Holy Spirit by wicked actions or wicked thoughts, lest you be deprived of this protecting light.' The Spirit, since He is eternal and life-creating, cannot be quenched; but if He is grieved – that is if He withdraws – He leaves the intellect without the light of spiritual knowledge, dark and full of gloom.

29. The loving and Holy Spirit of God teaches us, as we have said, that the perceptive faculty natural to our soul is single; indeed,

even the five bodily senses differ from each other only because of the body's varying needs. But this single faculty of perception is split because of the dislocation which, as a result of Adam's disobedience, takes place in the intellect through the modes in which the soul now operates. Thus one side of the soul is carried away by the passionate part in man, and we are then captivated by the good things of this life; but the other side of the soul frequently delights in the activity of the intellect and, as a result, when we practise self-restraint, the intellect longs to pursue heavenly beauty. If, therefore, we learn persistently to be detached from the good things of this world, we shall be able to unite the earthly appetite of the soul to its spiritual and intellectual aspiration, through the communion of the Holy Spirit who brings this about within us. For unless His divinity actively illumines the inner shrine of our heart, we shall not be able to taste God's goodness with the perceptive faculty undivided, that is, with unified aspiration.

30. The perceptive faculty of the intellect consists in the power to discriminate accurately between the tastes of different realities. Our physical sense of taste, when we are healthy, leads us to distinguish unfailingly between good food and bad, so that we want what is good; similarly, our intellect, when it begins to act vigorously and with complete detachment, is capable of perceiving the wealth of God's grace and is never led astray by any illusion of grace which comes from the devil. Just as the body, when it tastes the delectable foods of this earth, knows by experience exactly what each thing is, so the intellect, when it has triumphed over the thoughts of the flesh, knows for certain when it is tasting the grace of the Holy Spirit; for it is written: 'Taste and see that the Lord is good' (Ps. 34:8). The intellect keeps fresh the memory of this taste through the energy of love, and so unerringly chooses what is best. As St Paul says: 'This is my prayer, that your love may grow more and more in knowledge and in all perception, so that you choose what is best' (Phil. 1:9–10).

31. When our intellect begins to perceive the grace of the Holy Spirit, then Satan, too, importunes the soul with a sense of deceptive sweetness in the quiet times of the night, when we fall into a light kind of sleep. If the intellect at that time cleaves fervently to the remembrance of the glorious and holy name of the Lord Jesus and uses it as a weapon against Satan's deception, he gives up this trick

and for the future will attack the soul directly and personally. As a result the intellect clearly discerns the deception of the evil one and advances even further in the art of discrimination.

32. The experience of true grace comes to us when the body is awake or else on the point of falling asleep, while in fervent remembrance of God we are welded to His love. But the illusion of grace comes to us, as I have said, when we fall into a light sleep while our remembrance of God is half-hearted. True grace, since its source is God, gladdens us consciously and impels us towards love with great rapture of soul. The illusion of grace, on the other hand, tends to shake the soul with the winds of deceit; for when the intellect is strong in the remembrance of God, the devil tries to rob it of its experience of spiritual perception by taking advantage of the body's need for sleep. If the intellect at that time is remembering the Lord Jesus attentively, it easily destroys the enemy's seductive sweetness and advances joyfully to do battle with him, armed not only with grace but also with a second weapon, the confidence gained from its own experience.

33. Sometimes the soul is kindled into love for God and, free from all fantasy and image, moves untroubled by doubt towards Him; and it draws, as it were, the body with it into the depths of that ineffable love. This may occur when the person is awake or else beginning to fall asleep under the influence of God's grace, in the way I have explained. At the same time, the soul is aware of nothing except what it is moving towards. When we experience things in this manner, we can be sure that it is the energy of the Holy Spirit within us. For when the soul is completely permeated with that ineffable sweetness, at that moment it can think of nothing else, since it rejoices with uninterrupted joy. But if at that moment the intellect conceives any doubt or unclean thought, and if this continues in spite of the fact that the intellect calls on the holy name – not now simply out of love for God, but in order to repel the evil one – then it should realize that the sweetness it experiences is an illusion of grace, coming from the deceiver with a counterfeit joy. Through this joy, amorphous and disordered, the devil tries to lead the soul into an adulterous union with himself. For when he sees the intellect unreservedly proud of its own experience of spiritual perception, he entices the soul by means of certain plausible illusions of grace, so that it is seduced by that dank and debilitating sweetness

and fails to notice its intercourse with the deceiver. From all this we can distinguish between the Spirit of truth and the spirit of error. It is impossible, however, for someone consciously to taste the divine goodness or consciously to realize when he is experiencing the bitterness of the demons, unless he first knows with assurance that grace dwells in the depths of his intellect, while the wicked spirits cluster round only the outside of the heart. This is just what the demons do not want us to know, for fear that our intellect, once definitely aware of it, will arm itself against them with the remembrance of God.

34. The natural love of the soul is one thing, and the love which comes to it from the Holy Spirit is another. The activity of the first depends on the assent of our will to our desire. For this reason it is easily taken over and perverted by evil spirits when we do not keep firmly to our chosen course. But the love which comes from the Holy Spirit so inflames the soul that all its parts cleave ineffably and with utter simplicity to the delight of its love and longing for the divine. The intellect then becomes pregnant through the energy of the Holy Spirit and overflows with a spring of love and joy.

35. Just as a rough sea naturally subsides when oil is poured upon it, so the soul readily grows calm when anointed with the grace of the Holy Spirit. For it submits joyfully to the dispassionate and ineffable grace which overshadows it, in accordance with the Psalmist's words: 'My soul, be obedient to God' (Ps. 62:5. LXX). As a result, no matter how greatly it is provoked by the demons, the soul remains free from anger and is filled with the greatest joy. No man can enter or remain in such a state unless he sweetens his soul continually with the fear of God; for the fear of the Lord Jesus confers a measure of purity on those pursuing the spiritual way. 'The fear of the Lord is pure, and endures for ever' (Ps. 19:9. LXX).

36. Let no one who hears us speak of the perceptive faculty of the intellect imagine that by this we mean that the glory of God appears to man visibly. We do indeed affirm that the soul, when pure, perceives God's grace, tasting it in some ineffable manner; but no invisible reality appears to it in a visible form, since now 'we walk by faith, not by sight', as St Paul says (2 Cor. 5:7). If light or some fiery form should be seen by one pursuing the spiritual way, he should not on any account accept such a vision: it is an obvious deceit of the enemy. Many indeed have had this experience and, in

their ignorance, have turned aside from the way of truth. We ourselves know, however, that so long as we dwell in this corruptible body, 'we are absent from the Lord' (2 Cor. 5:6) – that is to say, we know that we cannot see visibly either God Himself or any of His celestial wonders.

37. The dreams which appear to the soul through God's love are unerring criteria of its health. Such dreams do not change from one shape to another; they do not shock our inward sense, resound with laughter or suddenly become threatening. But with great gentleness they approach the soul and fill it with spiritual gladness. As a result, even after the body has woken up, the soul longs to recapture the joy given to it by the dream. Demonic fantasies, however, are just the opposite: they do not keep the same shape or maintain a constant form for long. For what the demons do not possess as their chosen mode of life, but merely assume because of their inherent deceitfulness, is not able to satisfy them for very long. They shout and menace, often transforming themselves into soldiers and sometimes deafening the soul with their cries. But the intellect, when pure, recognizes them for what they are and awakes the body from its dreams. Sometimes it even feels joy at having been able to see through their tricks; indeed it often challenges them during the dream itself and thus provokes them to great anger. There are, however, times when even good dreams do not bring joy to the soul, but produce in it a sweet sadness and tears unaccompanied by grief. But this happens only to those who are far advanced in humility.

38. We have now explained the distinction between good and bad dreams, as we ourselves heard it from those with experience. In our quest for purity, however, the safest rule is never to trust to anything that appears to us in our dreams. For dreams are generally nothing more than images reflecting our wandering thoughts, or else they are the mockery of demons. And if ever God in His goodness were to send us some vision and we were to refuse it, our beloved Lord Jesus would not be angry with us, for He would know we were acting in this way because of the tricks of the demons. Although the distinction between types of dreams established above is precise, it sometimes happens that when the soul has been sullied by an unperceived beguilement – something from which no one, it seems to me, is exempt – it loses its sense of accurate discrimination and mistakes bad dreams for good.

39. As an illustration of what I mean, take the case of the servant whose master, returning at night after a long absence abroad, calls to him from outside his house. The servant categorically refuses to open the door to him, for he is afraid of being deceived by some similarity of voice, and so of betraying to someone else the goods his master has entrusted to him. Not only is his master in no way angry with him when day comes; but on the contrary he even praises him highly, because in his concern not to lose any of his master's goods he even suspected the sound of his master's voice to be a trick.

40. You should not doubt that the intellect, when it begins to be strongly energized by the divine light, becomes so completely translucent that it sees its own light vividly. This takes place when the power of the soul gains control over the passions. But when St Paul says that 'Satan himself is transformed into an angel of light' (2 Cor. 11:14), he definitely teaches us that everything which appears to the intellect, whether as light or as fire, if it has a shape, is the product of the evil artifice of the enemy. So we should not embark on the ascetic life in the hope of seeing visions clothed with form or shape; for if we do, Satan will find it easy to lead our soul astray. Our one purpose must be to reach the point when we perceive the love of God fully and consciously in our heart – that is, 'with all your heart, and with all your soul . . . and with all your mind' (Luke 10:27). For the man who is energized by the grace of God to this point has already left this world, though still present in it.

41. It is well known that obedience is the chief among the initiatory virtues, for first it displaces presumption and then it engenders humility within us. Thus it becomes, for those who willingly embrace it, a door leading to the love of God. It was because he rejected humility that Adam fell into the lowest depths of Hades. It was because He loved humility that the Lord, in accordance with the divine purpose, was obedient to His Father even to the cross and death, although He was in no way inferior to the Father; and so through His own obedience He has freed mankind from the crime of disobedience and leads back to the blessedness of eternal life all who live in obedience. Thus humility should be the first concern of those who are fighting the presumption of the devil, for as we advance it will be a sure guide to all the paths of virtue.

42. Self-control is common to all the virtues, and therefore whoever practises self-control must do so in all things. If any part, however small, of a man's body is removed, the whole man is disfigured; likewise, he who disregards one single virtue destroys unwittingly the whole harmonious order of self-control. It is therefore necessary to cultivate not only the bodily virtues, but also those which have the power to purify our inner man. What is the good of a man keeping the virginity of his body if he lets his soul commit adultery with the demon of disobedience? Or what is the good of a man controlling gluttony and his other bodily desires if he makes no effort to avoid vanity and self-esteem, and does not endure with patience even the slightest affliction? At the judgment what crown will he deserve, when a just reward is given only to those who have accomplished works of righteousness in a spirit of humility?

43. Those pursuing the spiritual way should train themselves to hate all uncontrolled desires until this hatred becomes habitual. With regard to self-control in eating, we must never feel loathing for any kind of food, for to do so is abominable and utterly demonic. It is emphatically not because any kind of food is bad in itself that we refrain from it. But by not eating too much or too richly we can to some extent keep in check the excitable parts of our body. In addition we can give to the poor what remains over, for this is the mark of sincere love.

44. It is in no way contrary to the principles of true knowledge to eat and drink from all that is set before you, giving thanks to God; for 'everything is very good' (cf. Gen. 1:31). But gladly to abstain from eating too pleasurably or too much shows greater discrimination and understanding. However, we shall not gladly detach ourselves from the pleasures of this life unless we have fully and consciously tasted the sweetness of God.

45. When heavy with over-eating, the body makes the intellect spiritless and sluggish; likewise, when weakened by excessive abstinence, the body makes the contemplative faculty of the soul dejected and disinclined to concentrate. We should therefore regulate our food according to the condition of the body, so that it is appropriately disciplined when in good health and adequately nourished when weak. The body of one pursuing the spiritual way must not be enfeebled; he must have enough strength for his labours,

so that the soul may be suitably purified through bodily exertion as well.

46. When, as a result of visits from some of our brethren or some strangers, we are fiercely attacked by thoughts of self-esteem, it is good to relax our normal regime to a certain extent. In this way the demon will be frustrated and driven out, regretting his attempt; moreover, we shall properly fulfil the rule of love, and by relaxing our usual practice we shall keep hidden the mystery of our self-control.

47. Fasting, while of value in itself, is not something to boast of in front of God, for it is simply a tool for training those who desire self-restraint. The ascetic should not feel proud because he fasts; but with faith in God he should think only of reaching his goal. For no artist ever boasts that his accomplishment is simply due to his tools; but he waits for the work itself to give proof of his skill.

48. When watered in due measure the earth yields a good, clean crop from the seed sown in it; but when it is soaked with torrential rain it bears nothing but thistles and thorns. Likewise, when we drink wine in due measure, the earth of the heart yields a clean crop from its natural seed and produces a fine harvest from what is sown in it by the Holy Spirit. But if it is soaked through excessive drinking, the thoughts it bears will be nothing but thistles and thorns.

49. When our intellect is swimming in the waves of excessive drink, it not only regards with passion the images formed in it by the demons while we sleep, but also itself forms attractive appearances, treating its own fantasies as if they were women whom it ardently loved. For when the sexual organs are heated by wine, the intellect cannot avoid forming in itself pleasurable pictures reflecting our passion. So we must keep due measure and escape the harm that comes from excess. For when the intellect is not affected by the pleasure that seduces it to the picturing of sin, it remains completely free from fantasy and debility.

50. People who wish to discipline the sexual organs should avoid drinking those artificial concoctions which are called 'aperitifs' – presumably because they open a way to the stomach for the vast meal which is to follow. Not only are they harmful to our bodies, but their fraudulent and artificial character greatly offends the conscience wherein God dwells. For what does wine lack that we

should sap its healthy vigour by adulterating it with a variety of condiments?

51. Jesus Christ, our Lord and Teacher in this holy way of life, was offered vinegar to drink during His Passion by those executing the devil's orders, and thus He left us, it seems to me, a clear example for spiritual combat. Those struggling against sin should not, He says, indulge themselves in agreeable food and drink, but should patiently bear the bitterness of the warfare. Hyssop, too, must be added to the sponge of ignominy (cf. John 19:29), so that the pattern of our purification may conform perfectly to His example; for sharpness pertains to spiritual combat, just as purification does to being made perfect.

52. No one would maintain that it is strange or sinful to take baths, but to refrain from them out of self-control I regard as a sign of great restraint and determination. For then our body will not be debilitated by this self-indulgence in hot and steamy water; neither shall we be reminded of Adam's ignoble nakedness, and so have to cover ourselves with leaves as he did. All this is especially important for us, who have recently renounced the vileness of this fallen life, and ought to be acquiring the beauty of self-restraint through the purity of our body.

53. There is nothing to prevent us from calling a doctor when we are ill. Since Providence has implanted remedies in nature, it has been possible for human experimentation to develop the art of medicine. All the same, we should not place our hope of healing in doctors, but in our true Saviour and Doctor, Jesus Christ. I say this to those who practise self-control in monastic communities or towns, for because of their environment they cannot at all times maintain the active working of faith through love. Furthermore, they should not succumb to the conceit and temptation of the devil, which have led some of them publicly to boast that they have had no need of doctors for many years. If, on the other hand, someone is living as a hermit in more deserted places together with two or three like-minded brethren, whatever sufferings may befall him let him draw near in faith to the only Lord who can heal 'every kind of sickness and disease' (Matt. 4:23). For besides the Lord he has the desert itself to provide sufficient consolation in his illness. In such a person faith is always actively at work, and in addition he has no scope to display the fine quality of his patience before others, because

he is protected by the desert. For 'the Lord settles the solitaries in a dwelling' (Ps. 68:6. LXX).

54. When we become unduly distressed at falling ill, we should recognize that our soul is still the slave of bodily desires and so longs for physical health, not wishing to lose the good things of this life and even finding it a great hardship not to be able to enjoy them because of illness. If, however, the soul accepts thankfully the pains of illness, it is clear that it is not far from the realm of dispassion; as a result it even waits joyfully for death as the entry into a life that is more true.

55. The soul will not desire to be separated from the body unless it becomes indifferent to the very air it breathes. All the bodily senses are opposed to faith, for they are concerned with the objects of this present world, while faith is concerned only with the blessings of the life to come. Thus one pursuing the spiritual way should never be too greatly preoccupied with beautifully branched or shady trees, pleasantly flowing springs, flowery meadows, fine houses or even vists to his family; neither should he recall any public honours that he happens to have been given. He should gratefully be content with bare necessities, regarding this present life as a road passing through an alien land, barren of all worldly attractions. For it is only by concentrating our mind in this way that we can keep to the road that leads back to eternity.

56. Eve is the first to teach us that sight, taste and the other senses, when used without moderation, distract the heart from its remembrance of God. So long as she did not look with longing at the forbidden tree, she was able to keep God's commandment carefully in mind; she was still covered by the wings of divine love and thus was ignorant of her own nakedness. But after she had looked at the tree with longing, touched it with ardent desire and then tasted its fruit with active sensuality, she at once felt drawn to physical intercourse and, being naked, she gave way to her passion. All her desire was now to enjoy what was immediately present to her senses, and through the pleasant appearance of the fruit she involved Adam in her fall. Thereafter it became hard for man's intellect to remember God or His commandments. We should therefore always be looking into the depths of our heart with continued remembrance of God, and should pass through this deceitful life like men who have lost their sight. It is the mark of true spiritual wisdom always to

clip the wings of our love for visible appearances, and this is what Job, in his great experience, refers to when he says: 'If my heart has followed my eye . . .' (Job. 31:7. LXX). To master ourselves in this way is evidence of the greatest self-control.

57. He who dwells continually within his own heart is detached from the attractions of this world, for he lives in the Spirit and cannot know the desires of the flesh. Such a man henceforward walks up and down within the fortress of the virtues which keep guard at all the gates of his purity. The assaults of the demons are now ineffective against him, even though the arrows of sensual desire reach as far as the doorways of his senses.

58. When our soul begins to lose its appetite for earthly beauties, a spirit of listlessness is apt to steal into it. This prevents us from taking pleasure in study and teaching, and from feeling any strong desire for the blessings prepared for us in the life to come; it also leads us to disparage this transient life excessively, as not possessing anything of value. It even depreciates spiritual knowledge itself, either on the grounds that many others have already acquired it or because it cannot teach us anything perfect. To avoid this passion, which dejects and enervates us, we must confine the mind within very narrow limits, devoting ourselves solely to the remembrance of God. Only in this way will the intellect be able to regain its original fervour and escape this senseless dissipation.

59. When we have blocked all its outlets by means of the remembrance of God, the intellect requires of us imperatively some task which will satisfy its need for activity. For the complete fulfilment of its purpose we should give it nothing but the prayer 'Lord Jesus'. 'No one', it is written, 'can say "Lord Jesus" except in the Holy Spirit' (1 Cor. 12:3). Let the intellect continually concentrate on these words within its inner shrine with such intensity that it is not turned aside to any mental images. Those who meditate unceasingly upon this glorious and holy name in the depths of their heart can sometimes see the light of their own intellect. For when the mind is closely concentrated upon this name, then we grow fully conscious that the name is burning up all the filth which covers the surface of the soul; for it is written: 'Our God is a consuming fire' (Deut. 4:24). Then the Lord awakens in the soul a great love for His glory; for when the intellect with fervour of heart maintains persistently its remembrance of the precious name, then that name

implants in us a constant love for its goodness, since there is nothing now that stands in the way. This is the pearl of great price which a man can acquire by selling all that he has, and so experience the inexpressible joy of making it his own (cf. Matt. 13:46).

60. Initiatory joy is one thing, the joy of perfection is another. The first is not exempt from fantasy, while the second has the strength of humility. Between the two joys comes a 'godly sorrow' (2 Cor. 7:10) and active tears;[1] 'For in much wisdom is much knowledge; and he that increases knowledge increases sorrow' (Eccles. 1:18). The soul, then, is first summoned to the struggle by the initiatory joy and then rebuked and tested by the truth of the Holy Spirit, as regards both its past sins and the vain distractions in which it still indulges. For it is written: 'With rebukes Thou hast corrected man for iniquity, and made his soul waste away like a spider's web' (Ps. 39:11. LXX). In this manner the soul is tested by divine rebuke as in a furnace, and through fervent remembrance of God it actively experiences the joy exempt from fantasy.

61. When the soul is disturbed by anger, confused by drunkenness, or sunk in deep depression, the intellect cannot hold fast to the remembrance of God no matter how hard we try to force it. Completely darkened by the violence of the passions, it loses totally the form of perception which is proper to it. Thus our desire that our intellect should keep the remembrance of God cannot make any impression, because the recollective faculty of our mind has been hardened by the rawness of the passions. But, on the other hand, when the soul has attained freedom from these passions, then, even though the intellect is momentarily deprived by forgetfulness of the object of its longing, it at once resumes its proper activity. The soul now has grace itself to share its meditation and to repeat with it the words 'Lord Jesus', just as a mother teaches her child to repeat with her the word 'father', instead of prattling in his usual way, until she has formed in him the habit of calling for his father even in his sleep. This is why the Apostle says: 'Likewise the Spirit also helps our infirmities; for we do not know what to pray for as we should, but the Spirit Himself makes intercession for us with cries that cannot be uttered' (Rom. 8:26). Since we are but children as regards perfection in the virtue of prayer, we have need of the Spirit's aid so that all our thoughts may be concentrated and

---

[1] Following certain manuscripts, des Places reads: 'tears unaccompanied by grief'.

gladdened by His inexpressible sweetness, and so that with all our being we may aspire to the remembrance and love of our God and Father. For, as St Paul says, it is in the Spirit that we pray when we are taught by Him to cry without ceasing to God the Father, 'Abba, Father' (Rom. 8 : 15).

62. The incensive power usually troubles and confuses the soul more than any other passion, yet there are times when it greatly benefits the soul. For when with inward calm we direct it against blasphemers or other sinners in order to induce them to mend their ways or at least feel some shame, we make our soul more gentle. In this way we put ourselves completely in harmony with the purposes of God's justice and goodness. In addition, through becoming deeply angered by sin we often overcome weaknesses in our soul. Thus there is no doubt that if, when deeply depressed, we become indignant in spirit against the demon of corruption, this gives us the strength to despise even the presumptuousness of death. In order to make this clear, the Lord twice became indignant against death and troubled in spirit (cf. John 12 : 27, 13 : 21); and despite the fact that, untroubled, He could by a simple act of will do all that He wished, none the less when He restored Lazarus' soul to his body He was indignant and troubled in spirit (cf. John 11 : 33) – which seems to me to show that a controlled incensive power is a weapon implanted in our nature by God when He creates us. If Eve had used this weapon against the serpent, she would not have been impelled by sensual desire. In my view, then, the man who in a spirit of devotion makes controlled use of his incensive power will without doubt be judged more favourably than the man who, because of the inertness of his intellect, has never become incensed. The latter seems to have an inexperienced driver in charge of his emotions, while the former, always ready for action, drives the horses of virtue through the midst of the demonic host, guiding the four-horsed chariot of self-control in the fear of God. This chariot is called 'the chariot of Israel' in the description of the taking up of the prophet Elijah (cf. 2 Kgs. 2 : 12); for God spoke clearly about the four cardinal virtues first of all to the Jews. This is precisely why Elijah ascended in a fiery chariot, guiding his own virtues as horses, when he was carried up by the Spirit in a gust of fire.

63. Whoever has participated in divine knowledge and tasted the sweetness of God should not defend himself in law, and still less

prosecute, even though someone should go so far as to strip him of his clothes. The justice of the rulers of this world is in every way inferior to that of God or, rather, it is as nothing when compared with it. For what is the difference between the children of God and those of this world, if it is not that the justice of the latter appears imperfect when compared with that of the former, so that we call the one human and the other divine? Thus it was that our Lord Jesus, 'when He was reviled, did not revile in return; when He suffered, He did not threaten' (1 Pet. 2:23); He even kept silent when stripped of His clothes and, what is more, prayed to His Father for the salvation of those who were maltreating Him. The men of this world, however, never stop going to court unless, as sometimes happens, they are given out of court more than they are actually claiming, especially if they have already been receiving interest on the sum involved. In such cases, their justice often becomes the occasion for great injustice.

64. I have heard certain pious men declare that, when people rob us of what we possess for our own support or for the relief of the poor, we should prosecute them, especially if the culprits are Christians; for, it is argued, not to prosecute might encourage crime in those who have wronged us. But this is simply a specious excuse for preferring one's possessions to one's self. For if I abandon prayer and cease to guard the door of my heart, and begin to bring cases against those who wrong me, frequenting the corridors of the courts, it is clear that I regard the goods which I claim as more important than my own salvation – more important even than the commandment of Christ. For how can I possibly follow the injuction: 'When someone takes away your goods, do not try to recover them' (Luke 6:30), unless I gladly endure their loss? Even if we do go to court and recover all we claim, we do not thereby free the criminal from his sin. Human tribunals cannot circumscribe the eternal justice of God, and the accused is punished only according to those laws under which his case is heard. It is therefore better to endure the lawlessness of those who wish to wrong us, and to pray for them, so that they may be released from their guilt through repentance, rather than through restoring what they have taken. Divine justice requires that we receive back not the objects of theft, but the thief himself, freed through repentance from sin.

65. Once the spiritual way has become a reality for us, we shall

find it proper and helpful to follow the Lord's commandment and sell all our possessions immediately, distributing the money we receive (cf. Matt. 19:21), rather than to neglect this injuction on the excuse that we wish always to be in a position to obey the commandments. In the first place, this will secure our complete detachment, and a poverty which is in consequence invulnerable and impervious to all lawlessness and litigation, since we no longer have the possessions which kindle the fire of crime in others. Then, more than all the other virtues, humility will warm and cherish us; in our nakedness she will give us rest in her bosom, like a mother who takes her child into her arms and warms it when, with childish simplicity, it has pulled off what it is wearing and thrown it away, innocently delighting more in nakedness than in pretty clothes. For it is written: 'The Lord preserves the little ones; I humbled myself and He saved me' (Ps. 116:6. LXX).

66. The Lord will demand from us an account of our help to the needy according to what we have and not according to what we have not (cf. 2 Cor. 8:12). If, then, from fear of God I distribute in a short space of time what I might have given away over many years, on what grounds can I be accused, seeing that I now have nothing? On the other hand, it might be argued: 'Who now will give help to the needy that depend on regular gifts out of my modest means?' A person who argues in this way must learn not to insult God because of his own love of money. God will not fail to provide for His own creation as He has done from the beginning; for before this or that person was prompted to give help, the needy did not lack food or clothing. Understanding this, we should reject, in a spirit of true service, the senseless presumption which arises from wealth and we should hate our own desires – which is to hate our own soul (cf. Luke 14:26). Then, no longer possessing wealth which we enjoy distributing, we shall begin to feel our worthlessness intensely, because we find we cannot now perform any good works. Certainly, provided there is some good in us, we gladly obey the divine command and, as long as we are well off, we enjoy giving things away. But when we have exhausted everything an ill-defined gloom and a sense of abasement come over us, because we think we are doing nothing worthy of God's righteousness. In this deep abasement the soul returns to itself, so as to procure through the labour of prayer, through patience and humility what it can no longer acquire by the

daily giving of help to the needy. For it is written: 'The poor and needy shall praise Thy name, O Lord' (Ps. 74:21. LXX). God is not prepared to grant the gift of theology to anyone who has not first prepared himself by giving away all his possessions for the glory of the Gospel; then in godly poverty he can proclaim the riches of the divine kingdom. This is made clear in the Psalm, for after the words 'O God, in Thy love Thou hast provided for the poor', it continues, 'The Lord shall give speech to those who proclaim the gospel with great power' (Ps. 68:10–11. LXX).

67. All God's gifts of grace are flawless and the source of everything good; but the gift which inflames our heart and moves it to the love of His goodness more than any other is theology. It is the early offspring of God's grace and bestows on the soul the greatest gifts. First of all, it leads us gladly to disregard all love of this life, since in the place of perishable desires we possess inexpressible riches, the oracles of God. Then it embraces our intellect with the light of a transforming fire, and so makes it a partner of the angels in their liturgy. Therefore, when we have been made ready, we begin to long sincerely for this gift of contemplative vision, for it is full of beauty, frees us from every worldly care, and nourishes the intellect with divine truth in the radiance of inexpressible light. In brief, it is the gift which, through the help of the holy prophets, unites the deiform soul with God in unbreakable communion. So, among men as among angels, divine theology – like one who conducts the wedding feast – brings into harmony the voices of those who praise God's majesty.

68. Our intellect often finds it hard to endure praying because of the straitness and concentration which this involves; but it joyfully turns to theology because of the broad and unhampered scope of divine speculation. Therefore, so as to keep the intellect from expressing itself too much in words or exalting itself unduly in its joy, we should spend most of our time in prayer, in singing psalms and reading the Holy Scriptures, yet without neglecting the speculations of wise men whose faith has been revealed in their writings. In this way we shall prevent the intellect from confusing its own utterances with the utterances of grace, and stop it from being led astray by self-esteem and dispersed through over-elation and loquacity. In the time of contemplation we must keep the intellect free of all fantasy and image, and so ensure that with almost all our

thoughts we shed tears. When it is at peace in times of stillness, and above all when it is gladdened by the sweetness of prayer, not only does it escape the faults we have mentioned, but it is more and more renewed in its swift and effortless understanding of divine truth, and with great humility it advances in its knowledge of discrimination. There is, moreover, a prayer which is above even the broadest scope of speculation; but this prayer is granted only to those who fully and consciously perceive the plenitude of God's grace within them.

69. At the start of the spiritual way, the soul usually has the conscious experience of being illumined with its own light through the action of grace. But, as it advances further in its struggle to attain theology, grace works its mysteries within the soul for the most part without its knowledge. Grace acts in these two ways so that it may first set us rejoicing on the path of contemplation, calling us from ignorance to spiritual knowledge, and so that in the midst of our struggle it may then keep this knowledge free from arrogance. On the one hand, we need to be somewhat saddened by feeling ourselves abandoned, so that we become more humble and submit to the glory of the Lord; on the other hand, we need to be gladdened at the right time through being lifted up by hope. For just as great sadness brings the soul to despair and loss of faith, so great joy incites it to presumption (I am speaking of those who are still beginners). Midway between illumination and abandonment lies the experience of trial, and midway between sadness and joy lies hope. This is why the Psalmist says: 'I waited patiently for the Lord; and He heard me' (Ps. 40:1); and again: 'According to the multitude of the sufferings in my heart, Thy blessings have gladdened my soul' (Ps. 94:19. LXX).

70. When the door of the steam baths is continually left open, the heat inside rapidly escapes through it; likewise the soul, in its desire to say many things, dissipates its remembrance of God through the door of speech, even though everything it says may be good. Thereafter the intellect, though lacking appropriate ideas, pours out a welter of confused thoughts to anyone it meets, as it no longer has the Holy Spirit to keep its understanding free from fantasy. Ideas of value always shun verbosity, being foreign to confusion and fantasy. Timely silence, then, is precious, for it is nothing less than the mother of the wisest thoughts.

71. Spiritual knowledge teaches us that, at the outset, the soul in pursuit of theology is troubled by many passions, above all by anger and hatred. This happens to it not so much because the demons are arousing these passions, as because it is making progress. So long as the soul is worldly-minded, it remains unmoved and untroubled however much it sees people trampling justice under foot. Preoccupied with its own desires, it pays no attention to the justice of God. When, however, because of its disdain for this world and its love for God, it begins to rise above its passions, it cannot bear, even in its dreams, to see justice set at nought. It becomes infuriated with evil-doers and remains angry until it sees the violators of justice forced to make amends. This, then, is why it hates the unjust and loves the just. The eye of the soul cannot be led astray when its veil, by which I mean the body, is refined to near-transparency through self-control. Nevertheless, it is much better to lament the insensitivity of the unjust than to hate them; for even should they deserve our hatred, it is senseless for a soul which loves God to be disturbed by hatred, since when hatred is present in the soul spiritual knowledge is paralysed.

72. The theologian whose soul is gladdened and kindled by the oracles of God comes, when the time is ripe, to the realm of dispassion; for it is written: 'The oracles of the Lord are pure, as silver when tried in fire, and purged of earth' (Ps. 12:6. LXX). The gnostic, for his part, rooted in his direct experience of spiritual knowledge, is established above the passions. The theologian, if he humbles himself, may also savour the experience of spiritual knowledge, while the gnostic, if he acquires faultless discrimination, may by degrees attain the virtue of theological contemplation. These two gifts, theology and gnosis, never occur in all their fulness in the same person; but theologian and gnostic each marvel at what the other enjoys to a greater degree, so that humility and desire for holiness increase in both of them. That is why the Apostle says: 'For to one is given by the Spirit the principle of wisdom; to another the principle of spiritual knowledge by the same Spirit' (1 Cor. 12:8).

73. When a person is in a state of natural well-being, he sings the psalms with a full voice and prefers to pray out loud. But when he is energized by the Holy Spirit, with gladness and completely at peace he sings and prays in the heart alone. The first condition is accom-

panied by a delusory joy, the second by spiritual tears and, thereafter, by a delight that loves stillness. For the remembrance of God, keeping its fervour because the voice is restrained, enables the heart to have thoughts that bring tears and are peaceful. In this way, with tears we sow seeds of prayer in the earth of the heart, hoping to reap the harvest in joy (cf. Ps. 126 : 5). But when we are weighed down by deep despondency, we should for a while sing psalms out loud, raising our voice with joyful expectation until the thick mist is dissolved by the warmth of song.

74. When the soul has reached self-understanding, it produces from within a certain feeling of warmth for God. When this warmth is not disturbed by worldly cares, it gives birth to a desire for peace which, so far as its strength allows, searches out the God of peace. But it is quickly robbed of this peace, either because our attention is distracted by the senses or because nature, on account of its basic insufficiency, soon exhausts itself. This was why the wise men of Greece could not possess as they should what they hoped to acquire through their self-control, for the eternal wisdom which is the fulness of truth was not at work within their intellect. On the other hand, the feeling of warmth which the Holy Spirit engenders in the heart is completely peaceful and enduring. It awakes in all parts of the soul a longing for God; its heat does not need to be fanned by anything outside the heart, but through the heart it makes the whole man rejoice with a boundless love. Thus, while recognizing the first kind of warmth, we should strive to attain the second; for although natural love is evidence that our nature is in a healthy state through self-control, nevertheless such love lacks the power, which spiritual love possesses, to bring the intellect to the state of dispassion.

75. When the north wind blows over creation, the air around us remains pure because of this wind's subtle and clarifying nature; but when the south wind blows, the air becomes hazy because it is this wind's nature to produce mist and, by virtue of its affinity with clouds, to bring them from its own regions to cover the earth. Likewise, when the soul is energized by the inspiration of the Holy Spirit, it is freed completely from the demonic mist; but when the wind of error blows fiercely upon it, it is completely filled with the clouds of sin. With all our strength, therefore, we should try always to face towards the life-creating and purifying wind of the

Holy Spirit – the wind which the prophet Ezekiel, in the light of spiritual knowledge, saw coming from the north (cf. Ezek. 1:4). Then the contemplative faculty of the soul will always remain clear, so that we devote ourselves unerringly to the contemplation of the divine, beholding the world of light in an air filled with light. For this is the light of true knowledge.

76. Some have imagined that both grace and sin – that is, the spirit of truth and the spirit of error – are hidden at the same time in the intellect of the baptized. As a result, they say, one of these two spirits urges the intellect to good, the other to evil. But from Holy Scripture and through the intellect's own insight I have come to understand things differently. Before holy baptism, grace encourages the soul towards good from the outside, while Satan lurks in its depths, trying to block all the intellect's ways of approach to the divine. But from the moment that we are reborn through baptism, the demon is outside, grace is within. Thus, whereas before baptism error ruled the soul, after baptism truth rules it. Nevertheless, even after baptism Satan still acts on the soul, often, indeed, to a greater degree than before. This is not because he is present in the soul together with grace; on the contrary, it is because he uses the body's humours to befog the intellect with the delight of mindless pleasures. God allows him to do this, so that a man, after passing through a trial of storm and fire, may come in the end to the full enjoyment of divine blessings. For it is written: 'We went through fire and water, and Thou has brought us out into a place where the soul is refreshed' (Ps. 66.12. LXX).

77. As we have said, from the instant we are baptized, grace is hidden in the depths of the intellect, concealing its presence even from the perception of the intellect itself. When someone begins, however, to love God with full resolve, then in a mysterious way, by means of intellectual perception, grace communicates something of its riches to his soul. Then, if he really wants to hold fast to this discovery, he joyfully starts longing to be rid of all his temporal goods, so as to acquire the field in which he has found the hidden treasure of life (cf. Matt. 13:44). This is because, when someone rids himself of all worldly riches, he discovers the place where the grace of God is hidden. For as the soul advances, divine grace more and more reveals itself to the intellect. During this process, however, the Lord allows the soul to be pestered increasingly by demons.

This is to teach it to discriminate correctly between good and evil, and to make it more humble through the deep shame it feels during its purification because of the way in which it is defiled by demonic thoughts.

78. We share in the image of God by virtue of the intellectual activity of our soul; for the body is, as it were, the soul's dwelling-place. Now as a result of Adam's fall, not only were the lineaments of the form imprinted on the soul befouled, but our body also became subject to corruption. It was because of this that the holy Logos of God took flesh and, being God, He bestowed on us through His own baptism the water of salvation, so that we might be reborn. We are reborn through water by the action of the holy and life-creating Spirit, so that if we commit ourselves totally to God, we are immediately purified in soul and body by the Holy Spirit who now dwells in us and drives out sin. Since the form imprinted on the soul is single and simple, it is not possible, as some have thought, for two contrary powers to be present in the soul simultaneously. For when through holy baptism divine grace in its infinite love permeates the lineaments of God's image – thereby renewing in the soul the capacity for attaining the divine likeness – what place is there for the devil? For light has nothing in common with darkness (cf. 2 Cor. 6:14). We who are pursuing the spiritual way believe that the protean serpent is expelled from the shrine of the intellect through the waters of baptism; but we must not be surprised if after baptism we still have wicked as well as good thoughts. For although baptism removes from us the stain resulting from sin, it does not thereby heal the duality of our will immediately, neither does it prevent the demons from attacking us or speaking deceitful words to us. In this way we are led to take up the weapons of righteousness, and to preserve through the power of God what we could not keep safe through the efforts of our soul alone.

79. Satan is expelled from the soul by holy baptism, but is permitted to act upon it through the body for the reasons already mentioned. The grace of God, on the other hand, dwells in the very depths of the soul – that is to say, in the intellect. For it is written: 'All the glory of the king's daughter is within' (Ps. 45:13. LXX), and it is not perceptible to the demons. Thus, when we fervently remember God, we feel divine longing well up within us from the depths of our heart. The evil spirits invade and lurk in

the bodily senses, acting through the compliancy of the flesh upon those still immature in soul. According to the Apostle, our intellect always delights in the laws of the Spirit (cf. Rom. 7 : 22), while the organs of the flesh allow themselves to be seduced by enticing pleasures. Furthermore, in those who are advancing in spiritual knowledge, grace brings an ineffable joy to their body through the perceptive faculty of the intellect. But the demons capture the soul by violence through the bodily senses, especially when they find us faint-hearted in pursuing the spiritual path. They are, indeed, murderers provoking the soul to what it does not want.

80. There are some who allege that the power of grace and the power of sin are present simultaneously in the hearts of the faithful; and to support this they quote the Evangelist who says: 'And the light shines in the darkness; and the darkness did not grasp it' (John 1 : 5). In this way they try to justify their view that the divine radiance is in no way defiled by its contact with the devil, no matter how close the divine light in the soul may be to the demonic darkness. But the very words of the Gospel show that they have departed from the true meaning of Holy Scripture. When John the Theologian wrote in this way, he meant that the Logos of God chose to manifest the true light to creation through His own flesh, with great compassion kindling the light of His holy knowledge within us. But the mentality of this world did not grasp the will of God, that is, it did not understand it, since 'the will of the flesh is hostile to God' (Rom. 8 : 7). Indeed, shortly afterwards the Evangelist goes on to say: 'He was the true light, who illumines every man that comes into the world '– meaning by this that He guides every man and gives him life – and: 'He was in the world, and the world was made by Him, and the world did not know Him. He came to His own, and His own did not receive Him. But to those who received Him He gave power to become the sons of God, even to those who believe in His name' (John 1 : 9–12). Paul, too, interprets the words 'did not grasp it' when he says, 'Not as though I had already grasped it or were already perfect, but I press on in the hope of grasping it; for it was to this end that I have been grasped by Jesus Christ' (Phil. 3 : 12). Thus the Evangelist does not say it is Satan who has failed to grasp the true light. Satan was a stranger to it from the beginning, since it does not shine in him. Rather, the Evangelist is censuring men who hear of the powers and wonders of

the Son of God, and yet in the darkness of their hearts refuse to draw near to the light of spiritual knowledge.

81. Spiritual knowledge teaches us that there are two kinds of evil spirits: some are more subtle, others more material in nature. The more subtle demons attack the soul, while the others hold the flesh captive through their lascivious enticements. Thus there is a complete contrast between the demons that attack the soul and those that attack the body, even though they have the same propensity to inflict harm on mankind. When grace does not dwell in a man, they lurk like serpents in the depths of the heart, never allowing the soul to aspire towards God. But when grace is hidden in the intellect, they then move like dark clouds through the different parts of the heart, taking the form of sinful passions or of all kinds of day-dreams, thus distracting the intellect from the remembrance of God and cutting it off from grace. When the passions of our soul, especially presumption, the mother of all evils, are inflamed by the demons that attack the soul, then it is by thinking on the dissolution of our body that we grow ashamed of our gross love of praise. We should also think about death when the demons that attack the body try to make our hearts seethe with shameful desires, for only the thought of death can nullify all the various influences of the evil spirits by bringing us back to the remembrance of God. If, however, the demons that attack the soul induce in us by this thought an excessive depreciation of human nature on the grounds that, being mortal, it is valueless – and this is what they like to do when we torment them with the thought of death – we should recall the honour and glory of the heavenly kingdom, though without losing sight of the bitter and dreadful aspects of judgment. In this way we both relieve our despondency and restrain the frivolity of our hearts.

82. In the Gospels the Lord teaches us that when Satan returns and finds his home swept and empty – finds, that is to say, the heart barren – he then musters seven other spirits and enters it and lurks there, making its last state worse than its first (cf. Matt. 12:44-45). From this we must understand that so long as the Holy Spirit is in us, Satan cannot enter the depths of the soul and remain there. Paul too clearly conveys this same spiritual understanding. When he looks at the matter from the viewpoint of those still engaged in the ascetic struggle, he says: 'For with the inward man I delight in the law of God; but I see another law in my members, warring against the law

of my intellect, and bringing me into captivity to the law of sin which is in my members' (Rom. 7:22–23). But when he looks at it from the viewpoint of those who have attained perfection, he says: 'There is therefore now no condemnation of those who are in Christ Jesus, who do not walk according to the flesh but according to the Spirit. For the law of the Spirit of life in Christ Jesus has freed me from the law of sin and death' (Rom. 8:1–2). Again, so as to teach us once more that it is through the body that Satan attacks the soul which participates in the Holy Spirit, he says: 'Stand, therefore, having girded your loins with truth, and having on the breastplate of righteousness, and having shod your feet with the gospel of peace; above all, taking the shield of faith with which you will be able quench all the fiery arrows of the evil one. And take the helmet of salvation and the sword of the Spirit, which is the word of God' (Eph. 6:14–17).

Captivity is one thing, battle is another. Captivity signifies a violent abduction, while battle indicates a contest between equally matched adversaries. For precisely this reason the Apostle says that the devil attacks with fiery arrows those who carry Christ in their souls. For someone who is not at close grips with his enemy uses arrows against him, attacking him from a distance. In the same way, when, because of the presence of grace, Satan can lurk no longer in the intellect of those pursuing a spiritual way, he lurks in the body and exploits its humours, so that through its proclivities he may seduce the soul. We should therefore weaken the body to some extent, so that the intellect does not slide down the smooth path of sensual pleasure because of the body's humours. We should believe the Apostle when he says that the intellect of those pursuing the spiritual way is energized by divine light, and therefore obeys and rejoices in the law of God (cf. Rom 7:22). But the flesh, because of its proclivities, readily admits evil spirits, and so is sometimes enticed into serving their wickedness.

Thus it is clear that the intellect cannot be the common dwelling-place of both God and the devil. How can St Paul say that 'with my intellect I serve the law of God, but with the flesh the law of sin' (Rom. 7:25), unless the intellect is completely free to engage in battle with the demons, gladly submitting itself to grace, whereas the body is attracted by the smell of mindless pleasures? He can only say this because the wicked spirits of deception are free to lurk

in the bodies of those pursuing a spiritual way; 'for I know that in
me – that is, in my flesh – there dwells nothing good' (Rom. 7:18),
says the Apostle, referring to those who are resisting and struggling
against sin. Here he is not merely expressing a personal opinion.
The demons attack the intellect, but they do so by trying through
lascivious temptations to entice the flesh down the slope of sensual
pleasure. It is for a good purpose that the demons are allowed to dwell
within the body even of those who are struggling vigorously against
sin; for in this way man's free will is constantly put to the test. If
a man, while still alive, can undergo death through his labours, then
in his entirety he becomes the dwelling-place of the Holy Spirit; for
such a man, before he has died, has already risen from the dead, as
was the case with the blessed Apostle Paul and all those who have
struggled and are struggling to the utmost against sin.

83. It is true that the heart produces good and bad thoughts from
itself (cf. Luke 6:45). But it does this not because it is the heart's
nature to produce evil ideas, but because as a result of the primal
deception the remembrance of evil has become as it were a habit.
It conceives most of its evil thoughts, however, as a result of the
attacks of the demons. But we feel that all these evil thoughts arise
from the heart, and for this reason some people have inferred that
sin dwells in the intellect along with grace. That is why, in their
view, the Lord said: 'But those things which proceed out of the
mouth come forth from the heart; and they defile the man. For out
of the heart proceed evil thoughts, adulteries', and so on (Matt.
15:18–19). They do not realize, however, that the intellect, being
highly responsive, makes its own the thoughts suggested to it by
the demons through the activity of the flesh; and, in a way we do not
understand, the proclivity of the body accentuates this weakness of
the soul because of the union between the two. The flesh delights
endlessly in being flattered by deception, and it is because of this
that the thoughts sown by the demons in the soul appear to come
from the heart; and we do indeed make them our own when we
consent to indulge in them. This was what the Lord was censuring
in the text quoted above, as the words themselves make evident.
Is it not clear that whoever indulges in the thoughts suggested to
him by Satan's cunning and engraves them in his heart, produces
them thereafter as the result of his own mental activity?

84. The Lord says in the Gospel that a strong man cannot be

expelled from a house unless someone stronger than himself disarms him, binds him and casts him out (cf. Matt. 12:29). How, then, can such an intruder, cast out in this shameful way, return and dwell together with the true master who now lives freely in his own house? A king, after defeating a rebel who has tried to usurp his throne, does not dream of allowing him to share his palace. Rather, he slays him immediately, or binds him and hands him over to his soldiers for prolonged torture and a miserable death.

85. The reason why we have both good and wicked thoughts together is not, as some suppose, because the Holy Spirit and the devil dwell together in our intellect, but because we have not yet consciously experienced the goodness of the Lord. As I have said before, grace at first conceals its presence in those who have been baptized, waiting to see which way the soul inclines; but when the whole man has turned towards the Lord, it then reveals to the heart its presence there with a feeling which words cannot express, once again waiting to see which way the soul inclines. At the same time, however, it allows the arrows of the devil to wound the soul at the most inward point of its sensitivity, so as to make the soul search out God with warmer resolve and more humble disposition. If, then, a man begins to make progress in keeping the commandments and calls ceaselessly upon the Lord Jesus, the fire of God's grace spreads even to the heart's more outward organs of perception, consciously burning up the tares in the field of the soul. As a result, the demonic attacks cannot now penetrate to the depths of the soul, but can prick only that part of it which is subject to passion. When the ascetic has finally acquired all the virtues – and in particular the total shedding of possessions – then grace illumines his whole being with a deeper awareness, warming him with great love of God. From now on the arrows of the fiery demon are extinguished before they reach the body; for the breath of the Holy Spirit, arousing in the heart the winds of peace, extinguishes them while they are still in mid-air. Nevertheless, at times God allows the demons to attack even one who has reached this measure of perfection, and leaves his intellect without light, so that his free will shall not be completely constrained by the bonds of grace. The purpose of this is not only to lead us to overcome sin through ascetic effort but also to help us advance still further in spiritual experience. For what is considered perfection in a pupil is far from perfect when compared with the

richness of God, who instructs us in a love which would still seek
to surpass itself, even if we were able to climb to the top of Jacob's
ladder by our own efforts.

86. The Lord himself declares that Satan fell from heaven like
lightning (cf. Luke 10:18); this was to prevent him, in his hideous-
ness, from looking on the dwelling-places of the holy angels. But if
he may not share the company of the righteous servants of God, how
then can he dwell in the intellect of man together with God Himself?
It will be said that this is possible because God recedes a little and
makes room for him. But this explanation is inadequate. For there
are two different ways in which God recedes. First He recedes in
order to educate us. But this receding does not by any means deprive
the soul of divine light. As I have said, all that happens is that grace
often hides its presence from the intellect, so that the soul may
advance through resisting the attacks of the demons by seeking help
from God with great humility and fear; and in this way it gradually
comes to know the wickedness of its enemy. A mother does much
the same when she finds her child rebellious over feeding: she
pushes it away for a moment so that, being alarmed by the sight of
some animals or rough-looking men, it will return crying with
fright to her breast. The second kind of receding is when God
withdraws altogether from the soul that does not want Him; and
this indeed delivers the soul captive to the demons. We, however,
are not children from whom God has withdrawn – heaven forbid!
We believe ourselves to be true children of God's grace, which
nurses us by briefly concealing its presence and then revealing itself
once more, so that through its goodness we may grow to our full
stature.

87. When God recedes in order to educate us, this brings great
sadness, humility and even some measure of despair to the soul.
The purpose of this is to humble the soul's tendency to vanity and
self-glory, for the heart at once is filled with fear of God, tears of
thankfulness, and great longing for the beauty of silence. But the
receding due to God's complete withdrawal fills the soul with
despair, unbelief, anger and pride. We who have experienced both
kinds of receding should approach God in each case in the appropriate way. In the first case we should offer Him thanks as we plead
in our own defence, understanding that He is disciplining our
unruly character by concealing His presence, so as to teach us, like

a good father, the difference between virtue and vice. In the second case, we should offer Him ceaseless confession of our sins and incessant tears, and practise a greater seclusion from the world, so that by adding to our labours we may eventually induce Him to reveal His presence in our hearts as before. Yet we must realize that when there is a direct struggle between Satan and the soul – and I am speaking here of the struggle that takes place when God recedes in order to educate us – then grace conceals itself a little, as I have said, but nevertheless supports the soul in a hidden way, so that in the eyes of its enemies the victory appears to be due to the soul alone.

88. When a man stands out of doors in winter at the break of day, facing the east, the front of his body is warmed by the sun, while his back is still cold because the sun is not on it. Similarly, the heart of those who are beginning to experience the energy of the Spirit is only partially warmed by God's grace. The result is that, while their intellect begins to produce spiritual thoughts, the outer parts of the heart continue to produce thoughts after the flesh, since the members of the heart have not yet all become fully conscious of the light of God's grace shining upon them. Because some people have not understood this, they have concluded that two beings are fighting one another in the intellect. But just as the man in our illustration both shivers and yet feels warm at the touch of the sun, so the soul may have both good and evil thoughts simultaneously. Ever since our intellect fell into a state of duality with regard to its modes of knowledge, it has been forced to produce at one and the same moment both good and evil thoughts, even against its own will; and this applies especially in the case of those who have reached a high degree of discrimination. While the intellect tries to think continually of what is good, it suddenly recollects what is bad, since from the time of Adam's disobedience man's power of thinking has been split into two modes. But when we begin wholeheartedly to carry out the commandments of God, all our organs of perception will become fully conscious of the light of grace; grace will consume our thoughts with its flames, sweetening our hearts in the peace of uninterrupted love, and enabling us to think spiritual thoughts and no longer worldly thoughts. These effects of grace are always present in those who are approaching perfection and have the remembrance of the Lord Jesus unceasingly in their hearts.

89. Divine grace confers on us two gifts through the baptism of regeneration, one being infinitely superior to the other. The first gift is given to us at once, when grace renews us in the actual waters of baptism and cleanses all the lineaments of our soul, that is, the image of God in us, by washing away every stain of sin. The second – our likeness to God – requires our co-operation. When the intellect begins to perceive the Holy Spirit with full consciousness, we should realize that grace is beginning to paint the divine likeness over the divine image in us. Artists first draw the outline of a man in monochrome, and then add one colour after another, until little by little they capture the likeness of the subject down to the smallest details. In the same way the grace of God starts by remaking the divine image in man into what it was when he was first created. But when it sees us longing with all our heart for the beauty of the divine likeness and humbly standing naked in its *atelier*, then by making one virtue after another come into flower and exalting the beauty of the soul 'from glory to glory' (2 Cor. 3 : 18), it depicts the divine likeness on the soul. Our power of perception shows us that we are being formed into the divine likeness; but the perfecting of this likeness we shall know only by the light of grace. For through its power of perception the intellect regains all the virtues, other than spiritual love, as it advances according to a measure and rhythm which cannot be expressed; but no one can acquire spiritual love unless he experiences fully and clearly the illumination of the Holy Spirit. If the intellect does not receive the perfection of the divine likeness through such illumination, although it may have almost every other virtue, it will still have no share in perfect love. Only when it has been made like God – in so far, of course, as this is possible – does it bear the likeness of divine love as well. In portraiture, when the full range of colours is added to the outline, the painter captures the likeness of the subject, even down to the smile. Something similar happens to those who are being repainted by God's grace in the divine likeness: when the luminosity of love is added, then it is evident that the image has been fully transformed into the beauty of the likeness. Love alone among the virtues can confer dispassion on the soul, for 'love is the fulfilling of the law' (Rom. 13 : 10). In this way our inner man is renewed day by day through the experience of love, and in the perfection of love it finds its own fulfilment.

90. If we fervently desire holiness, the Holy Spirit at the outset gives the soul a full and conscious taste of God's sweetness, so that the intellect will know exactly of what the final reward of the spiritual life consists. But later He often conceals this precious and life-creating gift. He does this so that, even if we acquire all the other virtues, we should still regard ourselves as nothing because we have not acquired divine love in a lasting form. It is at this stage that the demon of hate troubles the soul of the spiritual contestant more and more, leading him to accuse of hatred even those who love him, and defiling with hatred even the kiss of affection. The soul suffers all the more because it still preserves the memory of divine love; yet, since it is below the highest level of the spiritual life, it cannot experience this love actively. It is therefore necessary to work upon the soul forcefully for a while, so that we may come to taste divine love fully and consciously; for no one can acquire the perfection of love while still in the flesh except those saints who suffer to the point of martyrdom, and confess their faith despite all persecution. Whoever has reached this state is completely transformed, and does not easily feel desire even for material sustenance. For what desire will someone nourished by divine love feel for such things? It is for this reason that St Paul proclaims to us the future joy of the saints when he says: 'For the kingdom of God is not food and drink, but righteousness, peace and joy in the Holy Spirit' (Rom. 14:17), which are the fruits of perfect love. Those who have advanced to perfection are able to taste this love continually, but no one can experience it completely until 'what is mortal in us is swallowed up by life' (2 Cor. 5:4).

91. A man who loves the Lord with unflagging resolve once said to me: 'Because I desired conscious knowledge of divine love, God granted me a full and active experience of such love. I felt its energy so strongly that my soul longed with an inexpressible joy and love to leave the body and go to the Lord, and to become in a sense unaware of this transient form of life.' Once a man has experienced this love, he does not become angry however much he is insulted and harmed – for one pursuing the spiritual life still suffers such things – but he remains united in love to the soul of the man who has insulted or harmed him. His anger is kindled only against those who injure the poor or who, as the Scripture says, 'speak iniquity against God' (Ps. 75:5. LXX), or follow other forms of

wickedness. Whoever loves God far more than himself, or rather no longer loves himself but only God, no longer vindicates his own honour; for his sole wish is that the divine righteousness, which has accorded him eternal honour, should alone be held in honour. This he no longer wishes in a half-hearted way, but with the force of an attitude established in him through his deep experience of the love of God. We should know, moreover, that a person energized by God to such love rises, at that moment, even above faith, since by reason of his great love he now senses consciously in his heart the One whom he previously honoured by faith. The holy Apostle expresses this clearly when he says: 'Now there are three things that endure: faith, hope, love; but the greatest of them is love' (1 Cor. 13:13). For, as I have said, he who holds God in all the richness of love transcends at that moment his own faith, since he is wholly rapt in divine longing.

92. When spiritual knowledge is active within us to a limited degree, it makes us feel acute remorse if, because of sudden irritation, we insult someone and make an enemy of him. It never stops prodding our conscience until, with a full apology, we have restored in the person we have insulted the feelings he had towards us before. Even when a worldly person becomes angry with us for no reason, this intense compunction in our conscience fills us with uneasiness and anxiety because, in some way, we have become a stumbling-block to one of those who speak after 'the wisdom of this world' (1 Cor. 2:6). As a result the intellect also neglects contemplation; for spiritual knowledge, consisting wholly of love, does not allow the mind to expand and embrace the vision of the divine, unless we first win back to love even one who has become angry with us for no reason. If he refuses to lay aside this anger or avoids the places we ourselves frequent, then spiritual knowledge bids us visualize his person with an overflowing of compassion in our soul and so fulfil the law of love in the depths of our heart. For it is said that if we wish to have knowledge of God we must bring our mind to look without anger even on persons who are angry with us for no reason. When we have done this, not only can our intellect devote itself to theology, but it also ascends with great boldness to the love of God, rising unhindered from the second level to the first.

93. To those who are just beginning to long for holiness the

path of virtue seems very rough and forbidding. It appears like this not because it really is difficult, but because our human nature from the womb is accustomed to the wide roads of sensual pleasure. But those who have travelled more than half its length find the path of virtue smooth and easy. For when a bad habit has been subjected to a good one through the energy of grace it is destroyed along with the remembrance of mindless pleasures; and thereafter the soul gladly journeys on all the ways of virtue. Thus, when the Lord first leads us into the path of salvation, He says: 'How narrow and strait is the way leading to the kingdom and few there are who follow it' (cf. Matt. 7 : 14); but to those who have firmly resolved to keep His holy commandments He says: 'For My yoke is easy, and My burden is light' (Matt. 11 : 30). At the beginning of the struggle, therefore, the holy commandments of God must be fulfilled with a certain forcefulness of will (cf. Matt. 11 : 12); then the Lord, seeing our intention and labour, will grant us readiness of will and gladness in obeying His purposes. For 'it is the Lord who makes ready the will' (Prov. 8 : 35. LXX), so that we always do what is right joyfully. Then shall we truly feel that 'it is God who energizes in you both the willing and the doing of His purpose' (Phil. 2 : 13).

94. As wax cannot take the imprint of a seal unless it is warmed or softened thoroughly, so a man cannot receive the seal of God's holiness unless he is tested by labours and weaknesses. That is why the Lord says to St Paul: 'My grace is sufficient for you: for My power comes to its fulness in your weakness'; and the Apostle himself proudly declares: 'Most gladly therefore will I rather glory in my weaknesses, so that the power of Christ may rest upon me' (2 Cor. 12 : 9). In Proverbs, too, it is written: 'For whom the Lord loves He disciplines; He chastens every son He accepts' (Prov. 3 : 12. LXX). By weaknesses the Apostle means the attacks made by the enemies of the Cross, attacks which continually fell upon him and all the saints of that time, to prevent them from being 'unduly elated by the abundance of revelations', as he says himself (2 Cor. 12 : 7). Because of their humiliation they persevered still more in the life of perfection, and when they were treated with contempt they preserved the divine gift in holiness. But by weaknesses we now mean evil thoughts and bodily illnesses. In those times, since their bodies were submitted to deadly tortures and other afflictions, men pursuing the spiritual way were raised far above the passions which

normally attack human nature as a result of sin. Today, however, since by the Lord's grace peace prevails in the Church, the bodies of those contending for holiness have to be tested by frequent illnesses, and their souls tried by evil thoughts. This is the case especially for those in whom divine knowledge is fully and consciously active, so that they can be stripped of all self-esteem and conceit, and can therefore, as I said, receive in their hearts the seal of divine beauty through their great humility. As the Psalmist says, 'We have been marked by the light of Thy countenance, O Lord' (Ps. 4:6. LXX). We must therefore submit to the Lord's will thankfully; for then our frequent illnesses and our fight against demonic thoughts will be counted a second martyrdom. The devil, who once said to the holy martyrs through the mouths of lawless rulers, 'Deny Christ, choose earthly honours', is now present among us in person constantly saying the same to the servants of God. In times past he tortured the bodies of the saints, inflicting the utmost outrage upon spiritual teachers held in honour by using such people as served his diabolic schemes; and now he attacks the confessors of holiness with the various passions, and with much insult and contempt, especially when for the glory of the Lord they give determined help to the poor and downtrodden. So we should fulfil our inward martyrdom before God with confidence and patience, for it is written: 'I waited patiently for the Lord; and He heard me' (Ps. 40:1).

95. Humility is hard to acquire, and the deeper it is, the greater the struggle needed to gain it. There are two different ways in which it comes to those who share in divine knowledge. In the case of one who has advanced halfway along the path of spiritual experience, his self-will is humbled either by bodily weakness, or by people gratuitously hostile to those pursuing righteousness, or by evil thoughts. But when the intellect fully and consciously senses the illumination of God's grace, the soul possesses a humility which is, as it were, natural. Wholly filled with divine blessedness, it can no longer be puffed up with its own glory; for even if it carries out God's commandments ceaselessly, it still considers itself more humble than all other souls because it shares His forbearance. The first type of humility is usually marked by remorse and despondency, the second by joy and an enlightened reverence. Hence, as I have said, the first is found in those half-way along the spiritual path, while the second is given to those nearing perfection. That is why

the first is often undermined by material prosperity, while the second, even if offered all the kingdoms of this world, is not elated and is proof against the arrows of sin. Being wholly spiritual, it is completely indifferent to all material glory. We cannot acquire the second without having passed through the first; for unless God's grace begins by softening our will by means of the first, testing it through assaults of the passions, we cannot receive the riches of the second.

96. Those who love the pleasures of this present life pass from evil thoughts to actual sins. Since they lack discrimination, they turn almost all their sinful thoughts into wicked words or unholy deeds. Those, on the other hand, who are trying to pursue the ascetic life, struggle first against external sins and then go on to struggle against evil thoughts and malicious words. So when the demons find such people cheerfully abusing others, indulging in idle and inept talk, laughing at the wrong time, uncontrollably angry or desiring vain and empty glory, they join forces to attack them. Using love of praise in particular as a pretext for their evil schemes, the demons slip into the soul – as though through a window at night – and despoil it. So those who wish to live virtuously should not hanker after praise, be involved with too many people, keep going out, or abuse others (however much they deserve it), or talk excessively, even if they can speak well on every subject. Too much talk radically dissipates the intellect, not only making it lazy in spiritual work but also handing it over to the demon of listlessness, who first enervates it completely and then passes it on to the demons of dejection and anger. The intellect should therefore devote itself continually to keeping the holy commandments and to deep mindfulness of the Lord of glory. For it is written: 'Whoever keeps the commandment will know no evil thing' (Eccles. 8 : 5. LXX) – that is, will not be diverted to base thoughts or words.

97. When the heart feels the arrows of the demons with such burning pain that the man under attack suffers as if they were real arrows, then the soul hates the passions violently, for it is just beginning to be purified. It if does not suffer greatly at the shamelessness of sin, it will not be able to rejoice fully in the blessings of righteousness. He who wishes to cleanse his heart should keep it continually aflame through practising the remembrance of the Lord Jesus, making this his only study and his ceaseless task. Those who

desire to free themselves from their corruption ought to pray not merely from time to time but at all times; they should give themselves always to prayer, keeping watch over their intellect even when outside places of prayer. When someone is trying to purify gold, and allows the fire of the furnace to die down even for a moment, the material which he is purifying will harden again. So, too, a man who merely practises the remembrance of God from time to time, loses through lack of continuity what he hopes to gain through his prayer. It is a mark of one who truly loves holiness that he continually burns up what is worldly in his heart through practising the remembrance of God, so that little by little evil is consumed in the fire of this remembrance and his soul completely recovers its natural brilliance with still greater glory.

98. Dispassion is not freedom from attack by the demons, for to be free from such attack we must, as the Apostle says, 'go out of the world' (1 Cor. 5:10); but it is to remain undefeated when they do attack. Troops protected by armour, when attacked by adversaries with bows and arrows, hear the twang of the bow and actually see most of the missiles that are shot at them; yet they are not wounded, because of the strength of their armour. Just as they are undefeated because they are protected by iron, so we can break through the black ranks of the demons if, because of our good works, we are protected by the armour of divine light and the helmet of salvation. For it is not only to cease from evil that brings purity, but actively to destroy evil by pursuing what is good.

99. When the man of God has conquered almost all the passions, there remain two demons that still fight against him. The first troubles the soul by diverting it from its great love of God into a misplaced zeal, so that it does not want any other soul to be as pleasing to God as itself. The second demon inflames the body with sexual lust. This happens to the body in the first place because sexual pleasure with a view to procreation is something natural and so it easily overcomes us; and in the second place it happens because God allows it. When the Lord sees an ascetic maturing in all the virtues, He sometimes allows him to be defiled by this sort of demon, so that the ascetic will regard himself as lower than those living in the world. Of course, this passion troubles men not only after they mature in the virtues, but also before that; in either case the soul is made to appear worthless, however great its virtues may

be. We should fight the first of these demons by means of great humility and love, and the second by means of self-control, freedom from anger, and intense meditation on death, until we come to perceive unceasingly the energy of the Holy Spirit within us and rise with the Lord's help above even these passions.

100. Those of us who come to share in the knowledge of God will have to account for all our vain imaginings, even when they are involuntary. 'For Thou hast marked even my involuntary transgressions', as Job rightly says (Job 14:17. LXX). For if we had not ceased from the remembrance of God and neglected His holy commandments, we would not have succumbed to either voluntary or involuntary sin. We must therefore offer to the Lord at once a strict confession even of our involuntary failings in the practice of our normal rule – and it is impossible for a human being to avoid such human failings – until our conscience is assured through tears of love that we have been forgiven. 'If we confess our sins, He is faithful and just, and will forgive us our sins and cleanse us from all unrighteousness' (1 John 1:9). We should pay close attention to maintaining inward awareness during confession, so that our conscience will not deceive itself into believing that the confession it has made to God is adequate; for though we may not be aware that we have done anything wrong, the judgment of God is far more severe than our conscience. This is what Paul in his wisdom teaches us when he says: 'I do not judge myself; for although I am not conscious of anything against myself, yet I am not thereby acquitted. But it is the Lord who judges me' (1 Cor. 4:3–4).

If we do not confess our involuntary sins as we should, we shall discover an ill-defined fear in ourselves at the hour of our death. We who love the Lord should pray that we may be without fear at that time; for if we are afraid then, we will not be able freely to pass by the rulers of the nether world. They will have as their advocate to plead against us the fear which our soul experiences because of its own wickedness. But the soul which rejoices in the love of God, at the hour of its departure, is lifted with the angels of peace above all the hosts of darkness. For it is given wings by spiritual love, since it ceaselessly carries within itself the love which 'is the fulfilling of the law' (Rom. 13:10). At the coming of the Lord those who have departed the present life with such confidence as this will be 'caught up' together with all the saints (cf. 1 Thess. 4:17);

but those who feel fear even for an instant at the moment of their death will be left behind with the rest of mankind to be tried by the fire of judgment (cf. 1 Pet. 1:7), and will receive from our God and King, Jesus Christ, the lot due to them according to their works. For He is the God of justice and on us who love Him He bestows the blessings of His kingdom through all the ages. Amen.

An interpretation of the phrase in Text 100, 'tried by the fire of judgment', *given by St Maximos at the request of certain brethren*: Those who have acquired perfect love for God and have through their virtues risen with the wings of the soul, will be 'caught up in the clouds', as the Apostle says (1 Thess. 4:17), and will not be brought to judgment. On the other hand, those who have not acquired love in all its perfection, but have both sins and virtues on their account, will appear before the court of judgment. There they will be tried as it were by fire; their good actions will be put in the balance against the bad, and if the good outweigh the bad they will be delivered from punishment.

ST JOHN OF KARPATHOS

Introductory Note

St Nikodimos says that he has little information about St John of Karpathos: 'It is not known when he was active or where he underwent his ascetic struggles.' Our knowledge today is only a little more extensive. Presumably John came from the island of Karpathos, situated between Crete and Rhodes in the archipelago of the Sporades. It is thought that he lived there as a monk in a *coenobium*, and then became bishop of the island; he may be identical with a bishop John of the island 'Karpathion' who signed the acts of the sixth Ecumenical Council (680–1), but this is hypothetical. The monks in India, to whom his two writings are addressed, were perhaps living in Ethiopia. His primary aim is to offer encouragement to those tempted to abandon the monastic life.

For the Encouragement of the Monks in India who had Written to Him: One Hundred Texts

When making a request to an earthly king, sometimes men bring with them as an offering nothing more than a bunch of spring flowers; yet often, so far from rejecting their request, the king has even presented them with gifts in return. In the same way I, at your command, have gathered from various sources a century of spiritual texts: this is my offering to you who are 'citizens of heaven' (Phil. 3 : 20). I hope that you will accept what I offer and grant me in return the gift of your prayers.

1. The King of all reigns for ever, and there is neither beginning nor end to His kingdom. To those, then, who choose to serve Him and who for His sake strive to attain holiness, He grants a reward infinitely greater than that given by any earthly ruler. The honours of this present life, however splendid, come to an end when we die; but the honours bestowed by God on those whom He regards as worthy are incorruptible and so endure for ever.

2. David in one of his Psalms describes the praise offered to God by the whole of creation (cf. Ps. 104). He speaks of the angels and all the invisible powers, but he also descends to the earth and includes wild animals, cattle, birds and reptiles. All of them, he believes, worship the Creator and sing His praise; for it is God's will that everything He has made should offer Him glory. How, then, can the monk, who may be compared to the gold of Ophir (cf. 1 Kgs. 10:11), allow himself to be sluggish or apathetic when singing God's praise?

3. Just as the bush burned with fire but was not consumed (cf. Exod. 3 : 2), so those who have received the gift of dispassion are not troubled or harmed, either physically or in their intellect, by

the heat of their body, however ponderous or fevered it may be. For the voice of the Lord holds back the flames of nature (cf. Ps. 29:7): God's will and His word separate what by nature is united.

4. The moon as it waxes and wanes illustrates the condition of man: sometimes he does what is right, sometimes he sins and then through repentance returns to a holy life. The intellect of one who sins is not destroyed (as some of you think), just as the physical size of the moon does not diminish, but only its light. Through repentance a man regains his true splendour, just as the moon after the period of waning clothes itself once more in its full light. If a man believes in Christ, 'even though he dies, he shall live' (John 11:25); he shall know that 'I the Lord have spoken, and will do it' (Ezek. 17:24. LXX).

5. If you give in and are defeated when a swarm of evil thoughts rises up against you in your mind, you should know that for a time you have been cut off from the grace of God, and by His just sentence abandoned to your fate. Make every effort, then, never through your own negligence to be deprived of grace, even for a single moment. If you manage to avoid falling, if you succeed in leaping over the barrier formed by impassioned thoughts, and if you overcome the unclean provocations that the enemy in his ingenuity continually suggests to you, do not ignore the gift conferred on you from above. As the Apostle says, 'It was not I but the grace of God which was with me' (1 Cor. 15:10) that won this victory, raising me above the impure thoughts that assailed me. It was His grace that 'delivered me from the wicked man' (cf. Ps. 18:48. LXX), that is, from the devil and from the 'old man' within me (cf. Rom. 6:6). Lifted by the wings of the Spirit and freed from the weight of my body, I was able to soar above the predatory demons, who catch man's intellect with the bird-lime of sensual indulgence, tempting it in a forcible and violent manner. It was God who brought me out from the land of Egypt, that is, from the soul-destructiveness of the world; it was God who fought on my behalf and with His unseen hand put Amalek to flight (cf. Exod. 17:8–16), thus giving me cause to hope that He will also drive out the other tribes of impure passions before me. He is our God, and will give us both 'wisdom and power' (Dan. 2:23); for some have received wisdom but not the power of the Spirit to defeat their enemies. He will 'lift up your head above your enemies' (cf. Ps. 27:6); He will

give you 'the wings of a dove', so that you can 'fly away and be at rest' with God (Ps. 55:6). The Lord will make your arms as a 'bow of bronze' (Ps. 18:34. LXX), giving you strength and endurance against the enemy, subduing under your feet all that rise against you (cf. Ps. 18:39). It is to the Lord, then, that you should ascribe the grace of purity, for He did not surrender you to the desires of your flesh and your blood, and to the impure spirits that trouble and corrupt them; but He guarded you with His own right hand. Build Him, then, an altar as Moses did after defeating Amalek (cf. Exod. 17:15). 'Therefore will I give thanks to Thee, O Lord, and sing praises to Thy name' (Ps. 18:49), glorifying Thy mighty acts; for Thou hast 'redeemed my life from destruction' (Ps. 103:4), and snatched me from the midst of all the specious and deceptive snares and nets of evil.

6. The demons in their malice revive and rekindle the unclean passions within us, causing them to increase and multiply. But the visitation of the divine Logos, especially when accompanied by our tears, dissolves and kills the passions, even those that are inveterate. It gradually reduces to nothing the destructive and sinful impulses of soul and body, provided we do not grow listless but cling to the Lord with prayer and with hope that is unremitting and unashamed.

7. Why does Christ accept praise from the mouths of the faithful who are 'little children in regard to evil' (1 Cor. 14:20; cf. Matt. 21:16)? It is because through such praise He destroys the 'enemy and avenger' (Ps. 8:2), who tyrannizes us harshly; for the devil is an enemy of holiness and an avenger in the cause of evil. By praising the Lord with simplicity of heart we overthrow and destroy the schemes of this enemy; for 'in the fulness of Thy glory Thou hast crushed the enemy' (Exod. 15:7).

8. If someone is figuratively speaking an abortion, misshapen by sin, it is said that half his flesh is devoured in this life and half in the life to come (cf. Num. 12:12). For each of us will certainly experience the consequences of his own actions.

9. A monk should practise the virtue of fasting, avoid ensnarement by the passions, and at all times cultivate intense stillness.

10. In their hatred of our souls, the demons sometimes prompt others to pay us empty compliments, and thus cause us to grow slack because we are praised. If as a result we give way to conceit and self-esteem, our enemies have no difficulty in taking us prisoner.

11. Accept scornful criticism rather than words of praise; for a flatterer 'is no different from one who curses' (Prov. 27:14. LXX).

12. If you try to keep the rules of fasting and cannot do so because of ill health, then with contrition of heart you should give thanks to Him who cares for all and judges all. If you always behave with humility before the Lord, you will never show arrogance towards anyone.

13. The enemy knows that prayer is our invincible weapon against him, and so he tries to keep us from praying. He fills us with a desire for secular learning, and encourages us to spend our time on studies that we have already renounced. Let us resist his suggestions; otherwise, if we neglect our own fields and go wandering elsewhere, we shall harvest thorns and thistles instead of figs and grapes. 'For the wisdom of this world is folly in God's sight' (1 Cor. 3:19).

14. It is written: 'I bring you good tidings of great joy which shall come to all people' (Luke 2:10) – not just to some people. Again, it is written: 'Let all the earth worship Thee and sing to Thee' (Ps. 66:4. LXX) – not just part of the earth. This singing is an expression not of grief but of rejoicing. Since this is so, let us not despair, but pass through this present life cheerfully, conscious of its joys. Yet we should temper our gladness with the fear of God, keeping in mind the words: 'Rejoice in the Lord with trembling' (Ps. 2:11). Mary Magdalene and the women with her ran from Christ's tomb with both fear and great joy (cf. Matt. 28:8); and perhaps we, too, shall one day come out from our spiritual tomb with fear and joy. I should be surprised if we were to do so without fear, for there is no one without sin, not even Moses or the Apostle Peter. But, at the time of the departure of such men from this life, God's love proves victorious and casts out fear (cf. 1 John 4:18).

15. The Scriptures testify that if a man still under the sway of the passions believes humbly yet with all his heart, he will receive the gift of dispassion. For it is said: 'Today you shall be with Me in paradise' (Luke 23:43), and: 'Your faith has saved you; go in peace' (Luke 7:50) – the peace, that is, of blessed dispassion. Other texts express the same idea – for example: 'The grapes shall ripen at seedtime' (Amos 9:13. LXX), and: 'According to your faith so be it done to you' (Matt. 9:29).

16. When we fiercely oppose the passions, the demons trouble us all the more severely with shameful thoughts. At such a time, we

should reaffirm our faith in the Lord and set our hope steadfastly in the eternal blessings that He has promised us. In their jealousy our enemies wish to estrange us from these promised blessings and to deprive us of them; indeed, the very fact that the demons burn with such envy against us shows how great these blessings are. Continually bombarding us with unclean thoughts, the demons seek in this way to appease the frenzy within themselves, hoping to drive us to despair through these constant and unbearable attacks.

17. Some hold that the practice of the virtues constitutes the truest form of spiritual knowledge. In that case, we should make every effort to manifest our faith and knowledge through our actions. Whoever trusts blindly to knowledge alone should call to mind the words: 'They claim to know God, but in their actions they deny Him' (Titus 1:16).

18. For the most part it is at the time of Great Feasts and during the Divine Liturgy – especially when we are intending to receive Holy Communion – that the demons try to defile the ascetic with impure fantasies and the flow of semen. Yet they cannot break down the resistance of one accustomed to withstand all things firmly and courageously. Hunchbacks should not exult over us as if they stood upright.

19. The demons try to undermine your inward resolution by buffeting your souls with an untold variety of temptations. Yet out of these many tribulations a garland is woven for you; Christ's power 'comes to its fulness in us in our weakness' (2 Cor. 12:9). It is usually when our situation is most gloomy that the grace of the Spirit flowers within us. 'Light has shone in darkness for the righteous' (Ps. 112:4. LXX) – if, that is, 'we hold fast to our confidence and the rejoicing of our hope firmly to the end' (Heb. 3:6).

20. Nothing so readily obliterates virtue as frivolous talk and making fun of things. On the other hand, nothing so readily renews the decrepit soul, and enables it to approach the Lord, as fear of God, attentiveness, constant meditation on the words of Scripture, the arming of oneself with prayer, and spiritual progress through the keeping of vigils.

21. It is most necessary and helpful for the soul to endure with fortitude every tribulation, whether inflicted by men or by demons. We should recognize that our sufferings are no more than we deserve, and we should never blame anyone but ourselves. For

whoever blames others for his own tribulations has lost the power of judging correctly what is to his own advantage.

22. There are times when trials and temptations multiply and cause a man, despite his diligence, to deviate from the true path; for all his wisdom and skill are swallowed up. This happens so as to prevent us from trusting in ourselves: 'lest Israel boast, saying, My own hand has saved me' (Judg. 7:2). But once the evil one has withdrawn from us, driven away at God's command, we may hope to be restored to the good state that we possessed previously. Urging us to sin, the evil one encourages us to look at everything and listen to it with senses and thoughts imbued with passion. He coarsens our intellect, enveloping it in thick fog, and he makes our body seem an unspeakable weight and burden. Our innate intelligence, which at the outset is simple and undeveloped like a newborn child, he turns into something complex and highly experienced in every kind of sin, poisoning and distorting it through indecision and doubt.

23. When a man grows inwardly and increases in holiness, he is something great and marvellous. But just as the elephant fears the mouse, so the holy man is still afraid of sin, lest after preaching to others he himself 'should be cast away' (cf. 1 Cor. 9:27).

24. It is not only in the period close to the end of the world that the devil will 'speak words against the Most High' (Dan. 7:25). Even now, acting through our thoughts, he sometimes sends up to heaven monstrous blasphemies against the Most High, against all He has created and against the Holy Mysteries of Christ. But, climbing the rock of spiritual knowledge, we should not be terrified by this or astonished at the insolence of the avenger. Growing ever more fervent in our faith and prayer, we shall receive help from above and so resist the enemy.

25. When the soul leaves the body, the enemy advances to attack it, fiercely reviling it and accusing it of its sins in a harsh and terrifying manner. But if a soul enjoys the love of God and has faith in Him, even though in the past it has often been wounded by sin, it is not frightened by the enemy's attacks and threats. Strengthened by the Lord, winged by joy, filled with courage by the holy angels that guide it, encircled and protected by the light of faith, it answers the malicious devil with great boldness: 'Enemy of God, fugitive from heaven, wicked slave, what have I to do with you? You have no authority over me; Christ the Son of God has authority over me and

over all things. Against Him have I sinned, before Him shall I stand on trial, having His Precious Cross as a sure pledge of His saving love towards me. Flee far from me, destroyer! You have nothing to do with the servants of Christ.' When the soul says all this fearlessly, the devil turns his back, howling aloud and unable to withstand the name of Christ. Then the soul swoops down on the devil from above, attacking him like a hawk attacking a crow. After this it is brought rejoicing by the holy angels to the place appointed for it in accordance with its inward state.

26. There is a tiny fish called the remora, which is supposed to have the power to stop a large ship simply by attaching itself to the keel. In a similar manner, by God's permission a person advancing on the spiritual way is sometimes hindered by a small temptation. Remember how even the great Apostle said: 'We wanted to come to you – I, Paul – more than once, but Satan prevented us' (1 Thess. 2:18). Such a hindrance, however, should not upset you: resist firmly, with patient endurance, and you will receive God's grace.

27. When someone far advanced on the spiritual way deviates from it because of indolence, then he is attacked by all the evil 'children of the east', by 'the Amalekites and the Midianites', whose 'camels are without number' (Judg. 7:12). The Midianites signify the forces of unchastity, and their numberless camels are impassioned thoughts. These hostile armies 'destroy all the produce of the earth' (Judg. 6:4), that is, every good action and state. So Israel – that is, the man of whom we are speaking – is brought to destitution and utter discouragement, and is compelled to call upon the Lord. Then, because of his deep faith and humility, the man receives help from heaven, just as Gideon did. 'My clan is the humblest in Manasseh,' said Gideon (cf. Judg. 6:15) – too weak to face such a huge army; yet, against all expectation, with a weak force of three hundred men he defeated the enemy, because God's grace was fighting on his side.

28. You will not be able to 'tread upon the asp and cobra' (Ps. 91:13. LXX), unless in answer to your constant prayers God sends His angels to protect you. They will support you with their hands and raise you above the mire of impurity.

29. When someone is defeated after offering stiff resistance, he should not give up in despair; let him take heart, encouraged by the words of Isaiah: 'In spite of all your strength, you will be defeated,

wicked demons; and if you should again gather your strength together, again you will be defeated. Whatever plans you devise, the
Lord will bring them to nothing: for God is with us' (cf. Isa.
8:9–10). God 'raises up all who are bowed down' (Ps. 145:14)
and produces grief and consternation among our enemies, as soon
as we repent.

30. When you are being tested by trials and temptations, you
cannot avoid feeling dejected. But those who till the earth of
hardship and tribulation in their hearts are afterwards filled with
great joy, tears of consolation and holy thoughts.

31. Isaac wanted to bless Esau, and Esau was eager to receive his
father's blessing; but they failed in their purpose (cf. Gen 27). For
God in His mercy blesses and anoints with the Spirit, not necessarily
those whom we prefer, but those whom He marked out for His
service before creating them. Thus we should not be upset or
jealous if we see certain of our brethren, whom we regard as
wretched and insignificant, making progress in holiness. You know
what the Lord said: 'Make room for this man, so that he can sit in a
higher place' (cf. Luke 14:9). I am full of admiration for the
Judge, who gives His verdict with secret wisdom: He takes one of
the humblest of our brethren and sets him above us; and though we
claim priority on the basis of our asceticism and our age, God puts
us last of all. For 'each must order his life according to what the
Lord has granted him' (1 Cor. 7:17). 'If we live in the Spirit, let us
also walk in the Spirit' (Gal. 5:25).

32. Never acquiesce when someone under obedience to you
pleads: 'Give me time to resolve on such and such a virtuous action;
then I will be able to achieve it.' Whoever speaks like this is clearly
yielding to his own self-will and repudiating his promise of obedience.

33. However great they may have grown, the passions of body
and soul are destroyed, as you will see, by the passing of time and at
God's command. But the mercy of Christ never fails: 'the mercy
of the Lord is from everlasting to everlasting upon them that fear
Him' (Ps. 103:17), continuing with them from this present age
into the age to come.

34. A royal treasury is full of gold; and the intellect of a true
monk is filled with spiritual knowledge.

35. There are times when a teacher falls into disgrace and under-
goes trials and temptations for the spiritual benefit of others. 'For

we are despised and weak,' says the Apostle, 'brought to disgrace by the thorn in our flesh; but you are honoured and made strong in Christ' (cf. 1 Cor. 4:10; 2 Cor. 12:7).

36. Impassioned thoughts are the source and foundation of the corruption which comes to us through the flesh. But if, after sinning, we return to watchfulness through repentance, we expel such thoughts from our soul. It is a good thing that you have been 'filled with grief', so that the wicked and unholy thought that encouraged you to sin may be 'taken from your midst' (1 Cor. 5:2). Grief repulses the spirit of corruption.

37. To anyone among you who is oppressed by a sense of his worthlessness and inability to attain holiness, this is our message: if he attains dispassion he can see Jesus, not only in the future, but coming to him here and now 'with power and great glory' (Matt. 24:30). Though his soul, like Sarah, has grown old in barrenness, it can still bear a holy child, contrary to all expectation; like her he can still say: 'God has made me laugh' (Gen. 21:6) – that is, God has granted me great joy after the many years that I have spent in sorrow, dominated by the passions; God has shown His tender love to me, so that my youth 'is renewed like an eagle's' (Ps. 103:5). Previously I had grown old in sins and shameful passions, but now I am reborn in the fresh vigour of youth; material desires and actions had made me rough and hard, but now I am softened. God in His compassion has healed my intellect, and regaining my natural simplicity I can now see the things of this world clearly. My flesh, like that of Naaman the Syrian, has become as the flesh of a little child, because I have washed in the Jordan of spiritual knowledge (cf. 2 Kgs. 5:14). Now I am at one with myself, set free by God's grace from the guile of the serpent and from the great variety of evil thoughts that I had acquired in a manner contrary to nature.

38. Imagine that the Lord is saying to you: 'For a time I have taken away from you this or that gift of grace, in which you expected your intellect to find fulfilment, and so to be at peace. To make up for this, I have given you instead some other gift. Yet you think only about what has been taken away, not noticing what has been given you in its place; and so you feel dejected, pained and full of gloom. Nevertheless, I am glad because of this gloom which I have brought on you. I make you dejected for your own good. My purpose is not to destroy but to save you, since I regard you as My son.'

39. Suppose you have ordered yourself not to eat fish: you will find that the enemy continually makes you long to eat it. You are filled with an uncontrollable desire for the thing that is forbidden. In this way you can see how Adam's fall typifies what happens to all of us. Because he was told not to eat from a particular tree, he felt irresistibly attracted to the one thing that was forbidden him.

40. God saves one man through spiritual knowledge and another through guilelessness and simplicity. You should bear in mind that 'God will not reject the simple' (Job 8 : 20. LXX).

41. Anyone who devotes himself with special intensity to prayer is assailed by fearsome and savage temptations.

42. If you have resolved to clothe yourself in dispassion, do not be negligent, but strive to attain it with all your strength. 'For we groan, earnestly desiring to be clothed with our house that is from heaven . . . so that what is mortal in us may be swallowed up by life' (2 Cor. 5 : 2–4) – not only in the case of the body after the consummation of this age, but also by anticipation here and now, spiritually. For 'death is swallowed up in victory' (1 Cor. 15 : 54); all the pursuing Egyptians that harass us will be swallowed up in the waves, when power is sent down upon us from heaven.

43. Do not forget what St Paul says: 'I fear lest, after preaching to others, I myself should be cast away' (1 Cor. 9 : 27); 'Let anyone who thinks he stands firm take care lest he fall' (1 Cor. 10 : 12); 'You, who are spiritual . . . look to yourself, in case you also are tempted' (Gal. 6 : 1). Remember how Solomon, after receiving so much grace, turned aside to wickedness (cf. 1 Kgs. 11 : 1–8); remember how St Peter unexpectedly denied his Lord. If you allow yourself to forget all this, you will grow over-confident because of your spiritual knowledge; you will become boastful about your way of life and complacent because of your many years of strict asceticism, and so will give way to pride. Do not become puffed up, my brother, but continue in fear until your last breath, even though you should live as long as Moses. Pray in these words: 'Lord, cast me not off in the time of my old age; forsake me not when my strength fails; O God my Saviour, my praise shall be continually of Thee' (cf. Ps. 71 : 6, 9).

44. The Lord says to you what He said to Matthew: 'Follow Me' (Matt. 9 : 9). But when you follow the Lord with burning love, it may happen that on the road of life you strike your foot against the

stone of some passion and fall unexpectedly into sin; or else, finding yourself in a muddy place, you may slip involuntarily and fall headlong. Each time you fall and in this way injure your body, you should get up again with the same eagerness as before, and continue to follow after your Lord until you reach Him. 'Thus have I appeared before Thee in the sanctuary' – the sanctuary of my thoughts – 'that I might behold Thy power and glory', for they are my salvation. 'In Thy name will I lift up my hands', and I shall be heard; I shall think myself 'filled with marrow and fatness', and my lips will rejoice as they sing Thy praise (Ps. 63:2, 4, 5. LXX). It is a great thing for me to be called a Christian, as the Lord tells me through Isaiah: 'It is no light thing for you to be called My servant' (Isa. 49:6. LXX).

45. In one place it is said that the Father 'will give good things to those that ask Him' (Matt. 7:11); elsewhere, that He will 'give the Holy Spirit to those that ask Him' (Luke 11:13). From this we learn that those who pray to God with steadfast faith in these promises receive not only remission of sins but also heavenly gifts of grace. The Lord promised these 'good things' not to the righteous but to sinners, saying: 'If you then, being evil, know how to give good gifts to your children, how much more will your heavenly Father give the Holy Spirit to those that ask Him?' (Luke 11:13). Ask, then, unremittingly and without doubting, however poor your efforts to gain holiness, however weak your strength; and you will receive great gifts, far beyond anything that you deserve.

46. How can someone with little or no faith be made to realize that an ant grows wings, a caterpillar turns into a butterfly, and many other strange and unexpected things happen in nature, so that in this way he shakes off the sickness of unbelief and despair, himself acquires wings, and buds in spiritual knowledge like a tree? 'I am He', says God, 'who makes the dry tree flourish; I give life to the dry bones' (cf. Ezek. 17:24; 37:1–14.).

47. We should on no account wear ourselves out with anxiety over our bodily needs. With our whole soul let us trust in God: as one of the Fathers said, 'Entrust yourself to the Lord, and all will be entrusted to you.' 'Show restraint and moderation,' writes the Apostle Peter, 'and be watchful in prayer . . . casting all your care upon God, since He cares for you' (1 Pet. 4:7; 5:7). But if you still feel uncertainty, doubting whether He really cares about

providing for you, think of the spider and compare it with a human being. Nothing is more weak and powerless than a spider. It has no possessions, makes no journeys overseas, does not engage in litigation, does not grow angry, and amasses no savings. Its life is marked by complete gentleness, self-restraint and extreme stillness. It does not meddle in the affairs of others, but minds its own business; calmly and quietly it gets on with its own work. To those who love idleness it says, in effect: 'If anyone refuses to work, he should have nothing to eat' (2 Thess. 3:10). The spider is far more silent than Pythagoras, whom the ancient Greeks admired more than any other philosopher because of the control that he exercised over his tongue. Although Pythagoras did not talk with everyone, yet he did speak occasionally in secret with his closest friends; and often he lavished nonsensical remarks on oxen and eagles. He abstained altogether from wine and drank only water. The spider, however, achieves more than Pythagoras: it never utters a single word, and abstains from water as well as from wine. Living in this quiet fashion, humble and weak, never going outside or wandering about according to its fancy, always hard at work – nothing could be more lowly than the spider. Nevertheless the Lord, 'who dwells on high but sees what is lowly' (Ps. 113:5–6. LXX), extends His providence even to the spider, sending it food every day, and causing tiny insects to fall into its web.

48. One who is enslaved to greed may perhaps object: 'I eat a great deal, and since this involves me in heavy expenses, I am inevitably tied up with all kinds of worldly business.' Such a person should think of the huge whales that feed in the Atlantic Ocean: God gives them plenty to eat and they never starve, although each of them swallows daily more fish than a highly populated city would consume. 'All things wait upon Thee, to give them their food at the proper time' (Ps. 104:27). It is God who provides food both for those who eat much and for those who eat little. Bearing this in mind, anyone among you who has a capacious appetite should in future set his faith entirely in God, freeing his intellect from all worldly distractions and anxieties. 'Be no longer faithless, but have faith' (John 20:27).

49. If we truly wish to please God and to enjoy the grace of His friendship, we should present to Him an intellect that is stripped bare – not weighed down with anything that belongs to this

present life, with any skill or notion or argument or excuse, however highly educated we may be in the wisdom of this world. God turns away from those who approach Him presumptuously, puffed up with self-esteem. People who suffer from futile conceit we rightly describe as bloated and puffed up.

50. How can we overcome the sinfulness that is already firmly established within us? We must use force. A man labours and struggles, and so by the use of force he escapes from destruction, always striving to raise his thoughts to holiness. We are not forbidden to resist force with force. If in any ascetic task we exert force, however slight, then, 'remaining in Jerusalem', we can wait for the 'power from on high' which will come down upon us (cf. Luke 24:49). In other words, if we persevere in unceasing prayer and the other virtues, there will come upon us a mighty force, infinitely stronger than any we can exert. This force cannot be described in human language; in its great strength it overcomes our worst faults of character and the malice of the demons, conquering both the sinful inclinations of our soul and the disordered impulses of our body. 'There came a sound from heaven as of a rushing violent wind' (Acts 2:2); and this force from heaven drives out the evil that is always forcing us into sin.

51. The enemy lurks like a lion in his den; he lays in our path hidden traps and snares, in the form of impure and blasphemous thoughts. But if we continue wakeful, we can lay for him traps and snares and ambuscades that are far more effective and terrible. Prayer, the recitation of psalms and the keeping of vigils, humility, service to others and acts of compassion, thankfulness, attentive listening to the words of Scripture – all these are a trap for the enemy, an ambuscade, a pitfall, a noose, a lash and a snare.

52. When already well advanced in years, David offered thanks to God for choosing him, and he said this about the final fruits of God's blessing: 'Now has Thy servant found his own heart, so as to offer this prayer' (2 Sam. 7:27. LXX). This he said to teach us that a great effort and much time are needed in prayer, before through struggle we can reach a state in which our mind is no longer troubled, and so attain the inward heaven of the heart where Jesus dwells. As the Apostle says, 'Do you not know that Jesus Christ dwells within you?' (cf. 2 Cor. 13:5).

53. If Christ is our 'wisdom, righteousness, sanctification and

redemption' (1 Cor. 1:30), it is clear that He is also our rest. As He Himself says, 'Come to Me, all that labour and are heavy laden, and I will give you rest' (Matt. 11:28). He says also that the sabbath – and 'sabbath' means 'rest' – was made for man (cf. Mark 2:27); for only in Christ will the human race find rest.

54. Just as there is 'a cup of calamity and a goblet of wrath' (Isa. 51:17. LXX), so there is a cup of weakness which, at the proper time, the Lord takes from our hands and puts into the hands of our enemies. Then it is no longer we but the demons who grow weak and fall.

55. Outwardly men follow different occupations: there are money-changers, weavers, fowlers, soldiers, builders. Similarly, we have within us different types of thoughts: there are gamblers, poisoners, pirates, hunters, defilers, murderers, and so on. Rebutting such thoughts in prayer, the man of God should immediately shut the door against them – and most of all against the defilers, lest they defile his inward sanctuary and so pollute him.

56. The Lord can be robbed and made to grant salvation, not only by speech – as in the case of the thief who cried out from the cross (cf. Luke 23:42) – but also by thought. The woman who suffered from a haemorrhage merely thought within herself: 'If I can but touch the hem of His garment, I shall be healed' (Matt. 9:21). Another example is Abraham's servant, who spoke inwardly to God about Rebekah (cf. Gen. 24:12–28).

57. Sin itself drives us towards God, once we repent and have become aware of its burden, foul stink and lunacy. But if we refuse to repent, sin does not drive us towards God. In itself it holds us fast with bonds that we cannot break, making the desires which drive us to our own destruction all the more vehement and fierce.

58. Guard yourself from the witchcraft of Jezebel (cf. 2 Kgs. 9:22). Her most powerful spells are thoughts of delusion and vainglory. By God's grace you can overcome such thoughts, if you regard yourself as worthless and despicable, casting yourself down before the Lord, calling upon Him to help you, and acknowledging that every gift of grace comes from heaven. For it is written: 'A man can receive nothing, unless it is given him from heaven' (John 3:27).

59. The Law says about a bull which is given to goring other bulls: 'If men have protested to the owner and he has not destroyed

the animal, he shall pay' (Exod. 21 : 36. LXX). You should apply this to your thoughts and impulses. Sometimes during a meal the impulse of self-esteem springs up inside you, urging you to speak at the wrong moment. Then angelic thoughts protest within you and tell you to destroy this impulse to speak. If you do not resist the impulse by keeping silent as you should, but allow it to come out into the open because you are puffed up by delusion, then you will have to pay the penalty. As a punishment you will perhaps be tempted to commit some grave sin; alternatively, you may experience severe bodily pain, or be involved in violent conflict with your brethren, or else suffer torment in the age to come. We shall have to give account for every idle and conceited word spoken by our ill-disciplined tongue. Let us guard our tongue, then, with watchfulness.

60. The Psalm says of those who are tempted by thoughts of pleasure, anger, love of praise and the like, that the sun burns them by day and the moon by night (cf. Ps. 121 : 6). Pray, then, to be sheltered by the cool and refreshing cloud of God's grace, so that you may escape the scorching heat of the enemy.

61. Never form a close friendship with someone who enjoys noisy and drunken feasts, or who likes telling dirty stories, even though he may have been a monk for many years. Do not let his filth defile you; do not fall under the influence of people who are unclean and uncircumcised in heart.

62. Peter was first given the keys, but then he was allowed to fall into the sin of denying Christ; and so his pride was humbled by his fall. Do not be surprised, then, if after receiving the keys of spiritual knowledge you fall into various evil thoughts. Glorify our Lord, for He alone is wise: through setbacks of this kind He restrains the presumption that we tend to feel because of our advance in the knowledge of God. Trials and temptations are the reins whereby God in His providence restrains our human arrogance.

63. Often God takes away His blessings from us, just as He deprived Job of his wealth: 'The Lord gave and the Lord has taken away' (Job 1 : 21). But it is equally true that God will also remove from us the adversities He has brought upon us. 'Both blessings and adversities come from God' (Ecclus. 11 : 14); He has caused us to suffer adversities, but He will also give us eternal joy and glory. 'As I watched over you,' says the Lord, 'to destroy and afflict you,

so will I build you up again and will not pull you down; I will plant you and will not uproot you' (cf. Jer. 31:28; 24:6). Do not say: 'It's just my bad luck'; for the Lord, who changed our situation for the worse, can unexpectedly alter it again for the better.

64. If someone launches a fierce and determined attack on the demons through his self-control, prayer or any other form of holiness, they retaliate by inflicting deeper wounds upon him. Eventually he is reduced to despair, and feels in his soul that he has received a spiritual death-sentence. He is even brought to say: 'Who will deliver me from the body of this death? For I am compelled against my will to submit to the laws of my adversary' (cf. Rom. 7:23–24).

65. The demons say to themselves: 'Let us rise up, and fall upon a people that lives in hope and stillness; come, let us go and speak to them with words of spiritual deceit, seducing them from the truth over to our side' (cf. Judg. 18:27; Isa. 7:6. LXX). So they sharpen the sword of temptation against us who have chosen the life of stillness, and continue their attacks up to the last moment of our life. The more fervent our devotion and love for God, the more savage are their assaults; they urge us on to acts of sin, making war upon us in ways that we cannot endure, trying in this manner to deprive us of our faith in Christ, of prayer and every hope. But for our part we shall not cease to trust in God 'until He has mercy upon us' (Ps. 123:2), and those that devour us are driven far away. We shall not cease to trust in God, until He commands our tempters to depart, and we are given new life through patience and steadfast dispassion. For 'the life of man is a time of testing' (Job 7:1. LXX). God, who watches over the contest, often allows us for some definite period of time to be trampled underfoot by our enemies; but it is the mark of a courageous and noble soul not to despair in adversity.

66. If a demon has such strength as to force a man, even against his will, to change from his natural state of goodness into a state of sin, how great must be the strength of the angel who at the appointed time is commanded by God to restore that man's whole condition. If the icy blast of the north wind is strong enough to give to water the hardness of rock, what cannot the warmth of the south wind achieve? If extreme cold forces everything to submit to it – for 'who can withstand His cold?' (Ps. 147:17) – cannot heat in the

same way alter everything? 'Who can abide the burning heat?' (Ecclus. 43 : 3). So let us confidently believe that the cold, dark coals of our mind will sooner or later blaze with heat and light under the influence of the divine fire.

67. We should mention in this connection an inward state that shows the degree of dispassion attained by the Joseph hidden within each of us. Our intellect, departing from Egypt, leaves behind it the burden of the passions and the builder's basket of shameful slavery, and it hears a language that it does not understand (cf. Ps. 81 : 5–6. LXX). It hears no longer the demons' language, impure and destructive of all true understanding, but the holy language of the light-giving angels, who convert the intellect from the non-spiritual to the spiritual – a language which illumines the soul that hears and accepts it.

68. Once certain brethren, who were always ill and could not practise fasting, said to me: 'How is it possible for us without fasting to rid ourselves of the devil and the passions?' To such people we should say: you can destroy and banish what is evil, and the demons that suggest this evil to you, not only by abstaining from food, but by calling with all your heart on God. For it is written: 'They cried to the Lord in their trouble and He delivered them' (Ps. 107:6); and again: 'Out of the belly of hell I cried and Thou heardest my voice . . . Thou hast brought up my life from corruption' (Jonah 2 : 2, 6). Therefore 'until iniquity shall pass away' – that is, as long as sin still troubles me – 'I will cry to God most high' (Ps. 57 : 1–2. LXX), asking Him to bestow on me this great blessing: by His power to destroy within me the provocation to sin, blotting out the fantasies of my impassioned mind and rendering it image-free. So, if you have not yet received the gift of self-control, know that the Lord is ready to hear you if you entreat Him with prayer and hope. Understanding the Lord's will, then, do not be discouraged because of your inability to practise asceticism, but strive all the more to be delivered from the enemy through prayer and patient thanksgiving. If thoughts of weakness and distress force you to leave the city of fasting, take refuge in another city (cf. Matt. 10:23) – that is, in prayer and thanksgiving.

69. Pharaoh entreated, saying: 'May God take away from me this death' (Exod. 10:17), and he was heard. Similarly, when the demons asked the Lord not to cast them into the abyss, their request

was granted (cf. Luke 8 : 31). How much more, then, will a Christian be heard when he prays to be delivered from spiritual death?

70. It may happen that for a certain time a man is illumined and refreshed by God's grace, and then this grace is withdrawn. This makes him inwardly confused and he starts to grumble; instead of seeking through steadfast prayer to recover his assurance of salvation, he loses patience and gives up. He is like a beggar who receives alms from the palace, and feels put out because he was not asked inside to dine with the king.

71. 'Blessed are those who have not seen, and yet have believed' (John 20 : 29). Blessed also are those who, when grace is withdrawn, find no consolation in themselves, but only continuing tribulation and thick darkness, and yet do not despair; but, strengthened by faith, they endure courageously, convinced that they do indeed see Him who is invisible.

72. The humility which in due time and by God's grace, after many struggles and tears, is given from heaven to those who seek it is something incomparably stronger and higher than the sense of abasement felt by those who have lapsed from holiness. This higher humility is granted only to those who have attained true perfection and are no longer under the sway of sin.

73. 'Then the devil left Him, and angels came and ministered to Him' (Matt. 4 : 11). It does not say that the angels were with our Lord during the actual time when He was being tempted. In the same way, when we are being tempted, God's angels for a time withdraw a little. Then, after the departure of those tempting us, they come and minister to us with divine intellections, giving us support, illumination, compunction, encouragement, patient endurance, joyfulness, and everything that saves and strengthens and renews our exhausted soul. As Nathanael was told, 'You will see the angels ascending and descending upon the Son of man' (John 1 : 51); in other words, the ministry and assistance of the angels will be given generously to mankind.

74. Keep in mind that high priest at whose right hand the devil stood, opposing all his good thoughts and words and actions (cf. Zech. 3 : 1). Then you will not be astonished at what happens to yourself.

75. A monk should understand what it means to be weak, and he should remember the words: 'Have mercy upon me, O Lord, for

I am weak' (Ps. 6:2). He should understand what it means to be in rebellion against God; for this is the sickness with which the devil and his angels are afflicted.

76. Fire makes iron impossible to touch, and likewise frequent prayer renders the intellect more forceful in its warfare against the enemy. That is why the demons strive with all their strength to make us slothful in attentiveness to prayer, for they know that prayer is the intellect's invincible weapon against them.

77. When David went out from the city of Ziklag to fight the Amalekites, some of the men with him were so exhausted that they stayed behind at the brook Besor and took no part in the battle (cf. 1 Sam. 30:10). Returning after his victory, he heard the rest of his troops saying that no share in the spoils should be given to the men who had stayed behind; and he saw that these themselves were ashamed and kept silent. But David recognized that they had wanted to fight, and so in his kindness he spoke in their defence, saying that they had remained behind to guard the baggage; and on this ground he gave them as large a share in the spoils as he gave to the others who had fought bravely in the battle. You should behave in the same way towards a brother who shows fervour at first, but then grows slack. In the case of this brother and his salvation, the baggage consists of faith and repentance, humility and tears, patience, hope, long-suffering and the like. If in spite of his slackness he yet guards this baggage, waiting expectantly for Christ's coming, he is rightly given an eternal reward.

78. We give the name of Levites and priests to those who dedicate themselves totally to God, alike through the practice of the virtues and through contemplation. Those who do not have the strength to hunt down the passions may be called 'the cattle of the Levites' (Num. 3:41). They have a genuine and continuing thirst for holiness, and try to attain it so far as they can; but they frequently fail, hamstrung by sin. Yet we may expect that at the right moment God will grant the gift of dispassion to them as well, solely by virtue of His love; for 'the Lord has heard the desire of the poor' (Ps. 10:17. LXX).

79. We are aware of the torment that the enemy frequently inflicts upon us visibly or invisibly. But we do not perceive the torment and anguish that we inflict upon him, when we sometimes succeed in practising the virtues, when we repent over our trans-

gressions or show long-suffering and perseverance in our difficulties, or when we pray and do other things which pierce him to the heart, torture him and cause him bitter grief. God in His providence conceals all this from us, so as to prevent us from growing sluggish. Be sure, however, that 'God thinks it right to repay with affliction those who afflict you' (2 Thess. 1:6).

80. If the base of a felled tree that has grown old in earth and rock 'will bud at the scent of water . . . like a young plant' (Job 14:9), it is also possible for us to be awakened by the power of the Holy Spirit and to flower with the incorruptibility that is ours by nature, bearing fruit like a young plant, even though we have fallen into sin.

81. Sometimes our soul grows despondent at the huge swarm of its sins and temptations, and says, 'Our hope is gone and we are lost' (Ezek. 37:11. LXX). Yet God, who does not despair of our salvation, says to us: 'You shall live, and you shall know that I am the Lord' (Ezek. 37:6). To the soul that doubts how it can ever give birth to Christ through great acts of holiness, these words are said: 'The Holy Spirit shall come upon you' (Luke 1:35). Where the Holy Spirit is present, do not expect any more the sequence and laws of nature and habit. The Holy Spirit whom we worship is all-powerful, and in an astonishing way He brings into existence what does not as yet exist within us. The intellect that was previously defeated He now makes victorious; for the Paraclete who in compassion comes upon us from above 'is higher than all' (John 3:31), and He raises us above all natural impulses and demonic passions.

82. Struggle to preserve unimpaired the light that shines within your intellect. If passion begins to dominate you when you look at things, this means that the Lord has left you in darkness; He has dropped the reins with which He was guiding you, and the light of your eyes is gone from you (cf. Ps. 38:10). Yet even if this happens, do not despair or give up, but pray to God with the words of David: 'O send out Thy light and Thy truth to me in my gloom, for Thou art the salvation of my countenance and my God' (cf. Ps. 43:3, 5); 'Thou shalt send forth Thy Spirit and they shall be created; and Thou shalt renew the face of the earth' (Ps. 104:30. LXX).

83. Blessed is he who, with a hunger that is never satisfied, day and night throughout this present life makes prayer and the psalms

his food and drink, and strengthens himself by reading of God's glory in Scripture. Such communion will lead the soul to ever-increasing joy in the age to come.

84. Do all in your power not to fall, for the strong athlete should not fall. But if you do fall, get up again at once and continue the contest. Even if you fall a thousand times because of the withdrawal of God's grace, rise up again each time, and keep on doing so until the day of your death. For it is written, 'If a righteous man falls seven times' – that is, repeatedly throughout his life – seven times 'shall he rise again' (Prov. 24:16. LXX). So long as you hold fast, with tears and prayer, to the weapon of the monastic habit, you will be counted among those that stand upright, even though you fall again and again. So long as you remain a monk, you will be like a brave soldier who faces the blows of the enemy; and God will commend you, because even when struck you refused to surrender or run away. But if you give up the monastic life, running away like a coward and a deserter, the enemy will strike you in the back; and you will lose your freedom of communion with God.

85. It is more serious to lose hope than to sin. The traitor Judas was a defeatist, inexperienced in spiritual warfare; as a result he was reduced to despair by the enemy's onslaught, and he went and hanged himself. Peter, on the other hand, was a firm rock: although brought down by a terrible fall, yet because of his experience in spiritual warfare he was not broken by despair, but leaping up he shed bitter tears from a contrite and humiliated heart. And as soon as our enemy saw them, he recoiled as if his eyes had been burnt by searing flames, and he took to flight howling and lamenting.

86. The monk should wage a truceless war above all on these three things: gluttony, futile self-esteem, and avarice – which is a form of idolatry (cf. Col. 3:5).

87. There was once a king of Israel who subdued cave-dwellers and other barbarian tribes by using the psalms and music of David. You, too, have barbarian cave-dwellers living within you: the demons who have gained admittance to your senses and limbs, who torment and inflame your flesh. Because of them lust is in your eyes when you look at things; as you listen or use your sense of smell, passion dominates you; you indulge in dirty talk; you are full of turmoil inwardly and outwardly, like the city of Babylon. With great faith, then, and with 'psalms and hymns and spiritual songs'

(Eph. 5:19), you too must destroy the cave-dwellers who work evil within you.

88. The Lord desires one man to be saved through another, and in the same way Satan strives to destroy one man through another. So do not spend your time with somebody who is sloppy, a mischief-maker, not guarding his tongue, lest you be sent with him into punishment. It is hard enough for one who associates with a good man to attain salvation. If you do not watch yourself, but consort with people of evil character, you will be infected with their leprosy and destroyed. How can anyone expect pity if he recklessly approaches a poisonous snake? You should avoid those who cannot control their tongue, who are quarrelsome and full of agitation inwardly or outwardly.

89. If you wish to be called wise, intelligent and the friend of God, strive to present your soul to the Lord in the same state as you received it from Him: pure, innocent, completely undefiled. Then you will be crowned in heaven and the angels will call you blessed.

90. A single good word made the thief pure and holy, despite all his previous crimes, and brought him into paradise (cf. Luke 23:42–43). A single ill-advised word prevented Moses from entering the promised land (cf. Num. 20:12). We should not suppose, then, that garrulity is only a minor disease. Lovers of slander and gossip shut themselves out from the kingdom of heaven. A chatterbox may meet with success in this world, but he will not do so in the next. There he will trip and fall; 'evil will hunt him down and destroy him' (Ps. 140:11. LXX). It has been well said: 'Better to slip on the ground than to slip with your tongue' (Ecclus. 20:18). We should believe James the Apostle when he writes: 'Let every man be swift to hear and slow to speak' (Jas. 1:19).

91. So as not to be deceived and carried away by the vain and empty things that the senses bring before us, we should listen to the words of the prophet Isaiah: 'Come, my people, enter into your inner room' – the shrine of your heart, which is closed to every conception derived from the sensible world, that image-free dwelling-place illumined by dispassion and the overshadowing of God's grace; 'shut your door' – to all things visible; 'hide yourself for a brief moment' – the whole of man's life is but a moment; 'until the Lord's anger has passed by' (Isa. 26:20. LXX); or, as the

Psalms put it, 'until iniquity has passed' (Ps. 57:1). This anger of the Lord and this iniquity may be caused by demons, passions and sins; as Isaiah says to God, 'Behold, Thou art angry, for we have sinned' (Isa. 64:5). A man escapes this anger by keeping his attention fixed continually within his heart during prayer, and by striving to remain within his inner sanctuary. As it is written, 'Draw wisdom into your innermost self' (Job 28:18. LXX); 'all the glory of the king's daughter is within' (Ps. 45:13. LXX). Let us, then, continue to struggle until we enter the holy place of God, 'the mountain of Thine inheritance, the dwelling, O Lord, which Thou hast made ready, the sanctuary which Thy hands have prepared' (Exod. 15:17).

92. If you really wish to renounce the world, you should imitate the prophet Elisha, who in his intense and burning love for God kept nothing back for himself (cf. 1 Kgs. 19:21). You should distribute all your possessions to those in need and so take up the Cross of Christ, hastening eagerly and willingly to die to this world; and you will receive in exchange the eternal kingdom.

93. Once you have realized that the Amorite within you is 'as strong as an oak', you should pray fervently to the Lord to dry up 'his fruit from above' – that is, your sinful actions, and 'his roots from beneath' – that is, your impure thoughts. Ask the Lord in this way to 'destroy the Amorite from before your face' (Amos 2:9. LXX).

94. You should not be surprised when those who are themselves incapable of attaining stillness ridicule the stillness that we have achieved. Apply the words of the Psalter to them – but without any feeling of rancour. Resist them by intensifying your obedience to God, and repeat the words: 'My soul, be obedient to God' (Ps. 62:5. LXX); 'In return for my love, they made false accusations against me; but I continued to pray' – for their healing as well as my own (Ps. 109:4. LXX).

95. When there is no wind blowing at sea, there are no waves; and when no demon dwells within us, our soul and body are not troubled by the passions.

96. If you always feel the warmth of prayer and divine grace you may apply to yourself the words of Scripture: you have 'put on the armour of light' (Rom. 13:12) and 'your garments are warm' (Job 37:17). But your enemies are 'clothed with shame' (Ps. 109:29) and with the darkness of hell.

97. When recalling your sins, do not hestitate to beat your breast. With these blows you will dig into your hardened heart and discover within it the gold-mine of the publican (cf. Luke 18:13); and this hidden wealth will bring you great joy.

98. Let the fire of your prayer, ascending upwards as you meditate on the oracles of the Spirit, burn always on the altar of your soul.

99. If at every moment you strive to have 'your feet shod with the gospel of peace' (Eph. 6:15), you will always be building up your neighbour's house as well as your own. But if you are indolent, the demons will spit invisibly in your face and, as the Law states, you will be known as 'the man who had his sandal pulled off' (cf. Deut. 25:9–10).

100. If, as St John says, 'God is love', then 'he who dwells in love dwells in God, and God in him' (1 John 4:16). But he who hates his neighbour, through this hatred, is separated from love. He, then, who hates his brother is separated from God, since 'God is love, and he who dwells in love dwells in God, and God in him.' To Him be glory and power through all the ages. Amen.

Ascetic Discourse Sent at the Request of the Same Monks in India

A SUPPLEMENT TO THE ONE HUNDRED TEXTS

Never think that a person in the outside world – someone living contentedly with a wife and children – is more blessed than a monk because he is able to do good to others and to give generous alms, and seems never to be tempted by demons at all. Do not suppose that you are less pleasing in God's sight than he is; do not torture yourself, imagining that you are doomed. I do not say that your life is beyond reproach simply because you persevere in the monastic state; but even if you happen to be a very great sinner, the anguish of soul and hardship that you endure are more precious in God's sight than surpassingly great virtue on the part of someone living in the world. Your deep dejection and despondency, your tears and sighs of distress, the torments of your conscience and your doubts, your feelings of self-condemnation, the sorrow and lamentation of your intellect and heart, your contrition and wretchedness, your gloom and self-abasement – such experiences as these, which frequently overwhelm those cast into the iron furnace of trials and temptations, are far more precious and acceptable to God than any good actions by a person living in the world.

Take care, then, not to fall under God's rebuke like those who said: 'What have we gained by going as suppliants before the Lord, passing our time continually in his house?' (cf. Mal. 3 : 14. LXX). Obviously any slave who is near the master of the house receives from time to time a thrashing or a savage reprimand. But a slave who works outside avoids punishment for the time being, because he is not part of the household and so escapes his master's notice. What have we gained, they ask, we who suffer affliction in soul and body, always praying and singing psalms? Do not those who neither pray nor keep vigil enjoy happiness and success throughout their lives? Again they complain: 'Behold, the houses of others are built up, and we call others blessed'; and the Prophet adds: 'And servants of God who were not ignorant said these things' (cf. Mal. 3:15–16. LXX). Yet we should not think it strange that monks endure affliction and various forms of sorrow, patiently awaiting through many trials and temptations whatever their Master gives. For they have heard Him say in the Gospels: 'Truly I tell you, that you who are near Me shall weep and lament, but the world shall rejoice. Yet after a little while I will visit you through the Paraclete and drive away your despondency; I will renew you with thoughts of heavenly life and peace and with sweet tears, of all of which you were deprived for a short time when you were being tested. I will give you the breast of My grace, as a mother feeds her baby when it cries. When your strength fails in battle I will fortify you with power from on high, and I will sweeten you in your bitterness, as Jeremiah says in his Lamentations, speaking of the Jerusalem hidden within you. I will look upon you, and your hearts will rejoice at My secret visitation; your affliction will be turned to joy, and no one shall take that joy from you' (cf. John 16:20–22).

So let us not be blind or short-sighted, regarding those in the world as more blessed than ourselves; but, knowing the difference between true sons and bastards, let us rather embrace the apparent misery and afflictions of the monastic calling, since they lead to eternal life and to the Lord's unfading crown of glory. Let us, then, welcome the tribulations we endure as sinful ascetics (for we should not claim to be righteous). Let us choose to be 'an outcast in the house of God' – that is, to be a monk serving Christ continually – rather than to 'dwell in the tents of sinners' (Ps. 84:10. LXX) and associate ourselves with those in the world, even though they perform acts of great righteousness.

Listen, monk, to the words of your heavenly Father, who in His infinite love afflicts and oppresses you with various trials. 'Know this well, you pitiful monk,' He warns you, 'that as I said by My Prophet, I will be your chastiser (cf. Hos. 5:2. LXX). I will meet you on the road in Egypt, testing you with afflictions. I will block your evil ways with the thorns of My providence, pricking and obstructing you with unexpected misfortunes, so that you cannot fulfil the desires of your foolish heart. I will shut up the sea of your passions with the gates of My mercy (cf. Job 38:8); like a wild beast I will devour you with thoughts of guilt, condemnation and remorse, as you perceive things of which you were ignorant. All these tribulations are a great gift of grace from God. And I will be to you not only a beast of prey but a goad, pricking you with thoughts of compunction and with sorrow of heart. Anguish shall not depart from your house – that is, from your soul and body – but they will both undergo the salutary harrowing of the bitter-sweet torments of God.'

But all the grim things that befall us on the ascetic way – torments, pain, confusion, shame, fear and despair – lead finally to endless joy, inexpressible delight and unutterable glory. 'For this reason have I afflicted you,' God says, 'that I may feed you with the manna of spiritual knowledge; I have made you go hungry, so that at the end I may grant blessings to you and bring you into the kingdom on high.' When that time comes, lowly monks, you will skip like young calves loosed from their bonds (cf. Mal. 4:2. LXX), for you will be set free from carnal passion and the temptations of the enemy; you will trample on the wicked demons who now trample on you: 'they shall be ashes under the soles of your feet' (Mal. 4:3). For if you fear God and are humble – not puffed up with vanity, not headstrong, but in compunction and contrition regarding yourself as a 'useless servant' (cf. Luke 17:10) – then your sinfulness, monk, is better than the righteousness of those who live in the world, and your filthiness is more compelling than their purity.

What is it that so distresses you? No stain is intrinsic. If a man has tar on his hands, he removes it with a little cleansing oil; how much more, then, can you be made clean with the oil of God's mercy. You find no difficulty in washing your clothes; how much easier is it for the Lord to cleanse you from every stain, although you are bound to be tempted every day. When you say to the Lord, 'I have sinned', He answers: 'Your sins are forgiven you; I am He who wipes them out and I will remember them no more' (Matt. 9:2; Isa. 43:25); 'as far as the east is from the west, so far have I removed your sins from you; and as a father shows compassion to his sons, so will I show compassion to you' (cf. Ps. 103:12–13). Only do not rebel against Him who has called you to pray and recite psalms, but cleave to Him throughout your life in pure and intimate communion, reverent yet unashamed in His presence, and always full of thanksgiving.

It is God who, by a simple act of His will, cleanses you. For what God chooses to make clean not even the great Apostle Peter can condemn or call unclean. For he is told: 'What God has cleansed, do not call unclean' (Acts 10:15). For has not God in His love acquitted us? 'Who then will condemn us?' (cf. Rom. 8:33–34). When we call upon the name of our Lord Jesus Christ, it is not hard for our conscience to be made pure, and then we are no different from the prophets and the rest of the saints. For God's purpose is not that we should suffer from His anger, but that we should gain salvation through our Lord Jesus Christ, who died for us. So then, whether we are watchful in virtue or sometimes fall asleep, as is likely to happen because of our failings, yet shall we live with Christ. As we look up to Him with cries of distress and continual lamentation, it is He Himself that we breathe. Let us therefore put on the breastplate of faith, and take as our helmet the hope of salvation; then the arrows of dejection and despair will find no chink through which to wound us (cf. 1 Thess. 5:8–10).

You say: 'I feel infuriated when I see that those in the world are not tempted at all.' But realize this: Satan has no need to tempt those who tempt themselves, and are continually dragged down by worldly affairs. And know this too: the prizes and crowns are given to those who are tested by temptation – not to those who care nothing about God, to the worldly who lie on their backs and snore. 'But', you say, 'I am severely tempted by many things and my loins "are filled with mockings" (Ps. 38:7. LXX); I am bowed down in my distress and there is no healing for my flesh, no "remedy for my bones"' (Prov. 3:8. LXX). Yet in fact the great Physician of the sick is here beside us, He that bore our infirmities, that healed and still heals us by His wounds (cf. Isa. 53:5); He is here beside us and even now administers the medicine of salvation. 'For', He says, 'I have afflicted you by My absence, but I will also heal you. So do not fear: for when My fierce anger has passed, I will heal you again. As a woman will not forget to care for the offspring of her womb, even so will I not forget you', says the Lord (cf. Deut. 32:39; Isa. 7:4 and 49:15. LXX). 'For if a bird devotes itself with tender love to its nestlings, visiting them every hour, calling to them and feeding them, how much greater is My compassion towards My creatures!

How much more do I in tender love devote Myself to you, visiting you when you are forgetful, speaking with you in your intellect, feeding your reason when it opens wide its mouth like a young swallow. For as food I give you the fear of Him who is mightier than you; I give you longing for heaven and sighs that console you; I give you compunction and song, deep knowledge and divine mysteries. If I your Lord and Father am lying when I say these things to you, then convict Me of guilt and I will accept it.' It is in this way that the Lord always speaks to us inwardly.

I know that this letter is excessively long, but it is your request that has made it so. I have written at length in order to strengthen those in danger of falling away through apathy. For, as you wrote to me, there are certain brethren among you in India who find themselves more heavily oppressed by temptations than they expected; they have even renounced the monastic life, saying that it completely stifles a man and involves innumerable dangers. You told me that they openly regarded those in the outside world as more blessed than themselves, and cursed the day on which they took the habit. For this reason I have been compelled to write at length, using plain words, so that even a simple and unlettered person can understand what is said. And my aim in writing all this is to show that monks should not consider anything worldly as superior to their own monastic vocation; for, without any contradiction, monks are higher and more glorious than crowned monarchs, since they are called to be in constant attendance upon God. And, having written these things, I beseech you out of love to remember me continually in your prayers, that in my wretchedness I may be given grace from the Lord, so as to close my present life in holiness. May the Father of mercies and the God of all blessings grant you a hope well founded and everlasting blessings in Christ Jesus our Lord, to whom be glory and dominion through all the ages. Amen.

APPENDIX

A Work Attributed to St Antony the Great

The piece that follows, *On the Character of Men and on the Virtuous Life*, is regarded by St Nikodimos as a genuine work by St Antony of Egypt (251–356); and so on chronological grounds it is placed as the opening writing in the Greek *Philokalia*. The work contains many passages of deep spiritual insight, and no doubt this is why St Nikodimos included it. It is, however, almost certainly not of Christian origin, but seems to be a compilation of extracts from various Stoic and Platonic writers of the first to fourth centuries A.D.; there are passages which closely reflect the views of Seneca, Epictetus, Marcus Aurelius and Sallustius. The compiler, whoever he may have been, has made some small alterations so as to eliminate non-Christian terminology, but otherwise appears to have left the material substantially unchanged.

St Nikodimos had some doubts about the work, since twice he expresses reservations about the language used (see his editorial notes to §§ 127 and 138), and he also found it necessary to defend the Antonian authorship of the work in his short introduction. There he argues that the work is quoted as Antony's by Peter of Damaskos; but in fact, although there are eight references to Antony in Peter, none of them is to this present piece.[1] It will be noted that in the work there are no citations from Scripture. Although the Logos is sometimes mentioned (§§ 47, 156), there is nothing specifically Christian about these references. Nowhere is there any allusion to Jesus Christ, to the Church or to the sacraments. The Trinity is mentioned once (§ 141), but this appears to be an interpolation, as the sentence plays no organic part in the argument. Probably the reference to the guardian angel in § 62 is

[1] See I. Hausherr, 'Un écrit stoïcien sous le nom de Saint Antoine Ermite', in *De Doctrina Spirituali Christianorum Orientalium Quaestiones et Scripta*, v (*Orientalia Christiana*, 86, Rome, 1933), pp. 212–16.

likewise a Christian interpolation; all that we have in this passage is the notion, familiar in Greek pagan thought, of a 'personal daemon'.

Throughout the work the doctrine of man is Stoic or Platonic rather than Christian. Nothing is said about the fall or about man's dependence on divine grace; the soul seems to need no redemption, but advances towards God through its own inherent powers. The body is sharply contrasted with the soul (§§ 124, 142): it is regarded, not as a true part of man, but as a garment to be shed (§ 81) or as an enemy to be hated (§§ 50, 117), although there is also a hint that the body may eventually be saved (§ 93). Matter is considered inherently evil (§§ 50, 89). The doctrine of providence in the work is Stoic rather than Christian.

For these reasons, the Editors of the English translation do not regard the work *On the Character of Men and on the Virtuous Life* as a Christian writing, and they have therefore placed it in an appendix.

On the Character of Men and on
the Virtuous Life:
One Hundred and Seventy Texts

1. Men are often called intelligent wrongly. Intelligent men are not those who are erudite in the sayings and books of the wise men of old, but those who have an intelligent soul and can discriminate between good and evil. They avoid what is sinful and harms the soul; and with deep gratitude to God they resolutely adhere by dint of practice to what is good and benefits the soul. These men alone should truly be called intelligent.

2. The truly intelligent man pursues one sole objective: to obey and to conform to the God of all. With this single aim in view, he disciplines his soul, and whatever he may encounter in the course of his life, he gives thanks to God for the compass and depth of His providential ordering of all things. For it is absurd to be grateful to doctors who give us bitter and unpleasant medicines to cure our bodies, and yet to be ungrateful to God for what appears to us to be harsh, not grasping that all we encounter is for our benefit and in accordance with His providence. For knowledge of God and faith in Him is the salvation and perfection of the soul.

3. We have received from God self-control, forbearance, restraint, fortitude, patience, and the like, which are great and holy powers, helping us to resist the enemy's attacks. If we cultivate these powers and have them at our disposal, we do not regard anything that befalls us as painful, grievous or unbearable, realizing that it is human and can be overcome by the virtues within us. The unintelligent do not take this into account; they do not understand that all things happen for our benefit, rightly and as they should, so that our virtues may shine and we ourselves be crowned by God.

4. You should realize that the acquisition of material things and their lavish use is only a short-lived fantasy, and that a virtuous way

of life, conforming to God's will, surpasses all wealth. When you reflect on this and keep it in mind constantly, you will not grumble, whine or blame anyone, but will thank God for everything, seeing that those who rely on repute and riches are worse off than yourself. For desire, love of glory and ignorance constitute the worst passion of the soul.

5. The intelligent man, examining himself, determines what is appropriate and profitable to him, what is proper and beneficial to the soul, and what is foreign to it. Thus he avoids what is foreign and harmful to the soul and cuts him off from immortality.

6. The more frugal a man's life, the happier he is, for he is not troubled by a host of cares: slaves, farm-workers or herds. For when we are attached to such things and harassed by the problems they raise, we blame God. But because of our self-willed desire we cultivate death and remain wandering in the darkness of a life of sin, not recognizing our true self.

7. One should not say that it is impossible to reach a virtuous life; but one should say that it is not easy. Nor do those who have reached it find it easy to maintain. Those who are devout and whose intellect enjoys the love of God participate in the life of virtue; the ordinary intellect, however, is worldly and vacillating, producing both good and evil thoughts, because it is changeful by nature and directed towards material things. But the intellect that enjoys the love of God punishes the evil which arises spontaneously because of man's indolence.

8. The uneducated and foolish regard instruction as ridiculous and do not want to receive it, because it would show up their uncouthness, and they want everyone to be like themselves. Likewise those who are dissipated in their life and habits are anxious to prove that everyone else is worse than themselves, seeking to present themselves as innocent in comparison with all the sinners around them. The lax soul is turbid and perishes through wickedness, since it contains within itself profligacy, pride, insatiate desire, anger, impetuosity, frenzy, murderousness, querulousness, jealousy, greed, rapacity, self-pity, lying, sensual pleasure, sloth, dejection, cowardice, morbidity, hatred, censoriousness, debility, delusion, ignorance, deceit and forgetfulness of God. Through these and suchlike evils the wretched soul is punished when it is separated from God.

9. Those who aim to practise the life of virtue and holiness should not incur condemnation by pretending to a piety which they do not possess. But like painters and sculptors they should manifest their virtue and holiness through their works, and should shun all evil pleasures as snares.

10. A wealthy man of good family, who lacks inward discipline and all virtue in his way of life, is regarded by those with spiritual understanding as under an evil influence; likewise a man who happens to be poor or a slave, but is graced with discipline of soul and with virtue in his life, is regarded as blessed. And just as strangers travelling in a foreign country lose their way, so those who do not cultivate the life of virtue are led astray by their desires and get completely lost.

11. Those who can train the ignorant and inspire them with a love for instruction and discipline should be called moulders of men. So too should those who reform the dissolute, remodelling their life to one of virtue, conforming to God's will. For gentleness and self-control are a blessing and a sure hope for the souls of men.

12. A man should strive to practise the life of virtue in a genuine way; for when this is achieved it is easy to acquire knowledge about God. When a man reveres God with all his heart and with faith, he receives through God's providence the power to control anger and desire; for it is desire and anger which are the cause of all evils.

13. A human being is someone who possesses spiritual intelligence or is willing to be rectified. One who cannot be rectified is inhuman. Such people must be avoided: because they live in vice, they can never attain immortality.

14. When the intelligence is truly operative, we can properly be called human beings. When it is not operative, we differ from animals only in respect of our physical form and our speech. An intelligent man should realize that he is immortal and should hate all shameful desires, which are the cause of death in men.

15. Every craftsman displays his skill through the material he uses: one man, for instance, displays it in timber, another in copper, another in gold and silver. Likewise we who are taught the life of holiness ought to show that we are human beings not merely by virtue of our bodily appearance, but because our souls are truly intelligent. The truly intelligent soul, which enjoys the love of God, knows everything in life in a direct and immediate way; it lovingly

woos God's favour, sincerely gives Him thanks, and aspires with all its strength towards Him.

16. When navigating, helmsmen use a mark in order to avoid reefs or rocks. Likewise those who aspire to the life of holiness must mark carefully what they ought to do and what they ought to avoid; and, cutting off evil thoughts from the soul, they must grasp that the true, divine laws exist for their profit.

17. Helmsmen and charioteers gain proficiency through practice and diligence. Likewise those who seek the life of holiness must take care to study and practise what conforms to God's will. For he who so wishes, and has grasped that it is possible, can with this faith attain incorruptibility.

18. Regard as free not those whose status makes them outwardly free, but those who are free in their character and conduct. For we should not call men in authority truly free when they are wicked or dissolute, since they are slaves to worldly passions. Freedom and happiness of soul consist in genuine purity and detachment from transitory things.

19. Keep in mind that you must always be setting an example through your moral life and your actions. For the sick find and recognize good doctors, not just through their words, but through their actions.

20. Holiness and intelligence of soul are to be recognized from a man's eye, walk, voice, laugh, the way he spends his time and the company he keeps. Everything is transformed and reflects an inner beauty. For the intellect which enjoys the love of God is a watchful gate-keeper and bars entry to evil and defiling thoughts.

21. Examine and test your inward character; and always keep in mind that human authorities have power over the body alone and not over the soul. Therefore, should they command you to commit murders or other foul, unjust and soul-corrupting acts, you must not obey them, even if they torture your body. For God created the soul free and endowed with the power to choose between good and evil.

22. The intelligent soul endeavours to free itself from error, delusion, boastfulness, deceit, from jealousy, rapacity and the like, which are works of the demons and of man's evil intent. Everything is successfully achieved through persistent study and practice when one's desire is not impelled towards base pleasures.

23. Those who lead a life of frugality and of self-privation deliver

themselves from dangers and have no need of protection. By overcoming all desire, they easily find the path that leads to God.

24. Intelligent men have no need to listen to much talk, but should attend only to that which is profitable and guided by God's will. For in this way men regain life and eternal light.

25. Those who seek to lead a life of holiness, enjoying the love of God, should free themselves from presumption and all empty and false self-esteem, and should try to correct their life and way of thinking. For an intellect that steadfastly enjoys the love of God is a way of ascent to Him.

26. There is no profit in studying doctrines unless the life of one's soul is acceptable and conforms to God's will. The cause of all evils is delusion, self-deception and ignorance of God.

27. Concentration on holiness of living, together with attentiveness to the soul, lead to goodness and the love of God. For he who seeks God finds Him by overcoming all desires through persistence in prayer. Such a man does not fear demons.

28. Those who are deluded by worldly hopes, and know how to practise the life of holiness only in theory, are like those who employ drugs and medical instruments without knowing how to use them or bothering to learn. Therefore, we must never blame our birth, or anyone but ourselves, for our sinful actions, because if the soul chooses to be indolent, it cannot resist temptation.

29. A man who cannot discriminate between good and evil has no right to judge who is good and who evil. The man who knows God is good. If someone is not good, he knows nothing of God and never will; for the way to know God is by means of goodness.

30. Men who are good and enjoy the love of God rebuke evil-doers to their face. But when evil-doers are not present, such people neither criticize them nor allow others to do so.

31. When talking with others all harshness should be avoided; for modesty and self-restraint adorn an intelligent person even more than a young girl. An intellect that enjoys the love of God is a light that shines on the soul, just as the sun shines on the body.

32. Whatever passion arises in your soul, remember that those who have correct judgment, and want to keep secure what they have, take delight not in the ephemeral acquisition of material things, but in true and sound beliefs. It is these that make them happy. For wealth may be seized and stolen by more powerful men,

whereas holiness of soul is the only possession which is safe and cannot be stolen, and which saves after death those who have it. Fantasies about wealth and other pleasures do not delude those who understand this.

33. Those who are inconstant and uninstructed should not argue with intelligent men. An intelligent man is one who conforms to God and mostly keeps silent; when he speaks he says very little, and only what is necessary and acceptable to God.

34. Those who pursue a life of holiness, enjoying the love of God, cultivate the virtues of the soul, because the soul is their own possession and an eternal delight. In addition, whenever possible they take pleasure in such transitory things as come to them through God's will and gift. Even if these things are rather scanty, they use them gladly and gratefully. Luxurious meals nourish the body; but knowledge of God, self-control, goodness, beneficence, devoutness and gentleness deify the soul.

35. Rulers who use force to make men undertake foul and soul-corrupting acts have no dominion over the soul because it is created with freedom of will. They may fetter the body, but not the power of decision, of which the intelligent man is the arbiter through God who created him. Because of this he is stronger than any authority, necessity or force.

36. Those who consider it a misfortune to lose children, slaves, money or any other of their belongings, must realize that in the first place they should be satisfied with what is given them by God; and then, when they have to give it back, they should be ready to do so gratefully, without any indignation at being deprived of it, or rather at giving it back – for since they have been enjoying the use of what was not their own, they are now in fact returning it.

37. A good man does not sell his inner freedom for money, even if he happens to be offered a huge sum. For things belonging to this life are like a dream, and the fantasies of wealth are uncertain and short-lived.

38. Those who are truly men must endeavour to live with holiness and love of God, so that their holy life shines before others. Since men take pains to decorate white garments with narrow purple stripes which stand out and attract attention, how much more assiduously should they cultivate the virtues of the soul.

39. Sensible people should examine carefully both their strength

and the degree of alertness of their soul's powers; in this way they should make ready to resist the passions in accordance with the strength implanted in their nature by God. It is self-control which resists beauty and all desire harmful to the soul; it is fortitude which resists pain and want; it is forbearance which resists abuse and anger; and so on.

40. A man cannot become good and wise immediately, but only through much effort, reflection, experience, time, practice and desire for virtuous action. The man who is good and enjoys the love of God, and who truly knows Him, never ceases to do ungrudgingly all that accords with His will. Such men are rare.

41. Men of dull wits should not despair of themselves and become lazy, disdaining the life of virtue and of love for God as being un-attainable and incomprehensible to them. They should, instead, exercise such powers as they possess and cultivate themselves. For even if they cannot attain the highest level in respect of virtue and salvation, they may, through practice and aspiration, become either better or at least not worse, which is no small profit for the soul.

42. Through his intelligence man is linked to that power which is ineffable and divine; and through his bodily nature he has kinship with the animals. A few men – those who are perfect and intelligent – endeavour both to root their mind in God the Saviour and to keep their kinship with Him; and this is manifest through their actions and holiness of life. But most men, being foolish in soul, have renounced that divine and immortal sonship, turning towards a deadly, disastrous and short-lived kinship with the body. Concerning themselves, like animals, with material things and enslaved by sensual pleasures, they separate themselves from God; and through their desires they drag down their soul from heaven to the abyss.

43. The man of intelligence, being deeply concerned for partici-pation in the divine and union with it, will never become engrossed with anything earthly or base, but has his intellect always turned towards the heavenly and eternal. And he knows it is God's will that man should be saved, this divine will being the cause of all that is good and the source of the eternal blessings granted to men.

44. When you find someone arguing, and contesting what is true and self-evident, break off the dispute and give way to such a man, since his intellect has been petrified. For just as bad water ruins good

wines, so harmful talk corrupts those who are virtuous in life and character.

45. If we make every effort to avoid death of the body, still more should it be our endeavour to avoid death of the soul. There is no obstacle for a man who wants to be saved other than negligence and laziness of soul.

46. Those who scorn to grasp what is profitable and salutary are considered to be ill. Those, on the other hand, who comprehend the truth but insolently enjoy dispute, have an intelligence that is dead; and their behaviour has become brutish. They do not know God and their soul has not been illumined.

47. God, by His Logos, created the different kinds of animals to meet the variety of our needs: some for our food, others for our service. And He created man to apprehend them and their actions and to appraise them gratefully. Man should therefore strive not to die, like the non-rational animals, without having attained some apprehension of God and His works.

One must know that God is omnipotent; nothing can resist Him who is omnipotent. For man's salvation, out of nothing He created and creates by His Logos all that He wills.

48. Celestial beings are immortal because they have divine goodness within them; whereas earthly beings have become mortal because of the self-incurred evil within them. This evil comes to the mindless through their laziness and ignorance of God.

49. Death, when understood by men, is deathlessness; but, when not understood by the foolish, it is death. It is not this death that must be feared, but the loss of the soul, which is ignorance of God. This is indeed disaster for the soul.

50. Evil is a passion found in matter, and so it is not possible for a body to come into being free from evil. The intelligent soul, grasping this, strives to free itself from the evil burden of matter; and when it is free from this burden, it comes to know the God of all, and keeps watch on the body as being an enemy and does not yield to it. Then the soul is crowned by God for having conquered the passions of evil and of matter.

51. When the soul has come to recognize evil it hates it like the stench of a foul beast; but he who does not recognize evil loves it, and it holds him captive, making a slave of its lover. Then the unfortunate and wretched man can neither see nor understand his

true interest, but imagines that this evil is an adornment, and so he is happy.

52. The pure soul, because of its innate goodness, is illumined and made resplendent by God; and then the intellect apprehends what is good and begets thoughts that accord with God's will. But when the soul is defiled by evil, and God turns away from it, or rather the soul separates itself from God, evil demons enter its thought processes and suggest unholy acts to it: adultery, murder, robbery, sacrilege and other such demonic acts.

53. Those who know God are filled with good impulses; desiring the heavenly, they despise worldly objects. Such men neither like nor are liked by many people. Consequently numbers of idiots not only hate but also ridicule them. And they patiently endure all that comes from their poverty, knowing that what seems to many to be bad, for them is good. For he who comprehends the celestial believes in God, knowing that all are creatures of His will: whereas he who does not comprehend the celestial never believes that the world is a work of God and was made for man's salvation.

54. Those who are full of evil and drunk with ignorance do not know God, and their soul is not watchful. God is spiritual; and though He is invisible, He is clearly manifest in visible things, as the soul is manifest in the body. And just as it is impossible for a body to subsist without a soul, so it is impossible for any thing that is visible and has being to subsist without God.

55. Why was man created? In order that, by apprehending God's creatures, he might contemplate and glorify Him who created them for man's sake. The intellect responsive to God's love is an invisible blessing given by God to those whose life by its virtue commends itself to Him.

56. A man is free if he is not a slave to sensual pleasures, but through good judgment and self-restraint masters the body and with true gratitude is satisfied with what God gives him, even though it is quite scanty. If the soul and the intellect that enjoys the love of God are in harmony, the whole body is peaceful even against its wishes; then, should the soul so want, every bodily impulse is extinguished.

57. When men are not satisfied with what they need so as to remain alive but desire more, they enslave themselves to passions that disturb the soul, inflicting upon it thoughts and fantasies that what they have is inadequate. And just as tunics that are too large

hinder runners in a race, so the desire for more than one needs does not allow one's soul to struggle or to be saved.

58. Any circumstance in which a man finds himself unwillingly is a prison and a punishment for him. So be content with whatever circumstances you may now be in, lest by being ungrateful you punish yourself unwittingly. This contentment can be achieved in but one way: through detachment from worldly things.

59. Just as God has given us sight in order that we may recognize visible things – what is white, and what black – so, too, He has given us intelligence in order that we may discern what benefits the soul. Desire, detached from the intelligence, begets sensual pleasure, and does not allow the soul to be saved or to attain union with God.

60. What takes place according to nature is not sinful; sin always involves man's deliberate choice. It is not a sin to eat; it is a sin to eat without gratitude, and not in an orderly and restrained manner such as will enable the body to be kept alive without inducing evil thoughts. It is not a sin to use one's eyes with purity; it is a sin to look with envy, arrogance and insatiable desire. It is a sin to listen not peacefully, but angrily; it is a sin to guide the tongue, not towards thanksgiving and prayer, but towards backbiting; it is a sin to employ the hands, not for acts of compassion, but for murders and robberies. And thus every part of the body sins when by man's own choice it performs not good but evil acts, contrary to God's will.

61. If you doubt that every act performed is observed by God, you must reflect that although you are a man and but dust, nonetheless you can watch and perceive many places at the same time; how much more, then, can God observe, since all things appear to Him as a mustard seed appears to man, and He gives life and food to all creatures as He wills?

62. When you close the doors of your dwelling and are alone, you should know that there is present with you the angel whom God has appointed for each man; the Greeks call him the personal daemon. This angel, who is sleepless and cannot be deceived, is always present with you; he sees all things and is not hindered by darkness. You should know, too, that with him is God, who is in every place; for there is no place and nothing material in which God is not, since He is greater than all things and holds all men in His hand.

63. If soldiers remain loyal to Caesar because he feeds them, how

much more ought we to try ceaselessly to give thanks to God with lips that are never silent, and to praise Him who created all things for man's sake?

64. A virtuous way of life and gratitude towards God are fruits of man that are pleasing to God. The fruits of the earth are not brought to perfection immediately, but by time, rain and care; similarly, the fruits of men ripen through ascetic practice, study, time, perseverance, self-control and patience. And if, because of all you do, anyone should ever think that you are a devout man, distrust yourself so long as you are in the body, and think that nothing about you is pleasing to God. For you must know that it is not easy for anyone to keep himself sinless until the end.

65. Nothing is more precious to man than intelligence. Its power is such as to enable us to adore God through intelligent speech and thanksgiving. By contrast, when we use futile or slanderous speech we condemn our soul. Now it is characteristic of an obtuse man to lay the blame for his sins on the conditions of his birth or on something else, while in fact his words and actions are evil through his own free choice.

66. If we try to cure bodily passions in order to avoid the ridicule of people we chance to meet, how much more should we try to cure the passions of the soul; for when we are judged face to face by God we shall not wish to be found worthless and ridiculous. Since we have free will, although we may desire to perform evil actions, we can avoid doing so; and it is in our power to live in accordance with God's will. Moreover, no one can ever force us to do what is evil against our will. It is through this struggle against evil that we shall become worthy to serve God and live like angels in heaven.

67. If you so wish, you are a slave of the passions; and if you so wish, you are free and do not yield to the passions. For God created you with free will; and he who overcomes the passions of the flesh is crowned with incorruption. If there were no passions there would be no virtues, and no crowns awarded by God to those who are worthy.

68. Those who know what is good, and yet do not see what is to their benefit, are blind in soul and their power of discrimination has become petrified. Hence we should pay no attention to them, lest we too become blind and so are constrained to fall heedlessly into the same faults.

69. We should not become angry with those who sin, even if what they do is criminal and deserves punishment. On the contrary, for the sake of justice we ought to correct and, if need be, punish them ourselves or get others to do so. But we should not become angry or excited; for anger acts only in accordance with passion, and not in accordance with good judgment and justice. Moreover, we should not approve those who show more mercy than is proper. The wicked must be punished for the sake of what is good and just, but not as a result of the personal passion of anger.

70. To gain possession of one's soul is the only acquisition which is safe and inviolable. It is achieved through a way of life that is holy and conforms to God's will through spiritual knowledge and the practice of good actions. By contrast, wealth is a blind guide and a foolish counsellor, and he who uses wealth in an evil and self-indulgent manner loses his obtuse soul.

71. Men must not acquire anything superfluous or, if they possess it, must know with certainty that all things in this life are by nature perishable, and easily plundered, lost or broken; and they must not be disheartened by anything that happens.

72. You should know that the body's sufferings belong to it by nature, inasmuch as it is corruptible and material. The disciplined soul must, therefore, gratefully show itself persevering and patient under such sufferings, and must not blame God for having created the body.

73. Those who compete in the Olympic games are not crowned after achieving victory over their first opponent, or their second or third, but only after they have defeated every one of their competitors. In the same way, therefore, all who wish to be crowned by God must train their souls to be disciplined in respect not only of bodily matters, but also of love of gain, rapacity, mode of life, envy, self-esteem, abuse, death and all such things.

74. We should not pursue a godly and virtuous way of life in order to win human praise, but we should choose it for the sake of our soul's salvation: for death is daily before our eyes, and human affairs are unpredictable.

75. We can choose to live with self-discipline, but we cannot become wealthy simply by an act of choice. Must we then condemn our soul by pursuing or even desiring a wealth which we cannot acquire by an act of choice, and which in any case is but a short-

lived fantasy? How foolishly we act, not realizing that the first of all the virtues is humility, just as the first of all the passions is gluttony and desire for worldly things.

76. Intelligent people must ceaselessly remember that by enduring slight and passing sufferings in this life, we gain the greatest joy and eternal bliss after death. Therefore, if a man falls when struggling against the passions and wishing to be crowned by God, he should not lose heart and remain fallen, despairing of himself, but should rise and begin again the struggle to win his crown. Until his last breath he should rise whenever he has fallen; for bodily toil is a weapon used by the virtues, and brings salvation to the soul.

77. If they are worthy, ordinary people and ascetics are provided through the circumstances of their life with the opportunities to be crowned by God. Hence, during this life they must make their faculties dead to all worldly things; for a dead man never concerns himself with anything worldly.

78. A soul engaged in spiritual training, being deiform, must not cower with fear in the face of the passions, lest it be derided for cowardice; since if it is disturbed by fantasies of worldly things, the soul strays from its course. For the virtues of the soul lead to eternal blessings, while our self-willed vices result in eternal punishments.

79. Man is attacked by his senses through the soul's passions. The bodily senses are five: sight, smell, hearing, taste and touch. Through these five senses the unhappy soul is taken captive when it succumbs to its four passions. These four passions are self-esteem, levity, anger and cowardice. When, therefore, a man through sound judgment and reflection has shown good generalship, he controls and defeats the passions. Then he is no longer attacked but his soul is at peace; and he is crowned by God, because he has conquered.

80. When people come to an inn, some receive beds; others, having no bed, sleep on the ground, and these too snore just as much as those who sleep on beds. But when, after their night's stay, they leave the inn early next morning, all set off alike, each taking with him only what belongs to him. In the same way, all who come into this life, both those who live modestly, and those who enjoy wealth and ostentation, leave this life like an inn: each takes with him none of its pleasures and riches, but only his own past actions whether good or bad.

81. If you are in a position of high authority, do not lightly threaten someone with death, knowing as you do that by nature you, too, are subject to death and that the soul sheds the body as if shedding its last garment. Since you know this, be gentle and merciful, always giving thanks to God. For he who has no compassion has no virtue.

82. To escape death is impossible. Knowing this, those who are truly intelligent and practised in virtue and in spiritual thought accept death uncomplainingly, without fear or grief, recognizing that it is inevitable and delivers them from the evils of this life.

83. We must not hate those who ignore the way of life which is good and conforms to God's will, and who pay no heed to the teachings that are true and divine. Rather, we must show mercy to them as being crippled in discrimination and blind in heart and mind. For in accepting evil as good, they are destroyed by ignorance; and, being wretched and obtuse in soul, they do not know God.

84. Do not try to teach people at large about devoutness and right living. I say this, not because I begrudge them such teaching, but because I think that you will appear ridiculous to the stupid. For like delights in like: few – indeed, hardly any – listen to such instruction. It is better therefore not to speak at all about what God wills for man's salvation.

85. The soul suffers with the body, but the body does not suffer with the soul. Thus, when the body is cut, the soul suffers too; and when the body is vigorous and healthy, the soul shares its well-being. But when the soul thinks, the body is not involved and does not think with it; for thinking is a passion or property of the soul, as also are ignorance, arrogance, unbelief, greed, hatred, envy, anger, apathy, self-esteem, love of honour, contentiousness and the perception of goodness. All these are energized through the soul.

86. When meditating on divine realities, be full of goodness, free from envy, devout, self-restrained, gentle, as generous as possible, kindly, peaceable, and so on. For to conform to God through such qualities, and not to judge anyone or to say that he is wicked and has sinned, is to render the soul inviolate. One should search out one's own faults and scrutinize one's own way of life, to see whether it conforms to God. What concern is it of ours if another man is wicked?

87. He who is truly a man tries to be devout; and he is devout

when he does not desire what is alien to him. Everything created is alien to man. He is superior to all creatures because he is an image of God. A man is the image of God when he lives rightly and in a way that conforms to God. But he cannot live like this unless he detaches himself from worldly things. Now a man whose intellect enjoys the love of God is fully aware that everything beneficial to his soul and all his devoutness come from this detachment. Such a man does not blame another for sins he himself commits. This is the sign of a soul in which salvation is at work.

88. Those who contrive to gain possession of transitory things by force are also attached to their desire to act viciously. They ignore the death and destruction of their own soul, and do not consider what is to their interest or reflect on what men suffer after death because of wickedness.

89. Evil is a passion adherent to matter, but God is not the cause of evil. He has given men knowledge and understanding, the power of discriminating between good and evil, and free will. It is man's negligence and indolence that give birth to evil passions, while God is in no way the cause. The demons, like most men, have become evil as a result of the free choice of their own will.

90. The man who lives devoutly does not allow evil to slip into his soul; and, no evil being present, his soul is safe from danger and harm. Such a man is dominated neither by demon nor by fate, for God delivers him from all evil and, protected like a god, he lives unharmed. If he is praised, he laughs within himself at those who praise him; if he is execrated, he does not defend himself against those who mock him, and he never gets angry at what they say.

91. Evil clings closely to one's nature, just as verdigris to copper and dirt to the body. But the coppersmith does not create the verdigris, nor do parents create the dirt. Likewise, it is not God who has created evil. He has given man knowledge and discrimination so that he may avoid evil, knowing that it harms and punishes him. Thus when you see someone enjoying power and wealth, mind you are never deluded by some demon into thinking him happy. Quickly bring death before your eyes, and you will never have a desire for any evil or worldly object.

92. Our God has granted immortality to those in heaven, but for those on earth He has created mutability, giving life and movement to the whole of creation; and all this for man's sake. So do

not be ensnared by the worldly fantasies of the demon who in-
sinuates evil recollections into the soul, but immediately call to
mind the blessings of heaven and say to yourself: 'If I so wish, it is
in my power to win even this struggle against passion; but I shall
not win if I am set on fulfilling my own desire.' So struggle in this
way, since it can save your soul.

93. Life is the union and conjucture between intellect, soul and
body, while death is not the destruction of these elements so conjoined, but the dissolution of their inter-relationship; for they are
all saved through and in God, even after this dissolution.

94. The intellect is not the soul, but a gift of God that saves the
soul; and the intellect that conforms to God goes on ahead of the
soul and counsels it to despise what is transitory, material and
corruptible, and to turn all its desire towards eternal, incorruptible
and immaterial blessings. And the intellect teaches man while still
in the body to perceive and contemplate divine and heavenly
realities, and everything else as well, through itself. Thus the
intellect that enjoys the love of God is the benefactor and saviour of
the human soul.

95. When the soul is in the body it is at once darkened and
ravaged by pain and pleasure. Pain and pleasure are like the humours
of the body. But the intellect that enjoys the love of God, counter-
attacking, gives pain to the body and saves the soul, like a physician
who cuts and cauterizes bodies.

96. There are some souls which the intelligence does not control,
and the intellect does not govern, in such a way as to check and
restrain their passions – that is, pain and pleasure. These souls perish
like mindless animals, since the intelligence is carried away by the
passions like a charioteer who loses control over his horses.

97. The greatest sickness of the soul, its ruin and perdition, is
not to know God, who created all things for man and gave him the
gifts of intellect and intelligence. Winged through these gifts, man
is linked to God, knowing Him and praising Him.

98. Soul is in the body, intellect is in the soul, and intelligence
is in the intellect. When God is known and praised through all
these, He makes the soul immortal, granting it incorruptibility and
eternal delight; for God has granted the gift of being to all creatures
solely through His goodness.

99. God, being full of goodness and ungrudging bounty, not only

created man with free will but also endowed him with the capacity to conform to God if he so wishes. It is the absence of wickedness in man which conforms him to God. If, then, man praises the good actions and virtues of a soul which is holy and enjoys the love of God, and if he condemns ugly and wicked deeds, how much more so does God, who wishes for man's salvation.

100. Whatever is good man receives from God, who is goodness itself: this is why man was created by God. But he attracts evils to himself out of himself and out of the wickedness, desire and obtuseness within him.

101. The unintelligent soul, though immortal and the master of the body, becomes the body's slave through sensual pleasure. It does not realize that what delights the body harms the soul; but, stupid and obtuse, it seeks out such delight.

102. God is good, man wicked. There is no evil in heaven, and no goodness on earth. Therefore the intelligent man chooses the better part and acknowledges the God of all; he thanks and praises God, and before death he hates the body; and he does not allow his evil senses to carry out their desires, for he knows their destructiveness and their strength.

103. The wicked man delights in excess while he despises justice. He takes no account of the uncertainty, inconstancy and brevity of life, nor does he reflect that death cannot be bribed and is inexorable. And if an old man is shameless and stupid, he is like rotten wood and no use for anything.

104. We savour pleasure and joy to the degree to which we taste affliction. One does not drink with pleasure unless one is thirsty, nor eat with pleasure unless hungry, nor sleep soundly unless very drowsy, nor feel joy without grief beforehand. Likewise we shall not enjoy eternal blessings unless we despise transient things.

105. Intelligence is the servant of the intellect: whatever the intellect wills, the intelligence conceives and expresses.

106. The intellect sees all things, including the celestial. Nothing darkens it except sin. To the pure intellect nothing is incomprehensible, just as for the intelligence nothing is beyond expression.

107. By virtue of his body man is mortal; and by virtue of his intellect and intelligence he is immortal. Through silence you come to understanding; having understood, you give expression. It is in

silence that the intellect gives birth to the intelligence; and the thankful intelligence offered to God is man's salvation.

108. He who says foolish things has no intellect, for he speaks without understanding. So learn what it befits you to do in order to save your soul.

109. The intelligence which is wedded to the intellect and which gives help to the soul is a gift of God. But the intelligence which is full of babbling and which investigates the measurements and distances of sky and earth, and the size of the sun and the stars, characterizes a man who labours in vain. Fruitlessly vaunting himself, he pursues what is without profit, as if wishing to draw water with a sieve; for no man can resolve these matters.

110. Only the man who pursues holiness, who knows and glorifies God who created him for salvation and life, can perceive heaven and understand heavenly things. For a man who enjoys the love of God is fully aware that nothing exists without God. God, being infinite, is everywhere and in all things.

111. As man comes naked out of his mother's womb, so the soul comes naked out of the body. One soul comes out pure and luminous; another, blemished by faults; a third, black with its many sins. Thus the soul that is intelligent and enjoys the love of God reflects and meditates on the evils that follow death, and leads a devout life in order not to be entangled with them and so condemned. But unbelievers, fools that they are, commit impious and sinful acts, ignoring what is to come.

112. Just as when you leave the womb you no longer remember what pertains to the womb, so when you leave the body you no longer remember what pertains to the body.

113. When you left the womb you grew in bodily strength and excellence; equally, when leaving the body, if you are pure and unblemished you will grow in strength and incorruptibility, living in heaven.

114. Just as the body has to be born when it has completed its time in the womb, so the soul has to leave the body when it has completed in the body the time assigned to it by God.

115. According to how you treat the soul while it is in the body, so will it treat you when it leaves the body. He who has treated his body here softly and indulgently has treated himself ill after death. For, like a fool, he has condemned his soul.

116. Just as a body cannot grow perfectly if it leaves its mother's

womb in a crippled state, so a soul cannot be saved or united with God if it leaves the body without attaining to knowledge of God through a virtuous way of life.

117. The body, when it is united with the soul, comes from the darkness of the womb into the light. But the soul, when it is united with the body, is bound up in the body's darkness. Therefore we must hate and discipline the body as an enemy that fights against the soul. For over-indulgence in foods and delicacies excites the passions of vice in men, whereas restraint of the belly humbles these passions and saves the soul.

118. The body sees by means of the eyes, and the soul by means of the intellect. A body without eyes is blind, and cannot see the sun shining on earth and ocean or enjoy its light. Likewise the soul without a pure intellect and a holy way of life is blind: it does not apprehend God, Creator and Benefactor of all, or glorify Him, and it cannot enjoy His incorruptibility and eternal blessings.

119. Ignorance of God is obtuseness and stupidity of soul. For ignorance gives birth to evil, while from knowledge of God comes that goodness which saves the soul. If you are anxious to cut off your desires through watchfulness and knowledge of God, then your intellect will be concentrated upon the virtues. But if, drunk through ignorance of God, you try to fulfil your evil desires for self-indulgence, you will perish like a beast because you disregard the evils that will befall you after death.

120. Providence is manifested in events which occur in accordance with divine necessity – such as the daily rising and setting of the sun, and the yielding of fruits by the earth. Law, similarly, is manifested in events which occur in accordance with human necessity. Everything has been created for man's sake.

121. Since God is good, whatever He does, He does for man's sake. But whatever man does, he does for his own sake, both what is good and what is evil. Do not be astonished at the well-being of the wicked: you must realize that just as states employ executioners and, while not approving their terrible profession, use them to punish those who deserve it, in the same way God allows the wicked to tyrannize others in the worldly sphere as a means of punishing the impious. Afterwards He delivers the wicked also to judgment, because they have made people suffer in order to serve not God, but their own wickedness.

122. If those who worship idols knew and understood in their hearts what they worship, they would not be beguiled away from true reverence. Instead, seeing the beauty, order and divine providence of what God has made and is making, they would have acknowledged Him who created all this for man.

123. Man, in so far as he is bad and unjust, is capable of killing. But God never ceases granting life even to the unworthy. Bounteous and full of goodness by nature, He willed that the world should be made and it was made. And it is made for man and his salvation.

124. A true man is one who understands that the body is corruptible and short-lived, whereas the soul is divine and immortal and, while being God's breath, is joined to the body to be tested and deified. Now he who has understood what the soul is regulates his life in a way that is just and conforms to God; not submitting to the body, but seeing God with his intellect, he contemplates noetically the eternal blessings granted to the soul by God.

125. God, being eternally good and bounteous, gave man power over good and evil. He made him the gift of spiritual knowledge, so that, through contemplating the world and what is in it, he might come to know Him who created all things for man's sake. But the impious are free to choose not to know. They are free to disbelieve, to make mistakes and to conceive ideas which are contrary to the truth. Such is the degree to which man has power over good and evil.

126. God has ordained that the soul should be filled with intellect as the body grows, so that man may choose from good and evil what conforms to God. A soul which does not choose the good has no intellect. Hence, all bodies have souls, but not every soul has intellect. An intellect enjoying the love of God is present in the self-controlled, the holy, the just, the pure, the good, the merciful and the devout. The presence of intellect helps a man towards God.

127. One thing alone is not possible for man: to be deathless.[1] But it is possible for him to attain union with God, provided that he realizes that he can do so. For if he seeks God with his intellect, with faith and love and through a life of holiness, man can enter into communion with God.

---

[1] This should be understood as referring to the body and not to the soul; indeed, the body will also be rendered deathless after the final resurrection [note by St Nikodimos].

128. The eye perceives the visible; the intellect apprehends the invisible. The intellect that enjoys the love of God is the light of the soul. He who has such an intellect is illumined in his heart, and sees God with his intellect.

129. No good man is immoral; but if a man is not good, he will certainly be evil and a lover of the body. The first virtue is to reject the demands of the flesh. If we detach ourselves from transitory, corruptible and material things – by our own free choice and not through lack of means to indulge in them – this makes us heirs of eternal and incorruptible blessings.

130. If someone possesses intellect, he knows himself and what he is; and he knows, too, that man is subject to corruption. And he who knows himself knows all things: he knows that all things are created by God and made for man's salvation. For it lies in man's power correctly to apprehend all things and to hold correct beliefs concerning them. Such a man knows with certainty that those who detach themselves from worldly things must endure some slight hardship in this present life, but after death they receive from God eternal blessedness and peace.

131. Just as the body is dead without the soul, so the soul without the intellect is inert and cannot receive God.

132. Only to man does God listen. Only to man does God manifest Himself. God loves man and, wherever man may be, God too is there. Man alone is counted worthy to worship God. For man's sake God transforms Himself.

133. For man's sake God has created everything: earth and heaven and the beauty of the stars. Men cultivate the earth for themselves; but if they fail to recognize how great is God's providence, their souls lack all spiritual understanding.

134. Goodness is hidden, as are the things in heaven. Evil is manifest, as are earthly things. Goodness is that with which nothing can be compared. The man who possesses intellect always chooses what is best. Man alone, by virtue of his intellect, can attain an understanding of God and His creation.

135. The intellect manifests itself in the soul, and nature in the body. The soul is divinized through the intellect, but the nature of the body makes the soul grow slack. Nature is present in all bodies, but intellect is not present in every soul; and so not every soul is saved.

136. The soul is in the world because it is begotten; but the intellect transcends the world, because it is unbegotten. The soul which understands the world and wishes to be saved constantly reflects upon this as her inviolable rule: the time for combat and testing is now, and it is not possible to bribe the Judge, and a man's soul may be either saved or lost through some small and shameful indulgence.

137. On earth God has established birth and death; and in heaven, providence and necessity. All things were made for the sake of man and his salvation. Since God is not Himself in need of any good thing, it was for man that He created heaven, earth and the four elements, freely granting to him the enjoyment of every blessing.

138. The mortal is inferior to the immortal, yet the immortal serves the mortal: thus the four elements serve man, through the inherent goodness of God the Creator and His love for man.[1]

139. A man whose destitution deprives him of the power to inflict harm is not therefore to be regarded as holy. But when someone has the power to inflict harm yet refrains from doing so, out of reverence for God sparing those who are weaker, he is greatly rewarded after death.

140. Through the love of God our Creator, there are many ways that bring men to salvation, converting their souls and leading them up to heaven. For men's souls are rewarded for virtue and punished for sin.

141. The Son is in the Father, and the Spirit is in the Son, and the Father is in both. Through faith man knows all the invisible and intelligible realities. Faith involves a voluntary assent of the soul.

142. Men who are forced by need or circumstance to swim across a great river emerge safely if they are sober and watchful; and even if there are violent currents and they are briefly submerged, they save themselves by grasping the vegetation that grows on the banks. But if they happen to be drunk, then however well trained they may be as swimmers they are overcome by the wine; the current sucks them under and they lose their life. In the same way the soul, finding herself dragged down by the currents of worldly distractions, needs to regain sobriety, awakening from sinful materiality. She should come to know herself: that, though she is divine and immortal, yet

[1] 'Immortal' is to be understood here in the sense 'enduring over a long period of time' [note by St Nikodimos].

to test her God has joined her to a body, shortlived, mortal and subject to many passions. If, drunken with ignorance, indifferent to her true self, not understanding what she is, she lets herself be dragged down by sensual pleasures, she perishes and loses her salvation. For, like the current of a river, the body often drags us down into shameful pleasures.

143. When the soul endowed with intelligence firmly exercises her freedom of choice in the right way, and reins in like a charioteer the incensive and the appetitive aspects of her nature, restraining and controlling her passionate impulses, she receives a crown of victory; and as a reward for all her labours, she is granted life in heaven by God her Creator.

144. The truly intelligent soul is not disturbed when she sees the success of the wicked and the prosperity of the worthless. Unlike the stupid, she is not deluded by the gratification enjoyed by such people in this life. For she understands clearly the inconstancy of fortune, the uncertainty and brevity of life, and the unbribability of the Judge; and she is confident that God will not fail to provide her with the nourishment she needs.

145. The life of the body, and the enjoyment of great wealth and worldly power, are death to the soul. But toil, patient endurance, privation accepted with thankfulness, and the death of the body are life and eternal delight to the soul.

146. The soul endowed with intelligence, indifferent to the material world and this swiftly-passing life, chooses the delight of heaven and the eternal life that is conferred on her by God because of her holiness.

147. People with filthy clothes soil the coats of those who rub against them. Likewise, the immoral and wicked, when they come into contact with the simple-minded and speak to them about evil, defile such people's souls through their talk.

148. The beginning of sin is desire, and this destroys our soul. The beginning of salvation and of the heavenly kingdom for the soul is love.

149. Just as copper, when it has long lain unused and idle, and has not been cared for properly, deteriorates and becomes unserviceable and ugly with verdigris, so it is with the soul when she remains idle, neglecting holiness of life and conversion to God. By her evil actions she deprives herself of God's protection; and just as

copper is rotted away by verdigris, so is she rotted away by the evil that idleness produces in the material body, and she becomes ugly, unserviceable and incapable of attaining salvation.

150. God is good, dispassionate and immutable. Now someone who thinks it reasonable and true to affirm that God does not change, may well ask how, in that case, it is possible to speak of God as rejoicing over those who are good and showing mercy to those who honour Him, while turning away from the wicked and being angry with sinners. To this it must be answered that God neither rejoices nor grows angry, for to rejoice and to be offended are passions; nor is He won over by the gifts of those who honour Him, for that would mean He is swayed by pleasure. It is not right to imagine that God feels pleasure or displeasure in a human way. He is good, and He only bestows blessings and never does harm, remaining always the same. We men, on the other hand, if we remain good through resembling God, are united to Him; but if we become evil through not resembling God, we are separated from Him. By living in holiness we cleave to God; but by becoming wicked we make Him our enemy. It is not that He grows angry with us in an arbitrary way, but it is our own sins that prevent God from shining within us, and expose us to the demons who punish us. And if through prayer and acts of compassion we gain release from our sins, this does not mean that we have won God over and made Him change, but that through our actions and our turning to God we have cured our wickedness and so once more have enjoyment of God's goodness. Thus to say that God turns away from the wicked is like saying that the sun hides itself from the blind.

151. The truly devout soul knows the God of all. True devotion is simply to do God's will. This means to gain knowledge of God by being free from envy, self-restrained, gentle, as generous as possible, kindly, not quarrelsome, and by acquiring whatever else accords with God's will.

152. The knowledge and **fear** of God are a cure for material passions. As long as ignorance of God is present in the soul, the passions remain incurable and rot the soul away; for evil in the soul is like a festering wound. God is not responsible for this, since He has given to man spiritual understanding and knowledge.

153. God has filled man with spiritual understanding and knowledge, for He seeks to purify man from his passions and deliberate

wickedness; and in His love He desires to transform the mortal into the immortal.

154. The intellect in a pure, devout soul truly sees God the unbegotten, invisible and ineffable, who is the sole purity in the pure of heart.

155. Holiness, salvation and a crown of incorruption are given to the man who bears misfortunes cheerfully and with thankfulness. To control anger, the tongue, the belly and sensual pleasures is of the utmost benefit to the soul.

156. God's providence controls the universe. It is present everywhere. Providence is the sovereign Logos of God, imprinting form on the unformed materiality of the world, making and fashioning all things. Matter could not have acquired an articulated structure were it not for the directing power of the Logos, who is the Image, Intellect, Wisdom and Providence of God.

157. Desire that has its origin in the mind is the source of dark passions. And when the soul is engrossed in such desire, she forgets her own nature, that she is a breath of God; and so she is carried away into sin, in her folly not considering the evils that she will suffer after death.

158. Godlessness and love of praise are the worst and most incurable disease of the soul and lead to her destruction. The desire for evil signifies a lack of what is good. Goodness consists in doing with all our heart whatever is right and pleasing to the God of all.

159. Man alone is capable of communion with God. For to man alone among the living creatures does God speak – at night through dreams, by day through the intellect. And He uses every means to foretell and prefigure the future blessings that will be given to those worthy of Him.

160. For one who has faith and determination, it is not difficult to gain spiritual understanding of God. If you wish to contemplate Him, look at the providential harmony in all the things created by His Logos. All are for man's sake.

161. A man is called holy if he is pure from sin and evil. The highest attainment of man's soul and that which most accords with God's will is for there to be no evil in him.

162. A name designates one particular thing or person. Thus it is foolish to think that God, who is one and unique, has any other name.

The name 'God' designates Him who has no origin, and who created all things for man's sake.

163. If you are conscious of sinful actions in yourself, cut the sinfulness out of your soul by thinking of the blessings that you hope to receive. For God is just and compassionate.

164. A man knows God and is known by Him in so far as he makes every effort not to be separated from God; and he will succeed in this if he is good in every way and refrains from all sensual pleasure, not because he lacks the means to indulge such pleasure, but because of his own determination and self-control.

165. Do good to one who wrongs you, and God will be your friend. Never slander your enemy. Practise love, restraint and moderation, patience, self-control and the like. For this is knowledge of God: to follow Him through humility and other such virtues. These are the actions not of every man, but of one whose soul possesses spiritual understanding.

166. Because some people impiously dare to say that plants and vegetables have a soul, I will write briefly about this for the guidance of the simple. Plants have a natural life, but they do not have a soul. Man is called an intelligent animal because he has intellect and is capable of acquiring knowledge. The other animals and the birds can make sounds because they possess breath and soul. All things that are subject to growth and decline are alive; but the fact that they live and grow does not necessarily mean that they all have souls. There are four categories of living beings. The first are immortal and have souls, such as angels. The second have intellect, soul and breath, such as men. The third have breath and soul, such as animals. The fourth have only life, such as plants. The life of plants is without soul, breath, intellect or immortality. These four attributes, on the other hand, presuppose the possession of life. Every human soul is in continual movement.

167. When images of some sensual pleasure arise in you, watch yourself so as not to be carried away by it. Pause a little, think about death, and reflect how much better it is consciously to overcome this illusory pleasure.

168. Just as passion is present in the process of generation – for whatever comes into being in this world must also perish – so likewise evil is present in every passion. Do not therefore say that God is powerless to extirpate evil: to say that is to talk stupid

nonsense. All these passions pertain to materiality; yet there was no need for God to extirpate matter. He has, however, extirpated evil from men for their own good, by granting them intellect, **under-standing**, spiritual knowledge, and the power to discern what is good, so that, realizing the harm that comes from evil, they may avoid it. But the fool pursues evil and is proud of doing so: he is like someone caught in a snare, who struggles helplessly in its toils. So he is never able to look up, and to see and know God, who has created all things that man may be saved and deified.

169. Mortal creatures know in advance that they must die, and they resent the fact. The saintly soul is granted immortality because of her holiness, but mortality befalls the foolish and unhappy soul because of her sins.

170. When you go to bed with a contented mind, recall the blessings and generous providence of God; be filled with holy thoughts and great joy. Then, while your body sleeps, your soul will keep watch; the closing of your eyes will bring you a true vision of God; your silence will be pregnant with sanctity, and in your sleep you will continue consciously to glorify the God of all with the full strength of your soul. For when evil is absent from man, his thankfulness is by itself more pleasing to God than any lavish sacrifice. To Him be glory through all the ages. Amen.

GLOSSARY

AGE (αἰών – *aion*): the ensemble of cosmic duration. It includes the angelic orders, and is an attribute of God as the principle and consummation of all the centuries created by Him. The texts distinguish frequently between the 'present age' and the 'age to come' or the 'new age'. The first corresponds to our present sense of time, the second to time as it exists in God, that is, to eternity understood, not as endless time, but as the simultaneous presence of all time. Our present sense of time, according to which we experience time as sundered from God, is the consequence of the loss of vision and spiritual perception occasioned by the fall and is on this account more or less illusory. In reality, time is not and never can be sundered from God, the 'present age' from the 'age to come'. Because of this the 'age to come' must be thought of, not as something that belongs to the future, but as an ever-present mode of existence which we fail to realize so long as we persist in the state of spiritual blindness to which we are reduced by our alienation from God.

APPETITIVE ASPECT OF THE SOUL, or the soul's desiring power (τὸ ἐπιθυμητικόν – *to epithymitikon*): one of the three aspects or powers of the soul according to the tripartite division formulated by Plato (see his *Republic*, Book IV, 434D-441C) and on the whole accepted by the Greek Christian Fathers. The other two are, first, the intelligent aspect or power (τὸ λογιστικόν – *to logistikon*: see Intelligent); and, second, the incensive aspect or power (τὸ θυμικόν – *to thymikon*), which often manifests itself as wrath or anger, but which can be more generally defined as the force provoking vehement feelings. The three aspects or powers can be used positively, that is, in accordance with nature and as created by God, or negatively, that is, in a way contrary to nature and leading to sin (q.v.). For instance, the incensive power can be used positively to repel demonic attacks or to intensify desire for God; but it can also, when not controlled, lead to self-indulgent disruptive thought and action.

ASSENT (συγκατάθεσις – synkatathesis): see Temptation.

ATTENTIVENESS (προσοχή – prosochi): see Watchfulness.

COMPUNCTION (κατάνυξις – katanyxis): in our version sometimes also translated 'deep penitence'. The state of one who is 'pricked to the heart', becoming conscious both of his own sinfulness and of the forgiveness extended to him by God; a mingled feeling of sorrow, tenderness and joy, springing from sincere repentance (q.v.).

CONTEMPLATION (θεωρία – theoria): the perception or vision of the intellect (q.v.) through which one attains spiritual knowledge (q.v.). It may be contrasted with the practice of the virtues (πρακτική – praktiki) which designates the more external aspect of the ascetic life – purification and the keeping of the commandments – but which is an indispensable prerequisite of contemplation. Depending on the level of personal spiritual growth, contemplation has two main stages: it may be either of the inner essences or principles (q.v.) of created beings or, at a higher stage, of God Himself.

COUPLING (συνδυασμός– syndyasmos): see Temptation.

DELUSION (πλάνη – plani): see Illusion.

DESIRE, Desiring power of the soul: see Appetitive aspect of the soul.

DISCRIMINATION (διάκρισις – diakrisis): a spiritual gift permitting one to discriminate between the types of thought that enter into one's mind, to assess them accurately and to treat them accordingly. Through this gift one gains 'discernment of spirits' – that is, the ability to distinguish between the thoughts or visions inspired by God and the suggestions or fantasies coming from the devil. It is a kind of eye or lantern of the soul by which man finds his way along the spiritual path without falling into extremes; thus it includes the idea of discretion.

DISPASSION (ἀπάθεια – apatheia): among the writers of the texts here translated, some regard passion (q.v.) as evil and the consequence of sin (q.v.), and for them dispassion signifies passionlessness, the uprooting of the passions; others, such as St Isaiah the Solitary, regard the passions as fundamentally good, and for them dispassion signifies a state in which the passions are exercised in accordance with their original purity and so without committing sin in act or thought. Dispassion is a state of reintegration and spiritual freedom; when translating the term into Latin, Cassian rendered it 'purity of heart'. Such a state may imply impartiality and detachment, but not indifference, for if a dispassionate man does not suffer on his own account, he suffers for his fellow creatures. It does not consist in no longer feeling the attacks of the demons, but in no longer yielding to them. It is positive, not negative: Evagrios links it closely with the quality of love (*agapi*) and Diadochos speaks of the 'fire of dispassion' (§ 17). Dispassion is among the gifts of God.

ECSTASY (ἔκστασις – *ekstasis*): a 'going out' from oneself and from all created things towards God, under the influence of *eros* or intense longing (q.v.). A man does not attain ecstasy by his own efforts, but is drawn out of himself by the power of God's love. Ecstasy implies a passing beyond all the conceptual thinking of the discursive reason (q.v.). It may sometimes be marked by a state of trance, or by a loss of normal consciousness; but such psychophysical accompaniments are in no way essential. Occasionally the term *ekstasis* is used in a bad sense, to mean infatuation, loss of self-control, or madness.

FAITH (πίστις – *pistis*): not only an individual or theoretical belief in the dogmatic truths of Christianity, but an all-embracing relationship, an attitude of love and total trust in God. As such it involves a transformation of man's entire life. Faith is a gift from God, the means whereby we are taken up into the whole theanthropic activity of God in Christ and of man in Christ through which man attains salvation.

FALLEN NATURE (παλαιὸς ἄνθρωπος – *palaios anthropos*): literally, the 'old man'. *See* Flesh, sense (ii).

FANTASY (φαντασία – *fantasia*): denoting the image-producing faculty of the psyche, this is one of the most important words in the hesychast (q.v.) vocabulary. As one begins to advance along the spiritual path one begins to 'perceive' images of things which have no direct point of reference in the external world, and which emerge inexplicably from within oneself. This experience is a sign that one's consciousness is beginning to deepen: outer sensations and ordinary thoughts have to some extent been quietened, and the impulses, fears, hopes, passions hidden in the

subconscious region are beginning to break through to the surface.
One of the goals of the spiritual life is indeed the attainment of a
spiritual knowledge (q.v.) which transcends both the ordinary
level of consciousness and the subconscious; and it is true that
images, especially when the recipient is in an advanced spiritual
state, may well be projections on the plane of the imagination of
celestial archetypes, and that in this case they can be used cre-
atively, to form the images of sacred art and iconography. But more
often than not they will simply derive from a middle or lower
sphere, and will have nothing spiritual or creative about them.
Hence they correspond to the world of fantasy and not to the
world of the imagination in the proper sense. It is on this account
that the hesychastic masters on the whole take a negative attitude
towards them. They emphasize the grave dangers involved in this
kind of experience, especially as the very production of these
images may be the consequence of demonic or diabolic activity;
and they admonish those still in the early stages and not yet
possessing spiritual discrimination (q.v.) not to be enticed and led
captive by these illusory appearances, whose tumult may well
overwhelm the mind. Their advice is to pay no attention to them,
but to continue with prayer and invocation, dispelling them with
the name of Jesus Christ.

FLESH (σάρξ – *sarx*): has various senses: (i) the human in contrast to
the divine, as in the sentence, 'The Logos became flesh' (John
1 : 14); (ii) fallen and sinful human nature in contrast to human
nature as originally created and dwelling in communion with God;
man when separated from God and in rebellion against Him; (iii)
the body in contrast to the soul. The second meaning is probably
the most frequent. If the word is being employed in this sense, it is
important to distinguish 'flesh' from 'body' (σῶμα – *soma*). When
St Paul lists the 'works of the flesh' in Gal. 5 : 19–21, he mentions
such things as 'seditions', 'heresy' and 'envy', which have no
special connection with the body. In sense (ii) of the word,
'flesh' denotes the *whole* soul-body structure in so far as a man is
fallen; likewise 'spirit' denotes the *whole* soul-body structure in
so far as a man is redeemed. The soul as well as the body can
become fleshly or 'carnal', just as the body as well as the soul can
become spiritual. Asceticism involves a war against the flesh – in
sense (ii) of the word – but not against the body as such.

GUARD OF THE HEART, OF THE INTELLECT (φυλακὴ καρδίας, νοῦ – *phylaki kardias, nou*): *see* Watchfulness.

HEART (καρδία – *kardia*): not simply the physical organ but the spiritual centre of man's being, man as made in the image of God, his deepest and truest self, or the inner shrine, to be entered only through sacrifice and death, in which the mystery of the union between the divine and the human is consummated. '"I called with my whole heart", says the Psalmist – that is, with body, soul and spirit' (John Klimakos, *The Ladder of Divine Ascent*, Step 28, translated by Archimandrite Lazarus [London, 1959], pp. 257–8). 'Heart' has thus an all-embracing significance: 'prayer of the heart' means prayer not just of the emotions and affections, but of the whole person, including the body.

ILLUSION (πλάνη – *plani*): in our version sometimes also translated 'delusion'. Literally, wandering astray, deflection from the right path; hence error, beguilement, the acceptance of a mirage mistaken for truth. Cf. the literal sense of sin (q.v.) as 'missing the mark'.

INCENSIVE POWER or aspect of the soul (θυμός – *thymos*; τὸ θυμικόν – *to thymikon*): *see* Appetitive aspect of the soul.

INNER ESSENCES OR PRINCIPLES (λόγοι – *logoi*): *see* Logos.

INTELLECT (νοῦς – *nous*): the highest faculty in man, through which – provided it is purified – he knows God or the inner essences or principles (q.v.) of created things by means of direct apprehension or spiritual perception. Unlike the *dianoia* or reason (q.v.), from which it must be carefully distinguished, the intellect does not function by formulating abstract concepts and then arguing on this basis to a conclusion reached through deductive reasoning, but it understands divine truth by means of immediate experience, intuition or 'simple cognition' (the term used by St Isaac the Syrian). The intellect dwells in the 'depths of the soul'; it constitutes the innermost aspect of the heart (St Diadochos, §§ 79, 88). The intellect is the organ of contemplation (q.v.), the 'eye of the heart' (*Makarian Homilies*).

INTELLECTION (νόημα – *noïma*. νόησις – *noïsis*): not an abstract concept or a visual image, but the act or function of the intellect (q.v.) whereby it apprehends spiritual realities in a direct manner.

INTELLIGENT (λογικός – *logikos*): the Greek term *logikos* is so closely connected with Logos (q.v.), and therefore with the divine Intellect, that to render it simply as 'logical' and hence descriptive of the reason (q.v.) is clearly inadequate. Rather it pertains to the intellect (q.v.) and qualifies the possessor of spiritual knowledge (q.v.). Hence when found in conjunction with 'soul' (*logiki psychi*), *logikos* is translated as 'deiform' or as 'endowed with intelligence'. Intelligence itself (τὸ λογικόν – *to logikon*; τὸ λογιστικόν – *to logistikon*; ὁ λογισμός – *ho logismos*) is the ruling aspect of the intellect (q.v.) or its operative faculty.

INTENSE LONGING (ἔρως – *eros*): the word *eros*, when used in these texts, retains much of the significance it has in Platonic thought. It denotes that intense aspiration and longing which impel man towards union with God, and at the same time something of the force which links the divine and the human. As unitive love *par excellence*, it is not distinct from *agapi*, but may be contrasted with *agapi* in that it expresses a greater degree of intensity and ecstasy (q.v.).

INTIMATE COMMUNION (παρρησία – *parrisia*): literally, 'frankness', 'freedom of speech'; hence freedom of approach to God, such as Adam possessed before the fall and the saints have regained by grace; a sense of confidence and loving trust in God's mercy.

JESUS PRAYER ('Ιησοῦ εὐχή – *Iisou evchi*): the invocation of the name of Jesus, most commonly in the words, 'Lord Jesus Christ, Son of God, have mercy on me', although there are a number of variant forms. Not merely a 'technique' or a 'Christian mantra', but a prayer addressed to the Person of Jesus Christ, expressing our living faith (q.v.) in Him as Son of God and Saviour.

LOGOS (Λόγος – *Logos*): the Second Person of the Holy Trinity, or the Intellect, Wisdom and Providence of God in whom and through whom all things are created. As the unitary cosmic principle, the Logos contains in Himself the multiple *logoi* (inner principles or inner essences, thoughts of God) in accordance with which all things come into existence at the times and places, and in the forms, appointed for them, each single thing thereby containing in itself the principle of its own development. It is these *logoi*, contained principially in the Logos and manifest in the forms of the created universe, that constitute the first or lower stage of contemplation (q.v.).

MIND: *see* Reason.

NOETIC (νοητός – noïtos): that which belongs to or is characteristic of the intellect (q.v.). See also Intellection.

PASSION (πάθος – pathos): in Greek, the word signifies literally that which happens to a person or thing, an experience undergone passively; hence an appetite or impulse, such as anger, desire or jealousy, that violently dominates the soul. Many Greek Fathers regard the passions as something intrinsically evil, a 'disease' of the soul: thus St John Klimakos affirms that God is not the creator of the passions and that they are 'unnatural', alien to man's true self (The Ladder of Divine Ascent, Step 26, translated by Archimandrite Lazarus [op. cit.], p. 211). Other Greek Fathers, however, look on the passions as impulses originally placed in man by God, and so fundamentally good, although at present distorted by sin (cf. St Isaiah the Solitary, § 1: in our translation, Vol. I, p. 22). On this second view, then, the passions are to be educated, not eradicated; to be transfigured, not suppressed; to be used positively, not negatively (see Dispassion).

PRACTICE OF THE VIRTUES (πρακτική – praktiki): see Contemplation.

PREPOSSESSION (πρόληψις – prolipsis): see Temptation.

PROVOCATION (προσβολή – prosvoli): see Temptation.

REASON, mind (διάνοια – dianoia): the discursive, conceptualizing and logical faculty in man, the function of which is to draw conclusions or formulate concepts deriving from data provided either by revelation or spiritual knowledge (q.v.) or by sense-observation. The knowledge of the reason is consequently of a lower order than spiritual knowledge (q.v.) and does not imply any direct apprehension or perception of the inner essences or principles (q.v.) of created beings, still less of divine truth itself. Indeed, such apprehension or perception, which is the function of the intellect (q.v.), is beyond the scope of the reason.

REBUTTAL (ἀντιλογία – antilogia; ἀντίρρησις – antirrisis): the repulsing of a demon or demonic thought at the moment of provocation (q.v.); or, in a more general sense, the bridling of evil thoughts.

REMEMBRANCE OF GOD (μνήμη Θεοῦ – mnimi Theou): not just calling God to mind, but the state of recollectedness or concentration in which attention is centred on God. As such it is the opposite of the state of self-indulgence and insensitivity.

REPENTANCE (μετάνοια – metanoia): the Greek signifies primarily a 'change of mind' or 'change of intellect': not only sorrow, contrition or regret, but more positively and fundamentally the conversion or turning of our whole life towards God.

SENSUAL PLEASURE (ἡδονή – hidoni): according to the context the Greek term signifies either sensual pleasure (the most frequent meaning) or spiritual pleasure or delight. Sensual pleasure is often an illusory or deceptive form of spiritual delight.

SIN (ἁμαρτία – hamartia): the primary meaning of the Greek word is 'failure' or, more specifically, 'failure to hit the mark' and so a 'missing of the mark', a 'going astray' or, ultimately, 'failure to achieve the purpose for which one is created'. It is closely related, therefore, to illusion (q.v.). The translation 'sin' should be read with these connotations in mind.

SORROW (λύπη – lypi): often with the sense of 'godly sorrow' – the sorrow which nourishes the soul with the hope engendered by repentance (q.v.).

SPIRITUAL KNOWLEDGE (γνῶσις – gnosis): the knowledge of the intellect (q.v.) as distinct from that of the reason (q.v.). As such it is knowledge inspired by God, and so linked with contemplation (q.v.) and immediate spiritual perception.

STILLNESS (ἡσυχία – hesychia): from which are derived the words hesychasm and hesychast, used to denote the whole spiritual tradition represented in the Philokalia as well as the person who pursues the spiritual path it delineates (see Introduction, pp. 14–16): a state of inner tranquillity or mental quietude and concentration which arises in conjunction with, and is deepened by, the practice of pure prayer and the guarding of heart (q.v.) and intellect (q.v.). Not simply silence, but an attitude of listening to God and of openness towards Him.

TEMPERAMENT (κρᾶσις – krasis): primarily the well-balanced blending of elements, humours or qualities in animal bodies, but sometimes extended to denote the whole soul-body structure of man. In this sense it is the opposite to a state of psychic or physical disequilibrium.

TEMPTATION (πειρασμός – peirasmos): also translated in our version as 'trial' or 'test'. The word indicates, according to context: (i) a test or trial sent to man by God, so as to aid his progress on the spiritual way; (ii) a suggestion from the devil, enticing man into sin.

Using the word in sense (ii), the Greek Fathers employ a series of technical terms to describe the process of temptation. (See in particular Mark the Ascetic, *On the Spiritual Law*, §§ 138–41, in Vol. I of our translation, pp. 119–20; John Klimakos, *Ladder*, Step 15, translated by Archimandrite Lazarus [*op. cit.*], pp. 157–8; Maximos, *On Love*, I, §§ 83–4, in Vol. II of our translation of the *Philokalia*; John of Damaskos, *On the Virtues and Vices*, also in Vol. II of our translation.) The basic distinction made by these Fathers is between the demonic *provocation* and man's *assent*: the first lies outside man's control, while for the second he is morally responsible. In detail, the chief terms employed are as follows:

(i) *Provocation* (προσβολή – *prosvoli*): the initial incitement to evil. Mark the Ascetic defines this as an 'image-free stimulation in the heart'; so long as the provocation is not accompanied by images, it does not involve man in any guilt. Such provocations, originating as they do from the devil, assail man from the outside independently of his free will, and so he is not morally responsible for them. His liability to these provocations is not a consequence of the fall: even in paradise, Mark maintains, Adam was assailed by the devil's provocations. Man cannot prevent provocations from assailing him; what does lie in his power, however, is to maintain constant watchfulness (q.v.) and so to reject each provocation as soon as it emerges into his consciousness – that is to say, at its first appearance as a thought in his mind or intellect (μονολόγιστος ἔμφασις – *monologistos emphasis*). If he does reject the provocation, the sequence is cut off and the process of temptation is terminated.

(ii) *Momentary disturbance* (παραρριπισμός – *pararripismos*) of the intellect, occurring 'without any movement or working of bodily passion' (see Mark, *Letter to Nicolas the Solitary*: in our translation, Vol. I, p. 153). This seems to be more than the 'first appearance' of a provocation described in stage (i) above; for, at a certain point of spiritual growth in this life, it is possible to be totally released from such 'momentary disturbance', whereas no one can expect to be altogether free from demonic provocations.

(iii) *Communion* (ὁμιλία – *homilia*); *coupling* (συνδυασμός – *syndyasmos*). Without as yet entirely assenting to the demonic provocation, a man may begin to 'entertain' it, to converse or parley with it, turning it over in his mind pleasurably, yet still hesitating whether or not to act upon it. At this stage, which is

indicated by the terms 'communion' or 'coupling', the provocation is no longer 'image-free' but has become a *logismos* or
thought (q.v.); and man is morally responsible for having allowed
this to happen.

(iv) *Assent* (συγκατάθεσις – *synkatathesis*). This signifies a step
beyond mere 'communion' or 'coupling'. No longer merely
'playing' with the evil suggestion, a man now resolves to act upon
it. There is now no doubt as to his moral culpability: even if
circumstances prevent him from sinning outwardly, he is judged
by God according to the intention in his heart.

(v) *Prepossession* (πρόληψις – *prolipsis*): defined by Mark as 'the
involuntary presence of former sins in the memory'. This state of
'prepossession' or prejudice results from repeated acts of sin
which predispose a man to yield to particular temptations. In
principle he retains his free choice and can reject demonic
provocations; but in practice the force of habit makes it more
and more difficult for him to resist.

(vi) *Passion* (q.v.). If a man does not fight strenuously against
a prepossession, it will develop into an evil passion.

THEOLOGY (θεολογία – *theologia*): denotes in these texts far more
than the learning about God and religious doctrine acquired
through academic study. It signifies active and conscious participation in or perception of the realities of the divine world – in
other words, the realization of spiritual knowledge (q.v.). To be
a theologian in the full sense, therefore, presupposes the attainment of the state of stillness (q.v.) and dispassion (q.v.), itself the
concomitant of pure and undistracted prayer, and so requires gifts
bestowed on but extremely few persons.

THOUGHT (λογισμός – *logismos*): generally signifies not thought in
the ordinary sense, but thought provoked by the demons, and
therefore often qualified in translation by the adjective 'evil' or
'demonic'. It can also signify divinely-inspired thought.

WATCHFULNESS (νῆψις – *nipsis*): literally, the opposite to a state of
drunken stupor; hence spiritual sobriety, alertness, vigilance. It
signifies an attitude of attentiveness (προσοχή – *prosochi*), whereby
one keeps watch over one's inward thoughts and fantasies (q.v.),
maintaining guard over the heart and intellect (φυλακὴ καρδίας/
νοῦ – *phylaki kardias/nou*; τήρησις καρδίας/νοῦ – *tirisis kardias/
nou*). In Hesychios, *On Watchfulness and Holiness*, §§ 1–6 (in our

translation, Vol. I, pp. 162–3), watchfulness is given a very broad definition, being used to indicate the whole range of the practice of the virtues. It is closely linked with purity of heart and stillness (q.v.). The Greek title of the *Philokalia* is 'the Philokalia of the niptic Fathers', i.e., of the Fathers who practised and inculcated the virtue of watchfulness. This shows how central is the role assigned by St Nikodimos to this state.

WRATH, wrathfulness: *see* Appetitive aspect of the soul.

INDEX

[Major entries are given in bold type]

PERSONS

SUBJECTS